Educational Testing Service
Princeton, New Jersey

College Students' Knowledge and Beliefs:

A Survey of Global Understanding

**The Final Report
of the
Global Understanding Project**

by

Thomas S. Barrows
Project Director

with contributions by

Sheila M. Ager, Mary F. Bennett, Henry I. Braun, John L. D. Clark, Lois G. Harris
and
Stephen F. Klein

1981

Change Magazine Press

April 1981

This volume is the complete technical report of the 1980 Global Understanding Student Survey conducted by the Educational Testing Service of Princeton, New Jersey. This report and a series of related Council on Learning publications result from the Council's Education and the World View Project. Funding for the ETS survey of students' global understanding was provided by the Office of International Education of the U.S. Department of Education, with the support of the National Endowment for the Humanities. Funding for the total Council on Learning project was provided by the National Endowment for the Humanities and the Exxon Education Foundation. Additional copies of this report, as well as related publications listed at the end of this volume, can be ordered from Change Magazine Press, 271 North Avenue, New Rochelle, N.Y. 10801.

Contents

Foreword

Suspicions abound that American higher education, in light of changed world circumstances, does not sufficiently prepare the young for their civic roles as they enter the next century. This new educational challenge has led leaders across all walks of American life to advance the widening of understanding of these new global realities. On one front, Congressman Paul Simon, who has consistently called public attention to lack of global understanding in the United States, pressed for and obtained a presidential commission that reviewed the general state of the nation's foreign language and international studies education. One result from that endeavor was the consensus generated for enacting Senators Robert Stafford and Jacob Javits' proposals integrating international education with improving the United States' international economic position.

On another front, the Council on Learning, in its catalytic role of focusing national concern on critical higher learning issues, initiated a significant public action project, *Education and the World View* (E&WV), to strengthen international dimensions in the college experience. George W. Bonham, executive director of the Council, had succinctly proffered what many in higher education have been certain reflects actual student learning in this area:

> America's young face a set of new national and international circumstances about which they have only the faintest of notions. They are, globally speaking, blind, deaf, and dumb; and thus handicapped, they will soon determine the future directions of this nation.

To remedy this condition he called for a major review of international experiences at colleges and universities across the country.

Before any fundamental changes in the American undergraduate curriculum could be encouraged, it was necessary to assess the quality of campus programs and the degree to which college students understood world realities. The Educational Testing Service (ETS) was asked to design and conduct a national survey of college students' global understanding. (ETS had already broken new ground in this area with its earlier precollegiate study, *Other Nations, Other Peoples*.)

The results of this three-year effort are presented in this report. William W. Turnbull, until recently president of ETS, and Winton H. Manning, a senior vice president, have correctly stated that this new survey represents active evaluation in the service of and at the disposal of the entire higher education community. Not destined to gather dust on some shelf, the ETS Global Understanding Project report and other E&WV activities are being followed by regional workshops and individual campus self-assessments, so that international dimensions become strengthened throughout the curriculum. To do this, ETS is providing components included in an E&WV workshop kit that will be the centerpiece of these forthcoming campus self-evaluations.

Both the Council on Learning and Educational Testing Service greatly appreciate the widespread support and counsel received for the E&WV Project. Special thanks for funding of various segments goes to the National Endowment for the Humanities, the U.S. Department of Education, and the Exxon Education Foundation. Without such assistance, the objectives of this critical endeavor could never have been realized.

Robert Black
Project Director
Education and the World View

i

Acknowledgments

This volume is the final report of a survey of global understanding administered to a nationally representative sample of college students during February and March of 1980. Several organizations have been responsible for planning, supporting, and directing the effort.

The need for an up-to-date scientific survey was first suggested by the 50 prominent American leaders from the academy, business, government, foundations, and media, who constitute the National Advisory Board of the Council on Learning's Education and the World View (E&WV) Project. The actual status of students' knowledge, attitudes, and abilities to comprehend and deal with a new, emerging international order has not been assessed in any systematic way in recent years and, although the need for curricular reform has been broadly recognized, it has been based largely on informal impressions and anecdotal evidence. At the request of the E&WV task force, Educational Testing Service prepared a proposal for the desired survey which was subsequently submitted to the National Endowment for the Humanities for funding under the Council's project "umbrella." The resulting contract (NEH-C-93) provided support from the Office of International Education of the U.S. Department of Education and project monitoring and direction from both that office and the National Endowment. While the contract funded Educational Testing Service directly, the project has remained part of the Council on Learning's E&WV project by common agreement and through the National Endowment's coordinating efforts. Educational Testing Service has provided substantial financial support for the project in order to allow the scope of the Global Understanding Project to be expanded beyond the original proposal's specifications.

The support of senior individuals at each of these organizations has been critical to the project. The National Endowment's encouragement and interests must be specially recognized in the efforts of Joseph D. Duffey, Chairman, and Stanley F. Turesky, Assistant Director for Evaluation and Assessment Studies. Ernest L. Boyer, former U.S. Commissioner of Education, now President of the Carnegie Foundation for the Advancement of Teaching, and Robert C. Leestma, former Associate Commissioner for Institutional Development and International Education, provided support and direction; the continuing concern of Edward Meador and Julia A. Petrov of the Office of International Education has been greatly appreciated. The advice and counsel of George W. Bonham, Executive Director, and Robert Black, Director of Programs, of the Council on Learning has also been helpful and consistent; and, at Educational Testing Service the substantive and financial support provided by Winton H. Manning, Senior Vice President, Research and Development, has been critical.

From the outset of the project in early 1979, we have been assisted by a distinguished Assessment Committee and wish to express our gratitude for the valuable guidance of these outstanding scholars: Robert F. Dernberger, Professor of Economics, University of Michigan; A. David Hill, Professsor of Geography, University of Colorado; William J. McGuire, Professor of Psychology, Yale University; William H. McNeill, Robert A. Milliken Distinguished Service Professor of History, University of Chicago; Richard C. Snyder, formerly Mershon Professor of Education and Public Policy and Director, Mershon Center, The Ohio State University; Judith V. Torney-Purta, Professor of Psychology, University of Illinois at Chicago Circle; Richard G. Tucker, Jr., Director, Center for Applied Linguistics; Immanuel Wallerstein, Distinguished Professor of Sociology and Chairman, Department of Sociology, State University of New York at Binghamton.

The cooperation of staff and students at 185 colleges must also be recognized. Coordinators at each college drew samples of students, enlisted their participation, and administered the survey to them. These institutions are listed in Appendix F.

Finally, we must recognize unusual assistance from members of the staff at Educational Testing Service. Bruce Kaplan carried out our data analyses with exceptional speed, accuracy, and understanding, and both Paul Holland and Don Rubin provided analytic advice at critical points. Connie Pilla and her staff keytaped the survey responses on an impossible schedule. Anna Jackson, Nat Hartshorne, Elsa Rosenthal, and Sally Sharp assisted in the writing of our reports, and Christine Sansone and her text processing staff ably kept track of a seemingly endless series of revisions. The knowledge, cooperation, and expertise of these colleagues contributed immeasurably to the conduct of the survey and the preparation of this report, and the authors extend their deepest appreciation to each one.

Thomas S. Barrows
Stephen F. Klein
John L. D. Clark

Introduction

Surveys usually seek to establish levels of some well-defined phenomenon in a population of interest. Consumer-choice behavior, knowledge of American history, and even some political attitudes are fairly well-defined examples. Furthermore, methods for assessing them are generally available and supported by considerable experience. Global understanding by contrast has not been defined, although it has been the subject of a considerable literature. Measures of global understanding either have not existed or have not been recognized because of this.

Consequently, this report is not the usual survey fare. It covers the development of definitions of global understanding and the development and revision of survey measures. It also describes analyses that examine the fit between the original logical definitions and empirical, psychological models of the behavior defined. Because these steps were necessary, they are documented here, rendering the report unusually complex on the one hand but acceptably complete as a final report of the Global Understanding Project on the other.

Part I of this report discusses the development of the survey measures. It introduces the difficulties encountered in defining the concept of global understanding and traces the refinement of the definition and resultant survey measures. Part II deals with the procedures used to conduct the survey. It focuses on the scientific methods used to identify and select participating colleges and universities as well as the process of data collection. Part III presents a detailed analysis of the results and examines global understanding in terms of its components and their interrelationships—knowledge, student background, language learning, attitudes and perceptions. Part IV reviews and summarizes the survey's findings.

Readers who are not interested in methodological techniques or complete, detailed survey results may prefer to refer to Hartshorne's synopsis.* This emphasizes results and reduces the treatment of complex techniques that may not be of general interest.

---

*Barrows, Thomas S., Stephen F. Klein, and John L. D. Clark with Nathaniel Hartshorne, *What College Students Know and Believe About Their World*. New Rochelle, N.Y.: Change Magazine Press, 1981; E&WV Series V.

Part I

Survey Measures

Although much has been written about global understanding and its numerous aliases, little has been done to define it. Indeed, using the pronoun "it" may constitute a gross oversimplification. From the outset of this study, we have assumed that global understanding is more sensibly and tractibly approached as a multifaceted construct with components in both cognitive and affective domains. At the level of starting assumptions, it was clear that we would need to develop instruments to measure various domains of knowledge, skills, abilities, and so forth; and also attitudes, perceptions, interests, and other affective phenomena.

In addition to this intention of measuring many potential but as yet unspecified components of global understanding, the project's original objectives included exploration of some likely correlates of global understanding. Although correlates clearly could not be interpreted as causes, it was hoped that comprehensive background and experience data would provide some suggestions of how individual variation in levels of global understanding comes about. Foreign language study and foreign language proficiency were prime candidates here because of the relatively common belief that foreign language study or proficiency contributes to the understanding of other cultures.

In the following sections we describe the efforts that were undertaken to provide instruments for the survey. The lengths of the sections reflect the difficulty of adequately covering an ill-defined phenomenon—global understanding. Defining the cognitive components to be covered was primarily a rational, intellectual problem, while the affective area and foreign language proficiency presented primarily methodological challenges. The following sections, therefore, describe efforts that vary a good deal in terms of a rational or an analytic, empirical approach.

Chapter 1

Development of the Test of Knowledge

Stephen F. Klein and Sheila M. Ager

The assignment to develop a test of global knowledge immediately raised three questions:

- From what, or whose, perspective was the test to be developed?
- What knowledge and skills did global understanding comprise?
- At what level of sophistication was global understanding to be tested?

In order to insure that a broad range of perspectives was considered in answering these questions (and many others concerning the test's development), the project staff decided to enlist the help of several scholars, who came to constitute an assessment committee. Yet the range of likely answers would have to be known first in order to decide what kind of committee to appoint.

To the question of perspective, answers could plausibly be given that ranged from an American perspective to a global one. In defense of the latter, one could argue that national interest and ethnocentrism were themselves major impediments to the achievement of global understanding and that the agenda for global understanding, therefore, had to be written by those who were not biased by these considerations. Conversely, one could argue that there is no such thing, in practice, as a universal outlook, that every individual has an outlook modified by, if not rooted in, experiences of time, place, social position, and so on, and that global understanding, therefore, cannot be independent of those who perceive it. Not only the content of global understanding would be at issue, but the relative importance of the various aspects of content as well.

The range of answers to the question of perspective ultimately left us with two choices regarding the appointment of an assessment committee. The first was to appoint committee members from around the world, on the assumption that the test they would develop would be the best practical approximation to a universal instrument. The second was to recruit committee members from the United States whose world-mindedness would help to insure that a test relevant to American concerns was not at the same time parochial. The second course of action was taken, since financial constraints would have prevented all but a token effort to appoint committee members from abroad and since there seemed to be virtual unanimity within the global education community that American college students knew too little about even American concerns, much less those of other nations.

To the questions of what knowledge and what skills global understanding comprised, there was a better-defined range of answers to the former than the latter. From even cursory reading in this area, it became apparent that there were two fundamentally different approaches to structuring the knowledge domain, although they intersected at numerous points. The first approach was based on the established curricular traditions of international relations and area studies courses. The second was based on the concept of global issues that transcended particular nations or regions. Partisans of the latter sometimes exaggerated the differences between issues on the one hand and nations (or international actors) and regions on the other. Clearly a knowledge of international relations of one or more of the world's areas had to include knowledge of issues, even if those issues were not considered "whole", that is, in their full disciplinary and geographical complexity. Just as clearly, knowledge of issues had to include knowledge of the international arena in which these issues would or would not be worked out, as well as knowledge of the areas of the world in which these issues impacted. A knowledge of issues, therefore, could not possibly be devoid of references to particular institutional structures and relations, or to particular times, places, and cultures, even if these were considered to be somehow subsidiary to the issues themselves. And yet it would not be accurate to

2

go to the opposite extreme and view the two approaches to structuring the knowledge domain as simply different packaging for the same contents. Each approach has different implications for teaching and testing, if only in their different emphases on what is of primary importance in attempting to understand global developments today.

The range of answers to the question of what constituted the skills of global understanding was more constricted than the range of answers to the question of knowledge. In fact, it was difficult to distinguish skills in this area from analytical or problem-solving skills in the humanities and social sciences in general. As a result, the question of skills did not come to bear on the appointment of committee members whereas the question of knowledge did.

The problem in appointing a committee that, by its membership *alone*, would not foreclose either of the two approaches to structuring the domain of knowledge proved difficult to do. The number of committee members was limited by consideratio: : :' both efficiency and cost; hence expertise in all areas of the world (and in international relations), as well as expertise in all major world issues, could not possibly be provided within the confines of the committee itself. Instead, members were appointed who for the most part possessed two qualifications—knowledge of a major area of the world and knowledge of a major academic discipline important to the study of global affairs. Members appointed to the committee possessed expertise in the areas of Europe, Asia, Africa, and Latin America. The disciplines they represented were political science (more specifically, international relations), economics, sociology, geography, and history. The assumption behind these appointments was that a core group had been created that could deal effectively with either the international relations/area studies approach to the structuring of the knowledge domain or the issues approach. It was further assumed that fields of knowledge not represented on the committee could be covered by later engaging experts in these fields as question writers. Finally, the decision was made to expand committee membership to include two experts in attitudinal measurement and one in foreign language study who were to consult on those components of the survey.

The last of the questions raised before the committee's appointment concerned the level of sophistication at which global understanding should be tested. It was assumed that, however greater the degree of global understanding of college seniors as compared to college freshmen or two-year college students, the former would still fall short of some criterion level defined by the committee. Thus the question of the appropriate level at which to test had two potential answers: either at the level students were on or the criterion level defined by the committee. Both answers had assets and liabilities. To test at the level students were on would, in measurement terms, provide maximum discrimination among them and thereby facilitate sub-group comparisons and correlational analyses. Since many of the test questions would likely be at a relatively low level when compared to the criterion level of sophistication, the performance results would have considerable shock value—an asset to a project whose aim was to affect curricular change. The liability of such testing, however, was that the criterion level of global understanding would be confused in the public's mind with the lower level of the test. Taking the alternative approach, however, would simply reverse the assets and liabilities. A test that embodied a rigorous standard of achievement would inform the public about what it meant for college students to possess global understanding, but at the risk that scores on the test (and score variance as well) would be so low as to almost preclude making discriminations among students.

The Assessment Committee

When the committee was appointed, it discussed explicitly or implicitly each of the three questions at its first meeting. On the issue of perspective, no serious consideration was given to a test that would be universal as opposed to American in orientation. This lack of consideration reflected the assumption that major world problems were, in fact, American problems, that the increasing interdependence of nations and peoples made it likely that important developments elsewhere would sooner or later have impact on the United States. Conversely, what might superficially be viewed as purely American concerns often had significant implications for others. The committee proceeded, therefore, on the premise that a test of global understanding for Americans would inevitably have much in common with a test devised by and for others. This was in no way to deny the real importance to others of a host of local or regional issues that, for lack of space as much as any other consideration, would not find their way into the committee's test. Similarly, the United States agenda of

3

issues included some that were of more concern to it than to others, and these, as well as specifically American aspects of global developments, would receive a high priority on the test.

Two other matters pertaining to perspective were discussed by the committee. First was the importance of testing whether American students understood how other nations, peoples, or cultures viewed either the United States or issues of mutual concern to the United States and themselves. Second was the importance of testing a historical as well as a contemporary perspective on global developments. The members of the committee agreed that students' understanding of contemporary issues was often incomplete or distorted due to a lack of knowledge about the origins of these issues.

When it came to a discussion about how to structure the knowledge domain, the views of the members clearly inclined toward adopting the issues approach rather than that of international relations or area studies. The committee had little doubt that elements of the latter two should be tested, but preferred the issues approach because of its implicitly global scope and the multiple dimensions (e.g. economic, social, etc.) that characterized most issues. Particularly important, the members felt, was the opportunity afforded by the issues approach to trace the ramifications of issues across time, space, and societal institutions. Interestingly, the issues approach to global education was shortly thereafter endorsed by the President's Commission on Foreign Language and International Studies.

Little, if any, consideration was given by the committee to the question of what skills were germane to the acquisition of global understanding. In part, this was due to the extended discussion that took place about what knowledge to test. But the lack of attention to skills can also be seen as a reflection of the fact that a certain amount of knowledge about a subject is needed before analytical or problem-solving skills can usefully be applied. The committee was skeptical that students possessed even basic knowledge of numerous important issues and so addressed this as a priority concern.

There was also relatively little discussion of the tradeoffs between a test that was designed for measurement at the level of knowledge that students actually possessed versus one at a higher level that constituted a criterion standard of global understanding. The committee, of course, was made aware of these tradeoffs, and its subsequent work reflected an almost instinctive desire to steer a middle course generally veering toward the higher level.

Structuring the Issues Framework

Once the committee decided to use an issues framework for the test, considerable discussion ensued about how to insure that other dimensions of interest would be represented. How, in other words, would historical, geographical, disciplinary and other aspects of issues be assured of systematic coverage. The method chosen by the committee was to construct a "chain" of questions for each issue. Each chain would begin with a very basic question about the manifestation of a contemporary global issue in the United States or, conversely, with a contemporary issue abroad that reflected the actions or influence of the United States. From there the chain would quickly proceed outward in space (i.e., beyond the United States) and, more slowly, backward in time. By the end of the chain the questions would be dealing with the global ramifications of the issue and with its historical roots. As the chain proceeded through space and time, the questions would also have different disciplinary foci or, perhaps, be multi-disciplinary. Finally, the chain would demonstrate a rough progression from very basic to more sophisticated knowledge of the issue. The concept of the chain was not meant to be inflexible; it was noted, for example, that the historical roots of the issue might be addressed first, with the chain then moving forward toward the present. What was not seen at the time, however, was that the more variables that had to be encompassed by a chain the more constraints would be placed on any given question in the chain. In situations like this, item specifications become overprescribed with the result that item content that meets all of the specifications is increasingly arbitrary. This, as well as other problems, later caused significant revisions in the concept of the chain.

The committee had limited time in which to address the matter of which issues were to be tested. It was of course not difficult to tick off numerous global issues. What was difficult, however, was to organize the issues at a level of generality that took into account the total number of questions on the test. The broader the definition of the issues, the more questions that would have to be devoted to each issue and the fewer the number of issues that could be accommodated in the test. Also, as the definition of issues broadened, the number of different ways of combining sub-issues multiplied. If oil, for example, was too narrow to serve as an issue by itself (and the committee thought that it was), should oil be part of a broader issue called energy or one called depletable resources? Issue labels, in other words, had implications not only for the number of questions needed but for the overall conceptualization of the test.

At the end of the first committee meeting, it was apparent that considerably more discussion would be needed before agreement could be reached on defining the issues. Because it was not feasible to reassemble the committee on short notice, a different procedure was sought for accomplishing this crucial work. During the earliest phase of the project, it had come to the attention of ETS staff that Eisenhower College in Seneca Falls, NY (now the Eisenhower College of Rochester Institute of Technology), was one of the few institutions of higher education that had a core curriculum in world studies. After the first committee meeting, therefore, ETS staff contacted the college and arranged with about a dozen members of the world studies faculty to take up the task of defining the issues for the test where the committee had broken off. The work of the Eisenhower group would be sent to the members of the committee for review and possible revision.

During the course of two meetings at Eisenhower and a mail review in between by the committee, basic issues and sub-issues for the test were agreed upon, although later changes were made in sub-issues. On this point, it is interesting to note that as test development proceeded from specifying the larger issues to the sub-issues and finally to the writing of the questions, there were increasing amounts of committee debate and revision. It was easier, in other words, to reach agreement on the broad definition of issues than to identify sub-issues or the specific points to be tested. The following is the list of the issues that emerged from the meetings at Eisenhower (with only minor changes in wording that were made afterward):

Environment	Relations among States
Food	War and Armaments
Health	International Monetary and Trade Arrangements
Energy	Human Rights
Religious Issues	Racial and Ethnic Issues
Arts and Culture	Population
Distribution of Natural Characteristics	

When the Eisenhower group turned to identifying sub-issues, difficulties emerged that called into question the concept of the chain. First, the concept of the chain was appropriate only to those issues that presented a contemporary problem that had ramifications for the United States, either by emanating from or being thrust upon the country. Energy was promising in this regard, but Arts and Culture was not. Second, as already noted, the number of variables that had to be incorporated in each chain greatly constrained the process of letting an issue unfold according to a natural topical progression. It proved impossible to define each sub-issue in a way that moved the chain simultaneously across space, time, and disciplines, not to mention a steady increase in degree of sophistication. As a result, the Eisenhower group essentially abandoned the concept of the chain while taking care nonetheless to build into each list of sub-issues geographical, historical, and disciplinary variety as seemed natural to the issue. Incorporating disciplinary variety was the most difficult to do because each issue, by and large, heavily emphasized a particular discipline or field of knowledge. The Eisenhower group also took care to build into the subtopics several themes about which the committee was especially concerned: the problems of developing nations, interdependence among nations, and historical transformations important to an understanding of the modern world. While the committee made numerous revisions in the list of subtopics developed at Eisenhower, it did not make any effort to restore the concept of the chain.

Defining the issues to be tested gradually gave way to writing test questions, although these activities were never wholly separate in time. There was a reciprocal relationship between defining and writing, since question writers, whether inside or outside the committee, were usually given leeway to write questions on sub-issues that they thought should be listed, as well as on the sub-issues that already were. If the committee liked questions that it reviewed on sub-issues that had not been delineated, the list was revised. In that way, the total number of questions on the test expanded from an initially planned 50 or so to double that number.

Question writers were sometimes solicited by mail and sometimes invited to attend workshops in New York or Princeton. The workshop participants were particularly influential in bringing about revisions in the list of sub-issues, since their question-writing sessions almost inevitably turned into seminars on global issues.

One query that arose in both the workshops and committee meetings is especially worth noting. How ''technical'' does information have to be before one can say that it is too technical for broadly educated college students? Everyone agreed, for example, that the test ought not to assess a formal knowledge of economics as a discipline, but rather a knowledge of economic developments or issues that might be gleaned from a variety of courses or newspapers or newsmagazines with in-depth coverage of world affairs. Not everyone agreed, however, about the degree of scientific knowledge that could reasonably be required of college students, perhaps because fewer non-science majors take science courses than vice versa, or because coverage of science in the news media tends to be more limited than coverage of other aspects of the contemporary world. There was also some uneasiness expressed in the committee that ''too technical'' was what committee members did not know about fields other than their own.

During the question writing phase, a small number of questions were pilot tested along with attitudinal measures. While the major purpose of the pilot test was to see how the attitudinal measures functioned and what their relationship to the knowledge component was, a secondary purpose was to see how difficult the knowledge questions were. The results of pilot testing showed that although the questions were difficult, they were not so difficult as to jeopardize the measurement objectives of the survey.

When the pool of approved questions was ready for assembly into the final version of the test, the issue of test length had to be decided. In consideration of the fact that the total time available for administration of the complete survey was two hours, the decision was made to limit the test component to approximately one hour. In terms of the number of questions that could be handled by most students in an hour, this translated to about 100 questions. The actual number of questions that appeared in the test booklet was 113, of which 96 were from the pool, five from a somewhat similar test that had been administered to high school students several years ago (and on which comparative data were desired), and 12 from a pool of error-choice questions that were attitudinal rather than knowledge measures.

The fact that 96 questions was all that could be allocated to the list of issues defined by the committee meant that the amount of coverage for each issue was modest at best. The number of questions for each issue ranged from a low of four for Distribution of Natural Characteristics to a high of ten each for Relations among States and Population. The test should not be thought of, therefore, as an in-depth assessment of student knowledge about each issue, but as a survey instrument whose strength lies more in the dimension of breadth of coverage than depth.

Chapter 2

Attitudes and Perceptions

Thomas S. Barrows

While the required breadth of content coverage seems to have been the surprise in development of the knowledge or cognitive area, method was unquestionably the potential stumbling block of affective measurement. Consequently, our strategy was quite different, resembling "psychometric groping" to find something or some things that were not artifacts of our measurement methods. We employed existing measures and new ones, and relied heavily on successive revisions based upon multiple analyses of pilot and pretest data. Four distinct measurement methods were employed: Likert; Self-Report; Semantic Differential; Error Choice.

Likert

A large number of Likert scales appear in the general political attitude literature and a number of them appear to be related to global understanding. (Likert scales involve a series of statements to which respondents indicate agreement or disagreement on a 5-point response scale.) We initially chose 64 items from 10 existing scales: The Worldmindedness Scale, the Pacificism Scale, the Internationalism Scale, the Hostility in International Relations Scale, the Nationalism Scale, the Internationalism-Nationalism Scale, the Patriotism Scale, The Attitudes toward Patriotism Scale, the Peterson War Scale, and the Attitudes toward World Affairs Scale.* The 64 items we chose seemed to us to tap variables likely to be central to conceptions of global understanding. Items were discarded that seemed wide of the mark as well as those that appeared so dated as to be potentially useless at this time.

The items chosen were assembled into a pilot test and administered to 147 students at local colleges. Intercorrelations among all item responses were computed and then factor analyzed (see Figures 1.2.1. - 1.2.3.). Four factors emerged, and these were labeled Chauvinism, World Government, Cooperation, and War.

---

*These 10 scales, as well as many others, are available in two compilations: Robinson, J.P., Rusk, J.G, and Head, K.B. *Measures of Political Attitudes*. Ann Arbor, Michigan: Institute for Social Research, 1968 and Shaw, M.E. and Wright, J.M. *Scales for measurement of attitudes*. New York: McGraw-Hill, 1967.

Figure 1.2.1. Characteristic Roots for 64 Likert Items
(N = 147)

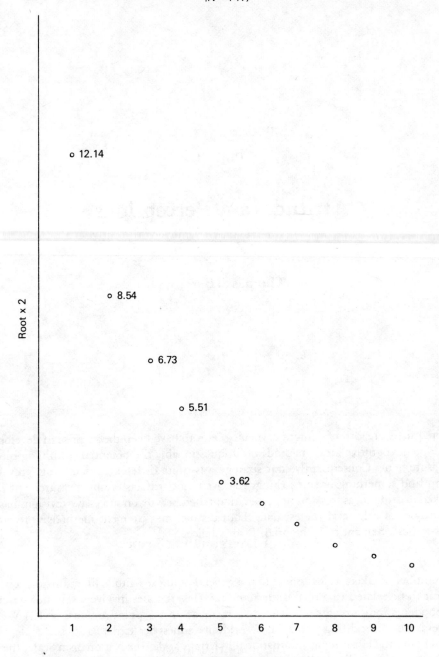

Note: 4 roots account for 72 percent of the common variance.

Figure 1.2.2. Promax Correlations with Primary Factors

Items	I	II	III	IV
1. All prices for imports and exports should be set by an international trade committee.	-.34	.03	.36	.16
2. It is unlikely that the U.S. will fight in another war within the next five years.	-.08	.02	-.15	-.19
3. The hatred of the U.S. by foreign countries is caused mostly by envy of our greatness.	.42	.07	.02	.06
4. The U.S. should not trade with any communist country.	.43	.29	.11	-.32
5. We should be willing to settle all differences with other nations within the framework of a World Government.	.05	-.01	.51	.00
6. The main threat to basic American institutions during this century has come from the infiltration of foreign ideas and doctrines.	.57	.41	-.01	-.21
7. Pacifism is simply not a practical philosophy in the world today.	.24	.05	.22	.11
8. If disarmament negotiations are not successful, the U.S. should begin a gradual program of unilateral disarmament—i.e., disarm whether other countries do or not.	-.09	-.09	.18	.35
9. The federal government should be prevented from giving away any more of our wealth to foreign governments.	.28	.50	.00	-.28
10. The U.S. is closer to being an ideal country than any other nation has ever been.	.40	-.14	.08	.15
11. Communism is the solution to our present economic problems.	.03	.00	-.44	-.03
12. An international authority should be established and given direct control over the production of nuclear energy in all countries, including the U.S.	.07	.09	.53	.04
13. Immigrants should not be permitted to come into our country if they compete with our own workers.	.18	.55	-.01	-.18
14. Under some conditions, war is necessary to maintain justice.	-.03	-.14	-.11	.69
15. I believe that the U.S. should send food and materials to any country that needs them.	-.05	.40	.17	.02
16. People should refuse to engage in any war, no matter how serious the consequences to their country may be.	-.11	-.11	.15	.54
17. I can accept the leadership of foreign countries in many fields.	.22	.21	.06	.06
18. Communism is a leftist version of rightist fascism.	-.35	-.01	.03	.00
19. It would be dangerous for our country to make international agreements with nations whose religious beliefs are antagonistic to ours.	.49	.33	-.09	-.25
20. Any healthy individual, regardless of race or religion, should be allowed to live in whatever country he or she chooses.	.05	.35	.15	.22
21. It is contrary to my principles to participate in war and the killing of other people.	-.08	.03	.03	.45
22. The best way to insure peace is to keep the U.S. stronger than any other nation in the world.	.43	.07	.13	.41
23. Most of the countries which have gotten economic help from America end up resenting what we have done for them.	.03	.20	.18	-.03
24. The American ideal of bigger, faster, and more doesn't appeal to me.	.30	.10	.03	.08
25. The ideals of communism are worth working for.	-.48	-.11	-.28	.04
26. The United Nations should be abandoned as unworkable.	.12	.06	.06	.14
27. Immigration should be controlled by an international organization rather than by each country on its own.	-.08	-.01	.37	.09
28. There will be no more wars when people become really civilized.	-.01	-.05	.50	-.05
29. We need compulsory universal military training to keep our country strong and safe from attack.	.35	.20	-.13	.10
30. I think the American people are the finest in the world.	.53	.07	.17	.03

9

Figure 1.2.2. Promax Correlations with Primary Factors (cont'd.)

Items	I	II	III	IV
31. The idea of a World Government as the future hope of international peace should be viewed with suspicion.	.31	.30	.30	.05
32. The U.S. should be open to all those who wish to settle here.	-.10	.49	.09	.00
33. The only way peace can be maintained is to keep America so powerful and well-armed that no other nation will dare to attack us.	.48	-.02	.09	.46
34. When I see so much corruption in the government of my country, I can't support it wholeheartedly.	.12	-.34	.27	.17
35. Our country should not participate in any international organization which requires that we give up any of our national rights or freedom of action.	.22	.07	.36	.01
36. The U.S. should be willing to provide the United Nations with troops to act, along with troops of other countries, as an international police force.	.19	.19	.23	-.23
37. World history should replace American history as a required course in U.S. schools.	.16	.03	.26	.13
38. I think that helping foreign countries is a waste of money.	.28	.65	.11	-.25
39. We should strive for loyalty to our country before we can afford to consider world brotherhood.	.50	.38	.08	-.05
40. Americans are willing to sacrifice anything to profit.	.07	-.26	.22	.35
41. The U.S. should concentrate upon keeping itself strong and should not get involved in the affairs of other countries.	.34	.61	.13	-.30
42. One should show greater loyalty towards humanity than towards the U.S. as a nation.	.26	.06	.13	.32
43. All military training should be abolished.	.00	-.06	.28	.10
44. It would not be dangerous for us to guarantee by international agreement that every person in the world should have complete religious freedom.	.11	.11	.10	.24
45. I'm for my country, right or wrong.	.51	.05	.08	.06
46. The U.S. ought to be willing to give up its independence and submit to the authority of a United States of the World.	.19	.01	.62	.07
47. If necessary, we ought to be willing to lower our standard of living to cooperate with other countries in getting an equal standard for every person in the world.	.28	.26	.53	.05
48. It would not be wise for us to agree that working conditions in all countries should be subject to international control.	-.14	-.15	-.20	.08
49. Patriotism and loyalty are the first and most important requirements of a good citizen.	.53	.07	.01	-.04
50. Underdeveloped areas should be helped through United Nations agencies like the World Health Organization and UNESCO.	.07	.30	.01	.02
51. America is committed to mediocrity by reason of the democratic ideal.	.10	.38	-.06	-.33
52. The communist is too radical and extreme in his views.	-.52	-.17	-.12	.11
53. The United Nations should be strengthened by giving it control of the armed forces of all member nations.	-.24	-.02	.42	.12
54. We should be open-minded about communism.	.49	.15	.45	-.05
55. It is unlikely that the U.S. will fight in another war within the next 25 years.	-.12	-.05	.16	-.05
56. Any form of international government is impossible.	.23	.16	.51	.01
57. The immigration of foreigners to this country should be kept down so that we can provide for Americans first.	.26	.76	.01	-.13
58. War is sometimes necessary because right is more important than peace.	.08	-.03	.01	.53
59. We should have a World Government with the power to make laws which would be binding to all its member nations.	.05	.11	.59	.11
60. Our country should have the right to prohibit certain racial and religious groups from immigrating.	.34	.54	-.07	.08
61. There is no conceivable justification for war.	-.08	-.12	.01	.67

10

Items	I	II	III	IV
62. George Washington's advice to stay out of agreements with foreign powers is just as wise now as it was when he was alive.	-.46	-.46	-.17	.37
63. One main trouble with American foreign policy today is that there is too much concern with military force and too little concern with political negotiation and economic reconstruction.	-.05	-.08	.04	.40
64. In the interests of humanity, America's doors should be opened wide to immigrants from all nations and current restrictive quotas should be abolished.	-.02	.49	.11	.09

Figure 1.2.3. Correlations Among Primary Factors

		II	III	IV
I	Chauvinism	.31	.15	-.07
II	Cooperation		.09	-.22
III	World Government			.09
IV	War			

For the next stage, pretesting, we decided that a minimum of five positively worded and five negatively worded items should mark each factor. Pilot test results, however, yielded only the following candidates:

> Factor I - 9 negative items;
> Factor II - 6 negative items, 4 positive items;
> Factor III - 1 negative item, 7 positive items;
> Factor IV - 3 negative items, 4 positive items.

For Factors I and II where there were more than five negative items with correlations over .38, those with the highest correlations were chosen. For Factor III, which had seven positive items with correlations over .38, the five highest-loading items were chosen. Where there were not enough positive or negative item correlations over .38, we reexamined those items that loaded the factor with slightly lower values. Only one was found, however, with a satisfactory correlation with the subject factor uncomplicated by appreciable correlations with other factors. At this point, where numbers of items were still too low, we returned to the various scales from which the pilot-test items were drawn and chose new items that were scored in the desired direction. In this manner 40 items were selected for the pretest.

Forty new Likert-type items were then written specifically for the global understanding pretest. These new items focused on the following topics: human rights, political freedoms, shortages of natural resources, environmental pollution, hunger and malnutrition, health care, overpopulation, intergroup conflict, international relations, war and armaments, and economic instability. The total collection of Likert items was then administered to 380 college students.

Item intercorrelations and subsequent factor analyses (see Figures 1.2.4. - 1.2.6.) yielded five factors but only four were interpretable, and these looked very much like the pilot-test factors. They were labeled "Chauvinism," "World Government," "Cooperation," and "War." The replication of the pilot-test factors was reassuring, and we chose seven Chauvinism, seven World Government, eight Cooperation, and six War items for the final survey instrument.

11

Figure 1.2.4. Characteristic Roots for 80 Likert Items
(N = 380)

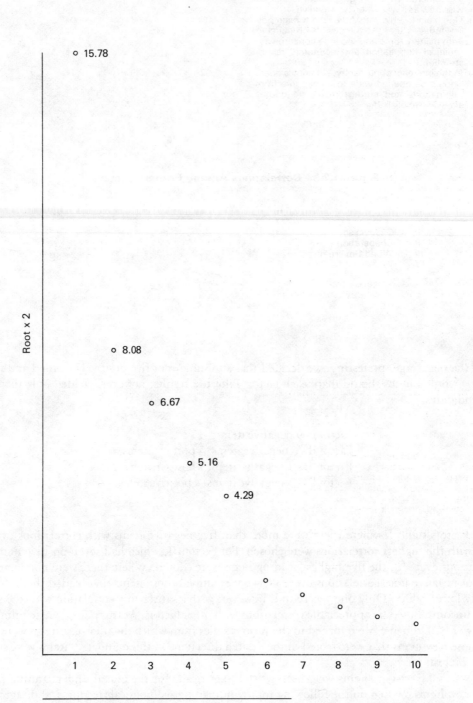

Note: 5 roots account for 75 percent of the common variance.

Figure 1.2.5. Promax Correlations with Primary Factors
(N = 380)

Items	I	II	Correlations III	IV	V
1. I think the American people are the finest in the world.	.45	.15	.29	.00	.25
2. Pacifist demonstrations—picketing missile bases, peace walks, etc.—are harmful to the best interest of the American people.	.52	.12	.27	.23	.09
3. The idea of a World Government as the future hope of international peace should be viewed with suspicion.	.30	.40	.20	-.05	-.05
4. Terrorism cannot be justified under any circumstances.	-.08	-.05	-.07	.30	.14
5. I believe that the U.S. should send food and materials to any country that needs them.	.17	.38	.53	.01	.19
6. Industries that have polluted rivers and lakes should be forced to clean them up no matter what the cost.	.01	.23	.08	.29	.14
7. The U.S. ought to commit more of its resources to raising the level of health care in underdeveloped nations.	.21	.48	.51	.03	.10
8. Americans are a mixture of all nationalities and are neither better nor worse than the nationalities that go into making them.	.14	.24	.28	.09	.23
9. The best way to insure peace is to keep the U.S. stronger than any other nation in the world.	.60	.22	.21	-.01	.25
10. The immigration of foreigners to this country should be kept down so that we can provide for Americans first.	.48	.09	.65	-.02	-.02
11. Underdeveloped areas should be helped through United Nations agencies like the World Health Organization and UNESCO.	.20	.07	.10	.42	.06
12. Effective worldwide family planning will allow the world's population to stabilize by the end of this century.	.06	-.26	-.03	-.13	-.01
13. Political freedom is a basic human right and no government should be permitted to abridge it.	-.01	-.08	.11	.41	-.04
14. It is contrary to my principles to participate in war and the killing of other people.	.30	.24	.17	.19	.35
15. The main threat to basic American institutions during this century has come from the infiltration of foreign ideas and doctrines.	.59	.05	.29	.10	-.06
16. I think that helping foreign countries is a waste of time.	.46	.09	.41	.33	.02
17. Since the world's supplies of essential minerals are limited, the mining and distribution of mineral resources should be controlled by an international authority.	.19	.48	.16	.05	.16
18. Everyone should have the right to leave any country, including his own, and to return to his country.	.15	-.02	.26	.30	.08
19. We should be willing to settle all differences with other nations within the framework of a World Government.	.09	.61	.13	.01	.15
20. In the interests of humanity, America's doors should be opened wide to immigrants from all nations and current restrictive quotas should be abolished.	.00	.30	.53	-.26	.19
21. War is a satisfactory way to solve international problems.	.37	.10	.16	.33	.40
22. We should cooperate fully with smaller democracies and should not regard ourselves as their leaders.	.33	.19	.24	.21	.02
23. It would be dangerous for us to guarantee by international agreement that every person in the world should have complete religious freedom.	.23	.08	.25	.07	.15
24. World population growth is a severe problem.	.07	.01	-.03	.21	-.12

Figure 1.2.5. Promax Correlations with Primary Factors (cont'd.)
(N = 380)

Items	Correlations				
	I	II	III	IV	V
25. In order to protect American workers' jobs, our government should raise the tariffs on imported goods which compete with American products.	.27	.04	.26	-.27	.06
26. Decreasing the United States' energy consumption should be our most important, immediate goal.	-.01	.17	.01	.37	-.06
27. No government should deny access to basic education to any of its citizens.	.22	-.01	.15	.41	.09
28. Intergroup conflicts cause problems in almost all areas of the world.	.03	-.07	.00	.30	.02
29. We should not allow foreign business enterprises to buy American farmland.	.15	.07	.39	-.32	-.07
30. A drought in India is a more serious occurrence than a drought in the midwestern U.S.	.19	.17	.25	.07	.11
31. Under some conditions, war is necessary to maintain justice.	.27	.15	.14	-.11	.72
32. Patriotism and loyalty are the first and most important requirements of a good citizen.	.54	-.01	.15	-.08	.08
33. Decreasing the United States' reliance on foreign oil should be our most important, immediate goal.	-.11	-.08	-.13	.44	-.06
34. The proliferation of nuclear arms is a serious threat to our continued existence on the planet earth.	.20	.14	.16	.43	-.01
35. Immigrants should not be permitted to come into our country if they compete with our own workers.	.39	.00	.53	.05	-.02
36. We should have a World Government with the power to make laws which would be binding to all its member nations.	.05	.56	.09	-.11	.01
37. Corporations that are polluting rivers and lakes should be forced to stop immediately even if it means that they must go out of business.	-.13	.35	.06	-.06	.30
38. War is sometimes necessary because right is more important than peace.	.21	.10	.07	-.02	.65
39. Any healthy individual, regardless of race or religion, should be allowed to live in whatever country he chooses.	.17	.16	.53	.27	.18
40. By the time the world's supplies of essential minerals are exhausted, scientists will have created synthetic substances to replace them.	.30	.05	.03	.14	.04
41. We should be willing to let American investments in foreign countries be lost if the only other alternative is war.	.27	.17	.17	.10	.17
42. Any form of international government is impossible.	.21	.30	.05	-.03	-.02
43. We need Arab oil so we had better find ways to get along with the Arabs, even if that means supporting Israel less.	-.17	-.07	-.09	-.20	-.15
44. Within twenty years, pollution from sulphur dioxide will have acidified lakes and rivers to such an extent that fish and plants can no longer live in them.	-.06	.32	.00	.00	.33
45. Investment of foreign capital in America is good for the United States.	-.01	.00	.18	-.08	.02
46. There is no conceivable justification for war.	-.03	.33	.13	-.18	.63
47. Our country should have the right to prohibit certain racial and religious groups from immigrating.	.39	.06	.55	.07	.04
48. The U.S. has the best health care delivery system in the world.	.36	.00	.11	.07	-.08
49. An international authority should be established and given direct control over the production of nuclear energy in all countries, including the United States.	.00	.37	.07	-.03	.15
50. Whereas some people feel that they are citizens of the world, that they belong to mankind and not to any one nation, a true American always feels that his primary allegiance is to his own country.	.41	.21	.21	-.23	.01

Items	Correlations				
	I	II	III	IV	V
51. There will be no more wars when people become really civilized.	-.09	.35	.07	-.09	.20
52. It is our responsibility to do everything possible to prevent people from starving anywhere in the world.	.24	.43	.51	.21	.14
53. One main trouble with American foreign policy is that there is too much concern with military force and too little with political negotiation and economic reconstruction.	.20	.34	.01	.06	.34
54. Many products imported from abroad are superior to those manufactured here, and they should not be priced out of the American market by high tariffs.	.03	.17	.12	-.25	.11
55. Changes in government should always be accomplished through peaceful means.	.03	.04	.10	.25	.42
56. The U.S. and other technologically advanced countries should do a great deal more than they have in the past to aid underdeveloped nations which are stricken by natural catastrophes.	.21	.33	.36	.23	.12
57. We should not allow foreign companies to own American natural resources (like forests and coal mines).	.16	.14	.33	-.36	.04
58. It is none of our business if other governments restrict the personal freedom of their citizens.	.36	-.10	.22	.35	-.11
59. The only way peace can be maintained is to keep America so powerful and well-armed that no other nation will dare to attack us.	.63	.19	.22	-.04	.34
60. The U.S. should be open to all those who wish to settle here.	.14	.17	.62	-.03	.16
61. Within the next twenty years, the increase in world population will lead to a serious shortage of food even in the industrialized countries.	-.05	.19	-.03	.05	.19
62. No duties are more important than duties toward one's country.	.65	.06	.18	.07	.03
63. Even if there were a prolonged drought in the U.S., it is unlikely that there would be a famine.	-.22	-.01	-.08	.08	.00
64. If disarmament negotiations are not successful, the U.S. should begin a gradual program of unilateral disarmament—i.e., disarm whether other countries do or not.	.03	.40	.20	-.33	.34
65. Within the next 20 years, considerable investment by developed nations in improving food production and health services in the Third World will dramatically increase the life span there.	.03	.03	.00	.29	-.01
66. Education should be directed primarily at promoting understanding, tolerance, and friendship among all nations, races, and religious groups.	.12	.34	.28	.25	.14
67. The U.S. should concentrate upon keeping itself strong and should not get involved in the affairs of other countries.	.47	.08	.39	.21	-.08
68. Each country in the world should limit its energy consumption to the amount it produces.	-.11	.16	.00	.06	.30
69. Many of the world's problems are caused by conflicts among diverse ethnic groups living close to one another.	-.07	-.03	-.07	.19	-.13
70. People should refuse to engage in any war, no matter how serious the consequences to their country may be.	-.03	.37	.11	-.29	.44
71. Increases in the price of oil have greater impact on the economies of *developed* countries than on the economies of *developing* countries.	.18	.02	.16	-.04	-.04
72. I prefer to be a citizen of the world rather than of any country.	.32	.49	.33	-.27	.23
73. Terrorist activities may be the only way for an oppressed minority to publicize its plight.	.08	-.09	.15	.34	.31

Figure 1.2.5. Promax Correlations with Primary Factors (cont'd.)
(N = 380)

Items	Correlations				
	I	*II*	*III*	*IV*	*V*
74. In the long run, it would be to our best interest as a nation to spend less money for military purposes and more money for education, housing, and other social improvements.	.45	.29	.15	.15	.29
75. The insistence of individuals living in democratic societies that no government should restrict the personal freedom of its own citizens is an example of sociocultural bias.	.00	.17	-.12	.02	.11
76. We should work for total, universal disarmament because the existence of arms encourages war.	.25	.35	.20	.20	.20
77. I'm for my country, right or wrong.	.64	.11	.29	.06	.10
78. The U.S. ought to be willing to give up its independence and submit to the authority of a United States of the World.	.16	.61	.22	-.27	.05
79. Violent revolution is sometimes the only way to eliminate an oppressive government.	.08	.11	.16	-.06	.53
80. Well-fed people in developed nations should voluntarily cut back on their food consumption and contribute food to the inadequately fed in underdeveloped nations.	.17	.40	.28	.24	.17

Figure 1.2.6. Correlations Among Primary Factors

	II	*III*	*IV*	*V*
I Chauvinism	.17	.41	.13	.12
II World Government		.30	-.06	.30
III Cooperation			.08	.14
IV Uninterpretable				.01
V War				

On the other hand, the fact that our 40 new items did not reveal any interpretable response structure was disappointing, and we decided to extend (perhaps overextend) our analyses of the pretest data. Thus, a second factor analysis of the 25x25 matrix of correlations among selected new item responses was carried out. Two latent roots were greater than one—2.30 and 1.11 respectively—and two factors were therefore rotated to orthogonal and oblique simple structures. Study of these structures yielded nothing interpretable, and so our attempts to add to the simple Chauvinism, World Government, Cooperation, War structure were unproductive.

One final group of four items was added to the 28 covering the four-factor structure. These were four human rights items that were added simply because their topical coverage was too important to neglect. Although they had not formed a factor, their intercorrelations were sufficiently high to support relaxed standards of convergent validity (see Figure 1.2.7.). The Likert item section thus was made up of 32 items ostensibly covering five factors.

Figure 1.2.7. Correlations Among Human Rights Items

	No. 18	*No. 2,*	*No. 58*
13. Political freedom is a basic human right and no government should be permitted to abridge it.	.19	.29	.21
18. Everyone should have the right to leave any country, including his own, and to return to his country.		.24	.17
27. No government should deny access to basic education to any of its citizens.			.19
58. It is none of our business if other governments restrict the personal freedom of their citizens.			

16

Self-Report

The second method of attitude measurement we employed is called "self-report." Like the Likert technique it too has a long history, although its use has been primarily in personality assessment rather than in political attitude work. Respondents are asked to mark "True" or "False" to a number of potentially self-descriptive statements such as "I enjoy meeting people from other cultures."

Numerous items of this sort were written, and eighteen of them were administered in our pretest (N = 380). Ten items, based largely upon the correlations of each item with the total scale score, were chosen for the survey (see Figure 1.2.8.). The ten items are numbers 3, 5, 7, 9, 11, 13, 14, 15, 17, and 18. In the final survey they are balanced between positive and negative wording to control "agreement" response bias. This was accomplished by reversing item 17. The word "not" was added.

Figure 1.2.8. Correlations of Self-Report Items with Total Scale Score

		bis
1.	I have a great deal in common with most other human beings.	.28
2.	My attitudes and interests are well-defined.	.15
3.	I am interested in international relations and acquire information about international developments whenever I can.	.42
4.	Most of my actions go unnoticed by the rest of the world.	.16
5.	I enjoy meeting people from other cultures.	.37
6.	My needs are specific to my individuality.	.38
7.	I have almost nothing in common with people in underdeveloped countries.	.42
8.	I am a rugged individualist.	.20
9.	I am most comfortable with people from my own culture.	.39
10.	I have considered numerous lifestyles.	.29
11.	I feel a strong kinship with the worldwide human family.	.50
12.	Some of my actions have systematic global implications.	.43
13.	I find the customs of foreigners difficult to understand.	.30
14.	I rarely read news articles about international events.	.32
15.	The fact that a flood can kill 25,000 people in India is very depressing to me.	.41
16.	My needs are like those of most of the rest of the people in the world.	.25
17.	I am interested in studying other cultures.	.55
18.	When I hear that millions of people are starving in India, I feel very frustrated.	.44

Semantic Differential

Osgood's (Osgood, Suci, and Tannenbaum, 1957) Semantic Differential was the third technique employed. In our early versions, students were asked to consider "problems" such as Depletion of Natural Resources or Environmental Pollution and to rate each on several bipolar, adjectival scales such as important-unimportant, simple-complex, and so on. Rather than being characterized as a simple attitude measure like the Likert and Self-report scales, this technique taps numerous dimensions of perception, although an evaluative component often emerges and may be thought of as at least akin to attitude. Systematic development of a Semantic Differential instrument is unusually demanding because it is necessary to choose both the rating scales and stimuli to be rated in some convincing manner. More specifically, our goal was to choose "world problems" for rating that would allow us to generalize to some domain of world problems and to choose rating scales that would cover the multivariate richness of students' perceptions.

The first pilot test was conducted at ETS (N = 15) using five stimuli: The Energy Crisis; Inflation; Overpopulation; Recognition of Universal Human Rights; and Conflict and Revolution. Subjects were asked to make up lists of up to 12 adjective pairs that they might use to compare and contrast the issues. They were then asked to write the adjectives on blank Semantic Differential scales and rate each issue on the scales they had chosen. "Good/Bad" and "Simple/Complex" were given as examples of adjective pairs and the latter pair was printed as the first scale under each issue. Following "Simple/Complex" were twelve blank scales for each subject's choices.

The fifteen subjects used 84 different adjective pairs. Fourteen pairs were used by two or more subjects: real/unreal (12); soluble/insoluble (7); critical/trivial (5); inevitable/avoidable (5); interesting/boring (5); divisive/unifying (3); understood/misunderstood (3); political/apolitical (3); temporary/permanent (3); frequent/infrequent (2); important/unimportant (2); threatening/nonthreatening (2); peaceful/warlike (2); and hopeless/hopeful (2).

As instrument development for the survey progressed, a longer list of issues was developed for the Semantic Differential. A second pilot test was administered to 35 subjects at two colleges. Two separate instruments were developed for this pilot test using the following ten "issues" as stimuli:

1. Recognition of Universal Human Rights
2. Equitable Allocation of the World's Material Wealth
3. Population Growth and Distribution
4. Depletion of Non-Renewable Resources
5. International Conflict War
6. Racial Cultural Conflict
7. Control of Air and Water Pollution
8. Ownership of the Seas
9. Coping with Natural Disasters
10. Monetary Instability

On the first instrument (N = 18), subjects were asked to think of adjective pairs that might be used to compare and contrast the issues. Nineteen adjective pairs were used by two or more subjects. On the second instrument (N = 17), subjects were asked to consider each issue separately and to list single adjectives that they might use to describe the stimulus. Thirty-three adjectives were used by two or more of these subjects (see Figure 1.2.9.).

Using the lists of adjectives from these two instruments and Osgood's list of "evaluation, activity, and potency" adjectives (Osgood, p. 53), we chose a number of scales for the pretesting. Later, members of the Assessment Committee suggested adding several "statement" pairs to the instrument and the following 15 scales were agreed upon.

Semantic Differential Scales

1.	Important	Unimportant
2.	National	International
3.	Political	Nonpolitical
4.	Simple	Complex
5.	Immediate	Long-term
6.	Necessary	Unnecessary
7.	Rational	Irrational
8.	Controllable	Uncontrollable
9.	Increasing	Decreasing
10.	American government can do a lot to solve this problem	American government can do very little to solve this problem
11.	International organizations can do a lot to solve this problem	International Organizations can do very little to solve this problem
12.	I know a lot about this problem	I know very little about this problem
13.	Interesting to learn about	Not interesting to learn about
14.	Of concern to people in many parts of the world	Of concern to people in only a few parts of the world
15.	Related to many other problems	Not related to many other problems

Figure 1.2.9. Semantic Differential, Second Pilot Test

COMPARATIVE (N = 18)

	Total
1) important/unimportant	11
2) national/international	8
3) simple/complex	8
4) immediate/long-term	7
5) solvable/unsolvable	6
6) possible/impossible	5
7) dangerous/not dangerous	4
8) good/bad	4
9) conflictual/peaceful	3
10) expensive/inexpensive	3
11) relevant/irrelevant	2
12) real/imagined	2
13) political/economic	2
14) political/social	2
15) rational/irrational	2
16) overestimated/underestimated	2
17) idealistic/realistic	2
18) governmental/non-governmental	2
19) rich/poor	2

SINGLE STIMULUS (N = 17)

	Monetary Instability	Coping with Natural Catastrophes	Ownership of the Seas	Control of Air and Water Pollution	Racial/Cultural Conflict	International Conflict/War	Depletion of Non-Renewable Resources	Population Growth and Distribution	Equitable Allocation of the World's Material Wealth	Recognition of Universal Human Rights	TOTAL
1) political (non)	8	–	7	8	5	12	5	5	8	8	66
2) international	7	7	10	7	3	3	8	2	4	3	54
3) economic	6	–	3	5	5	7	6	3	3	3	41
4) expensive	–	6	–	9	3	5	3	3	5	3	37
5) complex	5	–	5	4	4	2	4	3	4	3	34
6) necessary (un)	–	6	–	10	4	5	–	–	3	5	33
7) controversial	–	–	3	3	6	2	2	3	2	5	26
8) important	3	–	4	3	–	2	6	2	2	2	22
9) long-short term	4	2	3	5	4	2	2	2	–	–	21
10) widespread	–	–	–	2	2	2	3	4	–	–	19
11) disproportionate	2	–	–	–	–	–	–	11	–	–	13
12) wasteful	–	–	–	–	–	8	5	–	–	–	13
13) controllable (un)	2	2	3	2	3	–	–	6	4	2	13
14) possible (im)	–	–	2	2	–	–	5	–	–	–	10
15) social	–	–	–	–	2	2	–	2	–	–	9
16) under/over estimated	–	–	–	–	7	2	–	–	–	–	9
17) cultural	–	–	–	2	2	–	–	3	–	2	7
18) prejudice	–	–	–	–	–	–	–	–	–	–	7
19) education	–	–	–	3	–	–	–	2	–	–	6
20) frightening	–	–	–	–	3	–	–	2	–	–	6
21) humane (in)	–	2	–	2	–	–	–	–	–	–	6
22) governmental	2	3	–	3	–	–	3	–	–	–	6
23) unfortunate	–	–	–	–	–	–	3	–	–	–	6
24) conservation	–	–	–	–	–	–	2	–	–	–	6
25) immediate	–	–	–	–	–	–	–	–	–	–	5
26) ethnocentric	–	–	–	–	3	–	–	–	–	2	5
	37	28	40	70	56	54	57	53	35	43	473

In the language of working psychology, "backhandedness" refers to the extent to which *uncon-strained* behavior determines the outcomes of an investigation. At an early meeting, a member of the Assessment Committee pointed out that we had been admirably backhanded in our choice of adjectival scales for the Semantic Differential but that we had imposed our own structure on the instrument by choosing representative world problems according to our own perceptions. The observation was correct, of course, as each of the pilot test efforts had employed world problems furnished by project staff.

In order to rectify this situation, to build the backhanded quality into the stimuli as well as the scales, we worked with two members of the Assessment Committee and generated a list of 56 specific problems. These stimuli were printed on 3x5 index cards, ordered at random, and used in a third pilot test. Subjects (N = 147) at four colleges were asked to sort the 56 cards into as many categories as they wished, based on the similarities they perceived among them. Each subject was also asked to name the categories formed.

For analysis each subject's data constituted a 56x56 joint occurrence matrix. Pair-wise distances among the subjects' matrices were computed and subjects were arrayed in a two-dimensional space via M-D-SCAL (Kruskal, 1964 a and b). The resulting circumplex structure revealed two important structural qualities. First, outliers (those subjects at a great distance from the "eyeball centroid") had provided really bizarre data. They were excluded from further analyses. Second, within the central "cloud" of subjects', distance from the "centroid" looked like complexity or number of categories employed. Thus, having examined individual differences and excluded outliers, we employed Wiley's Latent Partition Analysis (Wiley, 1967) to obtain solutions of 6, 8, and 12 categories (see Figure 1.2.10.). The categories obtained were eminently interpretable and provided major problem labels that reflected subject perceptions rather than our own. For instance, "Racial Discrimination," "Age Discrimination," "Racial Segregation," "Sex Discrimination," "Apartheid," "Conflict Among Language Groups," "Conflict Among Religious Groups," and "Ethnic Conflict" became a major problem for the Semantic Differential with the label "Intergroup Conflict." Five other major problems that grew out of pilot testing were selected for the pretest: Denial of Basic Human Rights; Environmental Pollution and Depletion of Natural Resources; Malnutrition and Inadequate Health Care; International Conflict and War; and Economic Instability.

The pretest form of the semantic differential was administered to approximately 380 college students and the resulting scale intercorrelations were analyzed. Before the correlations were computed, stimulus means and subject means were swept out of the variance/covariance matrix so that the subsequent correlations indicated the degree of association among scales regardless of the problems (stimuli) being rated or the persons making the ratings. This procedure provides the best estimate of population structure in such a "persons-by-stimuli" design.

Figure 1.2.11. presents latent roots from a principle factors analysis of the correlations among scales. Although this plot may suggest as many as five factors, we chose a conservative 3-factor varimax solution (Figure 1.2.12.) as the basis for choosing scales for the survey. Rotations of larger numbers of factors and oblique rotations provided further differentiation among the scales but did not affect the choices of scales for the survey. Five scales representing Factor I were chosen for the final survey. Factor II loaded by "necessary" and "rational" was redefined as "solvable-unsolvable" and "avoidable-unavoidable." Factor III was adopted as it appeared, and a fourth component was incorporated—namely, "increasing-decreasing" and "immediate-long term," although they had not loaded any of the three factors appreciably. The scales were then transformed where necessary to a common statement format as follows:

Transformed Scales

1.	This problem is important.	1	2	3	4	5	This problem is unimportant.
2.	I know very little about this problem.	1	2	3	4	5	I know a lot about this problem.
3.	The American government can do a lot to solve this problem.	1	2	3	4	5	The American government can do very little to solve this problem.
4.	This problem will decrease in the next twenty years.	1	2	3	4	5	This problem will increase in the next twenty years.
5.	This problem is not interesting to learn about.	1	2	3	4	5	This problem is interesting to learn about.
6.	This problem is solvable.	1	2	3	4	5	This problem is unsolvable.

Figure 1.2.10. Latent Partition Analysis of Card-Sort Data; Three Degrees of Complexity

(N = 124)

RESTRICTION OF FREEDOM OF EXPRESSION
AND ACCESS TO INFORMATION
RESTRICTION OF FREEDOM OF RESIDENCE
AND MOVEMENT (WITHIN COUNTRY)
RESTRICTION OF PEACEFUL ASSEMBLY
AND ASSOCIATION
RESTRICTION OF PARTICIPATION IN
COMPETITIVE ELECTIONS
RESTRICTION OF FREEDOM TO LEAVE
HOME COUNTRY AND RETURN TO IT
RESTRICTION OF SOCIAL MOBILITY
RESTRICTION OF ACCESS TO BASIC
EDUCATION

RESTRICTION OF FREEDOM OF EXPRESSION
AND ACCESS TO INFORMATION
RESTRICTION OF FREEDOM OF RESIDENCE
AND MOVEMENT (WITHIN COUNTRY)
RESTRICTION OF PEACEFUL ASSEMBLY
AND ASSOCIATION
RESTRICTION OF PARTICIPATION IN
COMPETITIVE ELECTIONS
RESTRICTION OF FREEDOM TO LEAVE
HOME COUNTRY AND RETURN TO IT
RESTRICTION OF SOCIAL MOBILITY
RESTRICTION OF ACCESS TO BASIC
EDUCATION

RESTRICTION OF FREEDOM OF EXPRESSION
AND ACCESS TO INFORMATION
RESTRICTION OF FREEDOM OF RESIDENCE
AND MOVEMENT (WITHIN COUNTRY)
RESTRICTION OF PEACEFUL ASSEMBLY
AND ASSOCIATION
RESTRICTION OF PARTICIPATION IN
COMPETITIVE ELECTIONS
RESTRICTION OF FREEDOM TO LEAVE
HOME COUNTRY AND RETURN TO IT
RESTRICTION OF SOCIAL MOBILITY
RESTRICTION OF ACCESS TO BASIC
EDUCATION

OCCURRENCE OF NATURAL
CATASTROPHES
CATASTROPHIC WEATHER CONDITIONS
FLOOD
DROUGHT
INABILITY TO PREDICT NATURAL
CATASTROPHES
LACK OF DISASTER RELIEF
AIR POLLUTION
WATER POLLUTION
DEPLETION OF MINERAL RESOURCES
DEPLETION OF FOSSIL FUELS
NUCLEAR CATASTROPHE
ENERGY SHORTAGES

OCCURRENCE OF NATURAL
CATASTROPHES
CATASTROPHIC WEATHER CONDITIONS
FLOOD
DROUGHT
INABILITY TO PREDICT NATURAL
CATASTROPHES

AIR POLLUTION
WATER POLLUTION
DEPLETION OF MINERAL RESOURCES
DEPLETION OF FOSSIL FUELS
NUCLEAR CATASTROPHE
ENERGY SHORTAGES

OCCURRENCE OF NATURAL
CATASTROPHES
CATASTROPHIC WEATHER CONDITIONS
FLOOD
DROUGHT
INABILITY TO PREDICT NATURAL
CATASTROPHES

AIR POLLUTION
WATER POLLUTION
ENERGY SHORTAGES
OVERPOPULATION
OVERCROWDED HOUSING
UNEMPLOYMENT

DEPLETION OF FOSSIL FUELS
DEPLETION OF MINERAL RESOURCES

HUNGER
FAMINE
MALNUTRITION
EPIDEMICS
OVERPOPULATION
OVERCROWDED HOUSING
LACK OF ADEQUATE HEALTH CARE

HUNGER
FAMINE
MALNUTRITION
EPIDEMICS
OVERPOPULATIOIN
OVERCROWDED HOUSING
LACK OF ADEQUATE HEALTH CARE
LACK OF SOCIAL SECURITY
LACK OF DISASTER RELIEF

HUNGER
FAMINE
MALNUTRITION
EPIDEMICS

LACK OF ADEQUATE HEALTH CARE
LACK OF SOCIAL SECURITY
LACK OF DISASTER RELIEF
LACK OF A STABLE WORLD PEACE

RACIAL DISCRIMINATION
AGE DISCRIMINATION
RACIAL SEGREGATION
SEX DISCRIMINATION
APARTHEID
CONFLICT AMONG LANGUAGE GROUPS
CONFLICT AMONG RELIGIOUS GROUPS
ETHNIC CONFLICT

RACIAL DISCRIMINATION
AGE DISCRIMINATION
RACIAL SEGREGATION
SEX DISCRIMINATION
APARTHEID
CONFLICT AMONG LANGUAGE GROUPS
CONFLICT AMONG RELIGIOUS GROUPS
ETHNIC CONFLICT

RACIAL DISCRIMINATION
AGE DISCRIMINATION
RACIAL SEGREGATION
SEX DISCRIMINATION
APARTHEID

CONFLICT AMONG LANGUAGE GROUPS
CONFLICT AMONG RELIGIOUS GROUPS
ETHNIC CONFLICT

REVOLUTION
TERRORISM
VIOLENT CRIME
TORTURE
DICTATORSHIPS
ARBITRARY IMPRISONMENT
CIVIL DISOBEDIENCE
COLONIALISM
DISPUTES OVER TERRITORIAL WATERS
DISPUTES OVER FISHING RIGHTS
CONVENTIONAL ARMS PROLIFERATION
NUCLEAR ARMS PROLIFERATION
MUTUAL DEFENSE TREATIES
LACK OF A STABLE WORLD PEACE

REVOLUTION
TERRORISM
VIOLENT CRIME
TORTURE
DICTATORSHIPS
ARBITRARY IMPRISONMENT
CIVIL DISOBEDIENCE
COLONIALISM

CONVENTIONAL ARMS PROLIFERATION
NUCLEAR ARMS PROLIFERATION
MUTUAL DEFENSE TREATIES
DISPUTES OVER TERRITORIAL WATERS
DISPUTES OVER FISHING RIGHTS
LACK OF A STABLE WORLD PEACE

REVOLUTION
TERRORISM
VIOLENT CRIME
TORTURE
DICTATORSHIPS
ARBITRARY IMPRISONMENT
CIVIL DISOBEDIENCE
COLONIALISM

CONVENTIONAL ARMS PROLIFERATION
NUCLEAR ARMS PROLIFERATION
MUTUAL DEFENSE TREATIES
NUCLEAR CATASTROPHE

INFLATION
ECONOMIC DEPRESSION
CURRENCY REEVALUATIONS
ECONOMIC DEPENDENCY
ECONOMIC EXPLOITATION
ECONOMIC RECESSION
LACK OF SOCIAL SECURITY
UNEMPLOYMENT

INFLATION
ECONOMIC DEPRESSION
CURRENCY REEVALUATIONS
ECONOMIC DEPENDENCY
ECONOMIC EXPLOITATION
ECONOMIC RECESSION
UNEMPLOYMENT

INFLATION
ECONOMIC DEPRESSION
CURRENCY REEVALUATIONS
ECONOMIC DEPENDENCY
ECONOMIC EXPLOITATION
ECONOMIC RECESSION

DISPUTES OVER TERRITORIAL WATERS
DISPUTES OVER FISHING RIGHTS

Figure 1.2.11. Characteristic Roots for Semantic Differential Pretest
Within Correlation Matrix
(N = 380)

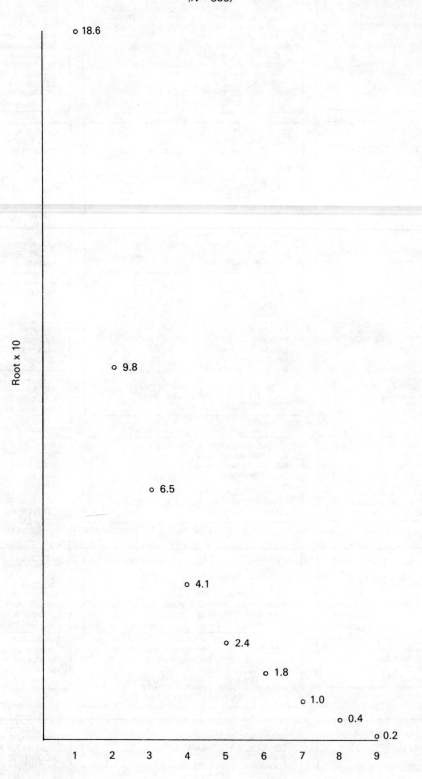

22

7.	International organizations can do very little to solve this problem.	1 2 3 4 5	International organizations can do a lot to solve this problem.
8.	This problem is unavoidable.	1 2 3 4 5	This problem is avoidable.
9.	This problem is related to many other problems.	1 2 3 4 5	This problem is not related to many other problems.
10.	This problem is temporary.	1 2 3 4 5	This problem is long-term.
11.	This problem is of concern to people in many parts of the world.	1 2 3 4 5	This problem is of concern to people in only a few parts of the world.

**Figure 1.2.12. Semantic Differential
Three Varimax Factors**

		1	2	3
1.	Important/Unimportant	.42	.04	.13
2.	National/International	-.02	.07	-.02
3.	Political/Nonpolitical	.18	-.02	.13
4.	Simple/Complex	-.26	.12	.04
5.	Immediate/Long-term	.00	.11	.05
6.	Necessary/Unnecessary	.08	.72	.03
7.	Rational/Irrational	.04	.66	.05
8.	Controllable/Uncontrollable	.07	.14	.29
9.	Increasing/Decreasing	.19	.02	.09
10.	American government can do a lot/can do very little to solve this problem.	.19	.02	.71
11.	International organizations can do a lot/can do very little to solve this problem.	.12	-.03	.48
12.	I know a lot/very little about this problem.	.53	.02	.14
13.	Interesting/not interesting to learn about.	.66	.05	.04
14.	Of concern to people in many/only a few parts of the world.	.45	.00	.11
15.	Related/not related to many other problems.	.54	-.02	.08

The six stimuli of the pretest were expanded to eight by separating "Environmental Pollution and Depletion of Natural Resources" into two distinct stimuli, and splitting "Economic Instability" into "Inflation" and "Unemployment." Thus, in the final instru...ents students made eleven ratings (scales above) of eight stimuli:

1.	Environmental Pollution	5.	Depletion of Natural Resources
2.	Denial of Basic Human Rights	6.	Inflation
3.	Unemployment	7.	Malnutrition and Inadequate Health Care
4.	Intergroup Conflict	8.	International Conflict and War

Error Choice

An affective measurement technique known as "error-choice" was the final one employed in the survey. Questions of this type appear to be factual and are in practice usually embedded among actual knowledge questions wherever they appear in a test or survey battery. Error-choice items present answer options that are ordered along the attitudinal variable that is of interest, and the correct answer is usually not provided as a response option. The response options provided usually bracket the correct response. In intergroup relations, error-choice has been used according to a rationale suggesting that consistently overestimating the prevalence of undesirable social characteristics or underestimating the prevalence of desirable ones within the target group constitutes an evaluative attitude towards the group. Thus, overestimating the crime rate for Hispanics has been interpreted as prejudice (Goldstein and Barrows, 1972).

For the Survey of Global Understanding, it was theorized that consistent overestimates or underestimates of the magnitude or prevalence of world problems might be indicative of a variable subsequently called "concern." Eleven error-choice items were written and pretested (N = 380) along with 20 cognitive items. Six of the items correlated highly (.35 or higher) with an error-choice total score derived by summing across all eleven items.

Figure 1.2.13. Correlations of Error-Choice Items with Error Choice Total Score

Pretest Item and Item Number

3. Proportion of countries with literacy rate below 50 percent	.41
6. Proportion of countries with GNP per capita less than 1/4 as large as U.S.	.50
9. "World price" of gasoline	.47
12. World average per capita cost of education	.50
15. Change in U.S. gasoline consumption	.35
18. Highest energy consumption	.32
19. Lowest energy consumption	
22. World population	-.02
25. Average proportion of GNP derived from foreign trade	.27
28. Proportion of the world's population living in countries that have nutritionally inadequate diets	.47
31. Proportion of world defense expenditure due to U.S. and Russia	.32

Those six items, along with six new ones written after the pretest, were embedded in the cognitive instrument for the final survey. The 12 items covered the following topics:

1. Proportion of countries with GNP per capita less that 1/4 as large as the United States;
2. Proportion of the world's population living in countries that have nutritionally inadequate diets;
3. Proportion of the world's population that has reasonable access to safe water;
4. The number of children who die every year from diseases that could be prevented by immunization;
5. The infant mortality rate in developing nations;
6. The average life expectancy in developing nations;
7. The "world price" of a gallon of gasoline;
8. The destructive power of the current world stockpile of nuclear arms;
9. The proportion of the countries of the world with literacy rates below 50 percent;
10. The estimated number of unemployed people in the world;
11. The change in United States gasoline consumption since the oil shortage of 1973; and
12. World average per capita expenditure for education.

Thus, four separate instruments, each employing distinct measurement methods, were developed to cover the affective area. It was expected that multiple proven techniques would enhance interpretations. In addition, multiple measures were intended to provide breadth of coverage so that the numerous potential affective components of global understanding could be tapped.

Chapter 3

Language

John L. D. Clark

. Rationale for Inclusion of Foreign Language Component

It is generally accepted, both by the lay public and the foreign language teaching profession, that the study of a foreign language is of considerable positive value to the student in developing a knowledge of and sensitiveness to countries and cultures other than his or her own. However, empirical data in support of this claim may be considered virtually non-existent, and the global understanding study offered an excellent opportunity for investigating the validity of this assumption and for determining, in some detail, the actual relationships between "foreign language variables" on the one hand and measured levels of global understanding, including affective orientation toward other countries and cultures, on the other. Such an investigation could have several possible outcomes, each with significant implications both for language teaching efforts in the United States and for curricular programs aimed at increasing the level of global understanding on the part of undergraduate students. Possible outcomes included the following:

- Global understanding level is not related to language background and/or personal interest, or to language proficiency;
- Global understanding is related to language background/interest but not to language proficiency;
- Global understanding is related to language proficiency but not to language background/interest;
- Global understanding is related to both level of background/interest and to language proficiency, either independently or on an additive basis.

It should be emphasized that within the scope of the study it was not possible nor intended to establish causal relationships between and among these variables in the sense of being able to say, for example, that a high level of global awareness comes about as a *consequence* of language interest, motivation, developed language skill, etc. (rather than the other way around). Nonetheless, to find

25

significant relationships among these survey variables—or perhaps equally revealing, to discover no such relationships—was felt to constitute a very important and potentially highly consequential project outcome in its own right.

Considerations in Selection of Data Collection Instruments

Data collection instruments for the foreign language portion of the survey were needed to obtain three different types of information:

- Foreign language background of the respondents—including both formal language study at the elementary, secondary, and college levels—and language contacts outside of the academic setting;
- Personal interest in and motivation for learning foreign languages;
- Actual proficiency in a modern foreign language—to the extent possible, expressed in terms of the ability to use the language in each of a variety of "real-life" situations that would be encountered in active, nonacademic use of the language.

Data gathering for the first two categories was considered straightforward, and a number of survey instruments were available that could easily be adapted for the purposes of the present study. Obtaining information on the actual language proficiency of survey respondents was considerably more complicated on both measurement and practical administrative grounds.

With respect to measurement considerations, currently available language tests were not, in general, appropriate to the data gathering purposes of the study. A major consideration in this regard was that carefully developed standardized tests of language proficiency were for the most part limited to the most widely taught languages: French, German, and Spanish (and, for some test batteries, Italian and Russian), and thus could not begin to cover the many different foreign languages that a large sample of the U.S. college population would be expected to have studied or acquired through other means.

Second, with the possible exception of the "Foreign Service Institute (FSI) interview technique," the major available language skills tests were not considered to have an especially high level of face or content validity as representative of the kinds of language-use tasks that the examinee would be expected to encounter in real-life situations. To give only one example, the listening comprehension test of the *MLA Foreign Language Proficiency Tests for Teachers and Advanced Students* battery (ETS, 1964) is based on the examinee's listening to brief tape-recorded utterances, short dialogues, and a few longer utterances in the test language. However, there is no simulation of other frequent and important listening comprehension situations such as television or radio broadcasts, telephone communication, "distorted speech" situations typical of airport, train, and other loudspeaker announcements, etc., and a variety of other "real world" listening tasks.

In addition to questions concerning the content coverage and appropriateness of available language tests were the considerable administrative difficulties that would be encountered in undertaking the administration of actual skills tests in a national survey. At any given institution, it would be necessary first to determine how many of the sampled students claimed even the slightest degree of foreign language proficiency and the particular language(s) represented, so that the necessary types and levels of tests could be made available.

With respect to test administration on-site, tests of reading comprehension and writing would be amenable to straightforward group administration, but administrative complexities would be raised by both listening comprehension tests (requiring separate audio materials for the different languages involved) and, especially, speaking tests (requiring recording-capable language laboratories or other procedures for individually recording the examinees' responses).

For all of these reasons, it did not appear possible to administer direct tests of language proficiency to the survey respondents. Consequently, an alternative means would have to be developed to obtain proficiency-related information for purposes of the study.

The decision was therefore made to make use of *student self-appraisals* of their own level of language proficiency. This approach was seen to have numerous advantages from both measurement-related and practical standpoints. First, the self-appraisal scales could be developed in such a way as to be uniformly applicable to any language. Second, these instruments could be prepared so as to directly reflect the "real-life" language-use situations of primary interest in the study. While available language tests (again, with the exception of the FSI interview) provide only normative information in the form of total test scores, behaviorally anchored self-assessment scales could be based on specific, criterion-related language-use situations, with the respondent asked to indicate whether or not (or the extent to which) he or she would be able to carry out the particular language-use activity in question. Language proficiency data of this latter type would be more straightforward and more immediately meaningful to both project staff and nonspecialist readers of the project report than would the normative data provided by available standardized language test scores.

Two cautions were in order concerning the adopting of this approach. First there was the possibility that respondents would not provide disinterested and frank appraisals of their foreign language ability, but would deliberately overestimate or underestimate their competence. This was not considered likely in the context of the Global Understanding Survey because the survey materials were to be completed anonymously (with ample assurances to the student of this fact) and they were to have no bearing whatsoever on course grades or other outcomes of interest to individual students.

The second caution was to insure that the self-appraisal scales developed and the data obtained from them would be generally in keeping with language proficiency information obtained from other independent objective sources—specifically, from actual tests of language skills. For reasons previously described, the available language skills tests were by no means considered ideal criterion measures against which the adequacy and usefulness of the self-appraisal scales could definitively be assessed. Indeed, it could with some justification be argued that the self-appraisal scales could properly be viewed as criterion measures in their own right, against which the relatively less face- and content-valid standardized proficiency tests should be compared, rather than the other way around.

Prestesting the Self-Appraisal Technique

Notwithstanding these considerations, it was felt by ETS project staff that before the proficiency self-appraisal technique was adopted for the survey, a preliminary study should be conducted in which both prototype self-appraisal scales and actual language skills tests would be administered to a group of students and comparable data obtained for the two types of measures. Although extremely high correlations between these two types of measures would not be anticipated (and indeed, would be undesirable to the extent that the skills tests were considered to depart from the precise measurement of real-life language proficiency), it was considered that a positive and reasonably substantial relationship would provide some confidence that the self-appraisal scales were indeed valid measures performing in a manner generally consistent with obtained performance on direct skills tests.

A preliminary study of this type could also provide information on the internal characteristics of the self-appraisal scales (for example, whether or not the *a priori* sequencing of the individual items into a Guttman-like scale of increasingly demanding language-use tasks was borne out by student response patterns) and would also permit the simultaneous pretesting of language background and language interest/motivation items for these respective sections of the survey questionnaire.

As outlined above, the questionnaire instruments to be used in the study were to include a language background section, a section addressing interest in and motivation for foreign language study, and the self-appraisal scales of language competence. Draft versions of all three sections were developed for preliminary testing. Development of the language background questions was relatively straightforward and involved the direct use or adaptation of relevant questions from other language survey materials, together with the drafting of several new items. Background questions for the preliminary form of the questionnaire requested information on the following:

1. Respondent's native language, native language of other family members and relatives (father and mother, paternal grandparents, maternal grandparents);
2. Place of birth;
3. If respondent not born in the United States, age in years on first arrival in the U.S.;
4. Prior study of Latin and classical Greek in high school, college, or other setting;
5. Study of a modern language other than English in a formal classroom setting "outside of the regular grade school/high school/college courses" (e.g., Hebrew school, language courses offered through cultural organizations such as the Alliance Française, Goethe House, etc.);
6. Travel to a country other than the United States, geographic areas visited and length of stay;

7. Participation in organized summer abroad or year abroad programs;
8. Residence abroad with members of own family for more than one month, travel abroad on "own hook";
9. Peace Corps service or similar kinds of service abroad;
10. Extent of use of a language other than English during stay(s) abroad;
11. History of formal study of foreign language(s) from 3rd grade through college senior (as indicated on a two-dimensional grade-level x language grid);
12. Identification of foreign language in which respondent considers himself or herself "most proficient" at the present time;
13. Average grades in high school and college in "most proficient" language;
14. "Traditional" vs. "audiolingual" orientation of "most proficient" language courses.

The foreign language interest/motivation section of the preliminary questionnaire was also developed from available instruments, with the drafting of a few additional items. With a few exceptions, the interest/motivation questions addressed one or another of the following categories:

1. General "enjoyment" of foreign languages and/or language study (e.g., "I really enjoy learning languages"; "In your school studies, how enjoyable did you find your foreign language classes by comparison to your other academic subjects in general?");
2. Judged importance of foreign language study from a "general public" standpoint (e.g., "How important do you consider it to be for Americans to learn foreign languages?" "Foreign languages are an important part of the school program.");
3. Personal motivation to study foreign languages ("If you had the opportunity to study a foreign language in the future (or to continue your language study) how would you react to this opportunity?", "I plan to learn one or more foreign languages as thoroughly as possible.");
4. "Instrumental" vs. "integrative" motivation for foreign language study (e.g., "Studying a foreign language can be important to me because I think it will someday be useful in getting a good job" vs. "Studying a foreign language can be important for me because it will allow me to meet and converse with more and varied people.").

A total of 22 items were included in the interest/motivation section.

A number of considerations were involved in the planning and preparation of the language proficiency self-appraisal scales. A basic question was that of the general response-elicitation format to be used. One possibility was to use the same verbal descriptions of competence that constitute the official scoring levels on the Foreign Service Institute proficiency scales for speaking ability and reading comprehension. These consist of five short paragraph descriptions of increasing levels of language competence ranging from a minimum (''survival'') level up to a competence level indistinguishable in all respects from that of an educated native speaker of the language. For example, the FSI descriptions of "level 2" ability in speaking proficiency and reading comprehension are, respectively:

> Can handle with confidence but not with facility most social situations including introductions and casual conversations about current events, as well as work, family, and autobiographical information; can handle limited work requirements, needing help in handling any complications or difficulties; can get the gist of most conversations on non-technical subjects (i.e., topics which require no specialized knowledge) and has a speaking vocabulary sufficient to express himself simply with some circumlocutions; accent, though often quite faulty, is intelligible; can usually handle elementary constructions quite accurately but does not have thorough or confident control of the grammar.

> With extensive use of a dictionary can get the general sense of routine business letters, international news items, or articles in technical fields within his competence.

One advantage in adopting the FSI scales more or less directly for use in the global understanding study would be that they could be quite readily understood and interpreted by foreign language researchers and others familiar with the meaning and interpretation of the FSI descriptions.

However, there were two perceived disadvantages. First, the relatively complicated wording and linguistic terminology used in these descriptions would be difficult for the respondents to understand and react to properly. Second (particularly for the speaking proficiency descriptions), the FSI descriptions tend to combine both "real-life" language-use situations and linguistically-oriented statements (e.g., "[can handle] elementary constructions quite accurately"; "accent...is intelligible," etc.). As such, they were not considered to represent as "pure" a measure of communicative or receptive proficiency (as distinct from the mastery of various linguistic aspects *per se*) as might be obtained through a scale developed specifically for the project and devoted entirely to situation-oriented behavioral descriptions.

In view of these considerations, it was felt that an alternative set of proficiency scales should be developed that would reduce or eliminate the difficulties associated with the FSI scale. In this regard, the project staff were aware of a questionnaire developed by the Experiment in International Living entitled "Your Objectives, Guidelines, and Assessment: An Evaluation Form of Communicative Competence," one section of which ("Behavioral Performance") asked the respondent to self-rate his or her ability to carry out each of a number of specific language-use tasks using the foreign language (e.g., "How well can you give or ask for directions?", "Can you ask and obtain biographical information from others?", "How well can you describe the geography of the United States or a familiar location?"). This approach seemed especially appropriate to the needs of the study, and was followed by project staff in preparing a set of three descriptive scales for respondent self-rating of speaking proficiency, listening comprehension (including both conversational contexts and "passive listening" situations such as watching movies or listening to news broadcasts), and reading comprehension of materials of various levels of complexity. (The draft scales are shown in Foreign Language Questionnaire—Pretest, Appendix C.)

For all three scales, a format was adopted which provided a behaviorally oriented statement of a particular language-use performance (e.g., "Say the days of the week") and respondents were asked in each instance to indicate whether they would be able to carry out that activity "quite easily," "with some difficulty," or "with great difficulty or not at all." Within a given scale, the language performance statements (which came to be referred to as "can do" statements by the project staff) were written and sequenced in such a way as to reflect the range from the most minimal of language skills to language-use situations that only a native speaker of the language or very highly qualified non-native would be presumed able to handle adequately.

For comparison purposes, and to provide an alternative measurement approach in the event that the "can do" scales were not found to operate effectively in the preliminary testing, it was decided also to include in the draft questionnaire "FSI-type" scales that would be based on the official FSI proficiency descriptions for speaking and listening comprehension, but would be rephrased in the first-person (i.e., from the respondent's perspective) and simplified in expression as much as possible without losing the essential descriptive content of the official definitions. The example below shows the rewritten "level 2" descriptions for speaking and reading:

> I can talk with native speakers of the MPL [most proficient language] about myself and my family, my job or studies, hobbies, and current events. I can understand most conversations in the MPL except when the speech is very fast. My grammar is fairly good but I make mistakes with complicated constructions. If I do not know the word for a particular thought or object, I can usually describe it by using other, easier words.

> I can get the general sense of routine business letters, news items, and articles in fields with which I am familiar, but I need to use a dictionary extensively in doing so.

As previously discussed, a major purpose of the preliminary administration was to relate student responses to the proficiency self-appraisal section of the questionnaire to externally measured performance as indicated by the results of actual proficiency test administration. With respect to the examinee group to be used for this purpose, it was considered that it would not be feasible, or for that matter desirable, to attempt to reflect the composition of the population that was of interest in the main part of the study (i.e., a representative nationwide sampling of freshman, two-year college, and senior undergraduate students). Because a large proportion of the students drawn from such a large and undifferentiated population would be expected to have no or very little active proficiency in a foreign language, it would therefore be necessary to administer the questionnaire/test materials to an unreasonably large number of students in order to insure adequate score variance on both types of instruments.

A much more advisable approach was felt to be to select an examinee group that would be expected in advance to cover a usefully wide range of language proficiency within a relatively small total number of examinees. In view of these considerations, it was decided to recruit only undergraduate students currently enrolled in a foreign language course, or, more specifically, to draw approximately equal numbers of students in "beginning," "intermediate," and "advanced" college language courses, which would provide a satisfactorily wide score range on both the language proficiency self-assessment instruments and the external skills tests.

The relative nonavailability of suitable external criterion instruments has already been discussed. Of the available instruments, the Foreign Service Institute (FSI) interviewing technique and scoring scale was a clear choice as the most appropriate measure of active speaking proficiency, not only for its high level of face and content validity but also because of its history of effective prior use in other language research studies, most notably the 1967 study by John B. Carroll on the foreign language proficiency of undergraduate language majors near graduation from college. Cross-comparisons of the results of this and other studies to those of the global understanding project would be of considerable interest.

For testing listening comprehension and reading, each of three possible test batteries were considered: the *MLA Foreign Language Proficiency Tests for Teachers and Advanced Students* (ETS, 1966); the *Pimsleur Modern Language Proficiency Tests* (Pimsleur, 1967); and the *MLA-Cooperative Foreign Language Tests* (ETS, 1965). Of these, the *MLA Foreign Language Proficiency Tests for Teachers and Advanced Students* (commonly referred to as the "MLA teacher tests") were expected to be somewhat too difficult, on the whole, for the examinee population of interest; although tests in this battery might be usefully administered to the "advanced" students in the preliminary study sample, they were viewed as probably out of range for the majority of students in the sample.

Tests in the remaining two batteries were considered quite similar in format and item types. Of the two, the Pimsleur tests were considered as probably too restricted in range toward the bottom of the potential examinee group. Although both "lower level" and "higher level" forms of the Pimsleur tests were available, the latter were designed and intended for students up through the second semester of college language study, whereas the corresponding *MLA-Cooperative Test* forms were intended for use by (and correspondingly normed for) students up through two full years (i.e., four semesters) of college-level language study.

In view of the potentially more appropriate difficulty levels represented by the MLA-Cooperative tests, and in view also of the more extensive normative and technical information that was available for the MLA tests by comparison to the Pimsleur tests, the former were selected for use in the preliminary administration. Specifically, the lower-level "L" forms of the listening comprehension and reading subtests were to be administered to the "beginning" and "intermediate" students in the preliminary study sample and the higher-level "M" forms to the "advanced" group. Conversion tables derived from vertical equating during the initial norming process were available for both "L" and "M" level scores, so that student scores on either of these forms could be expressed on a single common scale.

When it came to identifying subjects for validating the self-ratings, the project was quite fortunate. In connection with another separate project, a small group of college and university foreign language teachers, selected on a nationwide basis, had recently participated in intensive training workshops in the FSI technique conducted by the language staff of the Foreign Service Institute. The FSI staff made available the names of those participants whom they considered qualified to conduct FSI-type interviews in an appropriate and effective manner, using the same general procedures employed by the FSI staff interviewers.

From the listing provided by the Foreign Service Institute, workshop participants from six institutions were contacted on behalf of the project and their assistance requested in carrying out the preliminary questionnaire administration and skills testing using students on their own campuses. Specifically, each of these contact persons was asked to do the following:

- Identify three separate foreign language classes at "beginning," "intermediate,'' and "advanced" levels, defined, respectively, as having completed a one-semester "introductory" course (or the secondary school equivalent) and presently enrolled in the next course in the sequence; having completed a second-semester language course and enrolled in a higher-level course; and being presently enrolled in one or more specialized or "advanced" language courses generally intended for foreign language majors;

● Administer the MLA-Cooperative listening comprehension and reading tests to all students in the three classes;

● For approximately one-third of the students in each class, randomly selected insofar as possible, administer a face-to-face language proficiency interview using the FSI procedure, and tape record each interview for later evaluation by Global Understanding Survey staff;

● For all students in the three classes, arrange for administration (on a take-home basis if desired) of the draft "Foreign Language Questionnaire," including language background, language interest and motivation, and proficiency self-appraisal sections.

Participating institutions and the languages (French and/or Spanish) tested at each institution are shown below:

Brigham Young University (F)
Earlham College (S)
Georgetown University (S)
Ohio State University (F)
Pomona College (F; S)
Portland State University (F; S)

At each institution, questionnaire and test administration was carried out during September and October of 1979, following procedures specified by the project staff in a detailed administration guide. The specified administration order for the MLA tests was listening comprehension followed by reading. For the subgroup designated to take the FSI interview, the interview was administered following the MLA tests on a one-to-one basis, with the interview recorded on lapel-microphone equipped cassette recorders.

The language questionnaire, including the proficiency self-appraisal scales as well as the background and interest/motivation sections, was completed as the final activity on the student's part, either during a classroom session or on a take-home basis. The contact person was advised that "since careful and well-thought-out responses to the questionnaire items are important to the proper analysis of the study, it is very desirable to insure that the students do take the questionnaire seriously. A brief discussion in class of the nature and purpose of the study and the information that is hoped to be gained may be helpful in this regard."

To help insure students' anonymity, a sealable envelope was provided with each questionnaire. On the front cover of the questionnaire the student was instructed to insert and seal the questionnaire in the envelope immediately upon completion, and to put his or her name only on the outside of the envelope (not on the questionnaire itself). The students were told that the completed questionnaires would be forwarded unopened to the study staff, assuring them that their language teachers would *not* see their answers to the questions.

Language Pretest Results

Test scoring, questionnaire response tabulation, and data analysis for the preliminary language administration were carried out at ETS. The MLA Cooperative listening and reading tests were optically scanned and the three-digit "converted score" (which placed both "L" and "M" level test results on a common scale) calculated in each instance. For the FSI interview, each of the tape-recorded interviews was independently scored by two raters previously trained by ETS in the FSI rating technique. The mean of the two FSI scores for a given examinee was used as the entry data for the analysis, using the coding system 00, 07, 10, 17, 20....50. The "7" digit was used to represent "plus" values which the rater could assign to each of the regular FSI levels (except for 5) to indicate that the examinee's performance "substantially exceeds the minimum requirements for the level in-

Figure 1.3.1. N's, Means, Standard Deviations, and Intercorrelations of 5 Language Proficiency Self-Rating Scales and 3 Criterion Measures

		(1)	(2)	(3)	(4)	(5)	(6)	(7)	(8)	N	$\bar{x}$	S.D.
FSI-Type Speaking Self-Rating	(1)	1.000	.630	.729	.748	.715	.594	.599	.565	322	2.94	0.89
FSI-Type Reading Self-Rating	(2)	.630	1.000	.633	.610	.725	.543	.462	.509	326	4.06	0.72
"Can-Do" Speaking Self-Rating	(3)	.729	.633	1.000	.760	.791	.632	.586	.559	318	34.40	4.64
"Can-Do" Listening Self-Rating	(4)	.748	.610	.760	1.000	.776	.578	.594	.532	314	25.50	5.10
"Can-Do" Reading Self-Rating	(5)	.715	.725	.791	.776	1.000	.640	.548	.601	317	17.10	3.13
FSI Interview	(6)	.594	.543	.632	.578	.640	1.000	.725	.708	140	2.09	0.90
MLA-Coop Listening	(7)	.599	.462	.586	.594	.548	.725	1.000	.779	331	171.90	11.08
MLA-Coop Reading	(8)	.565	.509	.559	.532	.601	.708	.779	1.000	328	171.60	13.14

volved but falls short of those for the next higher level." Thus, 07 represents "0 + " on the official FSI scale; 17 equals "1 + ," and so forth.

Questionnaire data were coded and keypunched in formats appropriate to the nature of the scales involved. In addition to individual item responses, a total score for each examinee was calculated for each of the "can do" proficiency scales for speaking, listening comprehension, and reading by summing the "1," "2," and "3" responses to each question (where "1" indicated "with great difficulty or not at all"; "2," "with some difficulty"; and "3," "quite easily"). Increasing total scores on each of the "can do" scales thus represented increasing overall judged proficiency, in the sense that the examinee marked relatively more of the items as accomplishable "with some difficulty" or "quite easily."

Data from both French and Spanish examinees were combined for purposes of analysis. The first analysis of interest involved the relationships between the results of the self-appraisal scales (of both the FSI and "can do" types) and the observed test performance of the examinees. Figure 1.3.1. shows the N's, means, standard deviations, and intercorrelations of the five self-rating scales (FSI-type scales for speaking and reading; "can do" scales for speaking, listening, and reading) and the three "criterion" measures (FSI interview for speaking; appropriate MLA Cooperative test for listening and reading).

Observed correlations range from .462 (FSI-type self-appraisal of reading ability *vs*. MLA-Cooperative listening test score) to .791 ("can do" reading *vs*. "can do" speaking scales). Further analysis and discussion of the relationships between the self-appraisal scales and the external test measures is facilitated by reformatting the Figure 1.3.1. data to show the relationships for speaking proficiency, listening comprehension, and reading criteria separately as follows:

Speaking proficiency (FSI interview score) related to...

1.	"Can do" reading scale	.640
2.	"Can do" speaking scale	.632
3.	FSI self-rating of speaking	.594
4.	"Can do" listening scale	.578
5.	FSI self-rating of reading	.543

Listening comprehension (MLA-Cooperative listening test) related to...

1.	FSI self-rating of speaking	.599
2.	"Can do" listening scale	.594
3.	"Can do" speaking scale	.586
4.	"Can do" reading scale	.548
5.	FSI self-rating of reading	.462

Reading ability (MLA-Cooperative reading test) related to...

1.	"Can do" reading scale	.601
2.	FSI self-rating of speaking	.565
3.	"Can do" speaking scale	.559
4.	"Can do" listening scale	.532
5.	FSI self-rating of reading	.509

For reasons previously discussed, extremely high correlations were not anticipated between the self-rating scales and the language skills measures, especially for the MLA-Cooperative listening and reading tests, for which the test content and testing format are considered to be at some remove from the real-life contexts and behavioral conditions involved in actual language-use settings. The observed correlations are, however, considered sufficiently substantial to indicate that the self-rating scales, of both the FSI and "can do" types, show definite positive relationships with external measures in the same general skill areas.

With few exceptions, both the FSI and "can do" self-appraisal scales for a particular skill correlate more highly with the external test measuring that skill than do the FSI or "can do" scales addressed to some other skill. For example, for the MLA-Cooperative listening test, the "can do" scale for listening is more strongly related (.594) than are the "can do" scales for speaking (.586) and reading (.548). This holds true for four of the six possible comparisons (considering the FSI "speaking" self-appraisal scale as relevant to both speaking and listening comprehension). The two exceptions are: MLA-Cooperative reading test score predicted more strongly by the FSI self-rating of speaking (.565) than by the FSI self-rating of reading (.509); and essentially equivalent results in

33

predicting the FSI score by the "can do" reading scale (.640) and the "can do" speaking scale (.632).

With respect to whether the FSI-type self-appraisal scales or the "can do" scales are more closely associated with measured performance, for the skill areas of speaking proficiency and reading, the correlations of the "can do" scale for that particular skill with the corresponding external test were higher than for the FSI-type self-appraisal vs. the external test: .632 and .594 for listening comprehension, and .601 and .509 for reading. The FSI-type self-rating of speaking (which includes elements of listening comprehension) and the "can do" appraisal of speaking were essentially equally correlated with the FSI interview scores (.599 and .594, respectively).

These correlational results were considered to add some weight to the psychometric appropriateness of the self-appraisal approach as a non-direct means of assessing language proficiency for purposes of the study. They also suggest that of the two techniques—use of FSI-type self-ratings vs. a series of "can do" statements—the latter might be somewhat more closely related on the whole to actual proficiency. In view of the statistical results—and considering also that the "can do" statements, with their short, highly focused descriptions of particular language tasks, would be more easily interpreted and responded to by "non-specialist" students than would the considerably more complex FSI-type descriptions—it was decided that the FSI-type self-report procedure would not be investigated further, but that attention would be turned to further analyzing, and revising as necessary, the "can do" scales for each of the three language skills.

As originally drafted, the descriptive statements making up each "can do" scale were intended to represent increasingly sophisticated language-use situations, which it was presumed increasingly fewer respondents would consider themselves capable of handling adequately. Figure 1.3.2. shows the percentage of "quite easily" responses for each of the items on the "can do" speaking scale. With relatively few exceptions, the item response pattern shows increasingly fewer "quite easily" responses from the beginning to the end of the scale, and the same pattern, although somewhat less strikingly so, was found for the listening comprehension and reading scales. Visual inspection, together with the results of computer-based Guttman scale analyses, resulted in the reordering of certain items within each of the three scales (for example, exchanging the positions of the last two items of the speaking scale). In one instance, an item was deleted because of an unanticipated (and in the project staff's opinon, inappropriately) high percentage of "quite easily" responses: the item in question ("Understand train departure announcements and similar kinds of 'public address system' announcements") was considered most probably interpreted by the respondents in terms of classroom and language laboratory exercises in which such announcements are given with much greater care and clarity than are the "real-world" equivalents, with their attendant problems of noise, distortion, etc.

Figure 1.3.2. Percentage of Students Responding "Quite Easily" to "Can Do" Proficiency Statements for Speaking

Say the days of the week.	98.5
Count to 10 in the language.	100.0
Give the current date (month, day, year).	94.5
Order a simple meal in a restaurant.	83.5
Ask directions on the street.	80.4
Buy clothes in a department store.	69.3
Introduce myself in social situations, and use appropriate greetings and leave-taking expressions.	79.8
Give simple biographical information about myself (place of birth, composition of family, early schooling, etc.).	80.2
Talk about my favorite hobby at some length, using appropriate vocabulary.	38.1
Describe my present job, studies, or other major life activities accurately and in detail.	38.7
Tell what I plan to be doing 5 years from now using appropriate future tenses.	37.4
Describe the U.S. educational system in some detail.	18.3
Describe the role played by Congress in the U.S. government system.	7.7
State and support with examples and reasons a position on a controversial topic (for example, birth control, nuclear safety, environmental pollution).	10.4

Minor phraseology changes were also made in certain descriptions to provide more clarity or precision (for example, "Understand the words of popular songs on the radio" was revised to "On the radio, understand the words of a popular song I have not heard before"). For the most part, however, in view of the very encouraging preliminary administration results, the "can do" scales used in the preliminary study were incorporated with only relatively minor modifications into the final survey questionnaire.

Analysis of the language interest and motivation section of the preliminary study questionnaire was aided by a principal factor analysis of the 22 items comprising this section. The first factor extracted accounted for 79.3 percent of the common variance, and individual item loadings on this factor ranged from a high of .82 to .13. These factor loadings were used on an essentially advisory basis, and although two items with extremely low loadings were deleted from the revised scale on this basis, the majority of the revisions to or deletions of items in the preliminary scale when assembling the final questionnaire form were to reduce the number of items having closely similar content. (For two or more items of essentially equivalent content, items having the higher factor loadings were generally retained.) A final step in the revision process was to reformat the relatively few items having atypical response formats so that all could be used with a single "strongly agree," "agree," "neutral," "disagree," "strongly disagree" response scale. The final version of the language interest/motivation scale included 15 items, seven fewer than originally tested.

Virtually no changes were made in the language-related background questions as a direct result of the preliminary testing. However, it was necessary to reduce somewhat the total number of background questions included and, in some instances, to combine two separate questions into a single item or to "collapse" the response scale. The changes made included: eliminating a total of four questions on "grandparents' native language"; combining high school, college, and "other" Latin study situations into a single "Have you ever studied Latin" question; and deleting individual questions on travel abroad with members of own family and "on your own hook" in favor of a single question on living/studying abroad.

A somewhat more consequential change was to abandon the two-dimensional language course background grid which provided a chronological record of coursework in *all* foreign languages taken by the respondent from third grade through college senior, and to make use instead of a single vector of third grade through college senior courses taken in the respondents' "most proficient" foreign language. Overall survey time and booklet space limitations made this change necessary.

Chapter 4

Background and Interests

Mary F. Bennett

In order to discover whether any discrete personal characteristics are associated with levels of global understanding, an extensive background questionnaire was developed for the survey. Items were collected from previously conducted surveys and various ETS instruments such as the Scholastic Aptitude Test and Graduate Record Examination student background questionnaires. The project staff examined these items and selected those which appeared to be appropriate to the study's purposes. The staff also wrote numerous original items. The questionnaire thus developed was designed to ferret out those elements of students' backgrounds that might influence the development of global understanding.

Because sociocultural perspective appeared to be a potentially significant factor, data were collected on students' ethnicity, country of birth, and socioeconomic status. Questions on students' and their parents' political party preferences and political attitudes were also included. Because intellectual ability is consistently associated with most forms of academic achievement, the questionnaire was designed to collect information on levels of scholastic ability through students' self-report of high school grades, SAT and ACT scores, and college grade point averages.

It seemed highly probable that educational experiences, both formal and informal, in high school and college would influence students' levels of global understanding. Therefore, the survey included questions on how many years of study students had completed in high school in English, foreign languages, physical and biological sciences, and social sciences. For college, they were asked to indicate how many courses they had taken in each of 19 subject areas. Students were asked how often they discussed world problems or issues in their classes in high school and in college and to what extent they thought experiences outside the classroom had contributed to their awareness of world issues.

The survey gathered data on informal educational experiences through items concerning participation in extracurricular activities and foreign travel. The latter included questions on structured experiences such as summer-abroad and year-abroad programs. Students were also asked to indicate their college majors and their educational goals.

The ways in which students acquire information about current events and their interest (or lack thereof) in those events could possibly influence the development of global understanding. The survey, therefore, explored students' information acquisition habits. Questions were posed concerning the amount and type of television students usually watch, with specific items directed at the frequency with which they watch television news and listen to radio newscasts. Students were asked how often they read a newspaper, which sections of the paper they usually read, and which newspaper(s) they read. They were also asked if they regularly read weekly newsmagazines. Students were directed to indicate which they considered their main source of information concerning current events. The survey included an item on special interest periodicals, providing space for the respondents to list the name(s) of any magazines they read regularly, and asked students how many hours per week they spend reading for pleasure.

Three items designed to measure students' interest in world problems were built into the section of the survey dealing with information acquisition. The first two items were based upon a list of ten world problems: (1) Air and water pollution; (2) Malnutrition and inadequate health care; (3) Terrorism; (4) Inflation and unemployment; (5) Denial of basic human rights; (6) Depletion of natural resources; (7) Racial discrimination; (8) Nuclear and conventional arms proliferation; (9) Overpopulation; and (10) Intergroup conflict. The first item directed students to rank the problems in order of importance; the second asked that they rank them from most interesting to least interesting. The third item consisted of a list of sixteen fictitious headlines. Students were instructed to indicate which of the articles they would read if they had time to read only four. The topics of the articles, as indicated by the headlines, were equally divided among four categories: (1) international news; (2) national news; (3) science and technology news; and (4) sports news.

Part II

Survey Procedures

Chapter 5

Survey Design

Henry I. Braun

The students selected to respond to the Global Understanding Survey were a probability sample from a two-stage stratified design. The universe of first stage units consisted of all accredited institutions of postsecondary education offering undergraduate instruction. These were grouped into strata according to three factors: school type, location, and estimated mean student ability. Second stage units consisted of freshmen or seniors within four-year colleges and universities and all students within two-year colleges.

Sample selection relied on a master data tape constructed at ETS from three separate tape files containing information on institutions of higher education. The major file was one compiled in 1974 by Higher Education General Information Surveys (HEGIS) and this was supplemented, when necessary, by two smaller files produced by the American Council on Education (ACE) and Management Information Systems (MIS).

Stratification

Classical sampling theory suggests that groupings of units into roughly homogenous strata can measurably improve the precision of sample estimates for fixed cost. For this survey it was decided that such factors as the type of institution, its geographical location, and the quality of its students should be correlated with the response variables of interest. The precise nature of the stratification is outlined in Figures 2.5.1a., b., and c. below. The phrase "Carnegie Code" (c.c.) refers to the Carnegie Commission Higher Education Institutional Classification Code. Use of the first two factors (Figures 2.5.1a. and 2.5.1b.) was expected to simplify the analysis of certain domains of study questions. The third factor (Figure 2.5.1c.) seemed to be the only variable available for judging student quality.

Figure 2.5.1a. Institutional Type

Level	Explanation
A	c.c. = 1.1, 1.2, 1.3, 1.4 (Research and Doctoral Granting Universities, I and II; Doctoral Granting Universities, I and II)
B	c.c. = 2.1, 2.2, 3.1, 3.2 (Comprehensive Colleges and Universities, I and II; Liberal Arts Colleges, I and II)
C	c.c. = 4.1 (Two-year Colleges and Universities)
D	c.c. = 5.1 (Theological Seminaries; Bible Colleges; other institutions offering Degrees in Religion)
E	c.c. = 5.3, 5.4, 5.5, 5.6, 5.8 (Health Professional Schools, Schools of Engineering and Technology; Schools of Business Management, Schools of Art, Music, Design, etc.; Teachers Colleges)

Figure 2.5.1b. Location

Level	Explanation
1	New England and Mideast (Connecticut, Delaware, District of Columbia, Maine, Maryland, Massachusetts, New Hampshire, New Jersey, New York, Pennsylvania, Rhode Island, Vermont).
2	Great Lakes and Plains (Illinois, Indiana, Iowa, Kansas, Michigan, Minnesota, Missouri, Nebraska, North Dakota, Ohio, South Dakota, Wisconsin).
3	Southeast (Alabama, Arkansas, Florida, Georgia, Kentucky, Louisiana, Mississippi, North Carolina, South Carolina, Tennessee, Virginia, West Virginia).
4	Southwest, Rocky Mountains, Far West (Alaska, Arizona, California, Colorado, Hawaii, Idaho, Montana, Nevada, New Mexico, Oklahoma, Oregon, Texas, Utah, Washington, Wyoming).

Figure 2.5.1c. Mean SAT-V of Incoming Freshmen

Level	Explanation
L*	Less than 445
M	Between 445 and 525
U	Greater than 525

*Includes schools with no SAT-V records or requirements.

With these three factors, a total of 5x4x3 = 60 strata are theoretically possible. In fact, because of insufficient numbers in various classes, some of the original strata were pooled, creating a final set of 36 strata. These will be described in more detail later.

Allocation

We begin with some notation. Let:

H = no. of strata,

N_h = no. of schools in stratum h ($h = 1, ..., H$),

K_h = no. of enrolled students in stratum h,

k_{hi} = no. of enrolled students in school i of stratum h,

n_h = no. of schools sampled in stratum h,

m_{hi} = no. of students sampled in school i of stratum h,

y_{hij} = score of student j in school i in stratum h.

Then $y_{hi.} = \dfrac{1}{m_{hi}} \sum_{j=1}^{m_{hi}} y_{hij}$ = estimated mean of ith school in stratum h.

41

If schools are sampled with probability proportional to size, k_{hi}/K_h, and students are drawn randomly without replacement, we have:

$$y_{h..} = \frac{1}{n_h} \cdot \sum_{i=1}^{n_h} y_{hi.} = \text{estimate of mean in stratum } h$$

and $y_{...} = \sum_h K_h y_{h..} \big/ \sum_h K_h$ = estimated mean in the population, with

$$\text{Var}(y_{...}) = \sum_h K_h^2 \, \text{Var}(y_{h..}) \Big/ \left(\sum_h K_h \right)^2$$

Although slightly different estimators were employed in the actual analysis, the present forms are adequate to the task of determining a rough allocation scheme. Now from Cochran (1963, p. 308):

$$(1) \quad \text{Var}(y_{h..}) = \frac{1}{n_h} \left\{ \sum_{i=1}^{N_h} (k_{hi}/K_h)(Y_{hi.} - Y_{h..})^2 \right.$$

$$\left. + \sum_{i=1}^{N_h} (k_{hi}/K_h)(1 - f_{2i}) \sigma_{(w)hi}^2 / m_{hi} \right\}$$

where $Y_{hi.}$, $Y_{h..}$ = true means in school i and in stratum h,

f_{2i} = sampling fraction in school i,

$\sigma_{(w)hi}^2$ = variance among students in school i.

Equation (1) makes clear the relatively greater importance of increasing n_h, rather than m_{hi}, in reducing the variance of $y_{h..}$.

It was plausible to assume that $f_{2i} = 0$ and that the within school variances $\sigma_{(w)hi}^2$ were roughly constant ($= \sigma_{(w)h}^2$) within strata. We may then write:

$$\text{Var}(y_{h..}) = S_h^2 / n_h ,$$

where $S_h^2 = \sigma_h^2 + \sigma_{(w)h}^2 / m$ and $\sigma_h^2 = \sum_{i=1}^{N_h} (k_{hi}/K_h)(Y_{hi.} - Y_{h..})^2$,

the size-weighted variance between school means in stratum h. Thus,

$$\text{Var}(y_{...}) = \left(\sum_h K_h^2 S_h^2 / n_h \right) \Big/ \left(\sum_h K_h \right)^2.$$

An elementary calculation (Cochran, 1963, p. 95) shows that the variance is minimized for a fixed total sample size if n_h is chosen so that

$$(2) \quad n_h \propto K_h S_h .$$

It remained to determine the allocation of resources; that is, the number of schools, n_h, to be sampled within strata and the number of students, m_{hi}, to be tested in each school. It proved convenient to solve the latter problem first. For simplicity, a fixed number of students were selected from each school.

Allocation Within Strata

It has already been pointed out that equation (1) strongly suggested sampling as many schools as possible in order to reduce the variance of the estimated means. A countervailing consideration was the extra cost incurred by including another school in the sample, in comparison with the cost of selecting more students from schools already in the sample. The optimal allocation of resources between schools and students had to be determined.

Fix attention on a particular stratum, h. Let:

$$R_c = \frac{\text{cost of an additional school}}{\text{cost of an additional student}}$$

and $R_\sigma = \sigma_{(w)h}^2 / \sigma_h^2$.

If the sample consisted of n_h schools with m students tested in each school, the total cost would be proportional to $R_c\, n + m\, n$. Hence, the relevant optimization problem was to:

Minimize $\sigma_h^2 (1 + R_\sigma / m) \big/ n$ subject to the constraint $R_c\, n + m\, n = constant$. The

solution was easily found to require setting m to satisfy

(3) $m^2 = R_c\, R_\sigma$, and, consequently, we had

(4) $\dfrac{\text{money spent on schools}}{\text{money spent on students}} = \dfrac{R_c\ n}{m\ n} = \sqrt{\dfrac{R_c}{R_\sigma}}$

Given the resources available, this enabled us to compute the number of schools to be selected.

The appropriate values of R_c and R_σ had to be determined. The variability of SAT-V scores of incoming freshman was studied at a number of schools in several strata. It appeared that we might take $R_\sigma \approx 10$ in all strata. Turning to R_c, it was estimated that the direct costs of adding a school were about ten times that of an additional student. Administrative costs added another factor of 10. In strata containing four-year institutions, however, the school costs could be apportioned equally between the freshman and senior surveys. Hence, for these strata, $R_c \approx 10$ and $m^2 = R_c R_\sigma \approx 100 \rightarrow m \approx 10$. In strata containing only two-year institutions (level "C" strata), $R_c \approx 20$. Consequently, $m^2 \approx 200 \rightarrow m \approx 14$. For convenience, we took m = 15 in these strata.

Allocation Between Strata

The total number of schools to be sampled and the split between four-year institutions and two-year institutions had to be determined. To simplify the calculations, we constructed two "superstrata," T_1 and T_2, T_1 containing all two-year institutions and T_2 containing all others. Let us now introduce some notation which pertain only to allocation between strata:

σ_i^2 = size-weighted variance among school means in stratum T_i $(i = 1.2)$

n_i = number of schools to be sampled from stratum T_i $(i = 1.2)$.

The results of the allocation within strata calculations indicated that for the survey of seniors, the estimate of the population mean would have a variance:

$$V_\alpha = \frac{\sigma_2^2}{n_2}[1 + R_\sigma / m] = \frac{\sigma_2^2}{n_2}[1 + 10/10] = \frac{2\sigma_2^2}{n_2}$$

43

Similarly, for the survey of freshmen, the variance of the estimate would be

$$V_\beta = \frac{\sigma_2^2}{n_2}[1 + R_\sigma/m] = \frac{2\sigma_2^2}{n_2}$$

For the survey of students at two-year institutions, the variance would be

$$V_\gamma = \frac{\sigma_1^2}{n_1}[1 + R_\sigma/m] = \frac{\sigma_1^2}{n_1}[1 + 10/15] = \frac{5\sigma_1^2}{3n_1}$$

It seemed reasonable to demand that the allocation scheme minimize, for fixed cost, the total variance $V = V_\alpha + V_\beta + V_\gamma$. Because 20 students (10 freshmen and 10 seniors) were chosen from each school sampled in T_2, but only 15 from each school sampled in T_1, the relative costs were in the ratio $(R_c + 20) : (R_c + 15)$, or 8 : 7. Hence, the relevant optimization problem was to minimize V subject to the constraint $N_1 + (8/7) n_2 = constant$. The solution was easily found to be:

$$\frac{n_1}{n_2} = \sqrt{\frac{20}{21}} \times \frac{\sigma_1}{\sqrt{2\sigma_2}}$$

A suitable value for the ratio σ_1/σ_2 had to be determined. It seemed likely that differences across regions and school types would make T_2 substantially more variable than T_1. In addition, the schools in T_2 would be evenly distributed across the range of mean SAT-scores. A plausible and convenient choice was to take $\sigma_2^2 = 2\sigma_1^2$ or, $\sigma_1/\sigma_2 = 1/\sqrt{2}$. Hence, $n_1/n_2 \approx 0.5$. Under the budgetary constraints, this led to the choice $n_1 = 60$ and $n_2 = 125$. The final allocation of schools to the original strata described above was carried out separately for each superstratum and according to the proportional allocation scheme $n_h \propto K_h S_h$ derived previously. The process is described below.

Sample Selection

Ideally, the number of schools in the sample allocated to stratum h (independently within each superstratum) should be proportional to the product of K_h, the number of students in the stratum, and S_h, which is roughly proportional to the standard deviation among schools in the stratum. Since exact values for K_h and S_h were not available, estimates were employed in their place.

The HEGIS file provided the total 1974 enrollment for each school. These values, denoted by K'_h, are found in Figures 2.5.2a. - c. below. In determining the allocation, it was assumed that the desired 1979 freshman and senior enrollments were both proportional to K'_h. Secondly, within each Carnegie Code-Geographical region combination, the relative sizes of S_h for the classes L, M, and U were estimated to be in the ratio of 2:1:1.5. These estimates were derived from computations based on the range of mean SAT-V scores in the three classes as well as information about their variability.

The allocation proceeded as follows. The original strata comprising superstratum T_1 are listed in Figure 2.5.2c. For each stratum, the values of K'_h, the total two-year enrollment, and $K'_h S_h$ are listed. Recall that 60 schools of the sample were allocated to T_1. The proportion of these schools, $n_h/60$, to be selected from stratum h was equal to the ratio $K'_h S_h / \Sigma_h K'_h S_h$, where the sum was over all strata in T_1. Some strata were combined because they were individually too small to warrant the selection of even one school.

The same procedure occurred for the strata comprising superstratum T_2, which are listed in Figures 2.5.2a., b., d., and e. Note that the values of $K'_h S_h$ are not comparable across superstrata, since K'_h represents a two-year enrollment in T_1 but a four-year enrollment in T_2. In addition, the values of S_h are not commensurate across superstrata. The final allocation was modified slightly to ensure that strata of interest were represented in the sample.

Once the n_h had been determined, schools were selected in stratum h with replacement, with probability proportional to k'_{hi}/K'_h. This should reduce the variability of the estimates. Although with replacement sampling is not as efficient as without replacement sampling, it was expected that

Figure 2.5.2a. Carnegie Code A, Superstratum T_2

Region	Stratum SAT-V	K'_h	$K'_h S_h$	N_h	n_h*
1	L	56	11	2	1
	M	1426	142	16	3
	U	2121	318	33	8
2	L	131	26	1	1
	M	3382	338	27	8
	U	1465	219	13	5
3	L	312	62	3	1
	M	2117	212	19	4
	U	457	68	7	2
4	L	156	30	2	1
	M	3407	341	35	8
	U	1267	189	12	4
Total			1956		46

*K'_h = No. of students in stratum (1974), in hundreds of students
$K'_h S_h$ = Weighted size of stratum, in relative units
N_h = No. of schools in stratum (1974)
n_h = No. of schools to be selected for the sample from stratum

Table 2.5.2b. Carnegie Code B, Superstratum T_2

Region	Stratum SAT-V	K'_h	$K'_h S_h$	N_h	n_h*
1	L	447	89	49	2
	M	4746	474	211	12
	U	1290	194	73	4
2	L	1001	200	69	5
	M	4309	431	241	11
	U	606	90	37	2
3	L	2922	584	153	15
	M	2028	203	130	5
	U	243	36	15	1
4	L	1278	255	72	6
	M	3301	330	120	8
	U	284	42	24	1
Total			2928		72

* See notes to Figure 2.5.2a.

45

Table 2.5.2c. Carnegie Code C, Superstratum T_1

Region	Stratum SAT-V	K'_h **	$K'_h S_h$ ***	N_h	n_h *
1	L	2838	568	239	13
	M	343	35	30	
	U	15	0	1	
2	L	2803	560	284	
	M	23	2	8	13
	U	0	0	0	0
3	L	2298	460	263	
	M	57	6	13	10
	U	0	0	0	0
4	L	5335	1066	284	
	M	121	12	12	24
	U	0	0	1	
Total			2709		60

* See notes to Figure 2.5.2a.
** K'_h = No. of students in stratum (1974), in hundreds of students
*** The relative weights $K'_h S_h$ are not commensurate with those of the other figures (see text).

Table 2.5.2d. Carnegie Code D, Superstratum T_2

Region	Stratum SAT-V	K'_h	$K'_h S_h$	N_h	n_h *
1	L	31	6	29	
	M	59	6	20	
	U	3	0.5	3	1
2	L	5	1	6	
	M	72	7	20	
	U	0	0	0	
3	L	8	1.5	10	
	M	33	3	10	
	U	0	0	0	1
4	L	5	1	7	
	M	24	2	7	
	U	0	0	0	
Total			28.0		2

* See notes to Figure 2.5.2a.

Table 2.5.2e. Carnegie Code E, Superstratum T$_2$

Region	Stratum SAT-V	K'_h	$K'_h S_h$	N_h	$n_h{}^*$
1	L	167	32	24	1
	M	331	33	31	
	U	90	13	10	1
2	L	26	5	14	
	M	235	23	30	1
	U	0	0	0	
3	L	34	6	5	
	M	51	5	7	1
	U	0	0	0	
4	L	42	8.5	17	
	M	100	10	13	1
	U	13	2	1	
Total			137.5		5

* See notes to Figure 2.5.2a.

---

the loss would be small in this case. In addition, the original decision to select 175 schools was made in anticipation of a slight reduction in this number because of repeated selections. For example, in a stratum where ten schools were to be chosen, the final sample might have consisted of eight schools, two being selected twice. In the latter schools, the size of the student sample would be correspondingly doubled. Sampling institutions with replacement also facilitates the calculation of sampling variances. As is customary, students were to be sampled without replacement.

As must be clear to the reader, the allocation schemes derived were based on approximations of varying precision. Because of the present uncertainty about many of the variables (such as enrollments), it was felt that a more detailed analysis could not be justified. Secondly, the loss of efficiency in adopting a nearly optimal allocation, rather than an exactly optimal one, is usually fairly small. It was expected that the allocation scheme derived was a reasonable one and would provide most of the benefits that survey design theory can offer.

Sample Characteristics Estimation

From the data collected in the survey it is possible to obtain estimates of how the entire population of college freshmen, for example, would have performed on the various components of the Global Understanding questionnaire. When the population parameter to be estimated is an average or total, the corresponding estimate may be expressed as a weighted linear combination of the individual observations. The weights depend on the size of the sample in the school, the size of the school, and the size of the stratum. In the present instance, the stratum size is itself unknown and must be estimated separately.

In carrying out the survey, it was found to be nearly impossible at most schools to distinguish between full- and part-time students. Hence, the actual sampling frame consisted of all enrolled students at the appropriate level. Before providing the formulas for the estimators, we require some additional notation. In the interests of brevity, the freshmen survey will serve as an illustrative example.

M_h = number of enrolled freshmen (1979) in stratum h,
M_{hi} = number of enrolled freshmen (1979) in school i of stratum h,
m_{hi} = number of enrolled freshmen (1979) sampled in school i of stratum h,
K'_h = total number of enrolled students (1974) in stratum h,
K'_{hi} = total number of enrolled students (1974) in school i of stratum h.

An estimate of the mean score in stratum h is:

$$(5) \quad y_{h..} = \sum_{i=1}^{n_h} (M_{hi} / \sum_{i=1}^{n_h} M_{hi}) \, (\sum_j y_{hij} / m_{hi}) \quad ,$$

a weighted average of the means of the sample schools. Because this estimator does not take into account the unequal probabilities of selection, it is slightly biased. On the other hand, its variance should be quite a bit smaller than that of the classical unbiased estimator.

To obtain an estimate of the national mean, we first require an estimate of M_h. For the schools in the sample, the campus coordinators were asked to provide the current enrollments, M_{hi}. For schools not in the sample, the M_{hi} are unknown. Nonetheless, a simple ratio estimator of M_h is available. It is

$$\hat{M}_h = \hat{R}_h K'_h \quad ,$$

where $\hat{R}_h = \sum_{i=1}^{n_h} M_{hi} / \sum_{i=1}^{n_h} K'_{hi}$.

Thus, the national mean is estimated by

$$(6) \quad y_{...} = \sum_h \hat{M}_h y_{h..} / \sum_h \hat{M}_h \quad .$$

Combining equations (5) and (6), we find that

$$(7) \quad y_{...} = \sum_{h=1}^{H} \sum_{i=1}^{n_h} \sum_{j=1}^{m_{hi}} w_{hi} \, y_{hij} \left/ \sum_{h=1}^{H} \sum_{i=1}^{n_h} m_{hi} \, w_{hi} \right. \quad ,$$

where $w_{hi} = M_{hi} K'_h / m_{hi} \sum_{i=1}^{n_h} K'_{hi}$.

(Note that $\sum_h \sum_i \sum_j w_{hi}$ is an estimate of the size of the national freshmen population.) The form of equation (7) permits the direct computation of estimates from the data tape.

If national estimates over certain domains are required, the same weighting scheme, in conjunction with certain auxiliary variables, may be employed. For example, suppose that an estimate of the mean score among male college freshmen, $Y_{...}$ (male), is required. One such estimate is

$$y_{...} \, (\text{male}) = \sum_{h=1}^{H} \sum_{i=1}^{n_h} \sum_{j=1}^{m_{hi}} w_{hi} y^*_{hij} \left/ \sum_{h=1}^{H} \sum_{i=1}^{n_h} \sum_{j=1}^{m_{hi}} w_{hi} Z_{hij} \right. \quad ,$$

where $y^*_{hij} = \begin{cases} y_{hij}, & \text{if } j^{\text{th}} \text{ individual is male} \\ 0, & \text{otherwise,} \end{cases}$

and $Z_{hij} = \begin{cases} 1, \text{ if } j^{th} \text{ individual is male} \\ 0, \text{ otherwise.} \end{cases}$

Variance Estimation

Ordinarily, point estimates of population parameters are not sufficient for a proper analysis of the data. In order to assess the statistical significance of the difference between the estimated means for two groups, it is necessary to have estimates of the associated variances. Actually, one should speak of mean squared error (MSE) rather than variance, since $y_{...}$ is slightly biased. However, because of the large samples, it is expected that the bias will be small compared to other sources of variability.

To obtain an appropriate estimate of $\text{Var}(y_{...})$ we must rewrite $y_{...}$ in the following form:

$$(8) \quad y_{...} = \left[\sum_{h=1}^{H} K'_h \left(\sum_{i=1}^{n_h} y_{hi+} \Big/ \sum_{i=1}^{n_h} K'_{hi} \right) \right] \Big/ \sum_{h=1}^{H} \sum_{i=1}^{n_h} m_{hi} w_{hi} \, ,$$

where $y_{hi+} = M_{hi} y_{hi.}$,

is an unbiased estimate of the total score in school i. The numerator of $y_{...}$ is in the form of a ratio estimator, and from standard results in sampling (Theorems 2.5 and 11.2 of Cochran (1977)) we obtain an estimator of $\text{Var}(y_{...})$.

$$(9) \quad \hat{\text{Var}}(y_{...}) = \left[\sum_{h=1}^{H} (N_h^2 / n_h) \sum_{i=1}^{n_h} (y_{hi+} - \hat{\gamma}_h K'_{hi})^2 \Big/ (n_h - 1) \right.$$

$$\left. + \sum_{h=1}^{H} (K'_h / \sum_{i=1}^{n_h} K'_{hi}) \sum_{i=1}^{n_h} \hat{\sigma}_{hi}^2 \right] \Big/ \left[\sum_{h=1}^{H} \sum_{i=1}^{n_h} m_{hi} w_{hi} \right]^2 \, ,$$

where $\hat{\gamma}_h = \sum_{i=1}^{n_h} y_{hi+} \Big/ \sum_{i=1}^{n_h} K'_{hi}$

and $\hat{\sigma}_{hi}^2 = M_{hi}^2 \sum_{j} (y_{hij} - y_{hi.})^2 \Big/ \left[m_{hi} (m_{hi} - 1) \right]$.

The numerator of (9) has two components: the first represents the "between schools" contribution, pooled over strata, to the variance of $y_{...}$, and the second represents the "within schools" contribution. The latter appears to be much smaller than the former, justifying the emphasis in the survey design on sampling as many schools as possible. In the actual computations, the 10 strata in the four-year surveys with only one school sampled were grouped into 3 strata in order that plausible estimates of their contribution to the variance could be found.

49

Chapter 6

Data Collection

Lois G. Harris, Mary F. Bennett, Thomas S. Barrows

Recruitment

In each stratum, a prospective list of schools to be surveyed was obtained by sampling with probability proportional to estimated size. The number of possible schools in each stratum was larger than the number of schools needed. The project staff decided that the best way to obtain institutional cooperation would be to address invitations to individuals who had an interest in international education. A list of Fulbright Program Advisers was obtained from the Institute of International Education; and the American Association of Community and Junior Colleges provided a list of academic deans at two-year colleges. A letter describing the Council on Learning's "Education and the World View" project and the survey was sent to Fulbright Program Advisers or academic deans at 186 institutions during the last week in October, 1979. The letter asked the addressee to obtain institutional cooperation for the survey and to serve as survey coordinator on his or her campus. It also stated that each student would be paid $6.00 for participating in the survey and the campus coordinator would receive an honorarium of $50. A reply form was included and responses were received from about two-thirds of the institutions by November 15, 1979. Those persons who did not return the reply forms were sent Mailgrams urging them to telephone their responses to ETS. This Mailgram and a follow-up, along with numerous telephone calls, eventually elicited positive responses from 150 of the institutions contacted, giving us a response rate of 81 percent. In order to recruit the desired number of schools, other institutions were selected from the list of schools in the appropriate sample cell, and new invitation letters were sent to 99 academic deans in mid-December. Response to this second mailing brought the total number of acceptances to 197. However, there were shortages in some of the sample cells and overages in others. Administrators who declined invitations to take part in the survey offered various reasons for doing so: some were too busy; some thought the honorarium was insufficient compensation for the amount of work required; and some said they could not fit the survey administration into their school calendars. One school declined to participate because it had a large number of Iranian students and administration officials were concerned about dealing with the possible repercussions on the campus of the seizure of American hostages in Iran. (See Figure 2.6.1.)

Administration

On January 10, 1980, campus coordinators were sent letters which provided explicit instructions for student sampling, recruitment, and payments (reproduced in Appendix E). A *systematic sample*

Figure 2.6.1. Intended and Obtained Samples

Carnegie Code	Region	SAT	Institutions Needed	Institutions Obtained	Students Needed	Students Obtained			+ (-) Institutions	+ (-) Students
						Fr.	Sr.	Total		
1	1	1	1	0	20	0	0	0	(1)	(20)
		2	3	3	60	26	26	52	-	(8)
		3	8	8	160	71	71	142	-	(18)
			12	11	240	97	97	194	(1)	(46)
	2	1	1	1	20	9	10	19	-	(1)
		2	8	6	160	56	57	113	(2)	(47)
		3	5	5	120	42	42	84	-	(36)
			14	12	300	107	109	216	(2)	(84)
	3	1	1	1	20	3	4	7	-	(13)
		2	4	4	80	33	28	61	-	(19)
		3	2	2	40	16	20	36	-	(4)
			7	7	140	52	52	104	-	(36)
	4	1	1	1	20	10	10	20	-	-
		2	8	9	160	75	75	150	1	(10)
		3	4	2	80	16	13	29	(2)	(51)
			13	12	260	101	98	199	(1)	(61)
2	1	1	2	2	40	20	20	40	-	-
		2	12	7	240	62	63	125	(5)	(115)
		3	4	3	80	31	29	60	(1)	(20)
			18	12	360	113	112	225	(6)	(135)
	2	1	5	3	100	25	23	48	(2)	(52)
		2	11	12	220	106	111	217	1	(3)
		3	2	2	40	19	19	38	-	(2)
			18	17	360	150	153	303	(1)	(57)
	3	1	15	15	300	136	138	274	-	(26)
		2	5	6	100	59	52	111	1	11
		3	1	1	20	10	10	20	-	-
			21	22	420	205	200	405	1	(15)
	4	1	6	5	120	45	44	89	(1)	(31)
		2	8	10	160	87	81	168	2	8
		3	1	1	20	10	10	20	(-)	(-)
			15	16	300	142	135	277	1	(23)
4	1, 2	1, 2, 3	1	2	20	20	20	40	1	20
	3, 4	1, 2, 3	1	2	20	19	20	39	1	19
			2	4	40	39	40	79	2	39
5	1	1	1	2	20	16	12	28	1	8
	1	2, 3	1	1	20	10	10	20	-	-
	2	1, 2, 3	1	1	20	10	10	20	-	-
	3	1, 2, 3	1	1	20	10	10	20	-	-
	4	1, 2, 3	1	1	20	8	8	16	-	(4)
			5	6	100	54	50	104	1	4
3	1	1	13	19	195	-	-	264	6	69
		2, 3	1	1	15	-	-	15	-	-
			14	20	210	-	-	279	6	69
	2	1, 2, 3	13	14	195	-	-	178	1	(17)
	3	1, 2, 3	10	12	150			171	2	21
	4	1, 2, 3	24	22	360			280	(2)	(80)
Totals - 4-yr. Institutions			125	119	2520	1060	1046	2106	(6)	(414)
2-yr. Institutions			61	68	915			908	7	(7)
Total Recruitment			186	187	3435	1060	1046	3014	1	(421)

51

with a random starting point was obtained by employing the registrar's alphabetic listing. Although the universe of possible samples is not as large as that of true random sampling, there are no apparent biases with this approach. This stands in contrast to the technique involving a choice based on the random selection of the first two letters of the last name which, at first flush, seems more appealing when an alphabetical listing is available. This latter technique, however, results in unequal probabilities of selection for different students.

The student names thus obtained were listed in random order and contacted consecutively until the target number was reached. Campus coordinators were instructed not to send students' names to ETS, and a method of payment was devised which guaranteed student anonymity. Coordinators were urged to be as flexible as possible in scheduling survey administrations. Most schools did provide us with (nearly) the target number. However, no estimate of a response rate is available at this level. (See Appendix E for recruitment and administration materials.)

Survey booklets, administration instructions, and instructions for students were mailed to campus coordinators at the end of January, and the survey was administered during February or, in a few cases, early in March. Completed survey booklets were received from 187 of the 197 institutions recruited. Booklets from one institution were lost in the mail on the way back to ETS, and nine institutions dropped out of the survey and returned the unused materials. The numbers of student responses entering into our findings are noted with each analysis in the "Results" sections.

Illustrative Sampling Errors

In order to provide estimates of the precision of the survey, sampling errors for several variables have been calculated. Variables chosen illustrate the range of errors likely to occur throughout the complete study's numerous variables. The sampling errors of means are dependent on score variances, so a range of variances is reflected in the variables chosen to illustrate the likely sampling errors of the study's means. Sampling errors of proportions are a function of the break between the categories with the largest errors at a 50-percent/50-percent dichotomous break. Consequently, proportions chosen to illustrate the range of likely errors are varied in that respect. Finally, where subgroup parameters are estimated (for example, the mean knowledge score for history majors), the size of the subgroup comes into play. Therefore, several error estimates are provided for subgroups of varied size.

These standard errors may be interpreted quite simply in the following way: Classic sampling theory tells us that a sample derived estimate will not "miss" the population value by more than plus or minus one sampling error 68 times in 100. Thus, we can be sure that the chances are 68 in 100 that our Knowledge mean for freshmen, 41.9, does not miss the freshman population mean by more than plus or minus 1.2. The chances are roughly 2 in 3 that the freshman mean lies between 40.7 and 43.1.

Similarly, the chances are 96 in 100 that a sample derived estimate does not miss the population value by more than plus or minus two standard errors. Returning to the freshman Knowledge mean, we may be sure that the interval 39.5-44.3 encompasses the actual mean for all freshmen 96 times out of 100. The mental arithmetic required to arrive at the 96 percent confidence interval for each of the statistics tabled above is not great, and the general stability of the survey's estimates can be seen to be quite acceptable.

Figure 2.6.2.a. Standard Errors of Freshman Means and Proportions

		Mean	Standard Deviation	Standard Error
Knowledge		41.9	11.4	1.2
Foreign Language - Speaking*		26.3	7.0	.7
Foreign Language - Listening*		19.1	5.0	.5
Foreign Language - Reading*		14.3	3.7	.4
Age		19.4	4.2	.5

		Proportion	Standard Error
Sex:	male	.44	.02
	female	.56	.02
Ethnicity:	white	.86	.02
Student's political party preference:	Democratic	.38	.01
	Republican	.28	.01
	Independent	.14	.01
How often do you read a newspaper?	Daily	.30	.02
Have you ever been in a country other than the U.S.?	Yes	.58	.02
Have you ever participated in an organized summer abroad program?	Yes	.09	.01
Student's native language:	English	.94	.03

*Based upon students answering "YES" to II-6 (78.1 percent)

Figure 2.6.2.b. Standard Errors of Senior Means and Proportions

		Mean	Standard Deviation	Standard Error
Knowledge		50.5	12.1	1.5
Foreign Language - Speaking*		25.6	7.4	.7
Foreign Language - Listening*		25.6	5.4	.5
Foreign Language - Reading*		13.8	4.1	.4
Age		23.4	4.6	.6
History Majors' Knowledge**		59.3	9.0	1.5
Education Majors' Knowledge**		39.8	9.3	2.7

		Proportion	Standard Error
Sex:	male	.49	.02
	female	.51	.02
Ethnicity:	white	.86	.02
Born in U.S:		.94	.02
Student's political party preference:	Democratic	.41	.02
	Republican	.27	.01
	Independent	.20	.01
How often do you read a newspaper?	Daily	.36	.02
Have you ever been in a country other than the U.S.?	Yes	.64	.02
Have you ever participated in an organized summer-abroad program?	Yes	.08	.01
Student's native language:	English	.96	.03

*Based upon students answering "YES" to II-6 (89.9 percent)
**Based upon students responding History (1.9 percent) or Education (7.3 percent) to I-38

Figure 2.6.2.c. Standard Errors of Means and Proportions for Students at Two-Year Institutions

	Mean	Standard Deviation	Standard Error
Knowledge	40.5	12.6	.8
Foreign Language - Speaking*	27.0	7.9	.5
Foreign Language - Listening*	20.4	6.0	.4
Foreign Language - Reading*	14.6	4.7	.3
Age	25.0	10.6	.5

		Proportion	Standard Error
Sex:	male	.40	.01
	female	.60	.01
Ethnicity:	white	.74	.02
Born in U.S.:		.87	.02
Student's political party preference:	Democratic	.43	.01
	Republican	.24	.01
	Independent	.16	.01
How often do you read a newspaper?	Daily	.42	.01
Have you ever been in a country other than the U.S.?	Yes	.61	.01
Have you ever participated in an organized summer-abroad program?	Yes	.09	.01
Student's native language:	English	.89	.02

*Based upon students answering "YES" to II-6 (73.2 percent)

54

Part III

Survey Results

Chapter 7

Knowledge

Stephen F. Klein and Sheila M. Ager

The results of the Test of Global Knowledge will be discussed from three viewpoints: first, the structural characteristics of the domain of knowledge defined by the test; second, the level of student performance on the test or on parts of the test; and third, the level of student performance on individual test items. The presentation of the level of student performance will also include a report on student characteristics and experiences that correlate most highly with test performance.

Structure of the Domain

Analysis of the cognitive structure of global understanding begins with a consideration of the reliability of the test, or the extent to which the items in the test are consistent measures of one ability or knowledge domain. Reliability coefficients can range from -1.00 to +1.00. A positive reliability coefficient indicates that performances on specific items are consistent with performances on others, and that the summing across items is not a senseless summing of disparate performances. Similarly, generalizations about the domain may be derived from the test results only when internal consistency has been demonstrated.

The reliability coefficient for the Test of Global Knowledge is strongly positive for each of the student populations surveyed. The figure is .84 for freshmen, .86 for seniors, and .87 for two-year college students. These figures represent the ''internal consistency'' reliability of the test and were calculated using the Kuder-Richardson formula #20.

After the homogeneity of performance in the domain of knowledge defined by the test was established, an attempt was made to derive a finer-grained internal structure of the domain from further analysis of the interrelationships among item performances. Two techniques were used to delineate groups of items that, in terms of shared variance, maximized the similarity of student performance within each group and minimized the similarity between groups. These two techniques were factor analysis and cluster analysis.

The factor and cluster analyses were first carried out on item results from seniors, to see if the techniques held sufficient promise to be extended to freshmen and two-year college students. Although various numbers of factors were extracted and related analytically to simple structure and several forms of cluster analyses were tried, no structures amenable to substantive interpretation were found.

The failure to find an interpretable domain structure through the factor and cluster analyses triggered a backup strategy in which a logical structure was assumed and the relationships among the hypothesized structural elements and between each element and the test were studied. The logical structure imposed on the data was the 13 issues examined by the test, among which all the items on the test were assigned. Correlations between issues were then calculated, as was the correlation between each issue and the test. These correlations are shown in Figures 3.7.1a.-3.7.1c.

Figure 3.7.1a.   Intercorrelations Among Test Issues for Freshmen

	Environment	Food	Health	International Monetary and Trade Arrangements	Population	Energy	Racial and Ethnic Issues	Human Rights	War and Armaments	Arts and Culture	Religious Issues	Relations Among States	Distribution of Natural Characteristics	Total
Environment	-	.211	.288	.288	.180	.157	.318	.307	.353	.340	.109	.238	.291	.546
Food	.211	-	.228	.275	.202	.180	.261	.196	.288	.295	.030	.219	.196	.478
Health	.288	.228	-	.332	.333	.165	.369	.271	.346	.398	.008	.204	.302	.592
International Monetary and Trade Arrangements	.288	.275	.332	-	.294	.161	.367	.292	.388	.362	.049	.277	.332	.624
Population	.180	.202	.333	.294	-	.135	.247	.295	.251	.328	.028	.145	.232	.522
Energy	.157	.180	.165	.161	.135	-	.246	.210	.215	.210	.040	.247	.152	.434
Racial and Ethnic Issues	.318	.261	.369	.367	.247	.246	-	.336	.427	.401	.139	.386	.221	.670
Human Rights	.307	.196	.271	.292	.295	.210	.336	-	.342	.326	.016	.224	.261	.557
War and Armaments	.353	.288	.346	.388	.251	.215	.427	.342	-	.439	.073	.304	.327	.674
Arts and Culture	.340	.295	.398	.362	.328	.210	.401	.326	.439	-	.118	.335	.336	.699
Religious Issues	.109	.030	.008	.049	.028	.040	.139	.016	.073	.118	-	.128	.109	.220
Relations Among States	.238	.219	.204	.277	.145	.247	.386	.224	.304	.335	.128	-	.195	.553
Distribution of Natural Characteristics	.291	.196	.302	.332	.232	.152	.221	.261	.327	.336	.109	.195	-	.546
Total	.546	.478	.592	.624	.522	.434	.670	.557	.674	.699	.220	.553	.546	-

Figure 3.7.1b. Intercorrelations Among Test Issues for Seniors

	Environ- ment	Food	Health	Interna- tional Monetary and Trade Arrange- ments	Population	Energy	Racial and Ethnic Issues	Human Rights	War and Armaments	Arts and Culture	Religious Issues	Relations Among States	Distribution of Natural Characteris- tics	Total
Environment	-	.186	.229	.350	.259	.322	.353	.285	.315	.377	.142	.298	.339	.581
Food	.186	-	.149	.204	.219	.186	.231	.149	.178	.265	.066	.248	.207	.428
Health	.229	.149	-	.278	.233	.182	.266	.296	.273	.269	.059	.259	.274	.491
International Monetary and Trade Arrangements	.350	.204	.278	-	.288	.200	.359	.343	.411	.370	.199	.336	.318	.646
Population	.259	.219	.233	.288	-	.225	.288	.203	.293	.336	.141	.229	.318	.538
Energy	.322	.186	.182	.200	.225	-	.246	.210	.310	.322	.185	.342	.233	.522
Racial and Ethnic Issues	.353	.231	.266	.359	.288	.246	-	.284	.449	.468	.228	.423	.297	.666
Human Rights	.285	.149	.296	.343	.203	.210	.284	-	.295	.315	.131	.296	.214	.522
War and Armaments	.315	.178	.273	.411	.293	.310	.449	.295	-	.439	.242	.431	.358	.689
Arts and Culture	.377	.265	.269	.370	.336	.322	.468	.315	.439	-	.247	.402	.370	.709
Religious Issues	.142	.066	.059	.199	.141	.185	.228	.131	.242	.247	-	.248	.122	.375
Relations Among States	.298	.248	.259	.336	.229	.342	.423	.296	.431	.402	.248	-	.264	.656
Distribution of Natural Characteristics	.339	.207	.274	.318	.318	.233	.297	.214	.358	.370	.122	.264	-	.570
Total	.581	.428	.491	.646	.538	.522	.666	.522	.689	.709	.375	.656	.570	-

Figure 3.7.1c. Intercorrelations Among Test Issues for Two-Year College Students

	Environ-ment	Food	Health	International Monetary and Trade Arrangements	Population	Energy	Racial and Ethnic Issues	Human Rights	War and Armaments	Arts and Culture	Religious Issues	Relations Among States	Distribution of Natural Characteristics	Total
Environment	-	.269	.245	.383	.246	.303	.330	.271	.393	.457	.171	.264	.303	.584
Food	.269	-	.299	.364	.240	.196	.287	.136	.364	.409	.086	.242	.336	.529
Health	.245	.299	-	.373	.283	.196	.397	.196	.393	.389	.125	.219	.318	.565
International Monetary and Trade Arrangements	.383	.364	.373	-	.370	.298	.454	.323	.452	.478	.145	.330	.339	.698
Population	.246	.240	.283	.370	-	.294	.347	.203	.359	.393	.166	.211	.408	.589
Energy	.303	.196	.196	.298	.294	-	.322	.255	.282	.332	.068	.277	.200	.519
Racial and Ethnic Issues	.330	.287	.397	.454	.347	.322	-	.292	.481	.472	.168	.391	.348	.698
Human Rights	.271	.136	.196	.323	.203	.255	.292	-	.302	.340	.144	.313	.265	.504
War and Armaments	.393	.364	.393	.452	.359	.282	.481	.302	-	.558	.184	.337	.418	.731
Arts and Culture	.457	.409	.389	.478	.393	.332	.472	.340	.558	-	.162	.322	.502	.770
Religious Issues	.171	.086	.125	.145	.166	.068	.168	.144	.184	.162	-	.231	.207	.323
Relations Among States	.264	.242	.219	.330	.211	.277	.391	.313	.337	.322	.231	-	.245	.558
Distribution of Natural Characteristics	.303	.336	.318	.339	.408	.200	.348	.265	.418	.502	.207	.245	-	.627
Total	.584	.529	.565	.698	.589	.519	.698	.504	.731	.770	.323	.558	.627	-

The most interesting correlations are between each issue and the test, in that the issues that have the highest correlations are those that mirror most faithfully the distinctions between high scorers and low scorers. These issues essentially constitute global understanding, or its lack, for the test populations. It should be noted that a relatively high correlation between an issue and the test does not mean that students knew more about that issue than most others, only that those who did well on the test as a whole did well on that particular issue. Health, for example, generally proved to be the easiest issue, but performance on Health was not as accurate a reflection of performance on the test as several other issues.

If one rank orders the correlations between each issue and the test for each of the test populations, four issues are most frequently found at the top of each list: Arts and Culture, and War and Armaments, followed with somewhat less consistency by Racial and Ethnic Issues and International Monetary and Trade Arrangements. Further down in the rankings more divergence develops among the lists. Six issues are generally found in the middle of each list, though with inconsistent ranking from list to list. These six issues are Relations Among States, Distribution of Natural Characteristics, Environment, Health, Population, and Human Rights. Toward the bottom of each list are Energy and Food; Religion is consistently last.

Interestingly, the four issues in the first group and the first two in the middle group are generally encountered by college students in traditional courses of study, whereas the remaining issues, despite the rapid rise of interest in them, still tend to be somewhat exotic in the typical college curriculum. The one exception to this among the issues having lower correlations with the test is Religion, which one might have predicted would correlate in the same range as Arts and Culture, Racial and Ethnic Issues, and Relations Among States, but did not. When examined for its correlation with other issues rather than the test, Religion turns out to be most closely related to Relations Among States for seniors and two-year students and to Racial and Ethnic Issues for freshmen.

Although the question of what knowledge distinguishes students with global understanding from those without cannot be answered by reference to the levels of performance on the various issues, levels of performance have an intrinsic importance in that they tell us the extent to which an issue is known among a population. Before examining the levels of performance on each of the issues, however, the levels of performance on the test need to be considered.

Level of Test Performance

Figure 3.7.2. shows the cumulative frequency distribution of test scores for each of the three populations. For freshmen, scores ranged from 0 to 80; for seniors, 0 to 84; and for two-year college students, 6 to 78. The maximum score possible was 101. Mean scores were 41.9 for freshmen, 50.5 for seniors, and 40.5 for two-year college students. The standard deviation of scores (a measure of score variation) for each of the three populations was 11.4, 12.1, and 12.5, respectively. If scores are normally distributed, which was very close to the case for freshmen and seniors and only somewhat less so for two-year college students, we may say that two-thirds of the population earned a score on the test within the range of plus or minus one standard deviation from the mean. In the case of seniors, for example, since the mean of 50.5 plus the standard deviation of 12.1 is 62.6, and the mean minus the standard deviation is 38.4, almost two-thirds of the seniors scored between 38.4 and 62.6. Comparable ranges for freshmen were 30.5 to 53.3 and for two-year college students 28.0 to 53.0.

The percentage of scores that fell into the so-called "chance score range" below 25 (the score most likely to be achieved if an answer sheet were marked at random) was generally low. For freshmen, the figure was six percent; for seniors two percent, and for two-year students nine percent. The test functioned, therefore, as a measure of real rather than spurious achievement. This is not to deny, however, that the level of performance for many students was modest indeed.

In addition to the total score on the test, two series of subscores were calculated. The first series was defined by the issues that were the building blocks of the test. Figure 3.7.3. shows the issue mean scores as a percent of the number of items in each issue. Caution must be exercised, however, in interpreting the figures. While the committee chose questions in what it regarded as an appropriate range of difficulty for each issue, no special effort was made to balance the mean difficulty from issue to issue. The relative difficulty of each issue, therefore, reflects the selection of questions as well as the ability of the students. If one were to rank order the issues for each population according

Figure 3.7.2. Cumulative Percentage Distribution of Test Scores

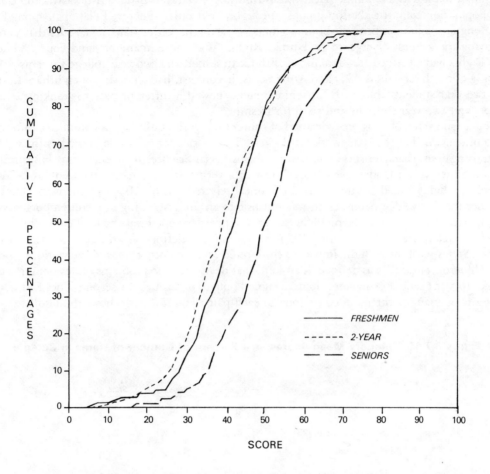

Figure 3.7.3. Issue Mean Scores as a Percent of Number of Items in Issue

	Freshmen	Seniors	Two-Year Students
Environment (5)	40.4	50.6	40.2
Food (7)	42.6	47.7	39.4
Health (6)	55.8	62.7	52.0
International Monetary and Trade Arrangements (9)	42.7	52.0	41.4
Population (10)	46.0	54.2	45.4
Energy (9)	35.9	41.4	38.0
Racial and Ethnic Issues (8)	40.8	51.1	40.9
Human Rights (6)	43.7	50.0	43.2
War and Armaments (8)	41.8	53.3	40.1
Arts and Culture (8)	49.3	60.0	46.1
Religious Issues (6)	22.3	25.2	20.2
Relations Among States (10)	27.9	36.9	27.8
Distribution of Natural Characteristics (4)	55.0	67.5	44.3

61

to the level of performance, there would be good agreement across the top and bottom of the lists but somewhat less in the middle. Health, Distribution of Natural Characteristics, Arts and Culture, and Population comprise the top groups in roughly that order. Energy, Relations Among States, and Religious Issues comprise the bottom group in exactly that order. The three issues that stand out as having the greatest divergence are Human Rights, War and Armaments, and Food. While Human Rights had a performance ranking of fifth for freshmen and two-year college students, it had a ranking of ninth for seniors. War and Armaments, in contrast, had a ranking of eighth for freshmen and two-year students, but fifth for seniors. Food showed a different pattern, ranking tenth for seniors and two-year students and sixth for freshmen.

The second series of subscores consisted of content categories built by the committee into the test but not construed as the framework for the test. The six categories can be viewed as three pairs of contrasting item characteristics: Humanities versus Social Sciences, Current versus Historical, and United States versus Underdeveloped. Humanities versus Social Sciences referred to the type of knowledge being tested. Current versus Historical referred not to a fixed moment in time but to whether the knowledge being tested was intrinsic to an understanding of a contemporary issue or simply part of the long view. United States versus Underdeveloped was the least contrastive, in that it did not really establish a polarity. "United States" was defined as an item that dealt with the United States itself, or with the impact of the United States on other areas of the world, or vice versa. "Underdeveloped" was defined as an item that dealt with the problems of developing nations. Unlike the first series of subscores (items assigned only to one issue) the second series had items assigned to as many as three categories (one in each pair). Figure 3.7.4. shows the results.

Figure 3.7.4. Category Mean Scores as a Percent of Number of Items in Category

	Freshmen	Seniors	Two-Year Students
Humanities (27)	40.9	48.7	39.1
Social Sciences (73)	41.7	50.4	40.3
Current (60)	41.6	50.4	40.8
Historical (35)	39.2	46.6	37.7
United States (26)	42.7	51.3	42.4
Underdeveloped (22)	48.0	56.4	47.1

Although the caution expressed in regard to Figure 3.7.4. about the imbalance of item difficulties from category to category is pertinent, nonetheless one of the category pairs—United States versus Underdeveloped—stands out as having the best performance across all three student populations. In Humanities versus Social Sciences, performance was just slightly better on the latter for all three groups, while in Current versus Historical, the performance gap was more pronounced—all three groups doing better on the former. Historical, it should be noted, elicited the lowest level of performance of any of the categories. Relatively poor performance on the historical items also partly explains why, in the first series of subscores, students in all three groups did most poorly on Relations Among States and Religious Issues. Half of the items in Relations Among States and two-thirds of the items in Religious Issues were categorized by ETS staff as being historical in nature. Not all issues in the first series that had relatively high proportions of historical items fared poorly, however. More than half of the items on Human Rights, Racial and Ethnic Issues, and International Monetary and Trade Arrangements were historical, yet they received middling performance from the students in all three groups.

In looking at performance on the test and performance on the two series of subscores, we find that the three student populations are quite similar to each other in the kinds of things that they know or do not know. The main difference among the populations is in the amount that they know. Seniors scored better than freshmen or two-year students on both the test and the two series of subscores.

Even senior performance on the test, however, must be viewed with reservations. A mean score of

50 percent correct for the population indicates a considerable lack of knowledge considered fundamental by the committee to an understanding of today's world. To some extent this conclusion can be tempered by recognition that global affairs is not a defined field of study in the college curriculum in the same way that history or economics is, and, therefore, not readily accessible through one or two courses or even a major, unless the major happens to be interdisciplinary. On the other hand, unlike many traditional fields of study, it is at least partially accessible through the news media, especially newspapers and magazines.

We turn now from the level of test performance to the correlates of test performance Figure 3.7.7. lists all the variables that correlated .20 or higher with scores on the test. The figure shows the strength of the relationship between test performance (i.e., doing well on the test) and variables that span student background, experiences, attitudes, and so on. Among the background variables, only race and parental education are significant. Since both of these generally correlate highly with socioeconomic status, their presence in the figure is simply another instance of the frequently observed relationship between socioeconomic status and educational achievement. The figure also suggests a weaker relationship between parental education and a student's global understanding the longer the student is in college, although only a longitudinal study of entering freshmen over a two- or four-year period could prove this. The relationship between race and global understanding, however, seems to persist and even grows stronger as an influence over time.

Among the experience variables, the highest correlations are recorded between global understanding and the aptitude measures used for college admissions. As with socioeconomic status, measures of aptitude like the SAT commonly evidence a moderate-to-strong relationship with measures of achievement like the Test of Global Knowledge. If anything, the relationship shown in the figure is weaker than that which exists between the SAT and College Board Achievement Tests in the social studies, thus indicating less of an aptitude component in global understanding than one might have expected. Also among the experience variables, though college grade point average is significant for all three groups, high school grade point average is significant only for freshmen. Courses or majors enter the picture only sporadically. Whereas history and math as majors are related to achievement for the two-year population, only economics is significant for seniors. There is also evidence in the figure that seniors who have traveled tended to do better on the test than seniors who have not.

The media variables that relate to high scores on the test are strongly weighted toward newspaper reading both in frequency of reading and the tendency to read national, international, and financial news. The only TV variable to make its way into the figure concerned the watching of science specials, which, like national, international, and financial news, generally convey serious content. It is interesting to note that more of these media variables crop up the longer a student is in college, though here, too, only a longitudinal study could determine whether there is a relationship over time or only a relationship unique to the three groups that were studied.

Political variables, especially in terms of party preferences, had only a slight relationship to scores on the test, although attitudes imbued with political content showed up more strongly. For all three populations, anti-chauvinism and pro-human rights attitudes were, for the most part, significant.

Finally, a number of language background variables proved to have a significant relationship to test scores for two-year students. These can be boiled down to having experience with, or proficiency in, Russian and having a mother whose native language was Hebrew. A further check of the data indicated that these two characteristics were independent of each other; that is, they did not relate to one and the same group of two-year students.

Despite the variables not shown in the table failing to meet the criterion of a .20 or higher correlation with score on the test, several of these were chosen for further study in terms of score differentials. Specifically, these variables were sex, political attitude, source of information about current events, and major area of study. For each of these variables, interesting relationships with the test emerged, albeit not strongly enough to meet the correlational criterion.

Males outperformed females in mean test score in each of the three populations: 44.8 to 39.8 among freshmen, 54.2 to 47.0 among seniors, and 43.1 to 38.7 among two-year students. These results parallel those found on College Board Achievement Tests in the social studies.

Political attitudes in terms of left and right also had a consistent relationship to performance on the test among the three groups. The left and the right each outscored the middle, the left achieving higher mean scores than the right. For freshmen, the left, middle, and right mean scores were

Figure 3.7.5.   Correlations (.20) Between Test Performance and Other Variables

Background Variables	Freshmen	Seniors	2-Year
1. White or Caucasian	.22	.24	.33
2. Level of formal education completed by father or male guardian	.24	-	-
3. Level of formal education completed by mother or female guardian	.21		-

Experience Variables	Freshmen	Seniors	2-Year
1. High School Grade Point Average	.26	-	-
2. SAT Verbal Score	.49	.40	.55
3. SAT Math Score	.42	.32	.42
4. ACT Score	.53	.64	.42
5. College Grade Point Average	.29	.26	.24
6. Economics course(s) taken in college contributing to global awareness	-	.21	-
7. Been in country other than U.S.	-	.22	-
8. Math intended major	-	-	.23
9. History courses taken in college	-	-	.26

Media Variables	Freshmen	Seniors	2-Year
1. When reading a newspaper, usually reads national news articles	.22	-	.25
2. When reading a newspaper, usually reads international articles	.26	.30	.34
3. When watching TV, usually watches science specials	-	.20	-
4. With time to read only 4 headlines would read "Soviet Jews Denied Exit Visas"	-	.20	-
5. Frequency of newspaper reading	-	.21	.21
6. When reading a newspaper, usually reads financial section	-	.22	-

Political Variables	Freshmen	Seniors	2-Year
1. "Other" political party preference	-	-	.20

Language Background Variables	Freshmen	Seniors	2-Year
1. Hebrew is mother's native language	-	-	.21
2. Studied Russian as foreign language in college	-	-	.25
3. Speaks, reads, or writes Russian	-	-	.21
4. Russian is most proficient foreign language (MPFL)	-	-	.26

Attitude Variables	Freshmen	Seniors	2-Year
Anti-Chauvinism	.26	.28	.36
Pro-Human Rights	.23	-	.32

Figure 3.7.6.   Mean Scores on Test According to Main Source of Information About Current Events

	Freshmen	Seniors	2-Year Students
Newspapers	43.1	54.4	43.4
Magazines	46.5	50.1	42.2
Television	41.5	48.6	38.2
Radio	41.3	50.5	40.2

45.0, 40.9, and 43.5, respectively. The comparable figures for seniors were 54.5, 48.1, and 50.9; and for two-year students 46.2, 38.9, and 39.9.

Students who indicated that their main source of information about current events was the print media outscored those who indicated the electronic media. For seniors and two-year students, newspaper readers outdistanced magazine readers, whereas for freshmen the reverse was true. Radio listeners were third highest and television watchers last, except among freshmen where the latter finished just slightly ahead. These results are shown in Figure 3.7.6.

The test results according to major or intended major are shown in Figure 3.7.7. The best performance was registered by history majors, who finished first among freshman and seniors and second among two-year students. Math and engineering majors were generally the next highest scorers, although among freshmen intended math majors were only fifth highest. At the low end of the spectrum were the education majors, who finished last among the freshmen and seniors and just two notches up among the two-year students. This poor performance is especially disturbing, since education majors will be the teachers of global understanding to the elementary and secondary school students of tomorrow.

Figure 3.7.7. Mean Score on Test According to Major or Intended Major

	Freshmen	Seniors	2-Year Students
Agriculture	42.7	48.2	34.0
Art	41.1	47.7	40.0
Biological Sciences/Physical Sciences	41.4	51.7	41.1
Business/Accounting/Finance	42.5	51.3	38.1
Education	36.6	39.8	38.3
Engineering	48.3	53.3	42.6
English/Drama/Communications	43.7	48.8	43.6
Foreign Languages	46.5	50.2	42.3
History	50.8	59.3	55.7
Mathematics	43.3	54.1	64.6
Music	42.3	50.2	38.4
Social Sciences	41.7	52.8	41.9
Vocational/Technical Training	39.4	45.0	40.2

Social science and foreign language majors, who might have been expected to be among the highest scorers on the test, finished somewhat lower, though still in the top half of the distribution when the mean scores for the various majors were averaged across the three populations and then rank ordered. Specifically, social science majors were fourth and foreign language majors sixth. These average ranks, however, mask a good deal of divergence from population to population. Social science majors were ninth among freshmen, fourth among seniors, and sixth among two-year students. The corresponding ranks for foreign language majors were third, seventh, and fifth.

Item Level Performance

An assessment of global understanding is as much a measure of how much students do not know as how much they do know. Every effort thus was made to construct cognitive questions whose incorrect answer choices would help identify the misinformed as opposed to students who could only guess at an answer. Although many of the test questions yielded a random guessing pattern among the incorrect responses and, therefore, little information beyond how many of the students knew and did not know the answer, a large number of questions gave clues to student misconceptions through the fact that able students grouped in their choice of one or more of the incorrect answers.

For the purposes of this discussion, able students are defined as those in each of the three student populations whose mean test score was higher than that of their peer group. Mean test scores for seniors, freshmen, and two-year college students were, respectively, 50.46, 41.94, and 40.45 questions correct out of 101.

Of the 101 cognitive questions in the assessment, 24 giving evidence of student misconceptions in that their incorrect responses drew able students in all three populations, have been selected for discussion. The breakdown of the questions among issues covered in the test is as follows:

Energy—	4 Questions (of a total of 9 questions on the test)
Religious Issues—	5 Questions (of a total of 6)
Population—	3 Questions (of a total of 10)
Food—	3 Questions (of a total of 7)
Human Rights—	3 Questions (of a total of 6)
Relations Among States—	2 Questions (of a total of 10)
International Monetary and Trade Relations—	2 Questions (of a total of 9)
War and Armaments—	1 Question (of a total of 8)
Health—	1 Question (of a total of 6)

Since the 24 questions under discussion had a wide range of difficulty—from 66 to 9 percent correct for seniors, 61 to 10 percent correct for freshmen and 52 to 9 percent correct for two-year college students—no consistent relationship between item difficulty per se and the existence of a misconception among the able could be determined. The attempt to find consistency within groups of issue-related questions in the relationship between misconceptions and item difficulty also proved fruitless. Moreover, irrespective of the subject matter being tested, the proportion of able students choosing specific incorrect responses seemed, in each population, independent of an item's difficulty level for that population. With respect to the 24 questions under discussion, the only general observation about item difficulty that can be made is that 20 of the qestions were easier for seniors than for the other two populations. Of the 4 remaining, 3 were more difficult for seniors—one substantially so—than for one or both of the other populations, and the fourth showed the same proportion of seniors and two-year college students answering correctly, with 8 percent fewer freshmen doing so.

Analyzed as individual measures, the 24 questions nevertheless give insights into some misconceptions common to all three student populations and some misconceptions particular to one or two. For ease of reference, the questions are printed below in the order in which they were enumerated by issue in the list above and numbered 1 to 24. The number of each question as it appeared in the assessment is shown in parenthesis. Beneath each question are shown the correct response (*), the percentage of students choosing a particular response (in roman typeface), and the mean score on the test (in italics) for the group of students choosing that response.

The thread of commonality that can be seen in the six questions (1, 10, 13, 14, 16, and 24) which attracted able students across all populations to the same incorrect response is that all are social science items concerned with recent or current global affairs. Three of the six questions proved relatively difficult for all populations, with 29 percent or fewer students answering correctly, and one of these three, 13, showed seniors performing less well than others, only 24 percent answering correctly compared to 27 percent freshmen and 28 percent two-year college students. Of all 24 questions under discussion, the latter, 13, also proved to be the question that, overall, drew the largest proportion of able students in each population to one incorrect answer. If all students responding to question 13 are considered as one population, the finding to be drawn from incorrect responses is that slightly more than half the population thought the global problem of inadequate nutrition a matter of inadequate food production rather than inequitable food distribution.

The incorrect responses of able students in all three populations to question 24—which showed approximately 14 percent of seniors and two-year college students and 10 percent of freshmen mistaking the distribution of malaria for that of cholera—may, like incorrect student responses to ques-

66

1. (36.) Which of the following curves best represents the estimates of experts about the pattern of the world's past and possible future consumption of fossil fuels such as petroleum, natural gas, and coal?

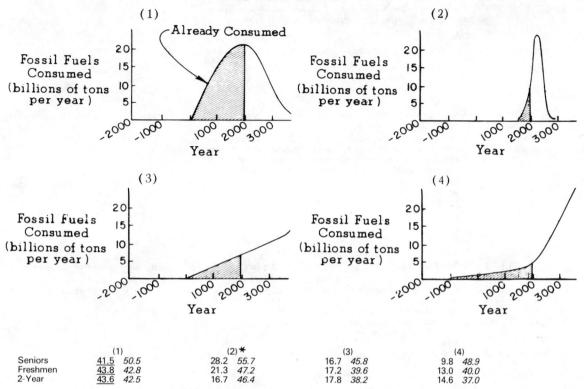

	(1)		(2) ✱		(3)		(4)	
Seniors	<u>41.5</u>	50.5	28.2	55.7	16.7	45.8	9.8	48.9
Freshmen	<u>43.8</u>	42.8	21.3	47.2	17.2	39.6	13.0	40.0
2-Year	<u>43.6</u>	42.5	16.7	46.4	17.8	38.2	14.6	37.0

2. (40.) President Carter was primarily concerned about which of the following when he urged all nations to defer nuclear fuel reprocessing and the development of the breeder reactor?

    (1) The possibility of nuclear weapons proliferation
    (2) The occurrence of a catastrophic accident
    (3) The emergence of a uranium cartel
    (4) The distortion of economic development priorities

	(1) ✱		(2)		(3)		(4)	
Seniors	43.5	53.4	37.6	48.4	5.5	50.5	11.6	48.0
Freshmen	36.0	44.6	<u>40.1</u>	43.2	6.3	39.6	13.1	38.6
2-Year	44.3	42.2	<u>35.2</u>	41.2	5.3	39.7	12.0	35.4

3. (104.) Which of the following lists is composed entirely of members of OPEC (Organization of Petroleum Exporting Countries)?

    (1) Iran, Iraq, Kuwait, Egypt
    (2) Great Britain, Norway, Mexico, United Arab Emirates
    (3) Syria, Lebanon, Libya, Ethiopia
    (4) Venezuela, Indonesia, Nigeria, Saudi Arabia

	(1)		(2)		(3)		(4) ✱	
Seniors	57.5	49.7	2.1	41.4	6.7	53.6	29.1	55.0
Freshmen	<u>56.2</u>	43.5	7.3	36.1	8.5	41.3	21.0	45.3
2-Year	<u>48.7</u>	40.7	8.1	34.2	7.9	39.8	27.9	45.9

4. (103.) Which of the following helps to explain the ability of OPEC (Organization of Petroleum Exporting Countries) to raise oil prices since 1973?

    (1) OPEC countries have become controlled uniformly by groups hostile to capitalism and the West.
    (2) OPEC countries have experienced a significant growth in their military strength.
    (3) There has been a large increase in total world industrial production and transport since the early 1960s.
    (4) The value of the dollar has declined.

	(1)		(2)		(3) ✱		(4)	
Seniors	<u>22.0</u>	51.3	8.4	45.8	40.2	53.7	23.8	49.1
Freshmen	<u>16.0</u>	42.9	12.7	39.2	32.9	45.8	30.7	41.9
2-Year	<u>14.4</u>	42.4	13.4	36.1	31.1	45.1	32.4	40.3

5. (70.) Which grouping of the religions below presents them in descending size of estimated world membership?
  (1) Christianity, Buddhism, Islam, Hinduism, Judaism
  (2) Islam, Christianity, Hinduism, Buddhism, Judaism
  (3) Hinduism, Islam, Christianity, Judaism, Buddhism
  (4) Christianity, Islam, Hinduism, Buddhism, Judaism

	(1)	(2)	(3)	(4) ✱
Seniors	16.2 48.3	23.9 55.0	24.7 50.2	31.8 50.1
Freshmen	20.9 40.4	21.8 46.3	17.2 44.5	36.0 41.2
2-Year	28.2 39.4	15.9 46.0	18.8 41.2	31.0 41.3

6. (72.) Each religion below is correctly matched with countries in *each* of which it either predominates or has a significant minority following EXCEPT
  (1) Christianity...Greece, Lebanon, the Philippines, Ethiopia
  (2) Islam...Saudi Arabia, the Soviet Union, Indonesia, Nigeria
  (3) Buddhism...Japan, Thailand, Vietnam, Sri Lanka (Ceylon)
  (4) Hinduism...India, Pakistan, Afghanistan, Kampuchea (Cambodia)

	(1)	(2)	(3)	(4) ✱
Seniors	31.9 48.6	42.0 51.4	7.2 44.3	13.1 59.4
Freshmen	29.2 42.7	39.8 44.3	13.2 38.6	12.5 43.7
2 Year	33.4 41.4	31.1 42.8	14.3 38.9	11.7 43.5

7. (73.) The World Zionist Organization, which sought the creation of a Jewish state, was founded in response to
  (1) the anti-Semitism that surrounded the Dreyfus case at the end of the nineteenth century.
  (2) the British government's 1917 declaration in support of the concept of a Jewish national homeland.
  (3) Stalin's anti-semitic purges in the 1930s.
  (4) Nazi persecution of the Jews.

	(1) ✱	(2)	(3)	(4)
Seniors	11.0 51.2	18.8 55.5	12.5 49.0	49.9 50.0
Freshmen	10.2 44.1	16.9 41.6	13.2 41.9	51.3 43.8
2-Year	9.7 36.2	12.3 42.1	11.1 42.4	55.9 43.0

8. (75.) One of Buddhism's most basic teachings is that
  (1) one can be saved from sin if one learns to suppress anger and fear.
  (2) human life is a cycle of suffering caused by individual desires.
  (3) everyone who wishes to be saved from sin must become a monk or a nun.
  (4) the Buddha was the final divinely inspired prophet sent to the human race.

	(1)	(2) ✱	(3)	(4)
Seniors	11.6 51.1	39.5 54.5	9.5 47.3	34.4 47.9
Freshmen	9.6 41.7	29.8 46.0	11.3 41.9	42.9 41.4
2-Year	12.1 39.0	29.2 46.7	9.7 40.7	40.1 39.4

9. (71.) Which of the following is shared by Christianity, Judaism, Islam, Buddhism, and Hinduism?
  (1) The concept of a messiah
  (2) A general tendency to proselytize
  (3) A tradition of mysticism
  (4) Insistence on personal identification with a single religion

	(1)	(2)	(3) ✱	(4)
Seniors	35.1 48.1	5.4 51.2	13.7 54.0	42.6 52.0
Freshmen	36.6 42.8	6.1 41.7	10.6 42.1	41.5 43.0
2-Year	34.9 39.9	6.2 40.3	9.3 42.1	43.0 43.0

10. (32.) Which of the following statements describes the trend in world population growth as of 1980?
  (1) It is accelerating and total population is expected to triple by the year 2000.
  (2) It is accelerating and total population is expected to double by the year 2000.
  (3) It has begun to decelerate, but total population is still expected to increase substantially by the year 2000.
  (4) It has started to decelerate, and therefore total population is expected to decline by the year 2000.

	(1)	(2)	(3) ✱	(4)
Seniors	6.6 50.1	36.8 51.0	52.6 51.3	3.1 38.6
Freshmen	9.9 39.9	33.1 43.2	48.9 43.5	5.1 35.4
2-Year	10.7 34.0	33.9 42.3	46.1 42.1	7.4 36.4

tion 13, be partly explained by the fact that the information tested is more likely to be acquired in academic courses to which all students do not have access than through non-academic sources such as the media. The same argument, however, cannot be applied in explanation of student misconceptions indicated in question 1, 10, 14, and 16, since the topics covered—fossil fuel consumption, world population trends, the difficulties of economic development in predominantly agricultural countries, and the Helsinki Accords—have received extensive news coverage. Despite the fact that the subject matter of these four questions could be reasonably classified as general information to which all students would have access, approximately two out of five students in the total population had an unrealistic view of past and future fossil fuel use, one out of three thought world population growth is accelerating, one out of five thought the mechanization of agriculture the only avenue to economic development in predominantly agricultural countries, and more than one out of four thought that a court where human rights complaints could be heard had been established by the Helsinki Accords.

The remaining questions in the 24 showed much greater diversity in the choice of incorrect responses by able students in the three populations, a frequent occurrence, for example, being one population's choice of one incorrect response and the other two populations' choice of another. Clear instances of the latter type of divergence were provided by two energy-related questions, (2 and 3) which were also unique among the questions under discussion in that able seniors answering incorrectly as a group were fewer than able students answering incorrectly from the other two populations. (It should be noted here, however, that question 2 was the question cited earlier as showing the same proportion of two-year college students as seniors, 44 percent, answering correctly and only 8 percent fewer freshmen doing so.) Thus in question 2, while 5.5 percent of seniors thought President Carter feared the emergence of a uranium cartel, more than two out of five freshmen and over one out of three two-year college students thought the possibility of a nuclear catastrophe the President's principal concern in urging nations to defer further nuclear development. Similarly, in question 3, while 6.7 percent of seniors incorrectly thought the membership of OPEC included Syria, Lebanon and Ethiopia as well as Libya, more than half the freshmen and nearly half the two-year college students revealed their misconception that OPEC is an all-Middle East organization by identifying Egypt as a member as well as Iran, Iraq, and Kuwait. Although the fourth and last energy question selected for discussion (4) does not display the same type of divergence in the incorrect responses of different student populations, it is interesting to note that while 22 percent of seniors, 16 percent of freshmen, and 14.4 percent of two-year college students thought OPEC countries were controlled by forces hostile to capitalism and the West, an additional 30.7 percent of freshmen thought OPEC's ability to raise oil prices since 1973 was the result of the dollar's decline. It is disconcerting to realize that despite the prominence given to the world energy situation since 1973, only two out of five seniors and roughly one out of three freshmen and two-year college students were aware of the impact of the total world increase in the use of oil since the early 1960s.

Among the five religious issue questions selected for discussion, an indication of the prevalence of student misconceptions is provided by the fact that three of the questions (6, 7, and 9) showed the proportion of each population answering correctly ranging as low as 9 to 14 percent, while the remaining two questions (5 and 8) showed a range extending no higher than 29 to 39 percent. Question 5 also proved to be an item on which seniors performed less well than freshmen (32 and 36 percent, respectively, answering correctly) and only slightly better than two-year college students (31 percent answering correctly). Incorrect responses from able students in the three populations included overestimates of the world membership of Islam and Hinduism compared to that of Christianity, ignorance of the countries in which Islam predominates or forms a significant minority, misunderstanding of the characteristics and precepts of the world's major religions, and a failure to understand the origins of Zionism.

Some distinctions can be drawn among the misconceptions held by the various populations. For example, in question 5, while sizable groups of seniors, freshmen, and two-year college students (approximately 24, 22, and 16 percent, respectively) thought Islam a larger religious community than Christianity, an additional 17.2 percent of freshmen and 18.8 percent of two-year college students thought Hindus outnumbered Christians. Similarly in question 6, while large groups of students in all three populations (42 percent of seniors and roughly 40 and 31 percent of freshmen and two-year college students) failed to recognize that Islam predominates or has many adherents in

11. (6.) The largest groups of people living outside their home countries in 1978-1979 were made up of

    (1)   political refugees leaving or fleeing their countries.
    (2)   foreign workers and their families working and residing in West European countries.
    (3)   legal and illegal immigrants to the United States.
    (4)   military forces of the United States and the Soviet Union stationed in the territories of allied countries.

	(1)		(2)*		(3)		(4)	
Seniors	36.0	52.1	10.9	53.4	31.2	46.7	19.9	52.3
Freshmen	31.0	44.0	10.2	42.0	41.2	40.2	15.8	44.4
2-Year	37.1	42.2	8.6	41.4	42.5	38.4	10.7	43.1

12. (54.) Which of the following is a correct statement about the historical sources of population in North and South America?

    (1)   During the mid-eighteenth century struggle between England and France for dominance in Canada, the French were a minority of the Canadian white population.
    (2)   By the beginning of the nineteenth century, all major areas of European settlement on the South American continent were under Spanish domination.
    (3)   The first sizable number of people of Mexican descent in the United States were resident in areas conquered or annexed by the United States in the mid-nineteenth century.
    (4)   In the massive influx of European immigrants into the United States during the late nineteenth and early twentieth centuries, Northern Europeans predominated over immigrants from Eastern and Southern Europe.

	(1)		(2)		(3)*		(4)	
Seniors	8.4	47.5	19.7	48.0	35.1	54.3	30.4	50.5
Freshmen	11.1	39.7	22.9	42.5	25.5	44.6	31.3	43.9
2-Year	13.4	38.0	21.2	38.7	30.3	45.0	27.4	41.9

13. (26.) As a global problem, inadequate nutrition is largely the result of

    (1)   large populations living in countries whose production of foodstuffs is insufficient to provide the minimum number of calories required by each person each day.
    (2)   world population having outgrown the world's ability to produce enough food to meet each person's daily caloric requirements.
    (3)   large populations living in countries in which inequalities of income result in a significant portion of the population being unable to buy the foods produced by others.
    (4)   trade controls that prevent food surpluses produced by some countries from being exported to other countries that want to buy them.

	(1)		(2)		(3)*		(4)	
Seniors	61.3	51.9	10.4	43.7	24.3	50.5	2.9	48.8
Freshmen	51.5	44.2	14.4	38.2	26.9	42.0	4.3	37.9
2-Year	48.7	43.5	15.7	6.0	28.0	39.1	5.5	36.3

14. (88.) Most countries that have a majority of their populations working in agriculture and earn most of their foreign exchange from agriculture exports are finding economic development difficult because

    (1)   there is a declining world market for agricultural products.
    (2)   they can only develop through mechanization of agriculture, but this will create large-scale unemployment.
    (3)   they are especially vulnerable to both crop failures and world price fluctuations.
    (4)   the income of the majority of the population depends upon export earnings.

	(1)		(2)		(3)*		(4)	
Seniors	2.5	44.1	21.5	51.2	65.8	51.8	6.9	47.6
Freshmen	6.2	39.7	19.5	42.3	57.9	44.5	9.2	38.4
2-Year	7.7	34.5	19.6	41.9	51.2	44.2	12.3	37.1

15. (90.) In China one-third of the farmland and sixty percent of the rural labor force are devoted to growing rice. The major advantage to China of growing rice is that

    (1)   China has surplus farm labor and few alternatives for employment.
    (2)   the weight, the nutrient, and the market value of rice per unit of land are much higher than those of other basic grain crops.
    (3)   rice, as the major grain involved in world trade, is principally grown for foreign markets to earn foreign exchange.
    (4)   the extra labor required for growing rice largely consists of women and children, a fact that makes the cost of growing rice less than that of growing other grains.

	(1)		(2)*		(3)		(4)	
Seniors	26.2	54.0	30.4	50.1	14.4	42.5	24.9	49.7
Freshmen	19.9	46.0	25.6	45.9	18.1	37.6	31.2	41.9
2-Year	17.4	44.7	22.3	47.2	25.8	36.1	28.4	40.5

16. (96.) In the area of human rights, the major accomplishment of the Helsinki Accords was the

    (1) establishment of a court where human rights complaints can be heard.
    (2) acknowledgement of the signatories' right to intercede in the event one of their members violates human rights.
    (3) commitment made by the United States to admit as an immigrant any Eastern European who can show that his or her human rights have been violated.
    (4) recognition accorded human rights as a legitimate subject of discussion in the East-West debate.

	(1)		(2)		(3)		(4)*	
Seniors	27.4	51.0	13.9	45.1	12.2	45.1	28.6	59.0
Freshmen	26.1	45.1	15.6	40.3	19.3	39.7	19.8	47.7
2-Year	27.9	42.1	14.1	39.5	18.0	36.4	25.0	48.3

17. (59.) In the period between 1945 and 1975, the United Nations adopted nearly 20 human rights treaties, such as the Genocide convention. These treaties must be ratified by a certain number of member countries before going into effect. About how many of these treaties did the United States ratify?

    (1) Nearly all of them
    (2) More than half of them
    (3) Fewer than half of them
    (4) Almost none of them

	(1)		(2)		(3)*		(4)	
Seniors	51.5	54.0	29.6	47.4	9.3	46.3	2.5	52.4
Freshmen	40.3	46.6	28.9	40.4	19.5	40.0	4.7	40.2
2-Year	38.6	43.8	29.9	39.8	19.1	39.1	5.0	39.5

18. (58.) Which of the following organizations promulgated the Universal Declaration of Human Rights?

    (1) The League of Nations in 1919 following the First World War
    (2) The World Council of Churches in 1936 following the outbreak of the Spanish Civil War
    (3) The United Nations in 1948 following the Second World War
    (4) Amnesty International in 1972 following a terrorist attack at the Olympic Games

	(1)		(2)		(3)*		(4)	
Seniors	21.6	50.0	5.9	45.9	51.6	51.7	10.3	52.9
Freshmen	21.0	2.7	7.9	37.3	49.9	44.5	10.7	41.6
2-Year	20.5	40.2	7.9	39.2	46.0	42.5	15.2	41.3

19. (45.) The establishment of the Western sovereign territorial state and the modern state system is usually dated from the

    (1) breakup of the Roman Empire in the fifth century.
    (2) development of feudalism in the early Middle Ages.
    (3) Peace of Westphalia in the mid-seventeenth century, which brought European conflicts fought in the name of religion to an end.
    (4) Peace of Versailles in the early twentieth century, which dealt with the aftermath of the breakup of the Russian, German, Austro-Hungarian, and Ottoman empires.

	(1)		(2)		(3)*		(4)	
Seniors	13.2	50.3	20.5	50.8	19.0	53.8	37.4	50.2
Freshmen	15.3	40.4	18.4	43.5	18.9	43.4	36.2	43.7
2-Year	16.8	42.1	21.4	40.7	17.6	41.2	34.4	41.8

20. (19.) A very high degree of interdependence is a basic fact of contemporary international life. Which of the following is NOT a significant consequence of interdependence?

    (1) Interdependence intermingles domestic with foreign policies.
    (2) Interdependence is associated with an increased willingness to renounce war as an instrument of national policy.
    (3) Interdependence makes it highly probable that significant events in, or actions by, nation A will have serious effects on nations B, C, D, etc., and vice versa.
    (4) Interdependence may make both self-sufficiency and dependency (e.g., reliance on imports of essential raw materials) difficult and costly.

	(1)		(2)*		(3)		(4)	
Seniors	15.8	49.5	33.2	53.9	14.6	45.6	28.1	51.4
Freshmen	14.6	43.7	23.2	46.1	24.2	39.1	25.1	44.3
2-Year	13.8	42.3	28.3	44.5	25.2	38.0	24.5	41.2

21. (16.) Unlike trade negotiations in the 1940s, 1950s, and 1960s, the main purpose of the recently completed multilateral trade negotiations was to

    (1) lower tariffs and customs duties.
    (2) establish stable prices for petroleum products.
    (3) reduce nontariff barriers to trade.
    (4) reduce the trade barriers of less developed countries.

	(1)		(2)		(3)✱		(4)	
Seniors	15.2	50.9	27.6	47.3	18.0	55.3	26.3	49.6
Freshmen	15.5	39.9	36.3	41.4	12.6	45.2	25.5	44.4
2-Year	19.4	39.2	32.4	40.3	13.0	43.4	26.2	42.3

22. (109.) In the North-South talks, representatives of developing countries have demanded all of the following EXCEPT

    (1) the reduction of their level of economic interdependence with the industrialized countries.
    (2) the stabilization of world prices for their basic commodity exports.
    (3) increased control over monetary lending institutions such as the International Monetary Fund.
    (4) lower tariffs in industrialized countries for their exports.

	(1)✱		(2)		(3)		(4)	
Seniors	24.9	55.5	16.9	51.3	27.5	50.3	12.1	47.3
Freshmen	22.4	46.7	18.2	41.2	29.4	42.9	15.7	40.3
2-Year	18.4	47.0	23.7	40.9	27.3	40.7	16.4	41.0

23. (61.) Between 1900 and 1979, numerous conferences and agreements intended to establish the conditions of international peace through prevention and control of war as well as through arms limitation fell short of their aims. Which of the following is LEAST important in explaining the lack of substantial progress toward world peace?

    (1) Sequences of arms buildup, followed by perceived threat, followed by another arms buildup by two rival nations or blocs of nations
    (2) Failure to design and implement a system of collective security that nations can trust to preserve their safety and to protect their interests
    (3) Destabilizing effects of war-related science and technology on arms limitation agreements
    (4) The increase in the number of governments established by military coup and the number of governments currently dominated by military regimes

	(1)		(2)		(3)		(4)✱	
Seniors	13.8	48.4	26.4	49.2	23.6	52.5	27.0	53.9
Freshmen	11.5	41.5	33.0	41.3	22.3	43.7	23.2	46.0
2-Year	12.8	38.8	32.6	41.0	22.5	40.8	21.4	46.0

24. (25.) The map above shows the distribution in the world today of which of the following diseases?

    (1) Bubonic plague
    (2) Malaria
    (3) Typhoid fever
    (4) Cholera

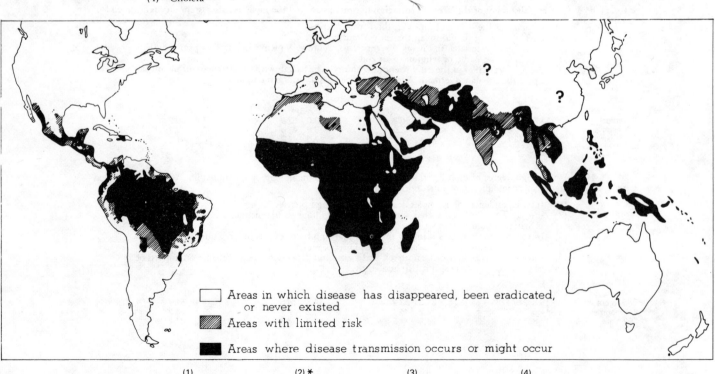

☐ Areas in which disease has disappeared, been eradicated, or never existed

▨ Areas with limited risk

■ Areas where disease transmission occurs or might occur

	(1)		(2)✱		(3)		(4)	
Seniors	1.7	38.8	63.7	51.6	13.2	47.7	14.3	51.0
Freshmen	5.9	37.6	61.2	43.8	15.8	38.5	9.6	44.4
2-Year	5.9	34.7	52.2	42.4	18.9	36.2	13.7	41.8

72

Saudi Arabia, the Soviet Union, Indonesia, and Nigeria, one out of three two-year college students and nearly as many freshmen were unaware of Christianity's predominance or strength in Greece, Lebanon, the Philippines, and Ethiopia. The distinction between misconceptions held by seniors and the other populations with respect to the origins of Zionism, the subject of question 7, is less clear-cut. While almost 19 percent of seniors incorrectly agreed with slightly more than 12 percent of two-year college students that the Balfour Declaration of 1917 was the origin, over half the freshmen and two-year college students thought the Nazi persecution of the Jews the source, and an additional 11.1 percent of two-year college students indicated their belief that Stalin's anti-Semitic purges of the 1930s had given rise to the Zionist movement.

That the three questions just discussed are humanities items—and that the two dealing with the relative size of the world's major religions and the origins of Zionism are academic in nature—suggests, perhaps, that students have had less exposure to the subject matter being measured than is the case with some social science topics, possibly accounting in part for the misconceptions evidenced. However, ignorance of the geographic distribution of Islam and Christianity, particularly given the strife in Lebanon, the current resurgence of Islam, events in Iran, and the Soviet invasion of Afghanistan, is ignorance of a subject frequently covered in the media.

Since the two remaining questions on religious issues (8 and 9) are also humanities items concerned with topics most likely to be encountered in academic courses (religious characteristics and precepts), again the extent of student misconceptions is perhaps less surprising than in the case of other subjects. In both questions, able students across the three populations once more divided in their choice of incorrect responses: in question 8, nearly 12 percent of seniors thought that in Buddhist belief one was saved from sin by the suppression of anger and fear, while roughly 11 percent of freshmen and 10 percent of two-year college students thought one was saved by becoming a monk or nun; and in question 9, over 40 percent of each population thought all the world's major religions insisted on personal identification with a single faith, while an additional 5.4 percent of seniors thought the religions shared a tendency to proselytize, and an additional 36.6 percent of freshmen thought they shared the concept of a messiah.

The remaining questions, ten items related singly or in pairs to an array of issues, show the pattern of diversity in the incorrect answer choices of able students continuing, regardless of whether the questions are current or historical, social science or humanities items, or measures of what might be learned through academic or nonacademic sources. For instance, question 11, a population question dealing with the current phenomenon of foreign populations living abroad, showed 36, 31, and 37 percent of seniors, freshmen, and two-year college students, respectively, thinking political refugees the largest groups of people living outside their home countries, while roughly 20, 16, and 11 percent of the student populations in the same order thought American and Soviet military forces posted abroad the largest group. It seems safe to infer that frequent media coverage of the refugee issue and troop movements influenced student response, and, unfortunately, obscured for students the attention paid in newspapers and newsmagazines to the large numbers of foreign workers living in Western Europe. On the other hand, question 12, an item dealing with the historical sources of population in North and South America, a topic usually learned in the classroom, showed approximately 30, 31, and 27 percent of seniors, freshmen and two-year college students, respectively, thinking Northern European immigrants to the United States outnumbered Eastern and Southern European immigrants during the late nineteenth and early twentieth centuries, and another 23 percent of freshmen thinking all major areas of European settlement on the South American continent under Spanish domination by the beginning of the nineteenth century. It is disheartening to observe that such large portions of the student populations did not know the correct answer—that people of Mexican descent were already resident in sizable numbers in certain areas of the United States when those areas were annexed by the United States. It is also of interest that students should have found little difference in difficulty between a relatively standard history item of this type and an item such as question 15 which asks why rice-growing is so advantageous to China, a topic one would suppose encountered in academic courses by far fewer students. In the latter question, the misconception that China has surplus farm labor and few alternatives for employment was evident among approximately 26, 20, and 17 percent of seniors, freshmen, and two-year college students, respectively, and the misconception that female and child labor made rice a cheap crop for China to grow was apparent among approximately 31 and 28 percent more of the freshmen and two-year college populations. In all, approximately 75 percent of students failed to recognize the yield, nutrient, and market values of rice vis-a-vis other crops.

The incorrect responses to question 17, a human rights item, seem particularly illuminative of the beliefs of students about their own country. The question is of further interest in that seniors performed less well than on any other item in the assessment, only 9 percent as compared to 19 percent of the freshmen and two-year college student populations knowing the answer: that of the nearly 20 human rights treaties adopted by the United Nations, fewer than half have been ratified by the United States. In contrast, 51.5 percent of seniors, 40.3 percent of freshmen, and 38.6 percent of two-year college students thought nearly all of the treaties had been so ratified. Despite an additional 2.5 percent of seniors thinking almost none of the treaties had received United States ratification, the misconception that anything having to do with human rights must have the official support of the United States was clearly evident among a majority of the able in the student population. Although students on the whole performed better on the second human rights question selected for discussion (18), nearly 50 percent of the total population knowing that the United Nations promulgated the Universal Declaration of Human Rights in 1948, student groups of some numerical significance thought otherwise. Approximately 10 percent of seniors and 15 percent of two-year college students believed Amnesty International to be the promulgator following the terrorist attack at the 1972 Olympic Games, and 21 percent of freshmen thought the Declaration was issued by the League of Nations in 1919.

Two questions relating to the issue of relations among states, 19 and 20, showed students in all populations weak in their knowledge of the historical origins of the Western territorial state and, with the exception of seniors among whom one out of three answered correctly, little better informed about the consequences of interdependence among nations. In the former question, slightly less than one out of five students in each population knew that the establishment of the modern state system is usually dated from the mid-seventeenth century Peace of Westphalia. Among those answering incorrectly, close to a fifth of each population thought the modern state had emerged with the development of feudalism, slightly more than another third of freshmen and two-year college students thought it derived from the Peace of Versailles, and an additional sixth of two-year college students thought it dated from the breakup of the Roman Empire. In question 20, approximately a quarter of the freshmen and two-year college populations and slightly more of the seniors failed to recognize that in an interdependent world both national selfsufficiency and dependency may be difficult and costly conditions. In addition, roughly 14 percent of each of the two former populations seemed unaware that interdependence results in an intermingling of domestic and foreign policies. The correct answer—that interdependence in contemporary international life has not induced nations to renounce war as an instrument of policy—was given by only 28 percent of the total student population.

Even fewer students, 23 percent of the total population, correctly answered question 23, a somewhat related item soliciting reasons in explanation of the largely failed efforts to build world peace in the present century. Incorrect responses indicated that in the neighborhood of 23 percent of each population underemphasized the destabilizing effects of war-related science and technology on arms limitation agreements, and roughly another third of two-year college students thought the international community's failure to build an effective system of collective security less important as a factor than the increase in the number of military regimes throughout the world.

The last two questions to be considered, 21 and 22, dealt with international monetary and trade relations and proved relatively difficult for all groups, only a quarter or less of the students in each population answering either question correctly. The former question, in which trade negotiations in the 1940s, 1950s, and 1960s are compared with recently completed multilateral negotiations, found about 15 percent of the seniors thinking the purpose of the latter to reduce tariffs and customs duties and slightly more than a quarter of the freshmen and two-year college populations thinking a reduction in the trade barriers of less developed countries the purpose. Only 18 percent of seniors and 13 percent of the other two populations correctly identified the lowering of nontariff trading barriers as the objective of recent agreements. Question 22 was the easier of the two monetary and trade questions, with 25, 22, and 18 percent of the senior, freshmen, and two-year college populations, respectively, answering correctly; it was designed to measure students' awareness of the demands of developing countries in the North-South talks. Incorrect answers showed a range of misconceptions at work, the one shared by all populations being the belief that developing countries wanted a reduction in their level of economic interdependence with the industrialized countries. Among those answering the question incorrectly, 17 percent of seniors and 24 percent of two-year college students failed to recognize that developing countries wanted stable world prices for their basic commodity exports; another 27 percent of two-year college students and 29 percent of freshmen ignored the wish of developing countries to increase their control over monetary lending institutions; and yet another 16 percent of two-year college students were unaware that developing countries wanted lower tariffs in industrialized countries for their exports.

The range of misconceptions about global affairs evidenced among able students in their incorrect responses to the two dozen questions discussed lends itself to few generalizations about student performance as a whole or student performance in the context of specific student groups. As noted in prefatory comments and in the discussion of individual questions, seniors found the great majority of the items easier than did the other student populations and, in a few items, able seniors revealed misconceptions different from those shared by the able in the other two populations. The number of cases of the latter, however, is too small to indicate trends in senior misconceptions vis-a-vis those of freshmen and two-year college students. Moreover, questions in which able seniors, sometimes in larger and sometimes in smaller percentages, shared misconceptions with one or both of the other populations outnumbered the former type of question by five to one. It was also observed that in ten questions in which there was a sharing and/or mix of misconceptions across all three populations, groups of able freshmen and two-year college students evidenced misconceptions not revealed by able seniors. Again, however, the cases are so few and spread among items of such a wide range of difficulty and subject matter that few conclusions can be drawn. Given these results, student misconceptions are best studied in the context of the question in which they were revealed and against the larger background of the issue to which the question, as one of a set, was related.

For purposes of comparison, five questions (shown on page 00) from a survey instrument administered to a national sample of twelfth-grade students in the fall of 1974 were included among the 101 cognitive questions in the Test of Global Knowledge. The purpose of the 1974 survey was to measure students' grasp of the information considered necessary to a rudimentary knowledge and understanding of other nations and people. Data on the selection of responses by the Other Nations, Other Peoples (Pike and Barrows) population are given below each question next to the data for the three student populations participating in the Survey of Global Understanding. Caution should be exercised in comparing the responses of twelfth-grade students and college freshmen in that the latter constitute a more select population than the former. The data from these five questions, however, demonstrate that even those American students who go on to college are surprisingly ignorant of some basic political, cultural, and geographic facts about the world in which they live.

1974 Questions on 1980 Global Understanding Survey
(Percentage of Students Selecting Responses [+])

(48.)   The republics of the Soviet Union were formed primarily on the basis of

    (1)   the ethnic groups or nationalities of the people.
    (2)   natural geographic boundaries.
    (3)   the political orientation of the people.
    (4)   agricultural and climatic zones.

| | ON, OP | GLOBAL UNDERSTANDING | | |
	12th Grade	Freshmen	Seniors	2-Year
*(1)	23	25	36	24
(2)	26	25	21	23
(3)	37	33	26	35
(4)	14	13	14	14

[+] Freshmen, seniors and students at two-year colleges are represented by samples of approximately 1,000 each. Twelfth-grade students are represented by samples of 550 to 600 each.

75

(111.) Which of the following is shared by all known culture groups?

*(1) a structured spoken language
(2) a written language
(3) a structured religion
(4) a prison system

	ON, OP	GLOBAL UNDERSTANDING		
	12th Grade	Freshmen	Seniors	2-Year
*(1)	42	54	64	50
(2)	14	10	6	11
(3)	27	18	13	16
(4)	17	14	13	17

(79.) Chinese culture has been characterized by all of the following EXCEPT:

*(1) a caste system
(2) patriarchal control
(3) a strong family cult
(4) ancestral concern

	ON, OP	GLOBAL UNDERSTANDING		
	12th Grade	Freshmen	Seniors	2-Year
*(1)	43	56	68	56
(2)	18	27	18	28
(3)	12	7	8	6
(4)	9	5	2	5

(67.) In which of the following countries do the regional governments have the most authority?

(1) The Soviet Union
(2) Great Britain
*(3) The United States
(4) France

	ON, OP	GLOBAL UNDERSTANDING		
	12th Grade	Freshmen	Seniors	2-Year
(1)	31	33	19	30
(2)	24	11	14	13
*(3)	34	40	53	39
(4)	10	11	9	11

(112.) Which country is in both Europe and Asia?

(1) China
*(2) Russia/The Soviet Union
(3) India
(4) Poland

	ON, OP	GLOBAL UNDERSTANDING		
	12th Grade	Freshmen	Seniors	2-Year
(1)	13	7	6	10
*(2)	54	68	75	67
(3)	15	6	4	7
(4)	17	14	11	9

The first of the ONOP questions (48) asked students to designate the primary basis upon which the republics of the Soviet Union were formed. In the Test of Global Knowledge, only among the seniors was the percentage of students choosing the correct option greater than the percentage who chose the option "the political orientation of the people." That incorrect option was selected by 33 percent of the freshmen, 26 percent of the seniors, and 35 percent of the two-year college students. Of the college seniors, 61 percent chose one of the three incorrect responses to this item, as did 71 percent of the freshmen and 72 percent of the two-year college students.

The second ONOP item (111) asked students to identify which of four characteristics is shared by

76

all known culture groups. Forty-two percent of the ONOP twelfth graders chose "a structured spoken language" (the correct option). Although at least 50 percent of the college students in each cohort in the Test of Global Knowledge did choose the correct answers, 32 percent of the seniors and 44 percent of the two-year college students selected incorrect options.

The third question (70) asked students to designate which one of four options has *not* been a characteristic of Chinese culture. The most interesting finding on this item is that although only 18 percent of the ONOP twelfth graders selected the incorrect option "patriarchal control," 27 percent of the freshmen and 28 percent of the two-year college students did so. Eighteen percent of the college seniors also selected this option.

The fourth ONOP question (67) asked students in which of four countries the regional governments have the most authority. Only among the college seniors was the proportion of students choosing the United States (the correct option) greater than 50 percent. Among ONOP twelfth graders, 31 percent of the students chose the Soviet Union, and this option was selected by 33 percent of the freshmen and 30 percent of the two-year college students.

The last ONOP question (112) asked students to designate which of four countries is in both Europe and Asia. It is the only one of the five ONOP questions that was answered correctly by a majority of students in the ONOP survey and in each cohort of the Test of Global Knowledge. It should be noted, however, that almost a third of both the freshmen and the two-year college students and fully a quarter of the seniors did *not* know the correct answer to this question.

Chapter 8

General Background and Interests

Mary F. Bennett

The general background section of the Global Understanding Survey contained 51 questions that probed students' personal backgrounds, habits, and interests. Response data for these items are tabled, question by question, in Appendix A.

The first three questions asked for students' age, sex, and ethnicity; the responses revealed some basic differences in the three populations surveyed. The mean age of freshmen at four-year institutions was 19.4, with a standard deviation of 4.2. The youngest freshman was 17 and the oldest was 62; the modal age was 18. The age of seniors at four-year institutions ranged from 18 to 52 years and the modal age was 21. The mean age for seniors was 23.4, with a standard deviation of 4.6. The mean age of students at two-year colleges was 25, but the standard deviation was 10.6, a reflection of the greater age diversity in that population. The youngest two-year college student was 17, the oldest was 74, and the modal age was 19.

The majority of students in each of the three groups was female. The seniors came closest to a 50:50 distribution, 48.7 percent of the sample being male and 51.3 percent female. The freshman population was 56.2 percent female and 43.8 percent male, and the two-year college sample was 60.2 percent female and 39.8 percent male.

Students who described themselves as "White or Caucasian" were preponderant in all three populations. Among four-year college students, they accounted for 85.7 percent of freshmen and 86.2 percent of seniors. In two-year colleges, however, only 73.6 percent of the students were "White or Caucasian." "Black or Afro American" students, the largest minority group, were represented in each cohort as follows: freshmen, 7.8 percent; seniors, 6.7 percent; 2-year, 11.4 percent. The second largest minority was different for each cohort.

Distribution of Minority Students

	Freshmen	Seniors	2-Year
Black or Afro American	7.8	6.7	11.4
Chicano or Mexican American	2.2	0.9	3.9
Oriental, Filipino, or Asian American	1.8	2.3	2.7
Puerto Rican, Cuban, or Hispanic	1.5	0.2	4.6
American Indian, Eskimo, or Aleut	0.1	0.1	0.7

The seventh option in the ethnic-racial background item was labeled "Other" and was followed by the instruction "Specify: ." Only 0.9 percent of the freshmen circled this option, but significant numbers of the seniors (3.5 percent) and two-year college students (3.1 percent) chose to specify an ethnic or racial identity other than those listed. The majority of these responses came from students whose mothers belong to one ethnic or racial group and their fathers to another. A number of presumably Caucasian students also used this option to specify their ancestry; i.e., they identified themselves as Italian-American, Polish-American, Armenian, Greek, and so on.

The next five questions in the survey dealt with place of birth and residence. Students were asked to identify the region of the world they were born in: North America, Central America, South America, Europe, Asia, Africa, Australia, or "Other (Specify:)." Almost 95 percent of the four-year college students were born in North America, but among two-year college students the figure was appreciably lower—87.9 percent. For the three populations as a whole, the largest group of students born outside of North America came from Asia (1.8 percent freshmen; 1.8 percent seniors; and 3.0 percent 2-year). European-born students were the next largest minority, accounting for 0.8 percent of the freshmen, 2.3 percent of the seniors, and 3.1 percent of the 2-year college students. Three percent of all the students were born in Central America and three percent in South America. The largest group in either case was composed of students attending two-year colleges (2.2 percent Central American; 2.1 percent South American). African-born students (1.2 percent of the total sample) were almost equally distributed among the three cohorts. No students reported having been born in Australia, and 2.5 percent circled "Other."

Question 5 asked students whether they were born in the United States. Among four-year college students, 6.4 percent of the freshmen and 6.0 percent of the seniors were not born here. The percentage of foreign-born students (13.2 percent) in two-year colleges was more than double the figure for either group at four-year institutions.

Examination of student responses to questions 4 and 5 brought to light a curious fact. Many of the students who said their place of birth was the United States circled either Central America or South America (instead of North America) when asked what region of the world they were born in. The research staff at first thought that these students might be Puerto Rican, Cuban, or Mexican. However, an analysis of the data, which excluded all students who described themselves as "Chicano or Mexican American" or "Puerto Rican, Cuban, or Hispanic," showed that 5.4 percent of the students who had reported the U.S. as their birthplace also had reported being born somewhere other than North America. As we examined the survey booklets of these students, it became apparent that many of those who reported "Central America" as their native region live in the midwestern United States and many of those who reported "South America" live in the southern United States. That more than five percent of this sample of American college students demonstrated such a misunderstanding of basic geographic nomenclature is appalling.

Question 6 asked students who were *not* born in the United States to print the name of the country in which they were born. The most surprising responses to this question came from students who *were* U.S. born but filled in the blank with the name of a *city* or *county* in the United States.

Students not born in the United States were also asked to state how old they were when they first came to this country. The mean ages were: freshmen, 11.3; seniors, 10.7; and two-year students, 11.5. However, the modal age of entry for both freshmen and seniors was one year, and for two-year students it was eight years. There was a foreign-born freshman who had come to the United States at 25, a senior who had come at 47, and a two-year student who had arrived here at 53. This wide spread explains the striking difference between the mode and the mean.

Finally, students not born in the United States were asked if they considered themselves permanent U.S. residents. Affirmative responses were made by 80.5 percent of the seniors, 85.1 percent of the freshmen, and 90.8 percent of the two-year students.

Students were asked to report the highest level of formal education completed by their fathers and their mothers, two items of information that are frequently used as measures of socioeconomic status. In the survey's results, the correlations between fathers' and mothers' levels of education were .62 for freshmen, .50 for seniors, and .58 for two-year students. These correlations were not considered high enough to justify combining the two indices into one variable.

There were students in the sample whose fathers or mothers (or both) had had no formal education—for freshmen 0.5 percent of the fathers and 0.5 percent of the mothers; for seniors 0.1 percent of the fathers and 0.4 percent of the mothers; and for two-year students 0.7 percent of the fathers and 1.3 percent of the mothers. Percentages of students in the sample whose fathers had not completed high school were: freshmen, 14.2; seniors, 14.6; and 2-year, 24.1. For freshmen and seniors the percentages of students whose *mothers* had not completed high school were *smaller*—11.2 percent and 13 percent, but for two-year students the percentage was slightly larger (25.2 percent). Students' fathers did, however, have considerably more postsecondary education than did the mothers, especially at the graduate school level. For example, the table below shows the distribution of those who had obtained a graduate or professional degree.

Parents With Graduate or Professional Degree

	Percent of Fathers	Percent of Mothers
Freshmen	21.6	7.1
Seniors	17.9	6.7
2-Year	15.3	5.9

The next set of questions in the survey focused on political background. Students were asked what their "usual political party preference" was and were given five response options: (1) Democratic, (2) Republican, (3) Independent, (4) Other (Specify:), and (5) I don't know. Students were also asked to indicate the political party preference of each of their parents. In the three cohorts, for both students and parents, Democrats outnumbered Republicans in all cases except for fathers of seniors, there being in this case 0.7 percent more Republicans than Democrats. Many students considered themselves Independents—13.6 percent of the freshmen; 20.2 percent of the seniors; and 15.5 percent of the two-year students. In each cohort, there were more students who labeled their mothers Independent than who labeled their fathers Independent. The percentages of students who "didn't know" their parents' political party preference were high, ranging from 14.5 percent to 19.1 percent. Very few students selected the option "Other" to describe their own or their parents' party preference. The seniors constituted the largest group of students who chose this option (3.7 percent), followed by the two-year students (3.2 percent), and the freshmen (1.7 percent); for parents, the percentages ranged from 0.6 percent for mothers of two-year students to 1.9 percent for fathers of two-year students. The most commonly specified "Other" response was "vote(s) for the person, not the party."

Correlations between "father's political party preference" and "mother's political party preference" were very high—.78 for freshmen, .71 for seniors, and .74 for two-year students. Correlations between students' party preference and that of their parents ranged from .33 to .39.

Students were also asked to indicate their own and their parents' political attitudes on a five-point "left/right" scale. The majority of the freshmen (60.2 percent) marked the midpoint of the scale, 20.3 percent leaned to the right and 19.4 percent leaned to the left. The seniors' responses were much more spread out on the scale, with only 42.8 percent at the midpoint, 26.2 percent favoring the right and 31.0 percent the left. The two-year college sample had the highest percentage of students at the midpoint (60.9 percent), but also had more respondents at the extremes than the rest of the sample. In all three groups appreciably more students noted that their parents' political attitudes were more right than left.

Correlations between fathers' and mothers' political attitudes were high—.64 for freshmen, .61 for seniors, and .56 for two-year students. Correlations between students' attitudes and their parents', however, were significantly lower than those for political party preference. The lowest correlation was between two-year college students and their fathers (.17), and the highest was between freshmen and their mothers (.32).

The next set of questions in the survey probed students' television-watching and newspaper-reading habits. These questions were included because it was deemed important to determine (a) the ways in which students acquire information concerning world affairs and (b) the relationship (or lack thereof) of patterns of information acquisition to knowledge and attitudes. Students were first asked to fill in the number of hours a week they usually spent watching television. The mean number of hours for each group was: freshmen, 9.9; seniors, 10.4; and two-year students, 12.0. In each cohort there were students who did not watch television at all, and the modal number of hours of television-watching per week was the same (10 hours) for each group. The highest number of hours of viewing reported among freshmen was 90, among seniors it was 75, and among two-year students, 81. Considering that these students were presumably also eating meals and sleeping, not to mention attending college, these high figures are astounding.

Next, students were asked to designate what they usually watched on television. Among freshmen, movies were the most popular (80.2 percent), followed by news (76.8 percent). Among seniors and two-year students, news was slightly ahead of the preference for movies.

Students were asked how often they watched world and national news programs on television, how often they watched local news programs, and how often they listened to radio newscasts. They were also asked how often they read a newspaper, which sections they usually read, whether they read a newspaper that carries a good deal of international news, and whether they regularly read a weekly newsmagazine or newspaper. Students were then asked whether they considered newspapers, magazines, television, or radio the main source of the information they acquired concerning current events. In each of the cohorts the largest percentage of students selected television in answer to this last question. It is interesting to note, however, that more students in each group indicated that they read a newspaper daily than said that they watched the news on television daily.

Figure 3.8.1. presents correlations greater than .20 among responses to items on television-viewing and newspaper-reading. Figures 3.8.2a., 3.8.2b., and 3.8.2c. present correlations greater than .15 for the item on types of television shows watched.

The section of the survey dealing with the media included a list of 16 fictitious headlines of articles and asked students to choose the four articles among them that they would most likely read. Of the 16 headlines, four were on international topics, four on events in the United States, four on science and technology, and four on sports. The headline selected most frequently by freshmen (57.7 percent) was "Team of New York Surgeons Reattach Man's Severed Leg." This article was also selected by 49.5 percent of the seniors and 46.8 percent of the two-year students. The article chosen by the largest number of seniors and two-year students (53.1 percent each) was "President Considering Wage-Price Freeze." The next most frequently selected headline in all three cohorts was "Astrophysicist's Findings Cast Light on 'Black Holes'." Next in popularity among freshmen and two-year students was "New Computer Terminal 'Talks' and 'Listens'," but among seniors it was "Indian Government Steps Up Voluntary Sterilization Campaign."

Students' selections of headlines did not correlate very highly with any of the other items in the media section. There were no correlations greater than .20, and the highest ones found were between the sports headlines and "reading the sports section of the newspaper" and "watching sports on television." Although three of the most popular headlines were in the science and technology category, none of them was significantly correlated with "watching science specials on television." Similarly, "reading international news articles" did not correlate highly with selection of the international news headlines.

Students were asked how many hours a week they spent reading for pleasure. The table below compares the means, standard deviations, and modes for responses to this question and the one on number of hours spent watching television.

Hours Reading or Watching TV

	Freshmen		Seniors		2-Year	
	T.V.	Reading	T.V.	Reading	T.V.	Reading
Mean	9.9	6.0	10.4	6.8	12.0	7.7
S.D.	9.5	6.0	8.9	5.7	9.8	7.2
Mode	10.0	5.0	10.0	5.0	10.0	10.0

In all cases, the mean number of hours per week spent watching television exceed the mean number of hours spent reading for pleasure. Among four-year college students (both freshmen and seniors), the mode for television watching (10 hours) is double the mode for reading (5 hours). For two-year college students, the mode for television watching and that for reading are the same—10 hours. This would appear to be a victory for reading except that the mean number of hours two-year college students spend reading for pleasure is only 7.7 hours. This indicates that although a sizeable number of students are spending 10 hours a week reading, most of their schoolmates are reading less than that.

Students were asked what their average grade in high school was, and over 50 percent in each cohort answered "B+ to B-." Among the freshmen, 32.8 percent said their average grade was "A to A-"; among seniors 35 percent reported being "A to A-" students. Only 15.3 percent of the two-year students had average grades of "A to A-" in high school, and 28.4 percent had been "C to C-" students. A few students in each cohort had average grades of "D or below"—0.4 percent of the freshmen, 0.4 percent of the seniors, and 0.9 percent of the two-year students.

Figure 3.8.1. Correlations > .20 Among Responses to Items on Television-viewing and Newspaper-reading

Item	Freshmen	Seniors	2-Year	Item
17. Number of hours per week spent watching television	.21	.20		20.4 watching situation comedies
	.23		.23	20.9 watching game shows
	.37	.36	.30	21. frequency of watching world and national news on television
	.37	.36	.30	22. frequency of watching local news on television
21. Frequency of watching world and national news on television	.71	.76	.74	22. frequency of watching local news on television
	.25		.31	25. frequency of newspaper reading
			.23	26.5 reading national news articles
22. Frequency of watching local news on television	.22		.21	25. frequency of newspaper reading
	.21			26.1 reading newspaper sports section
			.21	26.3 reading local news articles
25. Frequency of newspaper reading	.22	.21	.31	26.5 reading national news articles
		.20		26.6 reading international news articles
		.25		26.9 reading newspaper editorials
			.25	26.10 reading newspaper Letters to the Editor

Figure 3.8.2a. Correlations > .15 Among Types of Television Shows Watched
Freshmen

	20.1	20.2	20.3	20.4	20.5	20.6	20.7	20.8	20.9	20.10	20.11	20.12
20.1 Detective/police adventures												
20.2 Musical performances					.18						.19	.25
20.3 Curent events								.29		.21	.18	.20
20.4 Situation comedies	.19				.21				.22			
20.5 Dramatic series	.22	.18		.21					.24		.19	
20.6 Sports events								.20				
20.7 Movies	.22											
20.8 News			.29			.20					.16	.25
20.9 Game shows	.30			.22	.24							.24
20.10 Science specials			.21					.26				
20.11 Talk shows	.17	.19	.18		.19			.15	.24			
20.12 Specials about foreign countries and their cultures	.25	.20								.24		

82

Figure 3.8.2b. Correlations > .15 Among Types of Television Shows Watched
Seniors

	20.1	20.2	20.3	20.4	20.5	20.6	20.7	20.8	20.9	20.10	20.11	20.12
20.1 Detective/police adventures												
20.2 Musical performances					.21						.16	.21
20.3 Current events								.23		.5		.28
20.4 Situation comedies					.20		.16		.29		.16	.19
20.5 Dramatic series	.16	.21		.20			.17		.18		.25	
20.6 Sports events								.15				
20.7 Movies	.15			.16	.17							
20.8 News			.23			.15						
20.9 Game shows	.26			.29	.18						.24	
20.10 Science specials			.15									.32
20.11 Talk shows		.16		.16	.25				.24			
20.12 Specials about foreign countries and their cultures										.32		

Figure 3.8.2c. Correlations > .15 Among Types of Television Shows Watched
2-Year Students

	20.1	20.2	20.3	20.4	20.5	20.6	20.7	20.8	20.9	20.10	20.11	20.12
20.1 Detective/police adventures												
20.2 Musical performances			.23					.16		.21	.17	.20
20.3 Current events		.23						.25		.17		.27
20.4 Situation comedies	.15						.16		.20			
20.5 Dramatic series	.18						.16		.26		.19	
20.6 Sports events								.21	.18		.21	
20.7 Movies	.28			.16	.16							
20.8 News		.16	.25			.21					.16	
20.9 Game shows	.30			.20	.26	.18					.19	
20.10 Science specials		.21	.17			.21						.37
20.11 Talk shows		.17			.19			.15	.19			
20.12 Specials about foreign countries and their cultures		.20	.27							.37		

In the section of the survey dealing with high school experiences, students were asked how often they studied or discussed world problems or issues in class and to what extent their experiences outside the classroom contributed to their awareness of world issues. In the section containing questions on college experiences, the same two questions were asked. The Figure 3.8.3. compares the response data.

Figure 3.8.3. Experiences In and Outside the Classroom

	Freshmen		Seniors		2-Year	
	H.S.	College	H.S.	College	H.S.	College
Frequency of classroom discussion of world issues:						
1) At least once a day	29.1	13.8	19.6	18.4	30.3	21.1
2) Once or twice a week	50.2	40.2	54.2	39.2	45.0	41.1
3) Less than once a week	17.1	32.6	23.5	29.9	19.1	21.1
4) Never	3.6	13.4	2.8	12.5	5.6	16.5
Extent of outside experience contribution to awareness of world issues:						
1) A great deal	22.9	35.7	19.2	48.7	21.3	40.6
2) Some	43.5	39.6	36.3	36.3	40.4	41.2
3) A little	27.8	20.9	37.3	13.4	27.4	13.0
4) I don't know	5.8	3.8	7.1	1.4	10.8	5.2

It is apparent that students believed they had had considerably more exposure to world problems or issues in their high school classrooms than they had in their college classes. There are many plausible explanations for this finding: high school classes are generally smaller and more open to discussions; high school courses tend to be less restricted by disciplinary confines; and probably more high school than college courses are taught from a current events perspective. In contrast, students believed that their college experiences outside of the classroom contributed more to their awareness of world issues than their high school non-class experiences did. This could simply reflect increasing maturity and broader interests.

Students were asked to designate the area of study in which they were majoring or intended to major. The most frequently circled response was "Business/ Accounting/Finance," which was chosen by 18.4 percent of the freshmen, 20.3 percent of the seniors, and 22.5 percent of the two-year students. The second most frequently selected area of study was "Biological Sciences/Physical Sciences" (freshmen, 17.7 percent; seniors, 14.4 percent; two-year students, 13.0 percent). "Social Sciences" majors followed in popularity, attracting 11.2 percent of the freshmen, 13.5 percent of the seniors, and 12.4 percent of the two-year college students. Several areas were identified as majors by very small percentages of students. The table below presents the figures for the five least popular majors.

Least Selected Majors
(in percent)

	Freshmen	Seniors	2-Year
Agriculture	1.2	1.5	1.4
Foreign Languages	1.0	2.1	2.5
History	0.9	1.9	1.7
Mathematics	2.6	1.7	1.5
Music	2.4	2.2	1.8

It is interesting to note that four traditional liberal arts disciplines—foreign languages, history, mathematics, and music—each attracted less than three percent of the students in a given cohort.

Students were asked to note how many courses they had taken in college in each of the 19 subjects believed to have potential for contributing to students' global understanding. The table below orders the subjects taken by the largest numbers of students in each cohort.

Most Selected Courses

Freshmen	Seniors	2-Year
1) Literature	1) History	1) History
2) History	2) Literature	2) Literature
3) Sociology	3) Sociology	3) Sociology
4) Political Science	4) Economics	4) Political Science
5) Philosophy	5) Political Science	5) Economics
6) Modern Foreign Languages	6) Philosophy	6) American Studies
7) Economics	7) Modern Foreign Languages	7) Philosophy

Students were then given the same list of 19 subjects and asked which subjects, if any, they believed had contributed to their awareness of world problems or issues. History was identified by the largest percentage of students in each of the cohorts. Other subjects judged to have contributed to global understanding by large numbers of students were sociology, economics, political science, and American studies. Two subjects that were not among those taken by the greatest numbers of students but ranked high in this ordering were geography and environmental studies. Conversely, although modern foreign languages were among the seven most elected subjects, they were not highly rated by students as contributing to their global understanding.

Students were asked to report the scores they achieved on SATs and ACTs if they had taken the tests. Approximately 49 percent of the freshmen, 40 percent of the seniors, and 17 percent of the two-year college students reported SAT scores. ACT scores were reported by 31 percent of the freshmen, 19 percent of the seniors, and 16 percent of the two-year college students. The means and standard deviations for reported scores are presented in the table below.

Admission Test Scores

	Freshmen	Senior	2-Year
SAT Verbal: mean	517	547	485
s.d.	99	97	110
SAT Math: mean	536	546	511
s.d.	106	112	113
ACT (composite) mean	22	23	19
s.d.	5	5	5

Students were asked what their approximate college grade-point averages were. In each cohort, the largest percentage of students reported GPAs between 3.0 and 3.4. The highest percentage of students reporting GPAs between 3.5 and 4.0 was found among two-year college students (23.3 percent). Among students at four-year institutions, 16.3 percent of the freshmen and 22.1 percent of the seniors reported GPAs between 3.5 and 4.0.

Students were asked two questions regarding their educational objectives. The first, "What is your current (immediate) educational objective?", listed four response options: (1) nondegree study; (2) certificate; (3) two-year degree; and (4) four-year degree. Not surprisingly, the overwhelming majority of students at four-year institutions (93.8 percent of the freshmen and 99.0 percent of the seniors) said they planned to get four-year degrees. In two-year colleges, 44.1 percent of the students listed the four-year degree as their current educational objective, while a slightly higher percentage (45.4 percent) listed the two-year degree. Student responses to the second question, "What is your eventual (long-term) educational goal?", are summarized in the table below.

Long-Term Educational Goal
(in percent)

		Freshmen	Senior	2-Year
1.	Nondegree study	0.5	0.7	3.8
2.	Certificate	0.9	2.0	0.8
3.	Two-year degree	1.2	0.0	8.4
4.	Four-year degree	36.5	24.7	38.4
5.	Master's degree	33.7	48.5	29.3
6.	Doctoral degree	10.8	13.6	12.2
7.	Law degree	5.9	7.8	4.2
8.	Medical degree	6.4	2.7	4.9

The next section of the survey explored students' experiences in traveling or living abroad. Students were asked whether they had ever been in a country other than the United States, and the majority in each cohort responded affirmatively: 57.9 percent of the freshmen; 64.3 percent of the seniors; and 60.9 of the two-year college students. The country visited by the largest number of students was Canada, and Mexico was the next most popular; Europe and the British Isles were the next most visited areas, followed by the Caribbean. The percentages of students in each cohort who had been to each of the 19 areas listed in this item are presented in Appendix A (see Question 47).

Those students who had been out of the United States were asked whether most of their time abroad had been spent in military service. Only 4.4 percent of the freshmen, 5.1 percent of the seniors, and 6.0 percent of the two-year college students responded affirmatively. Students were also asked whether they had ever participated in an organized summer-abroad or year-abroad program or had been in the Peace Corps or any other program involving similar international service. The table below summarizes student responses to these three questions.

Experiences Abroad

Percent of students who had participated in:	Freshmen	Seniors	2-Year
1) summer-abroad programs	9.0	7.9	8.8
2) year-abroad programs	1.1	5.0	1.2
3) Peace Corps or similar programs	0.1	1.2	0.7

Chapter 9

Language

John L. D. Clark

For all of the questions in the final "Booklet A" survey instrument, the response percentages for the freshman, senior, and two-year cohort groups are shown in Appendix A. This chapter highlights those portions of the total data that appear to be especially relevant from foreign language background, proficiency, and attitude standpoints.

Background Variables

Although the great majority of questionnaire respondents were born in the United States (93.6, 94.0, and 86.8 percent for freshmen, seniors, and two-year groups, respectively), each of the three cohort samples does include a number of students who were born in some other country (6.4, 6.0, and 13.2 percent for the three groups). It would be anticipated that most of these students would be native speakers of some language other than English, and this is borne out in the first question on "language background," where 5.8 percent, 3.6 percent, and 10.6 percent of the freshman, senior, and two-year respondents indicate that they are non-native speakers of English. On the assumption that the "born abroad" and/or non-native English-speaking students would, on the whole, have had somewhat different language learning histories and exposures from U.S.-born native speakers of English, this should be taken into account in considering the total group data. The total group information is, of course, reflective of three separate nationwide college populations, and the whole-group statistics for self-appraised language proficiency may properly be considered to represent the total pool of foreign language competence available in these populations. However, in order to analyze the effects of regular, U.S.-based foreign language instruction on judged foreign language proficiency (and on other variables presumed to be influenced by country-of-birth and native language considerations), it would be useful to conduct additional analyses eliminating from the analysis sample those students whose backgrounds are atypical of "native English" speakers in the regular U.S. instructional context. Some of these additional analyses have already been conducted and are reported on later in this section.

Relatively few freshmen, seniors, and two-year students indicated that they were currently majoring or intended to major in foreign languages (1.0, 2.1, and 2.5 percent, respectively). Perhaps most disturbing to advocates of foreign language study is the especially low figure for current freshmen. Except for prospective history majors (0.9 percent of the freshmen), the foreign language data show the lowest percentage figure among the entire list of possible majors, including, for comparison, agriculture (1.2), music (2.4), art (4.4), education (9.9), social sciences (11.2), and business/accounting/finance (18.4).

Among 19 academic areas listed in the questionnaire, "modern foreign languages" appear to occupy an intermediate position with respect to the extent to which respondents believed that courses in that area contributed to their "awareness of world problems or issues." Of the areas listed, courses in sociology (26.8 percent for freshmen, 41.7 percent for seniors, and 31.0 percent for two-year), history (39.0, 54.8, and 43.9), and economics (22.7, 45.1, 31.1) were among the most frequently indicated in this regard, while extremely slight contributions were made by courses in archaeology (1.1, 1.8, 0.3), classical languages (1.1, 1.7, 1.5), and Slavic studies (0.5, 1.8. 0.9). Modern foreign languages (8.4, 15.4, and 8.7) appear generally on a par with anthropology (5.7, 14.9, 10.4), philosophy (9.1, 18.3, 13.9), and religion (8.2, 12.4, 10.9).

More than half of the students in each of the three cohort groups reported that they had been in a country other than the United States (57.9, 64.3, 60.9). However, a substantial amount of this travel had been to Canada and Mexico, and in the majority of cases for less than two weeks. Slightly less than 10 percent (9.0, 7.9, 8.8) of the respondents had participated in an organized summer-abroad program, and appreciably less (1.1, 5.0, 1.2) in a year-abroad program. (For the freshmen and two-year students, of course, a "year-abroad" opportunity would not ordinarily be available, since the usual pattern is to have the year abroad during the junior year.) Service in the Peace Corps or "any other program involving similar kinds of service abroad" was reported in only a very small number of instances (0.1, 1.2, 0.7), considered too few to justify separate detailed analysis.

Items in the "Language Background" section of the questionnaire are, on the whole, considerably more pertinent to the language-related concerns of the study than are the general background questions, and are discussed in detail below. As would be anticipated, English is by far the most frequently reported native language (94.2, 96.4, and 89.4 percent for freshmen, seniors, and two-year college students, respectively). For all three cohort groups, the percentage of native speakers of any of the 13 other languages listed is less than 1 percent, with the single exception of Spanish, which is reported as the native la..guage by 1.8 percent of the freshmen, 1.0 percent of the seniors and, rather surprisingly, 5.6 percent of the two-year students. The relatively large number of Spanish mother-tongue students may reflect the geographic distribution of two-year colleges in the United States, of which a considerable proportion are in the "border states." Questions on "father's native language" and "mother's native language" show generally similar patterning, except that the absolute values of the percentages for certain of the listed foreign languages (notably, German, Italian, and Polish) are higher than for the students' "own native language" data, presumably reflecting the "second-generation" status of a number of student respondents.

Study of classical Greek is reported by over 5 percent of each of the three cohort groups (5.6, 5.8, 5.3), suggesting secondary school as the major source of instructional contact. Latin study is two to three times more frequently reported than Greek (13.4, 15.9, 12.7), with the response pattern again suggesting that these courses were mainly taken in secondary school.

With respect to the study of modern foreign languages (defined as "a modern language other than your native language") virtually nine out of ten (89.9 percent) of the reporting seniors cited such study. Corresponding percentages for the freshman and two-year groups are 78.1 and 73.2.

For the remaining questions in the language background section, responses were calculated as the percentage of students responding positively to the "prior modern language study" question (i.e., excluding those students who had not studied any modern language other than their own). For those students reporting prior foreign language study, about 90 percent of both the freshman and senior group (91.5 and 89.3) indicated that they had had such study in elementary or secondary school. The percentage figure is somewhat lower for the two-year college group (81.2).

Slightly more than half (54.8) of the senior group reported foreign language study in college, and somewhat more than a quarter (27.3 percent) of the freshmen and about 4 out of 10 (39.5 percent) of the two-year students reported college-level study. At both elementary/secondary and college levels, the most frequently studied foreign language is Spanish, followed by French and German, in that order. Italian and Russian, the other two "traditional" foreign languages, are much less frequently reported. For ease in discussing several other interesting aspects of the elementary/secondary and college language study data, please see Figure 3.9.1.

For both elementary/secondary and college study data, English as a second language is modestly salient, exceeding Italian and Russian study (for all three cohort groups) at the elementary/secondary level. At the college level, English-second-language study is about on a par with Italian and Russian study for the freshman and senior groups, and substantially higher for the two-year college group. About twice as many current freshmen report elementary/secondary school study of English as a second language as do current seniors, possibly reflecting increased foreign student enrollments at the elementary/secondary level over the three-year period differentiating these two cohort

Figure 3.9.1. Percentages of Students Reporting Modern Foreign Language Study By Grade Level

	Freshmen	Seniors	2-Year
Elementary/Secondary			
English (as a foreign language)	3.1	1.8	8.3
French	36.4	41.1	30.7
German	15.9	13.3	7.9
Hebrew	3.8	0.9	1.7
Italian	1.4	0.7	1.2
Russian	1.3	1.3	0.9
Spanish	57.5	50.2	48.1
Other	1.8	1.5	2.9
College			
English (as a foreign language)	1.4	1.8	5.9
French	9.2	19.7	15.2
German	4.0	15.8	4.1
Hebrew	0.8	0.4	1.0
Italian	0.9	2.4	0.7
Russian	1.2	2.1	2.5
Spanish	22.0	24.5	16.7
Other	1.3	2.7	2.6

groups. An even more notable increase is seen for elementary/secondary school study of Hebrew across the senior (0.9 percent) and freshman (3.8 percent) cohort groups; there is no immediate explanation of this phenomenon.

The observed decrease in elementary/secondary French study between the senior and freshman groups (41.1 percent to 36.4 percent) and increase in Spanish study (50.2 percent to 57.5 percent) should also be noted. The existence of a similar French-decrease/Spanish-increase trend at the college level cannot be determined from the available survey data, since current freshmen would not, of course, have completed their college experience in this regard. The relatively large number of seniors reporting college-level study of German, interpreted in light of the other language data in the figure, suggests rather strongly that German is being chosen as a second (or subsequent) foreign language by students at the college level.

The final series of questions in the language background section asked for responses with respect to the student's "most proficient foreign language," which was operationally defined as the one modern foreign language that the student had learned or studied or, if more than one foreign language had been learned or studied, "the language in which you consider yourself currently most proficient (other than your native language)." The student was further cautioned that "you do *not* have to be *highly* proficient in your 'most proficient' language. This designation simply means that, of the modern foreign languages you have learned or studied, this is the one in which you feel best qualified at the present time."

Consistent with the previously described response patterns for elementary/secondary school and college foreign language study, Spanish was, by a large amount, the most frequently reported "most proficient" foreign language (abbreviated hereafter as MPFL). Percentages of the freshman, senior, and two-year groups reporting Spanish as the MPFL were 52.6, 42.6, and 49.5. Second in percentage order was French (26.4, 30.5, and 24.8), followed at some distance by German (12.1, 17.7, 7.0).

English (as a second language) was the most proficient foreign language for 3.1 percent of the freshman respondents, 2.4 percent of the seniors, and 9.1 percent of the two-year college students. The last presumably reflects the proportionately larger number of two-year college students whose native language was Spanish or other non-English language.

Approximately 90 percent of both the freshman (88.1) and senior (90.0) groups indicated that they had studied the MPFL in some kind of "formal educational setting," which was defined as elementary or secondary school, college, or other structured teaching situations such as Hebrew school, Alliance Francaise, Berlitz, and so on. The corresponding figure for two-year college respondents is 80.9 percent. All three percentages are consistent with previous questions on language-study history.

With respect to the learning (or strengthening) of the MPFL through "experience other than formal education," of four rubrics given ("family members speaking it," "friend(s) or people in the neighborhood speaking it," "living abroad," and "studying abroad"), the most frequently reported was "friends or people in the neighborhood" (21.9 percent, 19.4 percent, and 26.8 percent). "Family members speaking it" was appreciably less often reported (14.0, 11.9, 18.7). Living or studying abroad ranged from 3.4 to 13.4 percent.

As previously discussed, it had been found necessary for reasons of questionnaire space and student response time to forego obtaining a complete record of foreign language course history for *all* languages that the respondent may have studied. This information was, however, obtained for the MPFL itself by asking each respondent to indicate each grade level, from first grade through college senior, during which the MPFL had been studied.

For all three cohort groups, the reported pattern of course work for the MPFL is not at all unanticipated or surprising. Relatively few students report any MPFL study in first through third grades (maximum reported percentage is 8.0 for third grade study by the two-year college group). There is a slight increase in fourth- through sixth-grade enrollments (rising to 13.8 percent, 10.5 percent, and 13.9 percent for each of the three groups at the sixth-grade level), and a very salient increase at the seventh- and eighth-grade levels (33.2 percent, 25.6 percent, and 22.8 percent for the latter grade).

Across all three groups, ninth and tenth grades are the "peak" years for MPFL study, ranging from 45.7 percent to 61.2 percent. MPFL study declines slightly in the eleventh grade (41.5, 46.2, and 37.3) and more precipitously in the high school senior year (23.5, 26.9, and 23.7).

College freshman study of the MPFL (21.9, 26.8, 23.4) is about on a par with the twelfth-grade figures. For the remaining three college years, the senior group shows even slightly increased sophomore enrollment (27.1), followed by a not unanticipated drop in the junior and senior years (18.3 percent and 17.1 percent, respectively).

In comparing the responses of the senior and freshman groups, it is interesting to note that for each grade level from sixth through tenth, the seniors report a higher percentage of MPFL enrollment than do the current freshmen—almost 10 percentage points difference at the ninth-grade level. By contrast, a somewhat lower freshman enrollment by comparison to the senior data is seen at each level from eleventh grade through college freshman. As in all across-group comparions, caution in interpretation is required for the reported MPFL enrollment figurs; the available evidence, however, would at least suggest a tendency toward increased junior high school and early high school enrollment, and a slight decline in later high school and first-year college enrollment (the only college year for which paired figures are available) across the three-year span represented by the freshman and senior groups.

With respect to the general *type* of MPFL course experience for the three student groups, a single question was asked in which the respondents were requested to indicate "the emphasis of the instruction you received in formal courses in your MPFL." A five-point scale was provided, with the two endpoints defined as "Grammar-translation approach (mastery of rules of grammar and vocabulary)" and "Audio-lingual approach (emphasizing listening and speaking)." For all three groups, the most frequently selected response was the "neutral" category indicating that the instruction "was about equally divided" (26.1, 41.3, and 49.5 percent of the three groups selecting this option). Substantially more respondents chose the extreme grammar-translation position (11.1, 16.4, and 11.8 percent) than chose the extreme audio-lingual option (3.9, 4.3, and 4.2 percent). The moderate "tending toward" grammar-translation option was also appreciably more often selected than was the corresponding "tending toward" audio-lingual option (22.6, 25.7, and 23.2 percent vs. 9.4, 12.3, 11.3). It appears necessary to conclude that, on a total coursework basis, the foreign language classroom experiences of all three respondent groups tend for the most part to be "balanced" with respect to instructional approach or to favor the "grammar-translation" approach (as defined within the context of this particular survey question). It should be pointed out, however, that the question asked for an evaluative synthesis of all of the respondent's MPFL course experiences, and the aggregate data would not reveal individual courses with a highly audio-lingual orientation.

Proficiency Variables
The final portion of the "language background" section of Booklet A consisted of the three "can

do'' proficiency self-assessment scales for speaking, listening comprehension, and reading—each scale presenting a series of statements descriptive of various language-use situations and asking the respondent to indicate in each instance whether he or she would be able to handle that situation (from a language use point of view) "quite easily," "with some difficulty," or "with great difficulty or not at all." These descriptive statements were developed and refined in an earlier pilot study (see Part I, Chapter 3), and were intended to represent a wide range of proficiency from the most basic "survival" types of language use up through the communicative and receptive competencies that would be expected of a near-native speaker of the language.

Examination of the responses to each of the three self-appraisal scales by the three cohort groups indicates that the "can do" descriptions followed an order of generally increasing linguistic difficulty, in the sense that increasingly smaller percentages of students indicated that they could carry out the task in question "quite easily" or "with some difficulty," rather than "not at all." Complete percentage data for all three groups are shown in Appendix A.

For ease of discussion, the percentage of students responding "quite easily" to each "can do" statement for each of the cohort groups is reproduced in Figure 3.9.2. Interpreting these data in terms of the proportion of students who state that they can carry out the language tasks in question "quite easily" is considered appropriate in that this standard of performance would imply a naturalness and readiness in response on the student's part that would be in keeping with effective use of the language in the real-life situations. "With some difficulty," on the other hand, would suggest false starts, hesitancies, and other disfluencies that would impede the communication or reception process.

Figure 3.9.2. Percentage of Students Responding "Quite Easily" to "Can Do" Proficiency Statements

Speaking	Freshmen	Seniors	2-Year
a) Say the days of the week	62.6	56.5	57.7
b) Count to 10 in the language	92.6	93.1	91.5
c) Give the current date (month, day, year)	56.9	49.3	52.3
d) Order a simple meal in a restaurant	37.6	33.4	42.6
e) Ask for directions on the street	31.1	31.1	38.6
f) Buy clothes in a department store	26.6	26.2	31.6
g) Introduce myself in social situations, and use appropriate greetings and leave-taking expressions	48.4	45.4	48.1
h) Give simple biographical information about myself (place of birth, composition of family, early schooling, etc.)	34.1	29.8	35.2
i) Talk about my favorite hobby at some length, using appropriate vocabulary	11.5	11.8	18.2
j) Describe my present job, studies, or other major life activities accurately and in detail	13.4	12.1	17.2
k) Tell what I plan to be doing 5 years from now, using appropriate future tenses	11.7	10.6	14.9
l) Describe the United States educational system in some detail	5.2	7.2	11.2
m) State and support with examples and reasons a position on a controversial topic (for example, birth control, nuclear safety, environmental pollution)	3.5	5.0	6.8
n) Describe the role played by Congress in the United States government system	2.7	3.5	7.3

Listening Comprehension	Freshmen	Seniors	2-Year
a) Understand very simple statements or questions in the language ("Hello, "How are you?", "What is your name?", "Where do you live?", etc.)	93.4	88.9	91.3
b) In face-to-face conversation, understand a native speaker who is speaking slowly and carefully (i.e., deliberately adapting his or her speech to suit me)	56.3	48.7	56.1
c) On the telephone, understand a native speaker who is speaking to me slowly and carefully (i.e., deliberately adapting his or her speech to suit me)	41.8	37.5	43.5
d) In face-to-face conversation with a native speaker who is speaking slowly and carefully to me, tell whether the speaker is referring to past, present, or future events	36.8	33.4	40.7
e) In face-to-face conversation, understand a native speaker who is speaking to me as quickly and as colloquially as he or she would to another native speaker	7.7	7.8	16.7
f) Understand movies without subtitles	9.1	9.2	16.4
g) Understand news broadcasts on the radio	5.5	7.3	13.3
h) On the radio, understand the words of a popular song I have not heard before	6.1	5.4	10.2
i) Understand play-by-play descriptions of sports events (for example, a soccer match) on the radio	6.0	5.9	10.7
j) Understand two native speakers when they are talking rapidly with one another	4.8	6.1	12.7
k) On the telephone, understand a native speaker who is talking as quickly and as colloquially as he or she would to another native speaker	4.6	5.4	10.0

Reading Proficiency	Freshmen	Seniors	2-Year
a) Read personal letters or notes written to me in which the writer has deliberately used simple words and constructions	63.0	55.4	59.0
b) Read, on store fronts, the type of store or the services provided (for example, "dry cleaning," "book store," "butcher," etc.)	62.3	53.8	57.7
c) Understand newspaper headlines	46.5	41.1	45.5
d) Read personal letters and notes written as they would be to a native speaker	18.9	17.1	24.7
e) Read and understand magazine articles at a level similar to those found in *Time* or *Newsweek*, without using a dictionary	6.7	9.4	14.3
f) Read popular novels without using a dictionary	4.9	6.7	10.2
g) Read newspaper "want ads" with comprehension, even when many abbreviations are used	7.0	5.8	12.5
h) Read highly technical material in a particular academic or professional field with no use or only very infrequent use of a dictionary	1.6	2.6	7.7

An immediate observation is that for all three cohort groups, across all three skill areas, the responses begin (with the exception of two apparently atypical "can do" statements) at about the 60 percent level; that is to say, only about 60 percent of the respondents indicate that they can do even the simplest of the listed tasks "quite easily." The two exceptions are "count to 10 in the language" for the speaking scale, for which the percentage of freshmen, seniors, and two-year college students reporting themselves able to do so quite easily are 92.6, 93.1, and 91.5 percent, respectively; and, for listening comprehension, "understand very simple statements or questions in the language'' (such as "Hello," "How are you?," "What is your name?," etc.), for which the response percentages are 93.4, 88.9, and 91.3. The high "quite easily" response rate for "count to 10 in the language" is probably attributable to heavily drilled, rote learning of this particular element, which usually figures prominently in beginning language instruction and which it is assumed would be retained by virtually all students exposed even briefly to a foreign language course. By the same token, the unusually high "quite easily" rate for the comprehension of such simple utterances as "Hello," "How are you?," etc., can also be viewed as a consequence of widespread routine inclusion of these formulaic expressions in beginning language courses. It is interesting to note that the next "can do" statement in the listening comprehension series, which involves the comprehension of slow, deliberately simplified, but non-formulaic speech, shows the considerably lower response rates of 56.3, 48.7, and 56.1 percent.

Comparisons across cohort groups show generally similar response frequencies for both the freshman and senior groups for each of the three skill areas. With occasional slight percentage variations for individual "can do" statements, the proportion of seniors indicating that they can carry out a particular language task "quite easily" is about the same as that of the freshman group.

The two-year college responses, on the whole, show a somewhat higher percentage of "quite easily" judgments for each of the individual "can do" statements, especially toward the end of the respective scales, where the language use tasks are more complex and demanding. For example, on the speaking proficiency scale, 11.5 percent and 11.8 percent of the freshmen and seniors, respectively, indicated that they could "talk about my favorite hobby at some length, using appropriate vocabulary"; the corresponding figure for the two-year college group is 18.2 percent. For listening comprehension, the ability to easily "understand movies without subtitles" was reported by 9.1 percent of the freshmen, 9.2 percent of the seniors, and 16.4 percent of the two-year college students. The generally higher level of self-reported language proficiency for the two-year college group may be attributable to the greater number of foreign students in this cohort sample, for whom the MPFL (presumed to be English) would show a higher level of proficiency because of the selectivity of this "study-abroad" group.

Turning to each of the skill areas separately, it may be noted that language-use operations which about 50 to 60 percent of the respondents are able to carry out quite easily are very simple and highly delimited ("say the days of the week"; "give the current date"; and "introduce myself in social situations, and use appropriate greetings and leave-taking expressions"). The percentage of "quite easily" responses drops to about 30 to 35 percent for "give simple biographical information about myself (place of birth, composition of family, early schooling, etc.)"; "ask for directions on the street"; and "order a simple meal in a restaurant").

Activities requiring somewhat more extemporaneous speech on personal topics ("talk about my favorite hobby at some length, using appropriate vocabulary"; "describe my present job, studies, or other major life activities accurately and in detail"; and "tell what I plan to be doing 5 years from now, using appropriate future tenses") were quite easily accomplished by only about 11 to 14 percent of the freshmen and seniors (and somewhat more of the two-year college students). The ability to speak quite easily on relatively abstract and impersonal topics ("describe the United States educational system in some detail"; "state and support with examples and reasons a position on a controversial topic (for example, birth control, nuclear safety, environmental pollution)"; and "describe the role played by Congress in the United States government system") was reported by only about 3 to 7 percent of freshman and senior groups and somewhat more of the two-year college group.

With respect to listening comprehension, understanding a native speaker who is "speaking slowly and carefully (i.e., deliberately adapting his or her speech to suit me)" obtained "quite easily" indications by approximately 50 to 56 percent of the three groups, with similarly slowed speech in a telephone-use situation showing responses of about 38 to 44 percent. Comprehension of a native speaker at a normal conversational tempo (i.e., "speaking to me as quickly and as colloquially as he or she would to another native speaker") showed a precipitous drop to 7.7 percent of the freshmen and 7.8 percent of the seniors. Understanding two native speakers talking rapidly between themselves was a "quite easy" task for only 4.8 percent of the freshman group and 6.1 percent of the seniors.

News broadcasts on the radio were easily comprehensible to 5.5 percent of the freshmen and 7.3 percent of the seniors. For all three groups, the most difficult listening comprehension task was to understand, on the telephone, a native speaker talking quickly and colloquially (4.6, 5.4, and 10.0 percent, respectively).

Reading comprehension showed a relatively low percentage of "quite easily" responses across all of the "can do" statements (by comparison to the speaking and listening comprehension scales). Beyond reading personal letters or notes which the writer has deliberately simplified, store front signs, and newspaper headlines (for which the "quite easily" responses ranged from 41.1 to 63.0 percent), the next most frequently reported "quite easily" task ("read personal letters and notes written as they would be to a native speaker") showed response percentages of only 18.9 percent for the freshman group and 17.1 percent for the seniors (two-year college: 24.7 percent).

A functional, "reading for interest and/or information" level of proficiency, as might be represented by the statement "read and understand magazine articles at a level similar to those found in *Time* or *Newsweek*, without using a dictionary," reached the "quite easily" level for only 6.7 percent of the freshmen and 9.4 percent of the seniors (two-year college students: 14.3 percent). "Read popular novels without using a dictionary" was even less frequently indicated: 4.9 percent and 6.7 percent for the freshman and senior groups.

The most difficult task—reading "highly technical material in a particular academic or professional field with no use or only very infrequent use of a dictionary"—was reported as quite easy by 1.6 percent of the freshman respondents and 2.6 percent of the seniors. Two-year college percentages were somewhat higher (7.7 percent), again consistent with the presumed higher level of English-as-an-MPFL of the two-year college group.

Although the total extent of self-reported foreign language proficiency in the three survey populations may be relatively low, there are nonetheless variations across individuals in total scores on the speaking, listening, and reading proficiency scales. It would be of some interest to relate observed differences in the scale scores to the background, educational experiences, attitudes, and other characteristics of the survey participants, as embodied in their responses to the various relevant questions in Booklet A.

Attitude Variables

As previously described, Booklet A questions were grouped into six different categories or "blocks" for easier and more productive analysis: (1) Criteria, consisting of the variables to be "predicted" by those in the other blocks, and including the foreign language speaking, listening comprehension, and reading proficiency scales; (2) Background, including such personal characteristics as age, sex, ethnic group identification, geographic area of birth, and highest level of formal education attained by parents; (3) Educational Experiences, including, for example, years of high school study and number of college courses taken in various subject areas, high school and college grades, SAT or ACT scores obtained, immediate and long-term educational objectives, and (especially relevant to the foreign language analysis) length of time spent abroad and participation in summer- and year-abroad programs; (4) Information Acquisition: Media, covering newspaper-reading and television-watching habits, as well as the reading of newsmagazines and special-interest publications; (5) Politics, including own and father's/mother's political party preference and rating of the "left" vs. "right" political attitudes of student and parents; and (6) Language Background and Attitudes, including the student's own native language, foreign language study in elementary school through college, language learning exposure outside the formal academic setting, identification of "most proficient foreign language" (MPFL), chronology of elementary-through-college courses taken in the MPFL, relative emphasis of instruction in these courses ("grammar-translation" *vs* "audio-lingual" approach), and high school and/or college grade average in MPFL courses.

Figures 3.9.3. through 3.9.6. show, for each of blocks 2-6 (except for block 4, Politics, for which all correlations were below the cutoff point) all correlations of .20 or higher between the three "criterion" variables of self-reported speaking, listening, and reading proficiency in the student's MPFL and the individual background, experience, etc., variables comprised in these blocks. Although all correlations at or above .20 are shown in the figures, narrative discussion will be restricted to those correlations which are of *a priori* interest from a language-acquisition standpoint or show sufficient magnitude and/or consistency across cohort groups to warrant attention.

Age and sex of the student are not found to be correlated at a minimum level with self-reported MPFL proficiency in any of the three skill areas. Ethnic background is only sporadically and very

94

moderately related (correlations range from .20 to .28) to language proficiency within the nine cohort group/language skill combinations. Some tendency is observed for two-year college students' identification of themselves as of Puerto Rican, Cuban, Hispanic, or "other" ethnic-group origin to be positively related to scores on each of the three proficiency scales. A pattern of low but consistent correlations with MPFL proficiency is also seen for two-year college students reporting themselves to have been born in South America or Asia.

Figure 3.9.3. Background

	Speaking			Listening			Reading		
	Fr.	Sr.	2-yr.	Fr.	Sr.	2-yr.	Fr.	Sr.	2-yr.
Chicano or Mexican American				.27					
Puerto Rican, Cuban, or Hispanic			.24	.22		.28			.27
White or Caucasian				.20					
Other ethnic group			.27			.30			.24
Born in Central America			.25						
Born in South America			.21	.20		.27			.25
Born in Asia			.25			.24			.27
Not born in United States	.26	.28	.48	.33	.32	.51	.28	.27	.51
Born in other geographical area						.20			.22
If not born in U.S, age when came to U.S.	.27	.51	.31		.48	.43	.25	.50	.28
If not born in U.S., considers self permanent resident		.29			.24			.38	
Level of formal education completed by father			.26			.26			.28

Across all nine cohort/language skill combinations, correlations ranging from .26 to .48 and .51 (the latter two from the two-year college group) are found between self-reported MPFL proficiency and student answers to the question "Were you born in the United States?". Because of the coding procedure for this question (1 = "yes," 2 = "no"), positive correlations indicate that students reporting themselves to be born outside of the United States also report higher proficiency in their "most proficient foreign language" than do students born in the U.S.

Moderate to high positive correlations are also found for all cohort/language skill combinations except for freshman/listening to the question "If you were *not* born in the United States, please indicate how old you were when you first came to the United States." Since U.S.-born students would have left this question blank, the observed correlations would show a rather pure measure of "age on entry" into the U.S. (for non native-born students) as related to self-reported MPFL skill, with greater age on first entry corresponding to greater MPFL proficiency.

On the assumption that English is the "most proficient foreign language" of the great majority of those students who report other than "Black or Afro-American" or "White or Caucasian" as their ethnic group and/or state that they were born outside of the United States, the observed background correlations can for the most part be considered to reflect the relatively higher degree of English (second-language) proficiency of these students by comparison to the French, Spanish, etc., second-language proficiency of U.S.-born native speakers of English. This would, of course, not be surprising in light of the inherent selection process by which only students having at least a reasonable working command of English (and usually a substantially higher level of proficiency) would succeed in matriculating into (and remaining in) U.S. undergraduate institutions.

A number of quite interesting correlation patterns are found between self-judged MPFL proficiency and several variables in the Educational Experiences block. An immediate observation is that measures of general aptitude or overall high school or college achievement are not found to be related to MPFL skill. With respect to general scholastic aptitude, the SAT Verbal score correlates above the "not significant" threshold point for only one of the nine cohort group/skill combinations (freshmen/reading) and does so by only a very small margin (.21). By the same token, only one correlation above .20 is found for overall ACT score (.27, again for freshmen/reading). SAT Math does not reach the threshold.

Figure 3.9.4. Educational Experiences

	Speaking			Listening			Reading		
	Fr.	Sr.	2-yr.	Fr.	Sr.	2-yr.	Fr.	Sr.	2-yr.
Years of Foreign language completed in high school	.49	.34	.35	.39	.32	.39	.45	.39	.39
Years of physical and biological sciences completed in high school			.22			.31			.29
High school experiences outside the class contributed to global awareness			.25			.24			.26
SAT Verbal Score							.21		
ACT Score							.27		
College GPA	.21								
Foreign languages as intended major	.21	.27			.26		.20	.25	
American Studies courses taken in college			.21			.20			
Classical languages courses taken in college								.20	
Literature courses taken in college		.20						.24	
Modern foreign language course(s) taken in college	.35	.46	.22	.34	.41		.34	.46	.20
Modern foreign language course(s) contributing to global awareness	.23	.34	.36	.24	.28	.28	.23	.31	.31
Participated in high school or college ethnic activities or organizations		.23			.23				
Long-term educational goal					.22			.20	
Been in country other than U.S.		.28	.24		.28	.20		.23	
Length of time in foreign countries	.30	.27	.34	.33	.27	.33	.32	.20	.25

As a measure of general achievement, high school grade average shows no correlation of .20 or above, and college grade point average appears in only one of the nine figure cells (freshmen/speaking) at a level barely above the minimum (.21). By contrast, the number of modern foreign language courses taken in high school and in college are both fairly strong predictors of self-judged language proficiency, ranging from .32 to .49 for high school courses and .22 to .46 for college courses. It is also interesting to note that there is no pattern of differential prediction with respect to the specific language skill (i.e., the number of high school language courses taken shows about equal correlations with speaking, listening, and reading, and similarly for college language courses), suggesting that self-appraised proficiency increases comparably across the three skill areas with increasing numbers of courses.

"Years of foreign language completed in high school" is an appreciably stronger predictor of current MPFL proficiency for the freshmen in the survey population than for the seniors, in keeping with the additional (and correlation-lowering) diversity of language-related experiences of the senior group over the intervening college years. "Modern foreign language course(s) taken in college" is, on the other hand, more strongly related to self-appraised proficiency of the seniors, presumably because of the greater number of courses entering this variable for the seniors and the resulting increase in reliable variance.

While the number of courses taken in a modern foreign language is quite highly predictive of acquired proficiency, the taking of courses in other subject areas is not appreciably associated with foreign language proficiency. American studies, classical languages, and literature courses enter the correlation figure only very sporadically and at levels at or barely above the .20 criterion (.20 to .24). Students' indications that foreign language study was their "major or intended major" were modestly correlated with language proficiency scores for the senior cohort group (.27, .26, and .25 for speaking, listening, and reading), but essentially uncorrelated for the freshman and two-year college groups.

"Length of time spent abroad" was positively correlated with proficiency for all nine cohort/language skill combinations at levels from .20 to .34, with the lower correlations for the most part associated with the prediction of reading ability. Following years of foreign language study in high school or college, length of time abroad appears to be the strongest externally verifiable predictor of self-reported MPFL ability among all of the background variables in this section.

A very interesting outcome is noted for responses to the question "Please indicate which of the following courses, if any, you believe have contributed to your awareness of world problems or issues," for which 19 course areas including "modern foreign languages" were listed. MPFL proficiency was correlated with the selection of "modern foreign languages" in all 9 cells of the figure, at levels from .23 to .36. This indicates a definite tendency for those students who rated themselves relatively more proficient in their MPFL to consider that foreign language courses had contributed to their awareness of world issues—an appraisal that was not, however, borne out in the scoring results of the Test of Global Knowledge.

The Information: Media block consisted of 13 questions on television-watching habits, newspaper- or newsmagazine-reading practices, and other contacts with and preferences concerning both audiovisual and print media. As shown in Figure 3.9.5., correlations between responses to the various "media" questions and self-judged MPFL proficiency were, with only very few and for the most part apparently random exceptions, below the .20 minimum. However, based on quite slim evidence and with substantial caution in interpretation, it can be noted that several of the above-minimum correlations relate to items of an international nature, especially the "[I would watch on TV] specials about foreign countries and their cultures" response to television-viewing habits, which correlates with self-appraised language proficiency at levels of .20 to .27 across eight of the nine possible cohort/language skill combinations. Although by no means substantial evidence, there is at least a hint in these data that higher levels of language proficiency are associated with greater interest and involvement in obtaining information on international or "global" topics.

Figure 3.9.5. Information: Media

	Speaking			Listening			Reading		
	Fr.	Sr.	2-yr.	Fr.	Sr.	2-yr.	Fr.	Sr.	2-yr.
When watching television, usually watches specials about foreign countries and their cultures	.21	.27	.25	.22	.20	.20		.22	.21
With time to read only 4 newspaper headlines, would read "SOVIET JEWS DENIED EXIT VISAS"		.21							
When reading a newspaper, usually reads national news articles	.20								
When reading a newspaper, usually reads international news articles	.20					.25			
Regularly reads the *New York Times*		.24			.24			.25	

Correlations at or greater than .20 for all questions in the Language Background and Attitudes block are shown in Figure 3.9.6. This figure shows a fairly large number of what must frankly be considered sporadic artifacts of the particular sample of students included in the survey that have little observed consistency or interpretive value. For example, "German is mother's native language"—appearing only once in the nine figure cells above the minimum correlation level (for "senior/listening," at a level of .22), or "Studied French as a foreign language in elementary or secondary school" appearing once at a level of .20 for "senior/reading proficiency"—suggests no underlying pattern or relationship of significance and may reasonably be passed over in the discussion. Correlations for several other questions are of sufficient magnitude and distributed extensively enough to indicate or at least strongly suggest a genuine and consistent relationship between self-rated language proficiency and the particular language background item involved.

The first question in the language background section asked for student identification of "your own native language (mother tongue)," with a total of 14 languages (including English) listed, as well as a space for "Other." For two-year college students, the identification of "Spanish" as a native language was quite strongly associated with MPFL skill (.36, .37, and .37 for listening, speaking, and reading comprehension). This probably reflects the large number of two-year college students of Hispanic origin who report their native tongue to be Spanish but who are highly proficient in English as an MPFL. A similar but much weaker set of correlations (.20, .26, .21) is shown for the freshman group, again probably reflecting relatively greater English (MPFL) proficiency for members of this group who consider themselves native speakers of Spanish. Analogous interpretations of the correlational data are possible for students in both the senior and two-year college groups who report "Other" native languages.

An even more salient indication of the probable higher level of English MPFL proficiency of non-native speakers of English in the survey sample is the consistent pattern of above .20 correlations for students who reported studying English as a foreign language in elementary/secondary school or college. This is especially apparent for two-year college students, for whom the relevant correlations range from .33 to .50. Further support of the relatively more proficient non-native English speaker hypothesis is provided in the .29 to .53 correlations between MPFL proficiency and the student identification of his or her MPFL as being English.

As noted also in responses to some of the educational experiences (block 3) questions, foreign language contact opportunities outside of the United States are substantially related to self-judged language proficiency. To the question "Did you acquire any of your MPFL ability from experience other than formal education" (with two of the response options being "living abroad" and "studying abroad"), living abroad correlated at levels of .27 to .40 across all cohort/language skill groupings. Study abroad was somewhat less highly related to self-judged MPFL proficiency on an across-cohorts basis, but showed fairly substantial correlations in the senior group (.37, .39, and .39 for speaking, listening comprehension, and reading), most probably because this would be the only one of the three cohort groups that would have had the opportunity to participate in the popular (and presumably language-proficiency-enhancing) junior year-abroad programs.

Opportunities to acquire MPFL ability from "family members speaking it" and "friend(s) or people in the neighborhood speaking it" were also associated with self-appraised proficiency at levels of .21 to .43. With respect to formal language study, course grades in the MPFL in high school and/or college were consistently moderately good predictors of self-judged proficiency, with correlation levels of .28 to .37.

By far the best single predictor of MPFL scores on the three "can do" proficiency measures was the sum of the 15-item "language attitudes" scale, in which the student indicated, on a five-point scale, the extent of his own personal interest in and motivation for studying a foreign language, positive opinions concerning the general (public) value of foreign language study, absence of "linguistic ethnocentrism" (e.g., "learning a foreign language is unnecessary because English is spoken almost everywhere"), and orientation toward "integrative" rather than "instrumental" purposes for foreign language study. Across the nine cohort/skill cells, freshmen/speaking showed a correlation of .32; the other eight combinations showed correlations ranging from .46 to .53.

It bears repeating that the observed correlations do not and, unfortunately, cannot in and of themselves elucidate the question of whether increasing foreign language proficiency on the part of the student brings about a higher level of interest in and motivation for language study (as well as

Figure 3.9.6. Language Background and Attitudes

	Speaking			Listening			Reading		
	Fr.	Sr.	2-yr.	Fr.	Sr.	2-yr.	Fr.	Sr.	2-yr.
Spanish is native language	.20		.36	.26		.37	.21		.37
"Other" is native language		.21	.25		.25	.25		.23	.22
Spanish is father's native language	.24		.24	.37	.26	.25	.37		.30
"Other" is father's native language			.23		.23	.23			.20
German is mother's native language					.22				
Spanish is mother's native language	.21			.34	.21	.32	.21		.32
"Other" is mother's native language			.32						
Studied English as a foreign language in elementary or secondary school	.24	.26	.46	.30	.29	.50	.26	.29	.47
Studied French as a foreign language in elementary or secondary school									.20
Studied Spanish as a foreign language in elementary or secondary school			.21						
Studied "other" as a modern foreign language in elementary or secondary school			.43						.20
Studied a modern foreign language in college	.35	.40	.01	.29	.34	.33	.32	.37	.33
Studied English as a modern foreign language in college	.21	.21	.39	.23	.23	.42	.23	.22	.41
Studied French as a modern foreign language in college	.23		.26					.24	.23
Studied Spanish as a modern foreign language in college			.26	.21				.20	.24
Speaks, reads, or writes Arabic			.22			.25			.20
Speaks, reads, or writes French		.21	.27			.24		.25	.30
Speaks, reads, or writes German		.20			.24			.20	
Speaks, reads, or writes Hebrew						.20			
Speaks, reads, or writes Spanish	.23	.27	.24	.24	.23	.26		.27	.27
Speaks, reads, or writes "other" language		.27	.21		.31			.22	
English is most proficient foreign language (MPFL)	.32	.29	.48	.36	.31	.53	.32	.32	.49
Acquired MPFL ability from family members speaking it		.30	.26	.29	.36	.43		.36	.21
Acquired MPFL ability from friend(s) or people in the neighborhood speaking it	.24	.28	.33	.28	.32	.35	.21	.32	.36
Acquired MPFL ability from living abroad	.31	.37	.39	.31	.40	.40	.27	.40	.29
Acquired MPFL ability from studying abroad	.21	.37	.26		.39	.30		.39	.29
MPFL grade in high school or college	.37	.34	.32	.28	.30	.33	.33	.33	.31
Language attitude	.52	.53	.32	.52	.47	.49	.50	.46	.49

99

the other affective orientations associated with higher scores on the language attitude questions). Further studies oriented specifically toward investigating the causal underpinnings of the observed statistical relationship will be needed to more fully understand and interpret this correspondence.

Chapter 10

Attitudes and Perceptions

Thomas S. Barrows

In Chapter II we described the development of five affective measures. This chapter presents the results of the corresponding sections of the survey according to the titles of the measures that appeared in the survey materials. The Likert items' development described first in Chapter II becomes "Student Opinion Survey" here and is dealt with first here, too. The Self-Report items of Chapter II become "Student Self-Perceptions" here, the Semantic Differential becomes "Assessment of World Issues," and Error-Choice is dealt with last as it was in Chapter II. A final section deals with correlates of the effective scores.

This ordering will be seen as advantageous by the discerning reader, for the quality or amount of information derived from each of the four measures declines for largely technical reasons as we move from the second through the third to the fourth instrument.

Student Opinion Survey
Five scales in the common Likert format were included in this section, the items from the scales being mixed so that the objectives of the scales were not obvious. Thirty-two items were included in total.

Separate analyses of freshman, senior, and two-year student survey results indicate that the five factor structure found in pretesting is essentially replicated in the survey results. Figure 3.10.1 below provides latent roots that support the replicated five factor interpretation.

Figure 3.10.1. Characteristic Roots for 32 Likert Items

Root	Freshmen	Seniors	2-year
1	4.74	5.83	4.96
2	2.28	2.22	2.45
3	1.65	2.12	1.75
4	1.36	1.41	1.44
5	1.09	0.99	1.15
6	0.77	0.75	0.82
7	0.63	0.62	0.63

In the three groups (Ns are 850-1000) five factors account for 88 to 90 percent of the common variance.

We will not reproduce all the details of the factor analyses of student opinion survey results here for two reasons. First, the analyses replicate the structures obtained at pretest, and second, the results are strikingly similar for freshmen, seniors, and two-year students. The consistency of the results is reassuring, and we will assume, therefore, that the reader will accept our interpretations without copius statistical evidence.

In the Figures 3.10.2. - 3.10.6. we have grouped the 32 items according to the five factors. Twenty-seven of the 32 items are assigned unambiguously by their largest correlations ranging from .31 to .81 with primary factors in each of the three student groups. The remaining five items are assigned to scales according to two out of three largest correlations with a single factor. The five items are 8, 10, 19, 23, and 32. Response options for all the items were: 1. Strongly Agree; 2. Agree; 3. Indifferent; 4. Disagree; 5. Strongly Disagree.

Figure 3.10.2. Chauvinism Scale

(in percent)

	1	2	3	4	5
1. Pacifist demonstrations—picketing missile bases, peace walks, etc.—are harmful to the best interests of the American people.					
Fr.	7.2	15.7	25.6	34.1	17.3
Sr.	4.0	15.0	16.3	35.2	29.5
2-yr.	7.9	15.5	24.2	30.9	21.4
3. The best way to insure peace is to keep the United States stronger than any other nation in the world.					
Fr.	17.1	28.6	17.7	29.4	7.2
Sr.	15.0	24.6	14.5	40.0	5.9
2-yr.	24.7	28.6	15.9	25.8	5.0
6. The main threat to basic American institutions during this century has come from the infiltration of foreign ideas and doctrines.					
Fr.	3.4	15.1	36.7	31.6	13.2
Sr.	1.7	7.4	17.9	42.3	30.6
2-yr.	7.0	16.7	31.6	29.3	15.5
14. Patriotism and loyalty are the first and most important requirements of a good citizen.					
Fr.	16.9	37.5	25.1	15.0	5.5
Sr.	11.3	32.2	25.5	23.1	7.8
2-yr.	18.0	35.5	25.4	15.3	5.8
24. The only way peace can be maintained is to keep America so powerful and well-armed that no other nation will dare to attack us.					
Fr.	8.9	22.7	18.8	38.9	10.7
Sr.	7.3	21.7	13.2	41.8	16.1
2-yr.	10.6	26.8	18.7	34.1	9.8
26. No duties are more important than duties toward one's country.					
Fr.	10.7	29.1	25.5	29.1	5.6
Sr.	7.0	20.5	24.0	36.6	12.0
2-yr.	12.3	26.9	26.9	26.3	7.6
29. I'm for my country, right or wrong.					
Fr.	11.1	15.6	20.7	39.5	13.1
Sr.	5.5	13.1	18.7	38.7	24.0
2-yr.	11.0	16.3	22.2	38.6	12.0

Each of these questions resulted in a good spread of responses. Generally, seniors have the lowest percentage of "Indifferent" responses, and the highest proportion of disagreement with the chauvinist, nationalist statements offered. Freshmen and two-year students are close together in proportion disagreeing (response 4 or 5); the proportion of two-year students is higher on three of the seven items.

More interesting perhaps is the interpretation we may give to the spread of responses, for on each item an appreciable proportion agree or agree strongly with the chauvinist, ultranationalist statements. The *piece de resistance* in our view is "I'm for my country, right or wrong." Over one quarter of the freshmen and two-year students agree with that statement. Equally remarkable is that almost one fifth of the seniors do, too. Similar variety is shown by the other item response spreads, although the statements that serve as stimuli there do not seem as extreme to us.

The results in Figure 3.10.3. suggest first that appreciable proportions of the three student groups favor world government. Summing over "Agree" and "Strongly Agree," we note that about a third of each group favors international control of mining and distribution of mineral resources, about two-fifths believe that we should have a World Government that could make binding laws and that an international authority should control nuclear energy, and about two-thirds report that we should settle all differences with other nations within a World Government. However, approximately two-thirds in each group disagree or strongly disagree with the statement that we should give up United States independence or submit to World Government authority. Only about one in four would prefer to be a citizen of the world rather than of a country.

Figure 3.10.3. World Government Scale

	1	2	3	4	5
7. Since the world's supplies of essential minerals are limited, the mining and distribution of mineral resources should be controlled by an international authority.					
Fr.	10.5	25.7	26.5	27.2	10.1
Sr.	6.7	25.0	19.4	36.4	12.5
2-yr.	7.7	31.5	28.1	24.3	8.4
9. We should be willing to settle all differences with other nations within the framework of a World Government.					
Fr.	29.1	39.8	17.0	9.7	4.4
Sr.	23.4	45.2	14.0	12.6	4.8
2-yr.	32.8	42.7	15.5	5.6	3.3
16. We should have a World Government with the power to make laws that would be binding to all its member nations.					
Fr.	13.1	30.1	26.4	19.8	10.7
Sr.	11.8	33.0	20.0	25.6	9.5
2-yr.	16.7	32.3	28.5	16.1	6.5
20. An international authority should be established and given direct control over the production of nuclear energy in all countries, including the United States.					
Fr.	14.8	27.1	23.8	24.7	9.5
Sr.	16.0	31.9	16.9	21.5	13.7
2-yr.	16.6	24.0	28.3	23.2	7.9
28. I prefer to be a citizen of the world rather than of any country.					
Fr.	8.0	12.3	21.2	37.8	20.6
Sr.	9.6	15.7	17.2	39.1	18.5
2-yr.	13.8	18.4	21.4	31.0	15.4
30. The United States ought to be willing to give up its independence and submit to the authority of a United States of the World.					
Fr.	2.4	8.0	23.8	33.7	32.2
Sr.	4.0	10.1	20.8	35.6	29.5
2-yr.	3.8	10.3	28.2	30.0	27.7

One can only wonder what interdependence means to students and where they would stand on an independence-interdependence scale had we been clever enough to devise one. The current data suggest confusion if not contradiction, and we wonder how an effective curriculum might resolve it. The historic, cherished value of independence would seem quite a roadblock to the development of a knowledgeable, positive valuing of interdependence.

Responses to the War Scale items tabled below point out that while war is viewed quite negatively, there are important qualifications, and these qualifications are attended to most frequently by the seniors as a group. The first item shows this pattern, inasmuch as the preponderance of responses are "Strongly Agree" and "Disagree" in all three groups and that variation from "Strongly Agree" is greater for seniors than it is for the other two groups. Maintenance of justice is introduced as a qualifying condition in Item 13, and seniors respond to it more than the other groups. Similarly, on Item 27, seniors respond more than the other two groups to "serious consequences," and on Item 18 they appear more willing as a group to consider "conceivable justification" for war. On Items 22 and 31, more seniors seem willing to consider violence as a method of changing governments.

Figure 3.10.4. War Scale

	1	2	3	4	5
10. War is a satisfactory way to solve international problems.					
Fr.	0.7	3.2	4.3	22.9	69.0
Sr.	0.8	4.1	3.7	27.9	63.6
2-yr.	1.6	1.7	5.7	23.7	67.3
13. Under some conditions, war is necessary to maintain justice.					
Fr.	7.3	40.4	13.0	21.7	17.6
Sr.	7.2	47.3	10.8	20.5	14.2
2-yr.	9.0	37.5	14.0	21.2	18.4
18. There is no conceivable justification for war.					
Fr.	24.4	20.6	17.3	32.0	5.7
Sr.	20.2	17.3	10.5	41.4	10.6
2-yr.	22.1	23.3	19.7	26.5	8.4
22. Changes in government should always be accomplished through peaceful means.					
Fr.	32.7	47.3	12.4	7.1	0.6
Sr.	24.8	49.9	11.2	13.6	0.6
2-yr.	32.5	48.4	11.9	6.3	0.8
27. People should refuse to engage in any war, no matter how serious the consequences to their country may be.					
Fr.	5.0	8.7	16.5	53.0	16.9
Sr.	3.8	9.1	12.3	53.7	21.0
2-yr.	8.7	10.3	17.7	46.9	16.5
31. Violent revolution is sometimes the only way to eliminate an oppressive government.					
Fr.	5.6	39.4	19.2	21.6	14.3
Sr.	7.5	50.9	15.6	17.4	8.6
2-yr.	6.0	36.6	18.8	26.3	12.4

Five Cooperation Scale questions deal with immigration of foreign persons or capital to the United States. The results paint an alarmingly exclusionary attitude. Items 4 and 12 have response patterns that are especially provoking—less than a third of the students disagree with limiting immigration of foreigners, and about two-thirds agree with a policy forbidding foreign purchases of American farmland. Students appear more willing to assist foreigners when the question involves helping other countries with malnutrition problems (Items 2 and 21), or when the action or policy proposed does not specify the U.S. as an agent.

Figure 3.10.5. Cooperation Scale

		1	2	3	4	5
2. I believe that the United States should send food and materials to any country that needs them.						
	Fr.	7.8	28.9	16.9	38.4	8.1
	Sr.	5.1	31.4	12.7	39.5	11.3
	2-yr.	10.2	32.5	16.3	29.1	11.8
4. The immigration of foreigners to this country should be kept down so that we can provide for Americans first.						
	Fr.	18.0	31.2	20.3	23.0	7.5
	Sr.	10.4	31.5	18.7	32.9	6.5
	2-yr.	21.1	30.3	22.1	21.7	4.8
12. We should not allow foreign business enterprises to buy American farmland.						
	Fr.	28.7	37.7	21.7	9.7	2.2
	Sr.	26.0	37.9	17.3	14.8	3.8
	2-yr.	30.1	32.6	21.7	11.7	3.9
15. Immigrants should not be permitted to come into our country if they compete with our own workers.						
	Fr.	7.8	21.3	26.5	37.0	7.3
	Sr.	5.5	22.6	22.7	40.8	8.3
	2-yr.	8.9	17.4	28.7	38.3	6.7
17. Any healthy individual, regardless of race or religion, should be allowed to live in whatever country he chooses.						
	Fr.	28.5	40.2	14.3	14.2	2.8
	Sr.	31.0	39.7	16.4	10.1	2.8
	2-yr.	32.7	40.6	16.1	8.2	2.4
19. Our country should have the right to prohibit certain racial and religious groups from immigrating.						
	Fr.	5.0	13.0	17.2	37.1	27.1
	Sr.	4.6	11.2	14.0	40.1	30.1
	2-yr.	5.0	13.1	21.4	34.9	25.7
21. It is our responsibility to do everything possible to prevent people from starving anywhere in the world.						
	Fr.	14.6	34.4	23.0	20.1	7.8
	Sr.	15.7	37.1	13.6	24.9	8.7
	2-yr.	19.1	35.7	22.8	16.9	5.6
25. The United States should be open to all those who wish to settle here.						
	Fr.	7.4	31.4	22.4	32.1	6.7
	Sr.	7.7	32.1	21.3	34.6	4.4
	2-yr.	9.7	28.0	25.9	29.1	7.2
32. Well-fed people in developed nations should voluntarily cut back on their food consumption and contribute food to the inadequately fed in underdeveloped nations.						
	Fr.	11.2	38.5	28.9	17.7	3.6
	Sr.	7.4	41.1	23.9	22.8	4.9
	2-yr.	11.1	35.8	30.3	19.4	3.4

The Human Rights Scale finally provides results to warm the heart. Although we need such results badly to balance the less flattering results from the four preceding scales, we must point out that the items do not present value dilemmas or even controversial statements for agreement or disagreement. In view of that, the responses are not surprising.

Figure 3.10.6. Human Rights Scale

	1	2	3	4	5
5. Political freedom is a basic human right and no government should be permitted to abridge it.					
Fr.	39.6	40.6	12.8	5.9	1.1
Sr.	41.1	39.1	10.6	7.8	1.5
2-yr.	46.3	37.1	11.0	5.1	0.5
8. Everyone should have the right to leave any country, including his own, and to return to his country.					
Fr.	37.4	40.6	10.5	9.4	2.1
Sr.	41.4	39.4	9.1	8.5	1.7
2-yr.	41.8	39.9	9.2	7.2	1.9
11. No government should deny access to basic education to any of its citizens.					
Fr.	69.3	25.0	2.7	2.6	0.5
Sr.	68.9	26.8	2.5	0.5	1.3
2 yr.	69.9	22.2	5.5	2.8	0.8
23. It is none of our business if other governments restrict the personal freedom of their citizens.					
Fr.	4.6	15.1	23.7	40.3	16.3
Sr.	3.1	14.1	15.5	47.4	20.0
2-yr.	4.9	16.9	25.3	36.7	16.1

Student Self-Perceptions

This collection of items was originally written to tap interest, feelings of worldwide kinship, and empathy or concern using a response mode of "True" or "False" to descriptive statements about oneself. Although they were conceived as having these three components, analysis of pretest responses revealed that the items were so tightly interrelated psychologically as to render trivial distinctions among the three components. Factor analyses of the survey data replicate the pretest findings.

Figure 3.10.7. Characteristic Roots for 10 Self-Report Items
(cumulative percent of common variance)

Freshmen	Seniors	2-Year
1.49 (56)	1.76 (48)	1.81 (62)
.81 (87 +)	1.00 (78)	.68 (86)
.34 (100 +)	.48 (89)	.55 (105)
.18	.44 (101)	.21
.06	.14	.08
	.02	

The characteristic roots tabled above can be argued to support a multifactor interpretation of the ten items. However, when two factors are extracted, they are not very useful but merely point out that items 2 and 7 apparently have content that evokes responses that may vary discernably from responses to the other eight items. Item 4 correlates with both factors in the two factor solutions. When three or more factors are extracted and rotated, the resulting factors are characterized in too many cases by one or two appreciable correlations, and our interpretation and decision is, therefore, to stay with one factor. We view the scale as the best single, short measure of the affective component of global understanding inasmuch as it taps three rational components ("interest," "kinship," "concern") that can be summarized in a single score.

Means and standard deviations for the three survey groups are given in Figure 3.10.8. These data indicate that the average response to the ten items was to mark some combination of 6 + items indicating a positive global attitude (interest, kinship, and concern). For each group, approximately two-thirds of the students' scores lie in the interval of plus or minus one standard deviation. Two two-year student data yield both the highest average and highest variability, although the differences are slight and probably not of practical importance.

Figure 3.10.8. Student Self-Perceptions

	Mean	S.D.
Freshman	6.22	2.14
Seniors	6.43	2.12
2-year	6.44	2.30

Student responses appear in Figure 3.10.9., where we have grouped the scale's questions according to our original intentions to measure interest, kinship, and concern. Responses to questions 1, 5, and 8 reflect a moderate degree of reported interest in international relations, developments, and events, and high interest in studying other cultures. Specific wording probably accounts for some of the variation among the responses. For example, "whenever I can" in question 1 probably suggests consistency of behavior that few can honestly report.

Figure 3.10.9. Responses to Student Self-Perception Items

(in percent)

Interest		True	False
1. I am interested in international relations and acquire information about international developments whenever I can.	Fr.	60.3	39.7
	Sr.	65.3	34.7
	2-yr.	64.5	35.5
5. I rarely read news articles about international events.	Fr.	26.0	74.0
	Sr.	20.3	79.7
	2-yr.	21.6	78.4
8. I am not interested in studying other cultures.	Fr.	12.1	87.9
	Sr.	12.1	87.9
	2-yr.	12.3	87.7
Kinship			
3. I am most comfortable with people from my own culture.	Fr.	78.6	21.4
	Sr.	77.9	22.1
	2-yr.	70.7	29.3
4. I feel a strong kinship with the worldwide human family.	Fr.	41.4	58.6
	Sr.	42.4	57.6
	2-yr.	49.2	50.8
6. I find the customs of foreigners difficult to understand.	Fr.	27.8	72.2
	Sr.	22.8	77.2
	2-yr.	28.7	71.3
9. I have almost nothing in common with people in underdeveloped nations.	Fr.	28.0	72.0
	Sr.	27.7	72.3
	2-yr.	25.2	74.8
10. I make an effort to meet people from other countries.	Fr.	60.0	40.0
	Sr.	58.6	41.4
	2-yr.	63.8	36.2
Concern			
2. The fact that a flood can kill 25,000 people in India is very depressing to me.	Fr.	70.5	29.5
	Sr.	69.0	31.0
	2-yr.	71.5	28.5
7. When I hear that thousands of people are starving in Cambodia, I feel very frustrated.	Fr.	69.4	30.6
	Sr.	71.6	28.4
	2-yr.	65.3	34.7

Questions 3, 4, 6, 9, and 10 were selected to tap "kinship." This construct should not be thought of as the opposite of ethnocentrism because the roots of that construct have historically stressed ethnicity and prejudice. The flavor of our items seems less pointed toward this positive or negative eval-

107

uation, and we should caution the reader not to assign the connotations of ethnocentrism or its opposite to these items. The results, however, seem generally disappointing.

Items 2 and 7 are intended to reflect empathy, a term often used in the literature of global understanding. We are doubtful that we have captured the richness of the literature here, but again we must note that a sizeable proportion of the students do not report empathetic responses to the situations sampled by the items.

Assessment of World Issues

Students were asked to provide their perceptions of world issues or problems by rating eight problems according to eleven scales in this section of the survey and by ranking 10 world problems according to importance on Item 18 and interest on Item 19 of Part I. Percentages of students choosing each rating option for the Assessment of World Issues stimulus issues and scales are presented in Appendix A. Median rankings for Items 18 and 19 appear there too. Scoring the scales required reversing 1, 3, 6, 9, 10, and 11, and scores obtained reflect these reversals.

Figures 3.10.10a. through 3.10.10c. present mean ratings and ranks for each of 8 issues and 11 scales of the Assessment of World Issues. Note that mean ratings on several scales are uniformly high when we recognize that the scale values were 1 through 5 with 3 as a midpoint. For example, Intergroup Conflict has, for freshmen, the lowest mean on the Importance scale (3.75, ranked eighth), but it is still .75 points above the scale midpoint of 3. International Conflict and War has a mean rating of 4.88, indicating that almost all freshmen rated it as highly important and, indeed, data displayed in the appendix reveal the following response distribution after the required scoring reversal:

	5	4	3	2	1	
This problem is important.	92.3	5.7	.7	.1	1.1	This problem is unimportant.

The mean of all the importance ratings for freshmen is, in fact, above 4.5, indicating that most if not all of the problems were seen as highly important by most freshmen.

Figure 3.10.10a. Assessment of World Issues
Ranks (   ) and Mean Ratings
Freshmen

	Environmental Pollution	Denial of Basic Human Rights	Intergroup Conflict	Depletion of Natural Resources	Unemployment	Inflation	Malnutrition and Inadequate Health Care	International Conflict and War
1. This problem is important.	(6) 4.57	(7) 4.56	(4) 4.68	(8) 3.75	(2) 4.81	(3) 4.73	(5) 4.67	(1) 4.88
2. I know a lot about this problem.	(5) 3.22	(7) 3.13	(4) 3.50	(8) 2.25	(1) 3.65	(3) 3.59	(6) 3.17	(2) 3.61
3. The American government can do a lot to solve this problem.	(5) 4.02	(7) 3.86	(4) 4.19	(8) 3.13	(1) 4.18	(3) 4.21	(6) 3.98	(2) 4.16
4. This problem will increase in the next twenty years.	(3) 3.98	(8) 3.10	(5) 3.75	(7) 3.29	(1) 4.31	(4) 3.93	(6) 3.67	(2) 4.03
5. This problem is interesting to learn about.	(3) 3.98	(4) 3.93	(7) 3.65	(8) 3.25	(2) 4.21	(5) 3.74	(6) 3.73	(1) 4.24
6. This problem is solvable.	(1) 3.98	(3) 3.95	(4) 3.82	(8) 3.36	(7) 3.65	(5-6) 3.76	(2) 3.97	(5-6) 3.76
7. International organizations can do a lot to solve this problem.	(3-4) 3.81	(3-4) 3.81	(8) 3.06	(7) 3.31	(5) 3.72	(6) 3.43	(2) 4.08	(1) 4.19
8. This problem is avoidable.	(1) 3.27	(2) 3.26	(8) 2.75	(7) 2.77	(6) 2.87	(5) 2.94	(3) 3.23	(4) 3.16
9. This problem is related to many other problems.	(4) 4.29	(7) 4.08	(3) 4.41	(8) 3.85	(5) 4.22	(2) 4.47	(6) 4.09	(1) 4.48
10. This problem is long-term.	(1) 4.33	(7) 3.80	(6) 3.83	(8) 3.56	(2) 4.23	(5) 3.86	(4) 3.89	(3) 4.04
11. This problem is of concern to people in many parts of the world.	(4) 4.33	(5) 4.28	(7) 4.20	(8) 3.91	(3) 4.41	(6) 4.22	(2) 4.55	(1) 4.75

Figure 3.10.10b. Assessment of World Issues
Ranks ( ) and Mean Ratings
Seniors

	Environmental Pollution	Denial of Basic Human Rights	Unemployment	Intergroup Conflict	Depletion of Natural Resources	Inflation	Malnutrition and Inadequate Health Care	International Conflict and War
1. This problem is important.	(5-6) 4.64	(7) 4.56	(5-6) 4.64	(8) 3.91	(2) 4.84	(3) 4.72	(4) 4.68	(1) 4.86
2. I know a lot about this problem.	(5) 3.39	(6) 3.23	(3) 3.53	(8) 2.59	(1) 3.69	(4) 3.41	(7) 3.17	(2) 3.61
3. The American government can do a lot to solve this problem.	(2-3) 4.15	(7) 3.76	(6) 4.01	(8) 3.13	(1) 4.30	(4) 4.13	(5) 4.06	(2-3) 4.15
4. This problem will increase in the next twenty years.	(3) 4.04	(8) 3.18	(6) 3.68	(7) 3.45	(1) 4.47	(4) 3.99	(5) 3.69	(2) 4.06
5. This problem is interesting to learn about.	(3) 4.06	(4) 3.93	(7) 3.69	(8) 3.42	(1-2) 4.17	(5) 3.83	(6) 3.74	(1-2) 4.17
6. This problem is solvable.	(2) 3.98	(3) 3.77	(4) 3.72	(8) 3.32	(5) 3.71	(6) 3.60	(1) 4.03	(7) 3.56
7. International organizations can do a lot to solve this problem.	(3) 3.90	(4) 3.89	(8) 2.91	(6) 3.36	(5) 3.87	(7) 3.29	(1) 4.15	(2) 4.10
8. This problem is avoidable.	(3) 3.29	(2) 3.30	(7) 2.82	(8) 2.73	(6) 2.88	(5) 3.06	(1) 3.51	(4) 3.22
9. This problem is related to many other problems.	(4) 4.44	(6-7) 4.28	(3) 4.49	(8) 4.08	(5) 4.38	(1) 4.54	(6-7) 4.28	(2) 4.52
10. This problem is long-term.	(2) 4.42	(4) 4.05	(6) 3.99	(8) 3.77	(1) 4.53	(7) 3.95	(5) 4.03	(3) 4.26
11. This problem is of concern to people in many parts of the world.	(5) 4.32	(4) 4.44	(7) 4.22	(8) 4.08	(3) 4.54	(6) 4.26	(7) 4.67	(1) 4.81

Figure 3.10.10c. Assessment of World Issues
Ranks ( ) and Mean Ratings
Two-Year Students

	Environmental Pollution	Denial of Basic Human Rights	Unemployment	Intergroup Conflict	Depletion of Natural Resources	Inflation	Malnutrition and Inadequate Health Care	International Conflict and War
1. This problem is important.	(7) 4.56	(6) 4.58	(4) 4.72	(8) 3.88	(3) 4.77	(2) 4.80	(5) 4.63	(1) 4.86
2. I know a lot about this problem.	(5) 3.20	(6) 3.19	(1) 3.57	(8) 2.53	(4) 3.43	(2) 3.55	(7) 3.14	(3) 3.47
3. The American government can do a lot to solve this problem.	(5) 4.06	(7) 3.83	(3) 4.09	(8) 3.12	(2) 4.13	(1) 4.27	(6) 4.03	(4) 4.08
4. This problem will increase in the next twenty years.	(3) 3.91	(8) 3.19	(5) 3.66	(7) 3.34	(1) 4.16	(4) 3.88	(6) 3.65	(2) 4.02
5. This problem is interesting to learn about.	(3) 3.93	(4) 3.84	(7) 3.67	(8) 3.35	(2) 4.11	(5) 3.83	(6) 3.72	(1) 4.21
6. This problem is solvable.	(2) 3.97	(3) 3.92	(5) 3.85	(8) 3.37	(6) 3.71	(4) 3.87	(1) 3.98	(7) 3.62
7. International organizations can do a lot to solve this problem.	(3) 3.80	(4) 3.79	(8) 3.17	(7) 3.19	(5) 3.74	(6) 3.41	(2) 3.90	(1) 3.97
8. This problem is avoidable.	(4-5) 2.98	(2-3) 3.03	(7) 2.73	(8) 2.72	(6) 2.83	(4-5) 2.98	(1) 3.19	(2-3) 3.03
9. This problem is related to many other problems.	(4) 4.24	(7) 4.09	(2) 4.44	(8) 3.89	(5) 4.20	(1) 4.46	(6) 4.15	(3) 4.42
10. This problem is long-term.	(1) 4.27	(5-6) 3.84	(7) 3.80	(8) 3.60	(2) 4.16	(5-6) 3.84	(4) 3.87	(3) 4.07
11. This problem is of concern to people in many parts of the world.	(3-4) 4.22	(6) 4.15	(5) 4.17	(8) 3.88	(3-4) 4.22	(7) 4.14	(2) 4.35	(1) 4.59

Similar rating levels seem to be present for all three groups on the following scales:

"The American Government can do a lot to solve this problem."
"This problem is related to many other problems."
"This problem is long-term."
"This problem is of concern to people in many parts of the world."

and, as noted above,

"This problem is important."

Given the general level of ratings on these scales, we may conclude first that most world problems are seen as important, interrelated, long-term, and of broad or universal concern. On the other hand and somewhat naively, the three groups of students seem to view the problems as amenable to solution by "the American government." Of course specific problems or issues are differentiated to some degree on these five scales, but the means are so uniformly high that the attendant rankings should be treated with some caution. Responses to the 6 remaining scales are spread more evenly, and the means are not as extreme. Thus the rankings are more informative of students' perceptions.

Figures 3.10.11. and 3.10.12a. through 3.10.12c. present the results of another analysis of responses to the Perception of World Problems section. Here we have factored the correlations among scales after removal of person and stimulus means and have found two factors corresponding roughly to the first and third factors that emerged from pretest data. The second pretest factor has disappeared because the two pretest scales "Necessary/Unnecessary" and "Rational/Irrational" constituting it were not carried from pretesting into the survey, and the two factor solution is supported by the roots in the first of the figures.

Figure 3.10.11. Characteristic Roots for Assessment of Perceptions of World Problems Within Correlation Matrix

(cumulative percentage of variance)

Root	Freshmen	Senior	2-year
1	1.53 (54)	1.67 (54)	1.54 (56)
2	.79 (22)	.86 (82)	.74 (82)
3	.32 (94)	.36 (93)	.40 (97)
4	.26 (103)	.22 (100 +)	.21 (105)

Figures 3.10.12a. through 3.10.12c. depict the issues arrayed in a two-dimensional plot with each dimension corresponding to one of the factors. Numbers in parentheses give the varimax factor loadings for respective variables on the factors and the projection of each issue on each factor is equivalent to a stimulus factor score. Elevations (the vertical axis) correspond to higher-rated solvability and, as the legends indicate, avoidability (freshmen and seniors), and "the American government can do a lot to solve this problem" (seniors and two-year students). The horizontal dimensions are more complex composites. More component scales are collapsed into the single dimensions and, as the legends shows, the components vary from group to group. In spite of this variation, a common flavor seems interpretable—displacement to the right indicates interest in learning about the problem, its importance, knowing a lot about it, and its increasing or long-term nature. Problems' relatedness to other problems is also a component for freshmen and seniors. It enters into the horizontal projections for two-year students but at a level well below the criterion used for interpreting these results.

Perhaps the most striking characteristic of the three plots is their similarity. Apparently, perceptions of the problems are quite similar in the three groups of students. The appearance of similarity seems to be established by three or four common locations of a problem or group of problems. These include Intergroup Conflict as a consistent outlier; Denial of Basic Human Rights and Malnutrition and Inadequate Health Care as a consistent pair in the upper-middle area; the Environmental Pollution, Unemployment, and Inflation triplet that is fairly tightly grouped for freshmen and two-year students and spread—but in the same area—for seniors; and the consistent projection of International Conflict and War and Depletion of Natural Resources to the right of the space.

Intergroup Conflict is clearly rated as the least important, interesting, known, etc., problem and

110

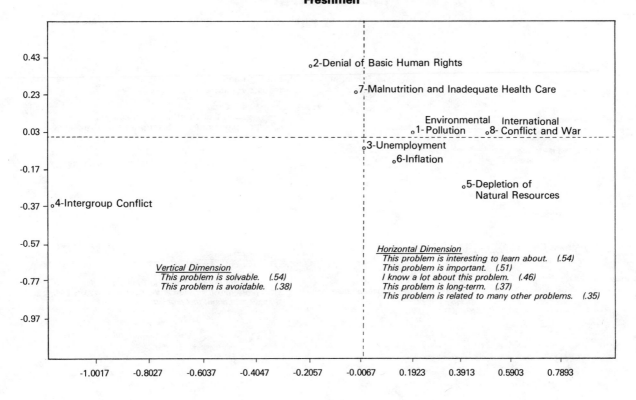

Figure 3.10.12a.   Assessment of World Issues
Stimulus Projections
Freshmen

Figure 3.10.12b.   Assessment of World Issues
Stimulus Projections
Seniors

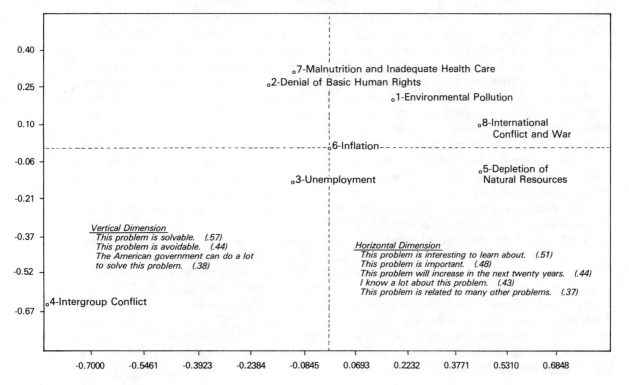

**Figure 3.10.12c. Assessment of World Issues
Stimulus Projections
Two-Year Students**

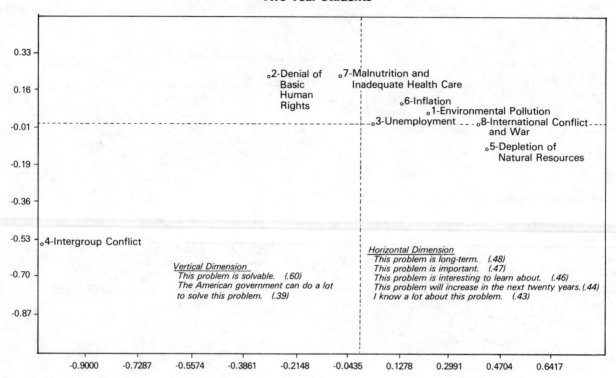

the one least amenable to solution, providing a characterization that we find surprising if not alarming. Similarly, the consistent perception that Malnutrition and Inadequate Health Care and Denial of Basic Human Rights are relatively solvable problems of moderate relative importance, interest, etc., suggests to us an interpretation of all three groups of results that is admittedly judgmental. The three problems (Intergroup Conflict, Malnutrition and Inadequate Health Care, and Denial of Basic Human Rights) seem to us to be basic in the sense of being fundamental to the social, economic, and political systems that have developed throughout history. Inflation, Unemployment, Environmental Pollution, International Conflict and War, and Depletion of Natural Resources, on the other hand, seem by comparison to be more immediate and symptomatic of current systems. From that personal perspective, we interpret the three arrays as reflecting a naive, ahistoric view. Certainly rating Denial of Basic Human Rights and Malnutrition and Inadequate Health Care as amenable to solution by the American government could be characterized as naive. Rating the triplet, Intergroup Conflict, Denial of Basic Human Rights, and Malnutrition and Inadequate Health Care, consistently lowest on the "interest in," "important," "know a lot about," and "long-term" is disappointing from our perspective and suggests to us that limited, immediate, American perspective characterizes the students.

Finally, items 18 and 19 of the survey called for ranking 10 world problems according to importance and interest respectively. The resulting data (Figures 3.10.13. and .10.14.) should not be expected to be completely equivalent to the ratings from the Assessment of World Issues section because the response methods, rating and ranking, differed. On the other hand the results should vary only slightly because method should have a very minor role in determining results or, ideally, no role at all.

Four problems were common to both the rating and ranking methods. Figure 3.10.15. compares relative rankings and ratings for these four common problems with respect to importance. Figure 3.10.16. compares them with respect to interest.

Figure 3.10.13. Medians of Ranked Importance

	Freshmen	Seniors	2-year
1. Malnutrition and inadequate health care	3.94	3.96	3.93
2. Nuclear and conventional arms proliferation	4.17	4.10	4.13
3. Depletion of natural resources	4.25	4.04	4.71
4. Inflation and unemployment	4.42	5.49	4.56
5. Denial of basic human rights	4.63	4.05	4.75
6. Air and water pollution	5.05	5.23	5.01
7. Overpopulation	6.38	5.65	5.72
8. Terrorism	6.53	6.87	6.50
9. Racial discrimination	7.01	7.01	6.82
10. Intergroup conflict	8.99	8.60	8.88

Figure 3.10.14. Medians of Ranked Interest

	Freshmen	Seniors	2-year
1. Depletion of natural resources	3.96	3.92	4.67
2. Denial of basic human rights	4.17	4.00	4.43
3. Inflation and unemployment	4.38	4.52	3.98
4. Nuclear and conventional arms proliferation	4.58	4.46	4.88
5. Malnutrition and inadequate health care	4.64	4.93	5.00
6. Air and water pollution	4.79	4.84	4.82
7. Racial discrimination	6.37	6.71	6.79
8. Terrorism	6.41	7.44	6.43
9. Overpopulation	7.14	6.70	6.20
10. Intergroup conflict	8.81	8.28	8.46

Figure 3.10.15. Comparisons of Ratings and Rankings of Four Problems' Importance

	Freshmen		Seniors		2-year	
	Ranked	Rated	Ranked	Rated	Ranked	Rated
Malnutrition and Inadequate Health Care	1	2	1	2	1	2
Depletion of Natural Resources	2	1	2	1	2	1
Denial of Basic Human Rights	3	3	3	3	3	3
Intergroup Conflict	4	4	4	4	4	4

Figure 3.10.16. Comparisons of Rating and Rankings of Four Problems' Interest

	Freshmen		Seniors		2-year	
	Ranked	Rated	Ranked	Rated	Ranked	Rated
Depletion of Natural Resources	1	1	1	1	2	1
Denial of Basic Human Rights	2	2	2	2	1	2
Malnutrition and Inadequate Health Care	3	3	3	3	3	3
Intergroup Conflict	4	4	4	4	4	4

In Figure 3.10.15. we note consistent changes in order for "Malnutrition and Inadequate Health Care" and "Depletion of Natural Resources." The mean importance ratings for the two issues differ only .14 for freshmen and twoyear students and .16 for seniors. All six ratings are above 4.60 on the five-point scale making the source of inconsistency quite obviously the previously noted uniformly high importance ratings. If we wish to differentiate among the problems with respect to perceived importance, the ranking data are probably better, but the safest stance is to note again the uniformity of perceptions of importance of all the problems and to approach differentiation cautiously.

Figure 3.10.16. shows one reversal—namely ranked interest in "Depletion of Natural Resources" and "Denial of Basic Human Rights" for two year students. The respective medians of ranks are 4.67 and 4.43, which may be compared to a range of values from 3.98 to 8.46. Obviously the difference is quite small, possibly unreliable, and certainly uninterpretable. Overall, the results are reasonably comparable suggesting acceptable validity for the rankings and ratings but cautioning against interpretations that rely on small differences.

Error-Choice

As noted previously in Chapter 2, the error-choice items specially written for this survey did not work as intended in the pretest. Error-choice total scores based on 12 items correlated substantially with knowledge test scores but not with any of the other six affective scales. Clearly our working hypothesis was that a consistent tendency to overestimate the magnitude of world problems would be related to scores on other attitude scales. What can we make of the fact that it did not?

The answer does not seem to lie in the characteristics of the items we developed. Notice that the spreads of responses across options (Figure 3.10.17.) for the items are generally good and that they generally bracket the unsupplied correct answer.

Figure 3.10.17. Error-Choice Items *

(in percent)

8. Gross National Product (GNP) is a commonly accepted measure of the wealth of countries. In the United States, GNP per capita in 1976 was about $7,884. What proportion of the world's countries had a GNP per capita less than one-quarter of this sum (i.e., less than $1,971)?

		Freshmen	Seniors	2-year
(1)	Four-fifths	18.6	29.2	21.4
(2)	Three-fifths	42.6	47.9	41.9
(3)	Two-fifths	29.7	17.4	25.3
(4)	One-fifth	5.2	2.8	8.0
Omit		4.1	2.6	3.5

The correct answer is approximately 70 percent.

---

* See Appendix D for sources of correct answers to error-choice items.

114

12. What proportion of the world's population lives in countries that have nutritionally inadequate diets?

		Freshmen	Seniors	2-year
(1)	More than two-thirds	17.2	25.8	26.7
(2)	About two-thirds	38.9	40.0	37.0
(3)	About one-half	22.7	22.8	21.4
(4)	Less than one-half	19.2	11.0	13.9
Omit		2.0	0.4	1.1

The correct answer is about two-thirds.

22. What proportion of the world's population has reasonable access to a safe water supply?

		Freshmen	Seniors	2-year
(1)	87 percent	7.5	7.1	7.6
(2)	75 percent	18.0	15.2	17.5
(3)	62 percent	39.8	33.8	36.5
(4)	48 percent	31.4	41.6	35.2
Omit		3.3	2.3	3.1

The correct answer is estimated to be 53 percent.

23. The number of children who die every year from diseases that could be prevented by immunization is about

		Freshmen	Seniors	2-year
(1)	8 million	16.6	26.2	21.5
(2)	5 million	34.8	32.5	30.7
(3)	3 million	32.9	26.9	31.3
(4)	1 million	10.8	8.4	13.0
Omit		4.9	6.0	3.5

The correct answer is about 5 million.

28. In 1976, 15 infants out of every 1,000 born in the United States died before reaching the age of one year. The comparable figure (infant mortality rate) for *developing* nations was

		Freshmen	Seniors	2-year
(1)	52	13.6	10.3	17.2
(2)	76	22.8	17.2	26.5
(3)	110	33.3	39.3	30.4
(4)	149	26.1	29.9	23.3
Omit		4.3	3.3	2.6

The correct answer is 111.

33. In 1976, the average life expectancy of infants born in *developed* nations was 72 years. In the same year, the average for *developing* nations was

		Freshmen	Seniors	2-year
(1)	65	12.4	5.9	19.2
(2)	57	31.8	32.9	32.1
(3)	49	30.5	40.9	25.4
(4)	42	21.8	18.5	21.1
Omit		3.5	1.8	2.2

The correct answer is 57 years.

38. The "world price" or average retail price of a gallon of gasoline in United States currency is

		Freshmen	Seniors	2-year
(1)	under $1.00	3.4	2.8	2.4
(2)	between $1.00 and $1.50	53.2	44.1	55.1
(3)	between $1.50 and $2.00	20.1	19.8	18.9
(4)	over $2.00	21.1	33.0	23.0
Omit		2.2	0.2	0.7

The correct answer to this question varies with "world price" fluctuation.

42. The bomb that leveled Hiroshima in the Second World War killed about 100,000 people. How many cities the size of Hiroshima could be destroyed by the current world stockpile of nuclear arms?

		Freshmen	Seniors	2-year
(1)	10,000	9.1	7.9	11.5
(2)	100,000	15.0	18.9	20.6
(3)	1,000,000	26.8	26.4	23.4
(4)	5,000,000	45.5	43.0	41.6
Omit		3.6	3.7	2.9

The correct answer is approximately 1,000,000.

81. What proportion of the countries of the world have literacy rates below 50 percent?

		Freshmen	Seniors	2-year
(1)	More than two-thirds	11.7	23.2	22.7
(2)	About two-thirds	41.3	46.7	37.1
(3)	About one-third	35.2	24.2	28.6
(4)	Less than one-third	6.0	3.9	5.3
Omit		5.7	2.1	6.4

The correct answer is about 46 percent.

89. The number of unemployed people in the world is estimated to be

		Freshmen	Seniors	2-year
(1)	between 50 and 100 million	12.9	9.9	16.9
(2)	between 150 and 200 million	39.9	30.0	34.8
(3)	between 300 and 400 million	29.1	33.9	23.4
(4)	over 500 million	10.4	16.0	18.5
Omit		7.8	10.1	6.4

The correct answer is between 300 and 400 million.

105. Since the oil shortage of 1973, United States gasoline consumption has

		Freshmen	Seniors	2-year
(1)	increased 10 percent or more	40.3	40.8	39.5
(2)	increased 5 percent	26.5	30.8	22.0
(3)	decreased 5 percent	19.1	20.4	22.0
(4)	decreased 10 percent or more	8.7	4.0	10.1
Omit		5.4	4.0	6.4

The correct answer to this question varies with consumption fluctuation.

110. The United States spent approximately $454 per capita on education in 1976. In that year, the world average was about

		Freshmen	Seniors	2-year
(1)	$310	9.2	4.8	13.4
(2)	$214	24.7	15.8	27.5
(3)	$122	32.1	30.0	22.9
(4)	$86	25.9	42.8	27.8
Omit		8.2	6.6	8.4

The correct answer is approximately $86.

In the main then, the items differentiate effectively among degrees of overestimation and underestimation as intended. This would not be the case if responses were piled up on a single option or on one or two. Further evidence that the error-choice items, taken together, measure something in common is presented in the first column of Figure 3.10.18.

Here we see that correlations of single items with ERCH, the scale score, are moderate and positive with the exception of items 42, 89, and 105. Accordingly, ERCHA was constituted by omitting these three items in order to increase the internal consistency of the error-choice total score. In spite of this effort, ERCHA correlations with the other affective scales are below .20 for all three student groups, and correlations with the knowledge test were .36, .33, and .48 for freshmen, seniors, and two-year students respectively.

Figure 3.10.18. Correlations of Error-Choice Items With:
Error-Choice Total Score (ERCH),
Error-Choice A Total Score (ERCHA),
and Knowledge Test Total Score (KNOWLEDGE)

	Freshmen			Seniors			2-year		
	ERCH	ERCHA	KNOW-LEDGE	ERCH	ERCHA	KNOW-LEDGE	ERCH	ERCHA	KNOW-LEDGE
Item 8	.36	.55	.24	.36	.51	.20	.35	.53	.29
Item 12	.33	.49	.09	.38	.50	.02	.35	.54	.18
Item 22	.35	.43	.08	.31	.37	-.02	.28	.41	.11
Item 23	.32	.42	.24	.43	.51	.28	.42	.50	.24
Item 28	.38	.51	.26	.38	.48	.20	.36	.49	.24
Item 33	.35	.45	.19	.43	.46	.13	.39	.45	.29
Item 38	.29	.45	.26	.36	.43	.37	.35	.47	.35
Item 42	-.15	.10	.12	-.20	.02	-.12	-.22	.03	-.03
Item 81	.34	.43	.14	.29	.46	.15	.38	.45	.12
Item 89	-.07	.25	.17	-.02	.24	.16	-.01	.24	.09
Item 105	-.15	.08	.12	-.17	.09	.16	-.10	.17	.13
Item 110	.41	.54	.39	.46	.59	.43	.50	.54	.50

Consistent overestimation or underestimation of the magnitude of world problems is therefore not interpretable as an affective trait in this survey. While the response behavior is consistent, we know that it is not associated with the affective variables tapped by our other measure but is related to level of knowledge. Understanding of these relationships will require further exploration.

Correlates of Attitudes

In this final section of Chapter 10 we examine the correlates of scores on the six attitude scales that functioned as intended. Figures 3.10.19a. through 3.10.19e. provide all correlations that are .20 or larger, and the reader may conclude that variables that do not appear were only negligibly correlated with the six attitude scores. Our comments—indications that we will risk making some cautious interpretation—are generally limited to those instances where correlations are found in two or three of the student groups, where they reveal counterintuitive relationships, or where they provide substantial explanations by their patterns or magnitudes.

Background/Affect

It is interesting to note that sex differences in attitudes appear only once in our data and that is with respect to the War Scale, where women appear more anti-war than men. These results may be expected to do some damage to stereotypic thinking about sex differences in attitudes. Students who came to the U.S. at older ages score higher on the Cooperation Scale and higher on the Concern Scale, with the exception of freshmen. Overall, these results are difficult to interpret given the negligible effect of "Born in the United States," a variable that would be viewed as basic if foreign birth had made a difference. We should also note that socioeconomic status as captured by parental education does not apear to have its ubiquitous potency in this attitude domain.

Experience/Affect

The relationships between ability and attitudes are strongest for the Chauvinism scale, as Figure 3.10.19b. demonstrates. Other correlations with the ability variables seem haphazard by comparison and, while some would venture the opinion that positive global attitudes are related to ability, we insist on the caveat that it is the anti-chauvinistic component that provides most of the overlap. The college and high school experiences listed in the figure do relate to both the Chauvinism and Concern Scales, but the pattern across groups seems too variable to support a theory woven for the occasion.

Figure 3.10.19a. Background/Affect Correlations $>$ .19

	Chauvinism			World Government			Cooperation			War			Human Rights			Concern		
	Fr.	Sr.	2-yr.	Fr.	Sr.	2-yr.	Fr.	Sr.	2-yr.	Fr.	Sr.	2-yr.	Fr.	Sr.	2-yr.	Fr.	Sr.	2-yr.
Sex										.27	.30	.20						
Born in the United States									.25									
If not born in the United States, age when came to the United States					.30		.20	.25	.20								.44	.39
If not born in the United States, considers self permanent resident			.26					.33			.26	.22			.39		.22	
Level of father's formal education	.23																	
Level of mother's formal education	.22																	

118

Figure 3.10.19b. Experience/Affect Correlations > .19

	Chauvinism			World Government			Cooperation			War			Human Rights			Concern		
	Fr.	Sr.	2-yr.	Fr.	Sr.	2-yr.	Fr.	Sr.	2-yr.	Fr.	Sr.	2-yr.	Fr.	Sr.	2-yr.	Fr.	Sr.	2-yr.
SAT Verbal	.28	.23	.27			.21							.27			.27		
SAT Math			.35												.22			
ACT	.37	.34	.22								.26			.20				
College GPA	.24	.22																
College experiences outside the class-room contribute to global understanding																		.20
Modern foreign languages contribute to global understanding																	.21	
Years of foreign language in high school	.24																	
Foreign language courses in college																	.22	
Time in foreign countries																.22		
Philosophy courses in college		.20																
Literature courses in college			.22															
Art, music, dance participation in high school or college																	.21	.22
Journalism, debating, literary, or drama-tic activities in high school or college																		.21
Long-term educational goal			.22															

119

Figure 3.10.19c. Politics/Affect Correlations > .19

	Chauvinism			World Government			Cooperation			War			Human Rights			Concern		
	Fr.	Sr.	2-yr.	Fr.	Sr.	2-yr.	Fr.	Sr.	2-yr.	Fr.	Sr.	2-yr.	Fr.	Sr.	2-yr.	Fr.	Sr.	2-yr.
Left political attitudes		.41	.28		.26			.20	.21		.20							

Figure 3.10.19d. Information – Media/Affect Correlations > .19

	Chauvinism			World Government			Cooperation			War			Human Rights			Concern		
	Fr.	Sr.	2-yr.	Fr.	Sr.	2-yr.	Fr.	Sr.	2-yr.	Fr.	Sr.	2-yr.	Fr.	Sr.	2-yr.	Fr.	Sr.	2-yr.
Frequency of watching local news on television	.21																	
Watching specials about foreign countries and their cultures on television									.29								.37	.37
Watching musical performances on television																.21		
Reading national news articles in newspaper																		.24
Reading international news articles in newspaper									.21						.20	.21	.36	.32
Selecting headline "Soviet Jews Denied Exit Visas"			.30				.21	.22								.28	.31	.21

Politics/Affect

Although the survey included several questions on politics, only one—the student's own "general political attitude"—correlated substantially with the global attitudes surveyed. For various groups Chauvinism, World Government, Cooperation, and War responses were related to "left" political attitudes. In each case, students to the left respond in the more aware or understanding direction, and it is interesting to note that "left-right" rather than Republican-Democrat appears to be salient.

Information—Media/Affect

Four of the numerous information acquisition variables incorporated in the survey appear to be related substantially to global attitudes. Six variables are tabled above, but three of them have only a single correlation greater than .19 with any of the scale-by-group intersections. Watching specials about foreign countries and cultures and reading international news appear to be associated with positive global attitudes—especially the Concern Scale score. The final variable, selection of a specific headline from 16 purported options for further reading, provides an encouraging partial replication of the relationship between reading international news articles and Concern. Both probably reflect the explicit interest component of the Concern Scale.

Language Background and Attitudes/Affect

The correlations of language background and attitudes with the six attitudes scales are numerous but largely inconsistent. That the majority of relationships obtained for 2-year students alone is provoking, underlining again that this population is different from freshmen and seniors with respect to foreign language background. The consistent correlation between language attitudes and the Cooperation and Concern Scales is not surprising given the coverage of the three scales.

Figure 3.10.19e. Language Background and Attitudes/Affect Correlations > .19

	Chauvinism			World Government			Cooperation			War			Human Rights			Concern		
	Fr.	Sr.	2-yr.	Fr.	Sr.	2-yr.	Fr.	Sr.	2-yr.	Fr.	Sr.	2-yr.	Fr.	Sr.	2-yr.	Fr.	Sr.	2-yr.
Studied modern foreign language other than native language			.24															
Studied English as a foreign language in elementary or secondary school									.23									
English is MPFL									.28									
A to A- average in MPFL courses in high school and/or college																	.20	
Studied MPFL in 4th grade																		.23
Studied MPFL in 5th grade																		.24
Studied MPFL in 8th grade						.23												
Studied MPFL as college freshman									.22									
Acquired some of MPFL ability from friends or people in the neighborhood speaking it									.25									
Acquired some MPFL ability from studying abroad																		.22
Acquired some MPFL ability from living abroad																.20		.20
Language attitudes	.22						.32	.24	.25				.25			.50	.48	.50

122

Chapter 11

Structure

Thomas S. Barrows and John L. D. Clark

What is global understanding? The issue of definition was an original, basic project concern, and the Assessment Committee and project staff returned to it repeatedly during the instrument development work already described. The final survey instruments may be viewed as the operational definition derived through the development work.

This operational definition is, however, subject to examination and modification based upon the survey's response data. For example, at the simplest level, we reasoned that global understanding consisted of cognitive and affective components and that these were related to foreign language study and proficiency. Response data can be explored to ascertain whether those components fit together in that hypothesized way. We cannot discover components of global understanding that we unwittingly left out of the survey, but we can determine if the variables that we included are, in fact, interrelated as we thought they would be. For example, if responses to cognitive items are essentially independent of responses to affective items, it will be difficult to argue that global understanding is a unitary or integrated phenomenon with cognitive and affective components.

In this final chapter of results we report analyses undertaken to "fit" response data and survey measures together. The general strategy develops a model of interrelationships among variables based upon response consistencies. This psychological, empirical model is then compared with the rational, hypothetical one underlying the survey's content.

As a first step we have reduced the number of variables to be considered. This was done in the interests of interpretability and could be accomplished without loss of information because many of the correlations among study variables have already been reported (Chapters 7-10). For each of the three groups of students we consider the 21 variables in Figure 3.11.1.

This collection of variables represents the major domains of study: knowledge (1), foreign language (3-8), and attitudes (2, 16-21). Variables 10 through 12 and 14 and 15 represent information acquisition activities, and 9 and 13 were included to allow the potentially interesting effects of general political attitude and general academic achievement to be represented.

A 21x21 matrix of correlations was computed for each group, and these were factor analyzed separately by the principal factor method. Plots of the characteristic roots are presented in Figure 3.11.2a. and the roots themselves in Figure 3.11.2b.

The plots of the roots reveal discontinuities between either 3 and 4 or 4 and 5 roots. In addition, Harman's (Harman, 1976, p. 141) rule that the sum of the roots for the factors extracted not exceed the sum of the communalities suggests a maximum of three factors for students at two-year institutions and four factors for freshmen and seniors. We chose to extract three factors for each group in order to obtain comparable solutions and to be reasonably conservative with regard to over-factoring. Four and five factor solutions examined did not add interpretive power nor did study of the residual correlations suggest the necessity of more than three factors to summarize the 210 interrelationships among the 21 variables.

Figure 3.11.1. Twenty-One Variables for Structural Analysis

Variable	Description	Freshmen		Seniors		2-year	
		Mean	S.D.	Mean	S.D.	Mean	S.D.
1. Knowledge	Appendix B, 101 items	41.94	11.36	50.46	12.11	40.45	12.54
2. Error-Choice A	Appendix B, items 8, 12, 22, 23, 28, 33, 38, 81, and 110. (A high score indicates consistent overestimation of the magnitude of world problems.)	20.31	5.43	22.12	4.99	20.95	5.42
3. Self-assessed foreign language speaking proficiency	Appendix A, Part II, item 18	26.32	6.89	25.60	7.35	26.97	7.88
4. Self-assessed foreign language listening proficiency	Appendix A, Part II, item 19	19.14	4.89	18.64	5.37	20.43	5.97
5. Self-assessed foreign language reading proficiency	Appendix A, Part II, item 20	14.18	3.73	13.79	4.07	14.64	4.68
6. Informal acquisition of foreign language proficiency	Appendix A, Part II, item 14. (Score is sum of positive responses to five possible contributing factors.)	0.56	0.81	0.57	0.88	0.78	0.97
7. Formal acquisition of foreign language proficiency	Appendix A, Part II, item 15. (Score is sum of years of language study from first grade through senior year in college.)	2.73	1.75	3.14	2.19	2.51	2.05
8. Language study attitude*	Appendix A, Part III, sum of 15 items	54.4	10.05	55.74	9.93	55.73	9.63
9. Politically left	Appendix A, Part I, item 14	2.98	0.73	3.04	0.85	3.03	0.77
10. TV world and national news viewing	Appendix A, Part I, item 21	2.84	1.27	3.18	1.37	3.30	1.39
11. Radio news listening	Appendix A, Part I, item 23	3.78	1.25	3.65	1.27	3.79	1.30
12. Newspaper international news reading	Appendix A, Part I, item 26.6	0.60	0.49	0.70	0.46	0.62	0.48
13. College GPA	Appendix A, Part I, item 37	4.23	1.23	4.74	0.90	4.70	1.04
14. Time spent outside United States	Appendix A, Part I, item 47	2.37	3.89	3.43	4.90	3.29	4.98
15. Selection of international news headlines	Appendix A, Part I, item 24	0.95	0.84	1.15	0.83	1.04	0.86
16. Concern*	Appendix A, Part VI, 10-item scale. (A high score indicates interest in and feelings of kinship for other people and their cultures.)	16.30	2.07	16.45	2.12	16.58	2.20
17. Chauvinism*	Appendix A, Part V, items 1, 3, 6, 14, 24, 26, and 29. (A high score indicates an anti-chauvinist attitude.)	21.48	5.29	23.70	5.34	21.11	5.52
18. World Government*	Appendix A, Part V, items 7, 9, 16, 20, 28, and 30. (A high score indicates a positive attitude toward world government.)	17.69	4.41	17.55	5.03	18.79	4.54
19. War*	Appendix A, Part V, items 10, 13, 18, 22, 27, and 31. (A high score indicates an anti-war attitude.)	20.21	4.18	19.07	4.32	20.37	4.18
20. Cooperation*	Appendix A, Part V, items 2, 4, 12, 15, 17, 19, 21, 25, and 32. (A high score indicates a positive attitude toward world cooperation.)	28.06	5.74	28.44	6.02	28.43	5.98
21. Human Rights*	Appendix A, Part V, items 5, 8, 11, and 23. (A high score indicates strong feelings against the denial of basic human rights.)	16.23	2.25	16.50	2.28	16.32	2.25

*Items for these attitude scales were worded both positively and negatively to avoid effects due to response tendency. Therefore, response to a number of items were reversed before being scored.

Figure 3.11.2a. Plot of Characteristic Roots for 21 Variables

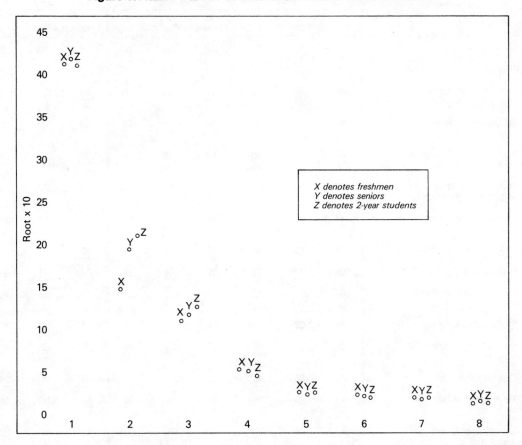

Figure 3.11.2b. Characteristic Roots for 21 Variables

	Freshmen	Seniors	2-year
1.	4.20	4.24	4.17
2.	1.56	2.10	2.13
3.	1.11	1.21	1.20
4.	0.57	0.57	0.48
5.	0.38	0.34	0.37
6.	0.32	0.29	0.25
7.	0.23	0.22	0.23
8.	0.16	0.17	0.13
9.	0.09	0.11	0.10
10.	0.06	0.08	0.05
11.	0.03	0.03	0.03
12.	0.02		

The three factors that emerge in each case (Figure 3.11.3a.) may be interpreted as Language, Affect, and Knowledge. Seven variables have their highest correlations with the first factor and the group is conceptually pleasing and clear, consisting of three language proficiency scales, the language attitude scale, and three acquisition variables—number of formal and informal language contacts and length of time spent outside the U.S. Replication of these correlations in each of three groups facilitates our labeling the language factor with unusual confidence. The factor provides empirical evidence that the seven variables are language related and that our foreign language proficiency/attitude/acquisition component of global understanding is coherent empirically as well as rationally. Before turning to another factor, we should point out consistently high correlation of the 10-item Concern scale with the language factor. Relationships among factors will be revisited as we proceed.

125

Figure 3.11.3a. Promax Correlations With Primary Factors

| | Freshmen | | | Seniors | | | 2-year | | |
Variable	I Language	II Affect	III Knowledge	I Language	II Affect	III Knowledge	I Language	II Affect	III Knowledge
1. Knowledge	.04	.10	.87	-.02	.18	.89	.16	.25	.85
2. Error-Choice A	-.06	-.07	.33	.01	-.10	.30	.14	.13	.50
3. Self-assessed foreign language speaking proficiency	.89	.37	.17	.95	.20	.09	.92	.07	-.05
4. Self-assessed foreign language listening proficiency	.92	.34	.05	.91	.16	.07	.86	.05	-.14
5. Self-assessed foreign language reading proficiency	.87	.34	.10	.89	.19	.09	.86	.05	-.19
6. Informal acquisition of foreign language proficiency	.47	.21	-.06	.61	.18	.10	.64	.23	-.10
7. Formal acquisition of foreign language proficiency	.44	.21	.18	.56	.06	-.05	.51	.13	-.07
8. Language study attitude	.65	.53	.18	.59	.36	.21	.59	.35	.13
9. Politically left	.05	.21	.10	.09	.44	.14	-.07	.37	.19
10. TV world and national news viewing	.04	-.06	.02	.02	-.12	-.01	.11	-.03	.07
11. Radio news listening	.15	.02	.07	.06	-.04	.06	-.02	-.08	.10
12. Newspaper international news reading	.22	.26	.40	.20	.24	.43	.29	.29	.42
13. College GPA	.22	.25	.45	.07	.20	.29	.00	.04	.26
14. Time spent outside United States	.40	.20	.06	.37	.18	.24	.44	.15	.26
15. Selection of international news headlines	.20	.36	.33	.22	.35	.34	.20	.10	.28
16. Concern	.47	.58	.12	.42	.55	.34	.50	.60	.16
17. Chauvinism	.18	.49	.32	.05	.70	.34	-.13	.52	.31
18. World Government	.11	.36	-.06	.12	.57	.08	.18	.46	-.13
19. War	.13	.39	-.19	.12	.50	-.14	.02	.34	-.27
20. Cooperation	.31	.68	.18	.23	.53	.21	.26	.65	.08
21. Human Rights	.20	.43	.27	.10	.38	.28	.10	.48	.25

Figure 3.11.3b. Correlations Among Primary Factors

Freshmen

	II. Affect	III. Knowledge
I. Language	.46	.14
II. Affect		.24

Seniors

	II. Affect	III. Knowledge
I. Language	.27	.13
II. Affect		.32

2-Year

	II. Affect	III. Knowledge
I. Language	.20	-.07
II. Affect		.25

The second factor has been labeled Affect, inasmuch as the six scales developed to measure affect have their major correlations with this factor in all three groups. Left political attitudes are apparently associated with these desired global attitudes, although this positive relationship is considerably stronger for seniors and students at two-year institutions than it is for freshmen. The indirect measure of interest consisting of the choice of headlines to be followed up (variable 15) has its major correlation with the affect factor in two of the three groups and in each of them the correlation with the third or "knowledge" factor is appreciable. It is not surprising to find interest forming this bridge between the two domains, but the negligible correlation with Affect for the two-year students is surprising and unexplainable without some reasonable theory about general differences among the three populations.

Finally with regard to Affect, we should point out the consistent, moderate correlations of lan-
les with Affect in the freshman group. The relationships are moderate for the proficien-
the senior group and are essentially zero for two-year students. On the other hand,
uisition's relationship is consistent though moderate, and Language Study Attitude is
high to moderate.

actor is best distinguished by the uniformly high correlations of the 101-item know-
e with it. We have labeled the factor "Knowledge" accordingly. Variables 9 through
wed as potential explanatory variables, and information-gathering activities (variables
e interesting contrasts from that point of view. Note that TV news and radio news have
o correlations with Knowledge while newspaper, international news-reading correlates
n each of the three groups. The apparent importance of that activity is enhanced by
additional low to moderate positive correlations with both the Affect and Language
group. Furthermore, the conceptually similar variable 15, Selection of International
es, shows fairly similar patterns of correlations with the three factors. Clearly the activ-
these two variables is associated with global understanding although it is not possible
whether the relationship is one of cause and effect. Grade point average consistently
moderate to high level with Knowledge, revealing, unsurprisingly, that academic
s also asociated with the global understanding knowledge component.

ent moderate to high correlation of the Error-Choice A score with the knowledge fac-
nagging reminder that all need not go as planned. Conceptual and interpretive prob-
s variable were reported in the sections on instrument development and the earlier
sults of the affective measures (Chapter 2). In the present analyses we see again that
the consistent tendency to overestimate the severity, magnitude, prevalence, or fre-
rld problems, is associated with the knowledge factor rather than the affect factor.
nalysis results seem more compelling than the simple correlations among scores on
affective scales, and the knowledge test. Here we see that ERCH A is associated most
ot only the knowledge score but also with the other variables that correlate with and
to the knowledge factor. ERCH A is thus in the domain psychologically defined by
ewspaper reading, and grade point average. In point of fact, two of the three correla-
A with the factor defined by the affective scales are negative. Clearly ERCH A is cog-
application, and further use of the error-choice technique for affective measurement
roached with renewed caution.

oint we have examined the make-up of the three factors that our analysis set forth. It
ay that most of the major measures employed in the survey functioned as expected and
ysis of response data has reproduced the components of our original rational model
le fidelity in three separate groups of students. On the other hand, we have not fully
tionships among the three components in order to determine the extent to which re-
pport the rational suggestions that knowledge and affect are integral to global under-
that foreign language proficiency, study, and so forth are sources of it.

natics confirm our rational model in part—namely, knowledge and affect and language and affect are moderately related in each of the three groups. On the other hand, language is 3.11.3a., and the indices of relationship among them are the correlations among the factors from Figure 3.11.3b.

These schematics confirm our rational model only in part—namely, knowledge and affect and language and affect are moderately related in each of the three groups. On the other hand, language is

ERRATUM

A printer's error appears in the bottom paragraph on page 127. The corrected version is as follows:

The schematics of Figure E.11.4. summarize the relationships among the three components for each of the three groups of students. The components are the factors described above and in Figure 3.11.3a., and the indices of relationship among them are the correlations among the factors from Figure 3.11.3b.

These schematics confirm our rational model in part—namely, knowledge and affect and language and affect are moderately related in each of the three groups. On the other hand, language is

Figure 3.11.4. Relationships Among Components

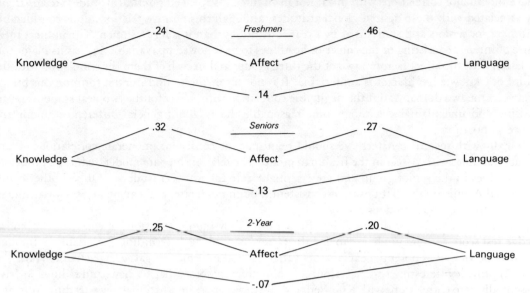

not related to knowledge as expected, the correlations between the two factors being either low or very low and negative. Although a substantial correlation between language and knowledge could not establish causality, the absence of such a relationship rules out the hypothesized role of language as a "source" of global understanding. In other words, a substantial language/knowledge relationship was a necessary but not sufficient condition to acceptance of our original, rational model. That necessary relationship was not found.

Two new hypotheses concerning these discouraging results were advanced. First, recognizing that all three of the original student groups contained a number of students for whom English was not a native language, it was suggested that their atypical educational patterns (by comparison to native-English speaking students undergoing a regular U.S.-based school program) might have had an effect on the observed interrelationships. For example, if a relatively high level of proficiency in English (as the MPFL) for these students was not accompanied by a correspondingly higher level of "global knowledge," this would serve to attenuate the relationship for the total group. The presence and extent of these effects, if any, in the groups could be fairly easily determined by conducting a further analysis in which the same correlations would be carried out for each of the groups minus those students who reported a native language other than English.

A second possibility was that there existed a "threshold" level of language proficiency, below which there would be essentially no relationship between proficiency and world knowledge, but above which (effectively masked by the total data) relatively substantial effects might be present.

The existence of such a threshold effect would be a reasonable hypothesis in view of the likelihood that a relatively high level of second language proficiency would be needed in order to make effective use of foreign printed materials such as newspapers or newsmagazines or to engage in "political," "economic," or other types of conversations with native speakers that would have a bearing on the acquisition of "world knowledge." Students whose foreign language proficiency was below the minimum level required to make these additional information sources available would not be expected to gain in knowledge, even though their self-reports might vary rather widely on the proficiency scales up to the threshold point.

For the first added analysis, students in each of the three cohort groups were separated into "native English" and "non-native English" groups on the basis of their responses to the question on "your own native language (mother tongue)" at the beginning of the Language Background section. As shown in Figure 3.11.5., the mean scores on the proficiency self-assessment scales for speaking, listening comprehension, and reading were consistently higher for the "non-native English" group than for the "native English" group, with rather large score differences in each instance.

Figure 3.11.5. Self-Appraisal MPFL Mean Proficiency Scores for "Native English" and "Non-native English" Students

	Native English			Non-Native English		
	Freshmen	Seniors	2-year	Freshmen	Seniors	2-Year
Speaking						
Mean:	26.00	25.15	25.38	35.26	36.70	37.05
S.D.:	6.61	7.01	7.11	7.47	7.17	4.96
Listening Comprehension						
Mean:	18.87	18.30	19.08	26.42	27.75	28.69
S.D.:	4.59	5.00	5.24	6.57	6.10	4.03
Reading Comprehension						
Mean:	14.04	13.55	13.71	19.46	20.13	20.88
S.D.:	3.58	3.83	4.24	4.24	4.66	3.24

Despite the substantially greater proficiency in the MPFL reported by the non-native English speakers, their removal from the correlational analysis was not found to affect the essentially complete lack of relationship between self-reported language proficiency and level of world knowledge, as shown in Figure 3.11.6. below.

Table 3.11.6. Correlations of Self-Appraised MPFL Proficiency and Scores on Global Understanding Test

(Native English Speakers)

	Freshmen	Seniors	2-Year
Speaking	.08	.01	.07
Listening Comprehension	.03	.01	.06
Reading Comprehension	.07	.04	-.05

To explore the hypothesis of a "threshold" effect for foreign language proficiency as related to world knowledge, the project staff developed a working definition of a student "proficient in a foreign language" as follows:

● Reports English as the native language;
● Responds "quite easily to" any one or more of the last five questions on the speaking self-appraisal scale;
● Responds "quite easily" to any one or more of the last seven questions on the listening comprehension scale;
● Responds "quite easily" to any one or more of the last four questions on the reading comprehension scale.

The setting of these relatively stringent criteria for "proficiency" in the MPFL was based on the desire to insure that any students falling into this group would have a sufficiently high level of competence in these three skill areas to permit them to make effective "real-world" use of them in face-to-face communication with native speakers of the language on non-trivial and reasonably sophisticated topics; listening, with easy, immediate comprehension, to news broadcasts, television programs, and other "genuine" audio information sources; and comprehending, at a reasonable speed and without the need for external aids, printed materials intended for a readership of educated native speakers of the language.

Although the "proficient" level for each of the scales was established on a judgmental basis reflecting the expectations for overall language competence implied by the "can do" statements involved, it was also noted that for the total-group data for each of the skill areas, "quite easily" responses for all three cohort groups showed a substantial percentage drop just at the point specified for the beginning of the "proficient" statements. This suggested an inherent dichotomy in the distribution of "can do" scale scores at the same points already judged on-face to represent the attainment of "proficiency" in the language.

Figure 3.11.7. Comparisons of Total Group and Language-Proficient Group on Selected Background Questions

	Total			Language-Proficient		
	Freshmen	*Seniors*	*2-Year*	*Freshmen*	*Seniors*	*2-Year*
Travel outside U.S. (%)	57.9	64.3	60.9	80.1	90.6	81.1
Average time abroad*	2.45	3.51	3.31	6.43	6.97	7.59
Participation in summer-abroad program (%)	9.0	7.9	8.8	3.4	19.2	14.5
Participation in year-abroad program (%)	1.1	5.0	1.2	0.0	13.0	2.8
Study of MPFL in formal setting (%)	88.1	90.0	80.9	78.2	86.2	90.0
Total years of high school FL study	1.91	2.07	1.70	3.08	3.01	2.72
Total FL courses in college	0.30	1.53	0.52	1.39	5.83	2.72
Major or intended major is FL (%)	1.0	2.0	2.5	13.6	17.5	0.0
FL contact with family members (%)	14.0	18.7	11.9	34.9	48.6	34.9
FL contact with friends (%)	21.9	19.4	26.8	37.2	47.3	73.3
FL contact through living abroad (%)	8.4	11.5	13.4	39.1	37.7	40.4
FL contact through studying abroad (%)	3.4	7.8	8.6	20.7	40.7	25.6

*see item 47, Part I, Booklet A in Appendix A for units describing "time."

On the basis of the criteria described above, we separated the group of "proficient" users of the MPFL in each of the three cohort groups from the overall group, for comparison purposes. Figure 3.11.7. shows, for pertinent questions in Sections 1 and 2 of Appendix A (General Background and Language Background), percentage responses or mean scores of both the total-group (all native English speakers in the group) and the "MPFL proficient" native English speakers from that group.

The "proficient" students, for all three cohort groups, were found to have had an appreciably greater amount of travel outside of the United States than the total groups. For the total cohort groups, 5.9, 64.3, and 60.9 percent of the freshmen, seniors, and two-year college students had "been in a country other than the United States," while 80.1, 90.6, and 81.1 percent of the "proficient" students had had this experience. Average time abroad was also considerably greater.

Much higher percentages of the "proficient" seniors and two-year college students reported that they had participated in an organized summer-abroad program (7.9 percent vs. 19.2 percent for senior; 8.8 vs. 14.5 percent for two-year). The percentage of MPFL-proficient freshmen who had had a summer abroad (3.4) was appreciably smaller than the corresponding total group figure (9.0), a finding that lacks satisfactory explanation at the present time, although it may simply be that freshmen had not yet had the opportunities. Participation in year-abroad programs was also much more frequently reported by the "proficient" students in all three groups: for freshmen 1.1 vs. 9.6 percent; seniors, 5.0 vs. 13.9 percent; and two-year college students, 1.2 vs. 2.8 percent.

Roughly equal percentages of the total and "proficient" groups had studied the MPFL in some kind of formal educational setting, but the amount of such study (as would be anticipated) was appreciably greater on the part of the latter group. The mean number of years of high school language study was 1.91, 2.07, and 1.70 for the total freshman, senior, and two-year college groups, and 3.08, 3.01, and 2.72 for the language-proficient students. At the college level, the differences were even more striking, the proficient freshmen reporting, on the average, 1.39 college foreign language courses, and the total group, only 0.30 courses. Proficient two-year college students took an average of 1.12 foreign language courses, compared to 0.52 courses for the total group.

By far the largest number of college foreign language courses was reported by the "proficient" seniors: an average of 5.83 courses, by comparison to 1.53 courses for the total senior group. This is probably due to the very large proportion of foreign language majors in the proficient group— 17.5 percent, compared to only 2.0 percent of the total seniors. The language-proficient freshmen also reported foreign languages as their intended major much more frequently (13.6 percent) than did the total freshman group (1.0 percent.)

In addition to the appreciably greater number of formal language courses reported by the "proficient" students, this group consistently showed a considerably higher level of contact with the MPFL in settings outside of the academic classroom. Contact through "family members speaking it" and "friend(s) or people in the neighborhood speaking it" was about two to three times more frequently reported by the "proficient" students than by the total group.

MPFL contact through "living abroad" was indicated by almost four out of ten of the language-proficient students in all three groups (39.1, 37.7, and 40.4 percent) as contrasted to the much lower total group percentages of 8.4, 11.5, and 13.4. Studying abroad was about six times more frequently reported by language-proficient freshmen than the total freshman group (20.7 vs. 3.4 percent), five times more frequently by language-proficient seniors (40.7 vs. 7.8 percent), and three times more often by proficient two-year college students.

The general profile of the MPFL-proficient student as outlined above rather clearly shows the appreciably greater amount of formal language study reported by these individuals, and also especially, considerably greater language contact opportunities outside of the regular classroom, including foreign travel and language-use opportunities offered by relatives and others in the student's immediate environment. Given both a considerably higher degree of self-reported competence in the MPFL by comparison to the larger cohort groups and correspondingly greater number of foreign language courses and other language contact opportunities, it could be considered an "acid test" of the contributions of developed language proficiency to increased "global understanding" to carry out the relevant comparisons on the MPFL-proficient students in the three cohort groups.

Examination of the mean total score on the Global Understanding Test obtained by the MPFL-proficient students (Figure 3.11.8.)shows scores that are not appreciably different from those of the total "native English speaking" groups or total study sample groups for any of the three student groups. The hypothesis that students "proficient" in a modern foreign language will show higher levels of knowledge does not appear to be upheld, on the basis of the results of the original total group analyses together with essentially similar results for the additional "native English speaker" and "threshold effect" analyses.

Figure 3.11.8. Mean Global Understanding Test Scores for Total Group and Language-Proficient Group

	Freshmen	Seniors	2-Year
Total Group	41.96	50.49	40.46
Language-Proficient Group	40.56	50.34	36.00

We conclude—on the basis of those data available to the study—that there is essentially no relationship between proficiency in a modern foreign language and the overall level of "global knowledge" on the part of current U.S. college freshmen, seniors, and two-year college students.

Part IV

Summary and Interpretations

Chapter 12

Global Understanding

Thomas S. Barrows

This chapter cannot possibly summarize what has been learned from the survey or even cover all of the results described in Part III. However, there are several major questions that the survey sought to answer, and interpretations may be organized around them.

What Is Global Understanding?

The range of possible answers to this question was limited at first by the initial definition adopted for the survey. Knowledge and affect were specified as broad, potential components of global understanding. Elaboration of the knowledge component proved to be a difficult intellectual task that required examination of numerous competing perspectives. A global issues approach was finally chosen because it encompassed and often required attention to competing dimensions of coverage. For example, ramifications of global issues are traceable across time, space, and social institutions, and they require multiple disciplinary perspectives for non-trivial understanding. In addition, the traditional approaches of international relations and area studies are incorporated easily into the issues approach. Environment, food, health, international monetary and trade arrangements, population, energy, race issues, relations among states, and distributions of natural characteristics were chosen as the topics for coverage. Facets of question content that were consciously varied included: U.S. and foreign perspectives, current and historical content, and varied geographic areas and disciplinary approaches.

Some reactions to the knowledge test have suggested that it is much too difficult and that much of its content cannot be expected to be known by college students. That impression misses the intent of the test—namely, to measure what *should* be known at a criterion level or to measure what *needs* to be known if global situations and processes are to be fully understood. Furthermore, when one considers the complexity of global issues, their historic roots and previous embodiments, and their attendant arrays of symptoms and interconnections throughout the world, it is not surprising to find content in the 101 test questions that looks novel and quite difficult for most of us. The knowledge required for global understanding is not common currency, and that fact may be reflected in reactions to the knowledge test as well as in students' performances on the test.

The affective component emerging from our work consists of attitudes toward five phenomena: chauvinism, war, world government, international cooperation, and human rights. Added to these are expressed interest in global developments and other cultures, and feelings of kinship with foreign peoples including being comfortable in their company and expressing empathy for them. These attitudes, interests, and feelings are interrelated to the extent that we may think of them as one component of global understanding with a moderate degree of internal consistency.

The two components, knowledge and affect, are themselves interrelated—students' responses in the knowledge and affect domains are correlated—to the extent that we may conceive of global understanding as a singular phenomenon or construct. While this two-component conception is very much like our original hypothesized definition, it has now survived empirical verification and is therefore more useful than purely rational definitions for describing the specific domain of behavior which we have called global understanding.

How "Globally Understanding" Are Students?

Each of the three groups of students surveyed fell short of achieving the criteria that were explicit or implicit in the survey's instruments. Seniors achieved an average score of only one half of the knowledge questions correct, while the average freshman and the average student at two-year institutions got only about 40 percent of them correct. Less than 15 percent of the seniors and less than 10 percent of the freshmen and two-year students got more than two-thirds correct. As noted above, the knowledge questions were designed to test knowledge necessary to global understanding. This suggests that a very small proportion of the students have the level of knowledge necessary for an adequate understanding of global situations and processes.

The meaning of the disappointing knowledge scores is elaborated profitably when we examine the results from specific questions or from groups of them. Questions on (1) Health, (2) Distribution of Natural Characteristics, (3) Art and Culture, and (4) Population elicited the highest levels of performance in that order, while questions on Energy, Relations Among States, and Religious Issues elicited the lowest levels of performance. Historical questions were answered with considerably less success than were questions having current content, and social science content generally proved easier than humanities content. These relationships between performance and question content were present in all three student groups.

Performances on 24 of the 101 items gave evidence of popular misconceptions held by able groups of students. All showed misconceptions in each of the three groups of students; six of these were concerned with current global affairs and drew able students in each group to the same wrong answer. Past and possible future consumption of fossil fuels, the current trend in population growth, and the general cause of malnutrition—topics of three of the questions—should be uniformly well known. Results show, however, that about 35 to 55 percent of the students hold common and obvious misconceptions and that these misinformed students are an above-average group.

It is more difficult to specify criterion levels of attitudes, feelings, and so forth than it is to specify criteria in the knowledge domain. In addition, scores obtained by summing responses to several attitude items are difficult to interpret, even though they are methodologically defensible and useful for relating attitudes to other variables. Attitude item responses obtained in the survey do indicate, however, that sizeable proportions of the three student populations have attitudes, feelings and perceptions that are unenlightened or unproductive from the perspective of global understanding, and attitudes are important because they may serve as "filters" in future information acquisition as well as indicators of students' continuing behavioral postures regarding global issues.

The Chauvinism Scale responses revealed that chauvinism—excessive patriotism—is a surprisingly popular sentiment. "I'm for my country, right or wrong" drew agreement from almost one-quarter of the freshmen and two-year students despite wording that emphasizes the "excessive" facet of chauvinism's definition. United States armed strength as the only insurance of peace drew over 30 percent agreement, illustrating the acceptability of militaristic strength that characterizes a number of Chauvinism Scale items.

World Government Scale responses revealed the general popularity of world government but also showed that about two-thirds of each student group do not favor giving up independence or national autonomy to supranational authority. These results may suggest confusion on the students' part; we wonder if an appreciation of the independence-interdependence relationship exists. The historic, cherished value of independence and national autonomy may be a powerful counterforce to the development of a knowledgeable, positive understanding of global interdependence.

War is viewed negatively in general, but exceptions occur to an appreciable extent where conditions that might justify war are specified. These include "maintenance of justice" and the elimination of an "oppressive government," suggesting, perhaps, that the purposes of and moral justifications for a war are more salient than the act of war itself. Human rights are viewed as basic rights and our proper concern when other governments restrict freedoms.

The Cooperation Scale included a set of items dealing with immigration of foreign persons to and foreign direct investments in the United States. The results indicate an alarmingly exclusionary attitude, but students appear to be more willing to help others when the United States is not specified as the agent or when helping others with problems of malnutrition is the proposed action.

The Concern Scale tapped interest in international developments and other cultures, and feelings of empathy and kinship with people from other nations and cultures. Generally about one-third of the students report that they do not have the desired interest or feelings, although specific item responses vary considerably from this one-third proportion. For example, about one in five students reported that they rarely read international news, while two in five reported that they do not acquire information "whenever possible." The kinship items yield the most disappointing results from this scale, with over half the students reporting that they do not have "a strong feeling of kinship with the world-wide human family" and over one-quarter indicating that they have "almost nothing in common with people in underdeveloped nations."

Generally speaking throughout the affective area, desirable responses—global understanding responses—attracted the majority of students. On the other hand, sizeable proportions in each student group chose less understanding responses; specific questions pointed out especially problematic areas such as an understanding of the interrelatedness of national autonomy and global interdependence and an inflated perception of the United States government's abilities to solve world problems.

Do Students' Characteristics/Backgrounds/Experiences Explain Their Varying Levels of Global Understanding?

From the outset of the study, it was hoped that variations in student characteristics and experiences would be associated with varying levels of global understanding. Although cause and effect would generally be impossible to establish, we hoped that some of the associations would suggest changes in the college experience that might serve to enhance global understanding.

A primary hypothesis in this regard grew from the commonly expressed opinion that foreign language study and proficiency are of considerable value to the student in developing a knowledge of and sensitiveness to countries and cultures other than his or her own. Considerable effort was expended developing the language proficiency and background measures necessary to assess this relationship, but exhaustive analyses of the resulting data revealed that there is no appreciable relationship between global knowledge as tested and either foreign language proficiency or extent of formal study, or informal study. On the other hand, the affective component of global understanding is associated with foreign language proficiency and language learning history to a moderate degree. Thus, there may be a causal or contributory relationship between foreign language and affect, though neither its necessity nor direction is assured. The language proficiency results also indicated that although language study is quite widespread, very few students have acquired a working proficiency in a foreign language. The discrepancy warrants the serious attention of the language teaching profession.

A second major conclusion is based upon an association observed repeatedly in the survey's results, that is, the association of the ways in which students acquire information with the knowledge and affect components of global understanding. Reading news articles, especially international news articles, in a newspaper and frequency of newspaper reading form a cluster of correlates of knowledge and affect scores that seems consistent and revealing. The relationships may indicate that international news in newspapers is the most informative source (electronic news was not related to knowledge or affect scores although television was the most frequent choice as the main source of information on current events) or that these articles are only turned to by persons whose interest and motivations are already high. The additional effort required by newspaper reading over passively responding to (or ignoring) the electronic media suggests the latter explanation, although it is not clearly superior.

By contrast, the lack of association between knowledge and course study is disappointing. Average knowledge scores did differ among the various academic majors, but these differences may not be unambiguously interpreted as curriculum effects. As expected, intellectual ability and socioeconomic status are highly related to knowledge test scores and self-selection into majors may well account for the observed score differences.

Finally, visiting other countries and time outside the United States are related to knowledge, affect, and foreign language variables. The pattern is not entirely consistent across the three student groups nor across all variables, but the relationship is replicated in enough situations to appear conclusive. Whether experience abroad leads to global understanding or globally understanding students travel is, of course, a question we cannot answer from the data in hand.

The small number of substantial relationships between experiences—especially educational experiences—and global understanding is disappointing in view of the prescriptive suggestions that were sought and might have been found in the survey data. For example, students reported the number of college courses they had taken in each of 19 areas that we thought might contribute to global understanding. The survey data indicated that study in these areas was not related to obtained knowledge or affect scores. Our disappointment with this result is mitigated, however, by the realization that very few courses in the areas were in fact reported by the students. The very rareness of the experiences renders it unlikely that they could have an overall effect, and our conclusions must accordingly be limited to what *was* effective rather than what experiences *could be* effective given greater student exposure. To cite one extreme instance, almost 95 percent of the seniors indicated that they had not taken any courses in archaeology, and less than 2 percent indicated that they had taken more than one. Given that distribution of experience with archaeology courses, it is most unlikely that archaeology could have had an effect.

Our perception of the college experience as deficient is not based solely on the numbers of students taking potentially enlightening courses but also upon students' reports of class discussions of global issues, irrespective of curricular area. Fewer than one in five students reported such discussions occurring on a daily basis, two-thirds reported them as occurring less than once a week or one or two times a week, and more than one in ten reported that they never occur. It is difficult to imagine that class discussion is entirely atypical of course content generally, and so it appears that most courses do not touch global issues frequently. In fact, students report more frequent discussion of global issues in their high school classes than in their college classes.

What Are The Implications Of This Project For The Future?

This project has provided national estimates of the levels of global understanding that describe freshmen, seniors, and two-year students in the United States. The estimates reveal deficits in knowledge and affect through comparisons with explicit criteria and reasonable implicit criteria. In addition, the survey has produced national estimates of foreign language proficiency that seem to call for similar attention from the higher education community.

The project has not provided suggestions of methods for improving upon current levels of global understanding because experiential correlates of global understanding were few, and those found were not suggestive of practical modifications to the college experience. Although it is disappointing, it is not unusual to find that naturally occurring program variation does not directly suggest program improvement strategies. In this situation it is necessary to look elsewhere for suggestions on how to improve effectiveness, and the Education and the World View Project provides several sources in its series of publications and in its task force recommendations. Series Nos. II, III, and IV should prove especially productive of suggestions.*

Changes in existing programs or the creation of new programs should be undertaken systematically. Institutional self-assessment can help review the needs of students on various campuses so that curricular change may be tailored accordingly. Studies of programs and their effects should also be carried out. Short versions of the survey instruments will be published by Educational Testing Service so that they may be used for both purposes. A forthcoming manual to accompany the instruments will describe methods for carrying out these studies. It will also provide national norms to aid score interpretation.

The full survey instruments will also be available should longitudinal research with 1979-80 as base year prove desirable. The full instruments and a data tape of the current survey responses will be made available to qualified researchers on request.

*Tonkin, Humphrey and Jane Edwards, *The World in the Curriculum: Curricular Strategies for the 21st Century*, New Rochelle, N.Y.: Change Magazine Press, 1981; E&WV Series II. *Education for a Global Century: Handbook of Exemplary International Programs*, New Rochelle, N.Y.: Change Magazine Press, 1981; E&WV Series III. *Education and the World View*, New Rochelle, N.Y.: Change Magazine Press, 1980; E&WV Series IV. In addition, see recommendations of the E&WV National Advisory Board, available from the Council on Learning.

Appendix A

Booklet A Item Responses

PART I – GENERAL BACKGROUND

			Distribution		
			Freshmen	Seniors	2-year
1.	Age:_____	mean:	19.4	23.4	25.0
	(in years)	s.d.*	4.2	4.6	10.6
		mode:	18.0	21.0	19.0
		min.:	17.0	18.0	17.0
		max.:	62.0	52.0	74.0

			Percent		
			Freshmen	Seniors	2-year
2.	Sex: Male female	Male:	43.8	48.7	39.8
		Female:	56.2	51.3	60.2

		Percent		
		Freshmen	Seniors	2-year
3. How would you describe yourself?				
1 American Indian, Eskimo, or Aleut		0.1	0.1	0.7
2 Black or Afro-American		7.8	6.7	11.4
3 Chicano or Mexican-American		2.2	0.9	3.9
4 Oriental, Filipino, or Asian-American		1.8	2.3	2.7
5 Puerto Rican, Cuban, or Hispanic		1.5	0.2	4.6
6 White or Caucasian		85.7	86.2	73.6
7 Other (Specify:_____)		0.9	3.5	3.1

		Percent		
		Freshmen	Seniors	2-year
4. Please circle the number in front of the region of the world in which you were born.				
1 North America		94.7	94.8	87.9
2 Central America		0.7	0.1	2.2
3 South America		0.6	0.3	2.1
4 Europe		0.8	2.3	3.1
5 Asia		1.8	1.8	3.0
6 Africa		0.3	0.4	0.4
7 Australia		----	----	----
8 Other (Specify:_____)		1.0	0.2	1.3

		Percent		
		Freshmen	Seniors	2-year
5. Were you born in the United States?				
1 YES		93.6	94.0	86.8
2 NO		6.4	6.0	13.2

* standard deviation

	Freshmen	Seniors	2-year

6. If you were _not_ born in the United States, please print the name of the country in which you were born.

	Freshmen	Seniors	2-year
	6.3	6.0	13.4

Distribution

	Freshmen	Seniors	2-year

7. If you were _not_ born in the United States, please indicate how old you were when you first came to the United States.

_____

(age in years)

	Freshmen	Seniors	2-year
mean:	11.3	10.7	11.5
s.d.:	7.5	9.1	7.3
mode:	1.0	1.0	8.0
min.:	1.0	1.0	1.0
max.:	25.0	47.0	53.0

Percent

	Freshmen	Seniors	2-year

8. If you were _not_ born in the United States, do you consider yourself a permanent resident of the United States?

	Freshmen	Seniors	2-year
1 YES	80.5	85.1	90.8
2 NO	19.5	14.9	9.2

Percent

	Freshmen	Seniors	2-year

9. Indicate the highest level of formal education completed by your father or male guardian.

	Freshmen	Seniors	2-year
1 None	0.5	0.1	0.7
2 Some grade school	2.1	2.5	5.2
3 Grade school	2.8	4.1	6.1
4 Some high school	8.8	7.9	12.1
5 High school diploma	24.1	22.8	21.5
6 Business or trade school	5.4	6.6	6.6
7 Some college	11.4	17.2	18.3
8 Bachelor's degree	18.5	17.6	10.0
9 Some graduate or professional school	4.8	3.2	4.3
10 Graduate or professional degree	21.6	17.9	15.3

		Percent		
		Freshmen	Seniors	2-year
10.	Indicate the highest level of formal education completed by your mother or female guardian.			
	1 None	0.5	0.4	1.3
	2 Some grade school	1.4	1.8	2.3
	3 Grade school	2.2	4.0	4.9
	4 Some high school	7.1	6.8	16.7
	5 High school diploma	35.1	36.5	33.5
	6 Business or trade school	7.2	9.6	6.9
	7 Some college	17.9	18.3	16.0
	8 Bachelor's degree	16.4	12.5	8.9
	9 Some graduate or professional school	5.2	3.4	3.6
	10 Graduate or professional degree	7.1	6.7	5.9

		Percent		
		Freshmen	Seniors	2-year
11.	What is your usual political party preference?			
	1 Democratic	37.8	40.6	42.8
	2 Republican	28.4	26.8	23.9
	3 Independent	13.6	20.2	15.5
	4 Other (Specify:_____)	1.7	3.7	3.2
	5 I don't know.	18.4	8.7	14.6

		Percent		
		Freshmen	Seniors	2-year
12.	What is the usual political party preference of your father or male guardian?			
	1 Democratic	38.7	38.2	43.1
	2 Republican	36.5	38.9	32.4
	3 Independent	6.6	7.4	4.2
	4 Other (Specify:_____)	1.1	1.0	1.9
	5 I don't know.	17.2	14.5	18.4

		Percent		
		Freshmen	Seniors	2-year
13.	What is the usual political party preference of your mother or female guardian?			
	1 Democratic	39.5	38.8	44.4
	2 Republican	33.7	35.8	31.2
	3 Independent	9.5	9.1	4.6
	4 Other (Specify:_____)	1.1	1.0	0.6
	5 I don't know.	16.3	15.3	19.1

14. Please indicate your general political attitudes by circling a number on the scale below. If you lean very strongly to the left or right, circle either 1 or 5 on the scale. If you lean somewhat to the left or right, circle 2 or 4. If you do not consider your political attitudes to be either left or right, circle 3.

	LEFT	1	2	3	4	5	RIGHT
% Freshmen		1.9	17.5	60.2	17.7	2.6	
% Seniors		2.3	28.7	42.8	23.5	2.7	
% 2-year		3.2	17.7	60.9	14.7	3.4	

15. How would you describe the political attitudes of your father or male guardian?

	LEFT	1	2	3	4	5	RIGHT
% Freshmen		3.2	12.8	45.2	30.8	7.9	
% Seniors		2.9	9.1	33.5	43.1	11.3	
% 2-year		5.1	10.8	49.7	26.2	8.2	

16. How would you describe the political attitudes of your mother or female guardian?

	LEFT	1	2	3	4	5	RIGHT
% Freshmen		2.7	14.6	52.5	24.8	5.4	
% Seniors		2.7	10.4	42.3	36.5	8.1	
% 2-year		2.9	10.1	59.6	22.3	5.1	

17. How many hours a week do you usually spend watching television?_____
(hours per week)

	Distribution		
	Freshmen	Seniors	2-year
mean:	9.9	10.4	12.0
s.d.:	9.5	8.9	9.8
mode:	10.0	10.0	10.0
min.:	0.0	0.0	0.0
max.:	90.0	75.0	81.0

18. Please rank the following world problems in order of importance. (Number from 1 to 10: 1 = most important; 10 = least important.)

		Median Rankings		
		Freshmen	Seniors	2-year
1	Malnutrition and inadequate health care	3.94	3.96	3.93
2	Nuclear and conventional arms proliferation	4.17	4.10	4.13
3	Depletion of natural resources	4.25	4.04	4.71
4	Inflation and unemployment	4.42	5.49	4.56
5	Denial of basic human rights	4.63	4.05	4.75
6	Air and water pollution	5.05	5.23	5.01
7	Overpopulation	6.38	5.65	5.72
8	Terrorism	6.53	6.87	6.50
9	Racial discrimination	7.01	7.01	6.82
10	Intergroup conflict	8.99	8.60	8.88

19. Which of the following world issues are you most interested in?
    (Please rank from 1 to 10: 1 = most interesting; 10 = least interesting).

		Median Rankings		
		Freshmen	Seniors	2-year
1	Depletion of natural resources	3.96	3.92	4.67
2	Denial of basic human rights	4.17	4.00	4.43
3	Inflation and unemployment	4.38	4.52	3.98
4	Nuclear and conventional arms proliferation	4.58	4.46	4.88
5	Malnutrition and inadequate health care	4.64	4.93	5.00
6	Air and water pollution	4.79	4.84	4.82
7	Racial discrimination	6.37	6.71	6.79
8	Terrorism	6.41	7.44	6.43
9	Overpopulation	7.14	6.70	6.20
10	Intergroup conflict	8.81	8.28	8.46

20. When you watch television, which of the following do you watch?

		Percent		
		Freshmen	Seniors	2-year
1	Detective/police adventures	36.8	28.4	40.3
2	Musical performances	32.3	30.7	35.4
3	Current events	50.8	54.6	50.9
4	Situation comedies	63.0	51.3	54.1
5	Dramatic series	36.5	35.0	32.3
6	Sports events	63.6	58.7	53.4
7	Movies	80.2	79.2	75.1
8	News	76.8	81.8	78.7
9	Game shows	23.9	17.3	22.4
10	Science specials	27.3	41.0	36.1
11	Talk shows	36.3	34.8	33.8
12	Specials about foreign countries and other cultures	19.3	28.0	35.2

21. How often do you watch world and national news on television?

		Percent		
		Freshmen	Seniors	2-year
1	Daily	14.5	25.1	31.1
2	5 times a week	14.4	14.3	10.4
3	3-4 times a week	27.4	27.7	28.4
4	1-2 times a week	27.8	18.8	18.0
5	Less than once a week	15.8	14.0	12.1

		Percent	
	Freshmen	Seniors	2-year

22. How often do you watch local news on television?

		Freshmen	Seniors	2-year
1	Daily	19.7	25.0	37.2
2	5-6 times a week	17.4	15.8	13.5
3	3-4 times a week	24.9	25.5	23.5
4	1-2 times a week	19.2	18.2	14.0
5	Less than once a week	18.9	15.5	11.7

		Percent	
	Freshmen	Seniors	2-year

23. How often do you listen to news broadcasts on the radio?

		Freshmen	Seniors	2-year
1	More than once a day	39.5	33.7	41.9
2	Once a day	22.0	23.5	21.2
3	Several times a week	23.2	25.4	22.1
4	About once a week	7.7	8.4	4.6
5	Less than once a week	7.5	9.0	10.1

24. Please read through the list of fictitious headlines below. If you had time to read only four (4) of the sixteen articles, which ones would you read?

		Percent of Students Selecting Article		
		Freshmen	Seniors	2-year
1	SOVIET JEWS DENIED EXIT VISAS	26.8	28.6	29.7
2	TEAM OF NEW YORK SURGEONS RE-ATTACH MAN'S SEVERED LEG	57.7	49.5	46.8
3	PRESIDENT THREATENS TO VETO APPRO-PRIATIONS BILL PASSED BY CONGRESS	14.3	12.9	22.0
4	STEELERS FAVORED TO WIN SUPER BOWL	24.9	17.5	16.6
5	MISSISSIPPI RIVER REACHES FLOOD STAGE	23.4	21.7	20.0
6	NEW COMPUTER TERMINAL "TALKS" AND "LISTENS"	40.0	38.1	44.5
7	PROFESSIONAL SOCCER DRAWING RECORD CROWDS	7.6	2.1	2.9
8	INDIAN GOVERNMENT STEPS UP VOLUNTARY STERILIZATION CAMPAIGN	26.7	39.6	29.4
9	ASTROPHYSICIST'S FINDINGS CAST LIGHT ON "BLACK HOLES"	43.0	46.7	45.1
10	SENATE COMMITTEE HEARS TESTIMONY ON CIVIL SERVICE REGULATIONS	8.0	11.7	9.6
11	U.S. BALANCE OF PAYMENTS GLOOMY	15.2	18.6	17.7
12	NEW LAND SPEED RECORD SET ON SALT FLATS	12.5	9.5	8.7
13	REFEREE TURNS McENROE-NASTASI MATCH OVER TO UMPIRE	9.3	9.9	7.7
14	PRESIDENT CONSIDERING WAGE-PRICE FREEZE	46.7	53.1	53.1
15	SALT II TALKS STALLED	26.9	27.8	29.9
16	U.S.-RUSSIAN WOMEN'S BASKETBALL PLAY-OFF EXPECTED IN OLYMPICS	12.6	10.3	8.0

	Percent		
	Freshmen	Seniors	2-year

25. How often do you read a newspaper?

		Freshmen	Seniors	2-year
1	Daily	29.8	35.9	41.5
2	5-6 times a week	13.2	9.8	10.1
3	3-4 times a week	20.5	23.4	19.5
4	1-2 times a week	21.7	19.9	19.5
5	Less than once a week	14.9	11.0	9.3

	Percent		
Freshmen	Seniors	2-year	

26. When you read a newspaper, which of the following do you usually read?

		Freshmen	Seniors	2-year
1	Sports section	54.2	44.0	35.6
2	Entertainment section	67.2	61.1	61.9
3	Local news articles	77.1	76.7	82.5
4	State news articles	49.7	61.4	58.4
5	National news articles	73.4	84.3	75.7
6	International news articles	59.9	69.7	62.7
7	Financial section	8.9	18.8	20.8
8	Home section	18.7	22.1	24.6
9	Editorials	33.4	34.7	38.2
10	Letters to the editor	29.5	31.4	33.5

	Percent		
Freshmen	Seniors	2-year	

27. Do you regularly read a newspaper that carries a good deal of international news? Circle any that you read.

		Freshmen	Seniors	2-year
1	The New York Times	17.2	17.2	12.5
2	The Los Angeles Times	2.3	3.9	26.5
3	The Chicago Sun-Times	4.6	4.6	10.2
4	The Washington Post	4.6	4.6	1.7
5	The St. Louis Post-Dispatch	1.2	0.3	3.9
6	The Wall Street Journal	9.0	15.0	9.3
7	The Christian Science Monitor	1.5	2.2	2.3
8	The International Herald Tribune	0.6	0.7	1.2
9	Other:_____	39.4	32.9	36.8

	Percent		
Freshmen	Seniors	2-year	

28. Do you regularly read a weekly news-magazine or newspaper? Circle any that you read.

		Freshmen	Seniors	2-year
1	Time	38.0	30.9	36.0
2	Newsweek	26.7	22.4	24.2
3	U.S. News and World Report	6.9	6.7	9.6
4	Business Week	1.4	3.1	3.8
5	Other (Specify:_____)	3.1	3.8	5.0

	Percent		
	Freshmen	Seniors	2-year

29. Which of the following do you consider the main source of the information you acquire concerning current events?

		Freshmen	Seniors	2-year
1	Newspapers	23.7	28.0	31.2
2	Magazines	6.0	7.3	6.0
3	Television	44.2	44.4	41.2
4	Radio	26.1	20.4	21.6

	Percent		
	Freshmen	Seniors	2-year

30. Do you regularly read a magazine devoted to a special interest (such as fashion, sports, photography, business, psychology, etc.)?

		Freshmen	Seniors	2-year
1	NO	41.5	38.4	34.9
2	YES (please list names of magazines)	58.5	61.6	65.0

	Distribution		
	Freshmen	Seniors	2-year

31. How many hours a week do you usually spend reading for pleasure?

	Freshmen	Seniors	2-year
mean:	6.0	6.8	7.7
s.d.:	6.0	5.7	7.2
mode:	5.0	5.0	10.0
min.:	0.0	0.0	0.0
max.:	70.0	50.0	99.0

	Percent		
	Freshmen	Seniors	2-year

32. What was your average grade in high school?

		Freshmen	Seniors	2-year
1	A to A-	32.8	35.0	15.3
2	B+ to B-	55.9	54.6	55.4
3	C+ to C-	10.9	10.4	28.4
4	D or below	0.4	0.4	0.9

33. Circle the total years of study you completed in <u>high school</u> (grades 9-12) in the following subject areas.

	no response	1	2	3	4 or more
1 English					
% Freshmen	0.8	0.2	1.1	12.9	85.0
% Seniors	1.3	1.1	4.9	18.5	74.2
% 2-year	2.7	0.7	6.2	20.4	70.0
2 Foreign Languages					
% Freshmen	18.9	17.3	32.3	17.3	14.3
% Seniors	15.8	14.6	33.4	19.6	16.6
% 2-year	25.7	18.8	28.7	13.0	13.8
3 Physical and Biological Sciences					
% Freshmen	1.3	6.5	25.6	28.4	38.3
% Seniors	1.7	8.7	25.9	30.2	33.4
% 2-year	6.6	17.9	36.7	20.7	18.1
4 Social Sciences					
% Freshmen	2.4	7.3	25.3	33.7	31.3
% Seniors	3.6	5.3	18.8	26.9	45.5
% 2-year	5.6	10.0	25.1	29.2	30.2

34. How often did you study or discuss world problems or issues in your <u>high school</u> classes?

	Percent		
	Freshmen	Seniors	2-year
1 At least once a day	29.1	19.6	30.3
2 Once or twice a week	50.2	54.2	45.0
3 Less than once a week	17.1	23.5	19.1
4 Never	3.6	2.8	5.6

35. To what extent did your <u>high school</u> experiences outside of the classroom contribute to your awareness of world issues?

	Percent		
	Freshmen	Seniors	2-year
1 A great deal	22.9	19.2	21.3
2 Some	43.5	36.3	40.4
3 A little	27.8	37.3	27.4
4 I don't know.	5.8	7.1	10.8

148

		Distribution		
		Freshmen	Seniors	2-year

36. If you took the SAT or ACT, approximately what were your scores?

			Freshmen	Seniors	2-year
1	SAT Verbal	mean:	517	547	485
		s.d.:	99	97	110
		min.:	250	250	230
		max.:	800	800	800
2	SAT Math	mean:	536	546	511
		s.d.:	106	112	114
		min.:	200	200	200
		max.:	800	800	800
3	ACT (composite)	mean:	22	23	19
		s.d.:	5	5	5
		min.:	1	8	6
		max.:	35	35	35

		Percent		
		Freshmen	Seniors	2-year

37. What is your approximate college grade point average (GPA)?

		Freshmen	Seniors	2-year
1	3.5-4.0	16.3	22.1	23.3
2	3.0-3.4	30.3	37.9	33.0
3	2.5-2.9	24.7	32.4	23.7
4	2.0-2.4	17.1	6.9	11.1
5	1.5-1.9	6.7	0.7	1.6
6	Less than 1.5	1.6	0.0	0.2
7	I don't know.	3.2	0.1	7.1

		Percent		
		Freshmen	Seniors	2-year

38. In what area of study is your major or intended major?

		Freshmen	Seniors	2-year
1	Agriculture	1.2	1.5	1.4
2	Art	4.4	2.9	2.3
3	Biological Sciences/Physical Sciences	17.7	14.4	13.0
4	Business/Accounting/Finance	18.4	20.3	22.5
5	Education	9.9	7.3	5.3
6	Engineering	8.1	7.8	7.4
7	English/Drama/Communications	8.0	6.6	5.7
8	Foreign Languages	1.0	2.1	2.5
9.	History	0.9	1.9	1.7
10	Mathematics	2.6	1.7	1.5
11	Music	2.4	2.2	1.8
12	Social Sciences	11.2	13.5	12.4
13	Vocational/Technical Training	1.4	6.2	10.3
14	Other (Specify:_____)	7.1	8.2	7.9
15	I don't know.	5.6	3.6	4.3

39. Indicate the total number of courses (one term or one semester) you have taken in college in each of the following subject areas.

	number of courses:	Percent of Freshmen				
		0	1	2	3	4 or more
1	American Studies	87.1	10.9	1.8	0.1	0.1
2	Anthropology	90.5	8.7	0.5	0.2	0.1
3	Archaeology	98.4	1.5	0.0	0.1	0.0
4	Classical Languages	96.3	2.9	0.5	0.2	0.1
5	Economics	81.6	14.2	3.9	0.1	0.2
6	Environmental Studies	88.8	8.5	2.9	0.1	0.3
7	Far Eastern Languages and Literature	98.5	1.3	0.2	0.0	0.0
8	Geography	89.6	10.1	0.3	0.0	0.0
9	History	56.0	31.1	11.3	1.1	0.5
10	International Relations	96.6	3.3	0.1	0.0	0.0
11	Journalism	92.6	5.2	1.1	0.6	0.5
12	Literature	52.7	31.1	13.3	1.9	1.0
13	Modern Foreign Languages	81.5	10.4	6.9	0.4	0.8
14	Near Eastern Languages and Literature	99.1	0.8	0.0	0.0	0.1
15	Philosophy	79.2	18.2	2.2	0.2	0.2
16	Political Science	78.2	17.7	3.3	0.7	0.1
17	Religion	90.5	7.0	1.6	0.6	0.3
18	Slavic Studies	99.1	0.8	0.1	0.0	0.0
19	Sociology	69.5	27.7	2.5	0.1	0.2

39.

	number of courses:	Percent of Seniors				
		0	1	2	3	4 or more
1	American Studies	60.6	18.0	14.8	3.1	3.5
2	Anthropology	70.8	21.9	5.3	0.7	1.3
3	Archaeology	94.7	4.1	1.1	0.1	0.0
4	Classical Languages	90.8	3.4	2.3	1.2	2.3
5	Economics	43.6	20.2	19.0	7.7	9.5
6	Environmental Studies	68.1	16.7	9.5	2.2	3.5
7	Far Eastern Languages and Literature	95.3	2.7	1.3	0.1	0.6
8	Geography	65.6	25.3	4.9	1.3	2.9
9	History	23.2	20.4	28.3	10.9	17.2
10	International Relations	83.5	11.3	3.7	0.6	0.9
11	Journalism	84.4	7.9	4.6	0.5	2.6
12	Literature	28.0	21.3	22.1	11.8	16.8
13	Modern Foreign Languages	53.8	13.5	11.6	6.5	14.6
14	Near Eastern Languages and Literature	97.5	1.5	0.7	0.2	0.1
15	Philosophy	53.0	28.7	11.5	4.4	2.4
16	Political Science	50.4	23.4	15.1	2.4	8.7
17	Religion	76.4	13.6	3.8	1.6	4.6
18	Slavic Studies	96.5	2.0	0.5	0.2	0.8
19	Sociology	32.6	38.6	11.4	8.6	8.8

150

39.	number of courses:	Percent of 2-year College Students				
		0	1	2	3	4 or more
1	American Studies	74.6	16.7	6.8	1.1	1.9
2	Anthropology	85.1	13.4	1.1	0.2	0.4
3	Archaeology	98.8	1.0	0.2	0.0	0.0
4	Classical Languages	93.8	3.9	1.7	0.2	0.4
5	Economics	69.9	19.1	9.7	0.8	0.5
6	Environmental Studies	82.7	13.4	2.3	0.7	0.9
7	Far Eastern Languages and Literature	98.0	1.0	0.7	0.0	0.3
8	Geography	83.6	13.3	2.4	0.3	0.4
9	History	51.5	29.5	11.5	3.2	4.3
10	International Relations	92.5	6.0	0.9	0.0	0.6
11	Journalism	88.3	8.0	2.8	0.5	0.4
12	Literature	54.0	23.2	12.9	2.7	7.2
13	Modern Foreign Languages	78.9	8.2	6.7	2.0	4.2
14	Near Eastern Languages and Literature	99.2	0.8	0.0	0.0	0.0
15	Philosophy	77.4	18.1	2.7	0.4	1.4
16	Political Science	69.7	23.2	4.5	1.2	1.4
17	Religion	90.4	6.7	1.6	0.4	0.9
18	Slavic Studies	99.2	0.6	0.2	0.0	0.0
19	Sociology	61.5	26.2	6.7	2.4	3.2

40. How often do you study or discuss world problems or issues in your college classes?	Percent		
	Freshmen	Seniors	2-year
1 At least once a day	13.8	18.4	21.1
2 Once or twice a week	40.2	39.2	41.1
3 Less than once a week	32.6	29.9	21.2
4 Never	13.4	12.5	16.5

41. To what extent have your college experiences outside of the class-room contributed to your awareness of world issues?	Percent		
	Freshmen	Seniors	2-year
1 A great deal	35.7	48.7	40.6
2 Some	39.6	36.6	41.2
3 A little	20.9	13.4	13.0
4 I don't know.	3.8	1.4	5.2

	Percent		
42. Please indicate which of the following courses, if any, you believe have contributed to your awareness of world problems or issues.	Freshmen	Seniors	2-year
1 American Studies	13.8	24.2	21.2
2 Anthropology	5.7	14.9	10.4
3 Archaeology	1.1	1.8	0.3
4 Classical Languages	1.1	1.7	1.5
5 Economics	22.7	45.1	31.1
6 Environmental Studies	9.0	19.0	13.5
7 Far Eastern Languages and Literature	1.1	1.4	0.9
8 Geography	10.6	19.2	17.3
9 History	39.0	54.8	43.9
10 International Studies	6.8	14.1	9.4
11 Journalism	6.4	7.7	8.7
12 Literature	15.8	17.7	15.2
13 Modern Foreign Languages	8.4	15.4	8.7
14 Near Eastern Languages and Literature	0.5	1.1	0.3
15 Philosophy	9.1	18.3	13.9
16 Political Science	24.2	38.7	30.6
17 Religion	8.2	12.4	10.9
18 Slavic Studies	0.5	1.8	0.9
19 Sociology	26.8	41.7	31.0
20 Other (Specify:_____)	11.3	9.4	11.1

	Percent		
43. Circle the number in front of each activity in which you participated while in high school or college	Freshmen	Seniors	2-year
1 Athletics (interscholastic, intramural, or community)	77.2	68.0	56.6
2 Ethnic activities or organizations	12.2	12.7	12.1
3 Journalism, debating, literary, or dramatic activities	35.3	34.6	26.4
4 Art, music, or dance	51.8	49.6	48.5
5 Preprofessional or departmental clubs	30.5	45.7	20.9
6 Religious activities or organizations	39.5	34.6	26.0
7 Fraternities or sororities	12.1	17.8	5.6
8 Community organizations	35.4	31.2	20.2
9 Student government	32.5	29.5	20.3
10 Other (Specify:_____)	11.1	11.4	6.0

	Percent		
	Freshmen	Seniors	2-year
44. What is your current (immediate) educational objective?			
1 Nondegree study	2.1	0.3	7.4
2 Certificate	1.1	0.1	3.1
3 Two-year degree (A.A., A.S., A.A.S.)	3.0	0.6	45.4
4 Four-year degree (B.A., B.S.)	93.8	99.0	44.1

	Percent		
	Freshmen	Seniors	2-year
45. What is your eventual (long-term) educational goal?			
1 Nondegree study	0.5	0.7	3.8
2 Certificate	0.9	2.0	0.8
3 Two-year degree (A.A., A.S., A.A.S.)	1.2	0.0	8.4
4 Four-year degree (B.A., B.S.)	36.5	24.7	38.4
5 Master's degree (M.A., M.S., M.Ed.)	37.7	48.5	29.3
6 Doctoral degree (Ph.D., Ed.D., D.D.)	10.8	13.6	12.2
7 Law degree (LL.D., J.D.)	5.9	7.8	4.2
8 Medical degree (M.D., D.D.S.)	6.4	2.7	4.9

	Percent		
	Freshmen	Seniors	2-year
46. Have you ever been in a country other than the United States?			
1 YES	57.9	64.3	60.9
2 NO	42.1	35.7	39.1

47. *Please see pages 154-157 for this data.*

	Percent		
	Freshmen	Seniors	2-year
48. Was the majority of your time abroad spent in military service?			
1 YES	4.4	5.1	6.0
2 NO	95.6	94.9	94.0

47. Please use the following codes to indicate the total length of time you
    have spent in each of the geographic areas listed below. Write in a code
    number for each separate area on the line to the left of the area desig-
    nation. For example, if you spent three weeks in France, two weeks in
    England, and a week in Ireland, you would write: ___2___ The British
    Isles; ___2___ Europe. Leave blank those areas you have not visited.

	omit	less than 2 weeks	2-4 weeks	1-2 months	3-6 months	7-12 months	1-2 years	3-4 years	5 years or more
	0	1	2	3	4	5	6	7	8
1. Canada									
% Freshmen	63.8	21.6	9.3	2.8	1.0	0.4	0.6	0.2	0.3
% Seniors	56.8	24.2	12.1	3.8	0.3	1.0	0.8	0.2	0.8
% 2-year	69.2	18.1	9.4	2.2	0.3	0.1	0.5	0.0	0.3
2. Mexico									
% Freshmen	79.0	13.8	5.4	1.1	0.2	0.0	0.2	0.0	0.2
% Seniors	72.9	18.0	6.2	1.4	0.5	0.4	0.3	0.1	0.2
% 2-year	71.3	16.2	8.1	2.1	1.5	0.1	0.3	0.1	0.4
3. The Caribbean									
% Freshmen	93.2	3.4	2.1	0.4	0.0	0.2	0.4	0.1	0.2
% Seniors	90.7	4.4	2.9	0.7	0.9	0.0	0.1	0.2	0.2
% 2-year	90.2	4.2	2.6	0.6	0.2	0.1	0.0	0.2	1.9
4. Central America									
% Freshmen	97.7	0.4	0.2	0.6	0.1	0.2	0.0	0.8	0.1
% Seniors	98.2	0.7	0.2	0.3	0.3	0.0	0.2	0.0	0.0
% 2-year	96.4	0.9	0.7	0.8	0.0	0.0	0.2	0.0	1.0
5. South America									
% Freshmen	97.7	0.9	0.3	0.1	0.2	0.0	0.0	0.1	0.7
% Seniors	96.6	1.5	0.4	0.5	0.3	0.2	0.3	0.0	0.3
% 2-year	97.0	0.6	0.4	0.3	0.1	0.0	0.0	0.0	1.7

	omit	less than 2 weeks	2-4 weeks	1-2 months	3-6 months	7-12 months	1-2 years	3-4 years	5 years or more
	0	1	2	3	4	5	6	7	8

6. Scandinavia

% Freshmen	97.6	0.7	0.5	0.5	0.3	0.1	0.1	0.0	0.0
% Seniors	96.3	2.0	0.9	0.1	0.6	0.0	0.1	0.0	0.0
% 2-year	96.8	1.9	0.6	0.5	0.0	0.0	0.1	0.0	0.0

7. The British Isles

% Freshmen	93.6	3.7	1.4	0.2	0.5	0.0	0.0	0.4	0.0
% Seniors	88.0	6.2	2.8	0.5	0.0	0.6	0.3	0.0	0.1
% 2-year	89.2	4.3	2.3	0.9	1.1	0.0	0.3	0.5	1.3

8. Europe

% Freshmen	85.3	2.9	3.7	2.9	1.4	1.2	1.2	0.9	0.5
% Seniors	75.0	2.8	7.7	2.7	2.9	1.7	3.1	2.4	1.7
% 2-year	80.4	3.0	4.9	4.6	2.9	1.3	1.3	0.6	0.9

9. The Soviet Union

% Freshmen	99.1	0.3	0.5	0.0	0.0	0.0	0.0	0.0	0.0
% Seniors	99.0	0.6	0.3	0.0	0.1	0.0	0.0	0.0	0.0
% 2-year	99.9	0.0	0.1	0.0	0.0	0.0	0.0	0.0	0.0

10. Africa

% Freshmen	97.9	0.8	0.2	0.3	0.0	0.0	0.1	0.2	0.4
% Seniors	97.4	1.7	0.0	0.2	0.1	0.1	0.1	0.0	0.4
% 2-year	98.7	0.9	0.2	0.0	0.0	0.0	0.0	0.0	0.2

11. Israel

% Freshmen	98.5	0.0	0.0	0.7	0.3	0.0	0.0	0.0	0.4
% Seniors	98.9	0.7	0.2	0.2	0.1	0.0	0.0	0.0	0.0
% 2-year	96.4	0.7	0.9	1.2	0.8	0.0	0.0	0.0	0.1

	omit	less than 2 weeks	2-4 weeks	1-2 months	3-6 months	7-12 months	1-2 years	3-4 years	5 years or more
	0	1	2	3	4	5	6	7	8

12. The Middle East

	0	1	2	3	4	5	6	7	8
% Freshmen	99.5	0.0	0.0	0.1	0.0	0.0	0.1	0.0	0.3
% Seniors	97.5	1.8	0.1	0.0	0.2	0.3	0.0	0.0	0.1
% 2-year	97.1	0.2	1.1	0.0	0.0	0.0	0.1	0.0	1.4

13. India

	0	1	2	3	4	5	6	7	8
% Freshmen	100.0	0.0	0.0	0.0	0.0	0.0	0.0	0.0	0.0
% Seniors	99.6	0.4	0.0	0.0	0.0	0.0	0.0	0.0	0.0
% 2-year	99.1	0.6	0.0	0.0	0.0	0.0	0.3	0.0	0.0

14. China

	0	1	2	3	4	5	6	7	8
% Freshmen	99.3	0.1	0.4	0.1	0.0	0.0	0.1	0.0	0.0
% Seniors	99.2	0.1	0.0	0.2	0.0	0.0	0.0	0.0	0.4
% 2-year	99.2	0.5	0.3	0.0	0.0	0.0	0.0	0.0	0.0

15. Korea

	0	1	2	3	4	5	6	7	8
% Freshmen	99.1	0.3	0.0	0.1	0.0	0.0	0.0	0.1	0.4
% Seniors	99.0	0.3	0.2	0.0	0.3	0.0	0.2	0.0	0.0
% 2-year	99.4	0.1	0.0	0.0	0.1	0.2	0.2	0.0	0.0

16. The Philippines

	0	1	2	3	4	5	6	7	8
% Freshmen	98.4	0.5	0.5	0.1	0.0	0.1	0.0	0.2	0.2
% Seniors	97.6	0.8	0.1	0.0	0.3	0.1	0.9	0.0	0.0
% 2-year	98.3	0.2	0.2	0.0	0.1	0.0	0.8	0.1	0.2

17. Southeast Asia

	0	1	2	3	4	5	6	7	8
% Freshmen	99.4	0.3	0.0	0.0	0.0	0.1	0.0	0.0	0.2
% Seniors	97.3	0.7	0.1	0.1	0.0	0.4	0.9	0.2	0.3
% 2-year	98.8	0.0	0.0	0.1	0.0	0.3	0.4	0.0	0.3

18. Japan

	0	1	2	3	4	5	6	7	8
% Freshmen	97.2	1.4	0.2	0.3	0.0	0.0	0.2	0.3	0.3
% Seniors	96.3	1.1	0.7	0.0	0.5	0.1	1.0	0.1	0.2
% 2-year	97.0	1.4	0.1	0.1	0.2	0.0	0.8	0.0	0.5

	omit	less than 2 weeks	2-4 weeks	1-2 months	3-6 months	7-12 months	1-2 years	3-4 years	5 years or more
	0	1	2	3	4	5	6	7	8

19. Australia;
   New Zealand

	omit	less than 2 weeks	2-4 weeks	1-2 months	3-6 months	7-12 months	1-2 years	3-4 years	5 years or more
% Freshmen	99.7	0.0	0.2	0.0	0.0	0.1	0.0	0.0	0.0
% Seniors	99.3	0.2	0.2	0.2	0.0	0.0	0.0	0.0	0.0
% 2-year	98.9	0.7	0.2	0.1	0.0	0.0	0.0	0.1	0.0

20. Other
   Countries

	omit	less than 2 weeks	2-4 weeks	1-2 months	3-6 months	7-12 months	1-2 years	3-4 years	5 years or more
% Freshmen	97.5	1.1	0.1	0.2	0.0	0.2	0.7	0.0	0.3
% Seniors	97.2	1.0	0.4	0.4	0.5	0.0	0.1	0.4	0.1
% 2-year	97.5	1.3	0.5	0.2	0.3	0.0	0.0	0.2	0.0

	Percent		
	Freshmen	Seniors	2-year

49. Have you ever participated in an organized _summer-abroad_ program?

	Freshmen	Seniors	2-year
1 YES	9.0	7.9	8.8
2 NO	91.0	92.1	91.2

	Percent		
	Freshmen	Seniors	2-year

50. Have you ever participated in an organized _year-abroad_ program?

	Freshmen	Seniors	2-year
1 YES	1.1	5.0	1.2
2 NO	98.9	95.0	98.8

	Percent		
	Freshmen	Seniors	2-year

51. Have you ever been in the Peace Corps or in any other program involving similar kinds of service abroad?

	Freshmen	Seniors	2-year
1 YES	0.1	1.2	0.7
2 NO	99.1	98.8	99.3

PART II - LANGUAGE BACKGROUND

	Percent		
	Freshmen	Seniors	2-year

1. What is your native language?

	Freshmen	Seniors	2-year
1 Arabic	0.6	0.2	0.0
2 Chinese	0.2	0.7	0.6
3 English	94.2	96.4	89.4
4 Farsi	0.3	0.0	0.6
5 French	0.2	0.0	0.2
6 German	0.5	0.3	0.0
7 Greek	0.0	0.0	0.0
8 Hebrew	0.4	0.0	0.0
9 Italian	0.2	0.0	0.0
10 Japanese	0.3	0.0	0.4
11 Polish	0.0	0.1	0.0
12 Portuguese	0.2	0.0	0.0
13 Russian	0.0	0.0	0.1
14 Spanish	1.8	1.0	5.6
15 Other (Specify:_____)	0.8	1.2	2.8
16 I don't know	0.2	0.0	0.2

		Percent		
		Freshmen	Seniors	2-year
2.	What is your father's native language?			
1	Arabic	0.8	0.2	0.0
2	Chinese	0.4	0.7	0.7
3	English	87.0	89.9	80.9
4	Farsi	0.3	0.1	0.6
5	French	0.6	0.3	0.6
6	German	1.6	1.2	3.3
7	Greek	0.5	0.0	0.0
8	Hebrew	0.0	0.0	0.0
9	Italian	1.2	0.3	0.7
10	Japanese	0.2	0.0	0.4
11	Polish	0.6	0.7	0.4
12	Portuguese	0.2	0.0	0.0
13	Russian	0.1	0.2	0.0
14	Spanish	3.3	2.0	7.8
15	Other (Specify:_____)	3.1	4.1	4.4
16	I don't know	0.2	0.2	0.2

		Percent		
		Freshmen	Seniors	2-year
3.	What is your mother's native language?			
1	Arabic	0.6	0.2	0.0
2	Chinese	0.4	0.7	0.6
3	English	87.4	86.8	79.7
4	Farsi	0.3	0.0	0.6
5	French	0.8	1.2	1.1
6	German	1.3	2.4	1.5
7	Greek	0.0	0.2	0.0
8	Hebrew	0.0	0.0	1.2
9	Italian	1.3	0.8	1.2
10	Japanese	0.7	1.3	0.4
11	Polish	1.2	0.9	0.4
12	Portuguese	0.2	0.3	0.0
13	Russian	0.2	0.1	0.1
14	Spanish	3.2	2.3	8.2
15	Other (Specify:_____)	2.3	2.7	4.8
16	I don't know	0.2	0.0	0.2

		Percent		
		Freshmen	Seniors	2-year
4.	Have you ever studied Classical Greek?			
1	YES	5.6	5.8	5.3
2	NO	94.4	94.2	94.7

	Percent		
	Freshmen	Seniors	2-year

5. Have you ever studied Latin?

		Freshmen	Seniors	2-year
1	YES	13.4	15.9	12.7
2	NO	86.6	84.1	87.3

	Percent		
	Freshmen	Seniors	2-year

6. Have you ever studied a modern language other than your native language?

		Freshmen	Seniors	2-year
1	YES	78.1	89.9	73.2
2	NO	21.9	10.1	26.8

Note: Responses reported for questions 7-20 are percentages of students who responded positively to question 6.

	Percent		
	Freshmen	Seniors	2-year

7. Did you study a modern foreign language in elementary or secondary school?

		Freshmen	Seniors	2-year
1	YES	91.5	89.3	81.2
2	NO	8.5	10.7	18.8

	Percent		
	Freshmen	Seniors	2-year

8. Please circle the number in front of each modern foreign language that you studied in elementary or secondary school.

		Freshmen	Seniors	2-year
1	English (as a foreign language)	3.1	1.8	8.3
2	French	36.4	41.1	30.7
3	German	15.9	13.3	7.9
4	Hebrew	3.8	0.9	1.7
5	Italian	1.4	0.7	1.2
6	Russian	1.3	1.3	0.9
7	Spanish	57.5	50.2	48.1
8	Other (Specify:_____)	1.8	1.5	2.9

	Percent		
	Freshmen	Seniors	2-year

9. Have you studied a modern foreign language in college?

		Freshmen	Seniors	2-year
1	YES	27.3	54.8	39.5
2	NO	72.7	45.2	60.5

	Percent		
	Freshmen	Seniors	2-year

10. Please circle the code number in front of each modern foreign language that you studied in college.

		Freshmen	Seniors	2-year
1	English (as a foreign language)	1.4	1.8	5.9
2	French	9.2	19.7	15.2
3	German	4.0	15.8	4.1
4	Hebrew	0.8	0.4	1.0
5	Italian	0.9	2.4	0.7
6	Russian	1.2	2.1	2.5
7	Spanish	11.0	24.5	16.7
8	Other (Specify:_____)	1.3	2.7	2.6

	Percent		
	Freshmen	Seniors	2-year

11. Please circle the number in front of any language that you speak, read, or write. Circle all that apply.

		Freshmen	Seniors	2-year
1	Arabic	0.3	0.5	1.9
2	Chinese	1.0	1.8	0.6
3	English	62.2	60.0	65.0
4	Farsi	0.2	0.4	1.1
5	French	25.4	26.3	24.5
6	German	13.4	15.3	9.4
7	Greek	0.6	0.8	0.2
8	Hebrew	3.1	0.9	4.1
9	Italian	2.2	3.5	2.7
10	Japanese	1.8	1.0	2.3
11	Polish	0.5	0.8	1.4
12	Portuguese	0.7	0.8	0.2
13	Russian	1.5	2.4	2.3
14	Spanish	45.0	35.6	42.8
15	Other (Specify:_____)	3.0	3.1	6.2

161

	Percent		
	Freshmen	Seniors	2-year

12. Please circle the code number in front of the language you consider your "most proficient" foreign language. Circle only one.

		Freshmen	Seniors	2-year
1	Arabic	0.0	0.1	0.0
2	Chinese	0.4	0.7	0.0
3	English	3.1	2.4	9.1
4	Farsi	0.1	0.1	0.0
5	French	26.4	30.5	24.8
6	German	12.1	17.7	7.0
7	Greek	0.3	0.1	0.3
8	Hebrew	0.4	0.2	3.1
9	Italian	1.2	1.5	0.8
10	Japanese	0.2	0.6	1.7
11	Polish	0.0	0.7	0.2
12	Portuguese	0.5	0.1	0.0
13	Russian	1.2	1.8	1.0
14	Spanish	52.6	42.6	49.5
15	Other (Specify:_____)	1.5	1.1	2.4

Note: In questions 13-20, "MPFL" stands for "most proficient foreign language."

	Percent		
	Freshmen	Seniors	2-year

13. Did you study your MPFL in any kind of formal educational setting (i.e., elementary or secondary school, college, Hebrew school, Alliance Francaise, Goethe House, Berlitz, etc.)?

		Freshmen	Seniors	2-year
1	YES	88.1	90.0	80.9
2	NO	11.9	10.0	19.1

	Percent		
	Freshmen	Seniors	2-year

14. Did you acquire any of your MPFL ability from experience other than formal education? Circle all that apply.

		Freshmen	Seniors	2-year
1	Family members speaking it	14.0	11.9	18.7
2	Friend(s) or people in the neighborhood speaking it	21.9	19.4	26.8
3	Living abroad	8.4	11.5	13.4
4	Studying abroad	3.4	7.8	8.6
5	Other (Specify:_____)	7.9	6.7	9.2

15. If you studied your MPFL in elementary school, secondary school, or college, circle the number in front of each grade level at which you studied the language. Circle all that apply.

		Percent		
		Freshmen	Seniors	2-year
1	First grade	4.1	3.1	4.7
2	Second grade	4.6	3.3	6.2
3	Third grade	6.3	4.4	8.0
4	Fourth grade	6.4	8.0	10.8
5	Fifth grade	7.7	9.1	11.5
6	Sixth grade	13.8	10.5	13.9
7	Seventh grade	29.5	21.7	20.9
8	Eighth grade	33.2	25.6	22.8
9	Ninth grade	59.8	50.0	45.7
10	Tenth grade	61.2	55.4	51.4
11	Eleventh grade	41.5	46.2	37.3
12	Twelfth grade	23.5	25.9	23.7
13	College freshman	21.9	26.8	23.4
14	College sophomore	1.0	27.1	16.4
15	College junior	0.3	18.3	4.5
16	College senior	0.2	17.1	1.3

16. If you studied your MPFL in high school and/or college, please indicate what grade, on the average, you received in your MPFL course(s).

		Percent		
		Freshmen	Seniors	2-year
1	A to A-	46.9	41.2	30.6
2	B to B-	32.8	39.2	46.2
3	C to C-	18.0	15.5	18.8
4	Below C-	1.4	2.9	2.6
5	I don't know	0.9	1.2	1.9

17. Please use the scale below to indicate the emphasis of the instruction you received in formal courses in your MPFL. If the courses you took strongly emphasized learning rules of grammar and vocabulary, circle 1 on the scale. If your courses strongly emphasized listening and speaking, circle 5 on the scale. If your instruction was about equally divided, circle 3. Use 2 or 4 to indicate a moderate emphasis in one direction or the other.

Grammar-translation approach (mastery of rules of grammar and vocabulary)

Audio-lingual approach (emphasizing listening and speaking)

	1	2	3	4	5
% Freshmen	11.1	29.6	46.1	9.4	3.9
% Seniors	16.4	25.7	41.3	12.3	4.3
% 2-year	11.8	23.2	49.5	11.3	4.2

18. Listed below are a number of "can do" statements about speaking ability in the MPFL. Please read each description carefully and circle the appropriate number to indicate whether, at the present time, you would be able to carry out each task "quite easily" (1), "with some difficulty" (2), or "with great difficulty or not at all" (3). Circle only one response for each task.

Percent of Freshmen

		Quite Easily	With Some Difficulty	With Great Difficulty or Not at All
a)	Say the days of the week	62.6	24.7	12.7
b)	Count to 10 in the language	92.5	6.7	0.8
c)	Give the current date (month, day, year)	56.9	29.7	13.5
d)	Order a simple meal in a restaurant	37.6	37.6	24.7
e)	Ask for directions on the street	31.1	37.6	31.3
f)	Buy clothes in a department store	26.6	38.8	34.6
g)	Introduce myself in social situations, and use appropriate greetings and leave-taking expressions	48.4	29.5	22.1
h)	Give simple biographical information about myself (place of birth, composition of family, early schooling, etc.)	34.1	33.5	32.4
i)	Talk about my favorite hobby at some length, using appropriate vocabulary.	11.5	30.4	58.1
j)	Describe my present job, studies, or other major life activities accurately and in detail	13.4	25.8	60.9
k)	Tell what I plan to be doing 5 years from now, using appropriate future tenses	11.7	22.9	65.4
l)	Describe the United States educational system in some detail	5.2	19.5	75.2
m)	State and support with examples and reasons a position on a controversial topic (for example, birth control, nuclear safety, environmental pollution)	3.5	11.6	84.9
n)	Describe the role played by Congress in the United States government system	2.7	11.3	86.0

19. Regardless of how well you currently speak the MPFL, please answer each of the following in terms of your present level of <u>listening comprehension</u> in the language. Circle only <u>one</u> response for each task.

<u>Percent of Freshmen</u>

		Quite Easily	*With Some Difficulty*	*With Great Difficulty or Not at All*
a)	Understand very simple statements or questions in the language ("Hello," "How are you?", "What is your name?", "Where do you live?", etc.)	93.4	6.0	0.6
b)	In face-to-face conversation, understand a native speaker who is speaking slowly and carefully (i.e., deliberately adapting his or her speech to suit me)	56.3	35.1	8.6
c)	On the telephone, understand a native speaker who is speaking to me slowly and carefully (i.e., deliberately adapting his or her speech to suit me)	41.8	39.4	18.8
d)	In face-to-face conversation with a native speaker who is speaking slowly and carefully to me, tell whether the speaker is referring to past, present or future events	36.8	37.8	25.3
e)	In face-to-face conversation, understand a native speaker who is speaking to me as quickly and as colloquially as he or she would to another native speaker	7.7	24.4	67.9
f)	Understand movies without subtitles	9.1	32.8	58.0
g)	Understand news broadcasts on the radio	5.5	24.5	70.0
h)	On the radio, understand the words of a popular song I have not heard before	6.1	27.7	66.2
i)	Understand play-by-play descriptions of sports events (for example, a soccer match) on the radio	6.0	18.2	75.9
j)	Understand two native speakers when they are talking rapidly with one another	4.8	14.2	80.9
k)	On the telephone, understand a native speaker who is talking as quickly and as colloquially as he or she would to another native speaker	4.6	12.0	83.4

20. Please answer each of the following in terms of your present level of reading proficiency in the MPFL. Circle only one response for each task.

		Quite Easily	*With Some Difficulty*	*With Great Difficulty or Not at All*
a)	Read personal letters or notes written to me in which the writer has deliberately used simple words and constructions	63.0	27.9	9.1
b)	Read, on store fronts, the type of store or the services provided (for example, "dry cleaning," "book store," "butcher," etc.)	62.3	29.6	8.1
c)	Understand newspaper headlines	46.5	36.0	17.5
d)	Read personal letters and notes written as they would be to a native speaker	18.9	37.7	43.4
e)	Read and understand magazine articles at a level similar to those found in *Time* or *Newsweek*, without using a dictionary	6.7	29.4	63.9
f)	Read popular novels without using a dictionary	4.9	17.8	77.3
g)	Read newspaper "want ads" with comprehension, even when many abbreviations are used	7.0	16.2	76.8
h)	Read highly technical material in a particular academic or professional field with no use or only very infrequent use of a dictionary	1.6	7.9	90.6

18. Listed below are a number of "can do" statements about speaking ability in the MPFL. Please read each description carefully and circle the appropriate number to indicate whether, at the present time, you would be able to carry out each task "quite easily" (1), "with some difficulty" (2), or "with great difficulty or not at all" (3). Circle only one response for each task.

<u>Percent of Seniors</u>

		Quite Easily	With Some Difficulty	With Great Difficulty or Not at All
a)	Say the days of the week	56.5	28.9	14.5
b)	Count to 10 in the language	93.1	5.7	1.1
c)	Give the current date (month, day, year)	49.3	33.9	16.8
d)	Order a simple meal in a restaurant	33.4	36.3	30.3
e)	Ask for directions on the street	31.1	33.3	35.6
f)	Buy clothes in a department store	26.2	28.6	45.2
g)	Introduce myself in social situations, and use appropriate greetings and leave-taking expressions	45.4	31.5	23.1
h)	Give simple biographical information about myself (place of birth, composition of family, early schooling, etc.)	29.8	30.7	39.5
i)	Talk about my favorite hobby at some length, using appropriate vocabulary.	11.8	22.2	66.1
j)	Describe my present job, studies, or other major life activities accurately and in detail	12.1	22.5	65.4
k)	Tell what I plan to be doing 5 years from now, using appropriate future tenses	10.6	19.0	70.4
l)	Describe the United States educational system in some detail	7.2	16.3	23.5
m)	State and support with examples and reasons a position on a controversial topic (for example, birth control, nuclear safety, environmental pollution)	5.0	10.2	84.7
n)	Describe the role played by Congress in the United States government system	3.5	10.4	86.2

19. Regardless of how well you currently speak the MPFL, please answer each of the following in terms of your present level of <u>listening comprehension</u> in the language. Circle only <u>one</u> response for each task.

		Percent of Seniors		
		Quite Easily	*With Some Difficulty*	*With Great Difficulty or Not at All*
a)	Understand very simple statements or questions in the language ("Hello," "How are you?", "What is your name?", "Where do you live?", etc.)	88.9	9.3	1.7
b)	In face-to-face conversation, understand a native speaker who is speaking slowly and carefully (i.e., deliberately adapting his or her speech to suit me)	48.7	36.6	14.7
c)	On the telephone, understand a native speaker who is speaking to me slowly and carefully (i.e., deliberately adapting his or her speech to suit me)	37.5	31.9	30.6
d)	In face-to-face conversation with a native speaker who is speaking slowly and carefully to me, tell whether the speaker is referring to past, present or future events	33.4	34.8	31.8
e)	In face-to-face conversation, understand a native speaker who is speaking to me as quickly and as colloquially as he or she would to another native speaker	7.8	23.8	68.4
f)	Understand movies without subtitles	9.2	27.5	63.3
g)	Understand news broadcasts on the radio	7.3	23.2	69.4
h)	On the radio, understand the words of a popular song I have not heard before	5.4	26.6	68.0
i)	Understand play-by-play descriptions of sports events (for example, a soccer match) on the radio	5.9	15.7	78.4
j)	Understand two native speakers when they are talking rapidly with one another	6.1	14.5	79.4
k)	On the telephone, understand a native speaker who is talking as quickly and as colloquially as he or she would to another native speaker	5.4	11.3	83.3

20. Please answer each of the following in terms of your present level of reading proficiency in the MPFL. Circle only one response for each task.

		Percent of Seniors		
		Quite Easily	*With Some Difficulty*	*With Great Difficulty or Not at All*
a)	Read personal letters or notes written to me in which the writer has deliberately used simple words and constructions	55.4	29.8	14.8
b)	Read, on store fronts, the type of store or the services provided (for example, "dry cleaning," "book store," "butcher," etc.)	53.8	33.2	13.0
c)	Understand newspaper headlines	41.1	40.6	18.3
d)	Read personal letters and notes written as they would be to a native speaker	17.1	34.2	48.8
e)	Read and understand magazine articles at a level similar to those found in *Time* or *Newsweek*, without using a dictionary	9.4	21.5	69.1
f)	Read popular novels without using a dictionary	6.7	12.6	80.7
g)	Read newspaper "want ads" with comprehension, even when many abbreviations are used	5.8	15.8	78.4
h)	Read highly technical material in a particular academic or professional field with no use or only very infrequent use of a dictionary	2.6	9.4	88.0

18. Listed below are a number of "can do" statements about speaking ability in the MPFL. Please read each description carefully and circle the appropriate number to indicate whether, at the present time, you would be able to carry out each task "quite easily" (1), "with some difficulty" (2), or "with great difficulty or not at all" (3). Circle only one response for each task.

Percent of 2-Year

		Quite Easily	With Some Difficulty	With Great Difficulty or Not at All
a)	Say the days of the week	57.7	27.4	14.9
b)	Count to 10 in the language	91.5	6.6	2.0
c)	Give the current date (month, day, year)	52.3	28.5	19.2
d)	Order a simple meal in a restaurant	42.6	32.4	25.1
e)	Ask for directions on the street	38.6	30.8	30.6
f)	Buy clothes in a department store	31.6	32.8	35.6
g)	Introduce myself in social situations, and use appropriate greetings and leave-taking expressions	48.1	28.5	23.3
h)	Give simple biographical information about myself (place of birth, composition of family, early schooling, etc.)	35.2	31.6	33.3
i)	Talk about my favorite hobby at some length, using appropriate vocabulary.	18.2	26.5	55.3
j)	Describe my present job, studies, or other major life activities accurately and in detail	17.2	23.1	59.7
k)	Tell what I plan to be doing 5 years from now, using appropriate future tenses	14.9	22.5	62.6
l)	Describe the United States educational system in some detail	11.2	21.7	67.1
m)	State and support with examples and reasons a position on a controversial topic (for example, birth control, nuclear safety, environmental pollution)	6.8	16.3	76.8
n)	Describe the role played by Congress in the United States government system	7.3	15.3	77.3

19. Regardless of how well you currently speak the MPFL, please answer each of the following in terms of your present level of <u>listening comprehension</u> in the language. Circle only <u>one</u> response for each task.

		Percent of 2-Year		
		Quite Easily	*With Some Difficulty*	*With Great Difficulty or Not at All*
a)	Understand very simple statements or questions in the language ("Hello," "How are you?", "What is your name?", "Where do you live?", etc.)	91.3	7.2	1.5
b)	In face-to-face conversation, understand a native speaker who is speaking slowly and carefully (i.e., deliberately adapting his or her speech to suit me)	56.1	31.3	12.6
c)	On the telephone, understand a native speaker who is speaking to me slowly and carefully (i.e., deliberately adapting his or her speech to suit me)	43.5	34.5	21.9
d)	In face-to-face conversation with a native speaker who is speaking slowly and carefully to me, tell whether the speaker is referring to past, present or future events	40.7	30.7	28.6
e)	In face-to-face conversation, understand a native speaker who is speaking to me as quickly and as colloquially as he or she would to another native speaker	16.7	24.8	58.5
f)	Understand movies without subtitles	16.4	35.1	48.5
g)	Understand news broadcasts on the radio	13.3	28.9	57.8
h)	On the radio, understand the words of a popular song I have not heard before	10.2	32.2	57.6
i)	Understand play-by-play descriptions of sports events (for example, a soccer match) on the radio	10.7	23.3	66.0
j)	Understand two native speakers when they are talking rapidly with one another	12.7	18.6	68.8
k)	On the telephone, understand a native speaker who is talking as quickly and as colloquially as he or she would to another native speaker	10.0	19.0	71.0

171

20. Please answer each of the following in terms of your present level of
reading proficiency in the MPFL. Circle only one response for each
task.

		Percent of 2-Year		
		Quite Easily	*With Some Difficulty*	*With Great Difficulty or Not at All*
a)	Read personal letters or notes written to me in which the writer has deliberately used simple words and constructions	59.0	22.4	18.6
b)	Read, on store fronts, the type of store or the services provided (for example, "dry cleaning," "book store," "butcher," etc.)	57.7	25.1	17.2
c)	Understand newspaper headlines	45.5	31.9	22.7
d)	Read personal letters and notes written as they would be to a native speaker	24.7	32.1	43.2
e)	Read and understand magazine articles at a level similar to those found in *Time* or *Newsweek*, without using a dictionary	14.3	27.4	58.3
f)	Read popular novels without using a dictionary	10.2	21.7	68.1
g)	Read newspaper "want ads" with comprehension, even when many abbreviations are used	12.5	23.5	64.0
h)	Read highly technical material in a particular academic or professional field with no use or only very infrequent use of a dictionary	7.7	11.0	81.3

PART III - LANGUAGE ATTITUDES

On the following pages you will find a series of statements. Read each statement and decide whether or not you agree with it. At the top of each page
numbered responses appear as follows:

STRONGLY AGREE	AGREE	INDIFFERENT	DISAGREE	STRONGLY DISAGREE
1	2	3	4	5

After you have read each statement, please circle the number (1, 2, 3, 4, or 5)
that indicates your response to it.

1. I enjoy meeting people who speak other languages.

	1	2	3	4	5
% Freshmen	29.3	42.0	22.9	5.3	0.5
% Seniors	33.2	44.3	17.9	4.3	0.3
% 2-year	28.3	45.2	22.6	3.4	0.5

2. It is important for Americans to learn foreign languages.

	1	2	3	4	5
% Freshmen	32.8	42.5	18.8	5.0	0.9
% Seniors	41.2	39.9	11.8	6.1	1.0
% 2-year	35.4	40.7	18.4	5.2	0.2

3. Studying a foreign language can be important for me because I think it
will someday be useful in getting a good job.

	1	2	3	4	5
% Freshmen	22.3	31.4	24.8	19.0	2.4
% Seniors	22.5	28.9	23.6	21.1	3.9
% 2-year	32.4	25.6	24.9	13.2	3.9

4. Foreign languages are not an important part of the school program.

	1	2	3	4	5
% Freshmen	2.1	11.1	15.0	45.1	26.7
% Seniors	2.1	11.5	13.5	44.8	28.1
% 2-year	4.1	12.3	14.2	42.9	26.5

5. Studying a foreign language can be important for me because it will
enable me to better understand and appreciate the art and literature
of another country.

	1	2	3	4	5
% Freshmen	22.3	45.6	24.7	6.0	1.5
% Seniors	29.8	43.9	19.4	6.7	0.2
% 2-year	31.5	43.7	19.5	4.8	0.4

6. I plan to learn one or more foreign languages as thoroughly as possible.

	1	2	3	4	5
% Freshmen	18.0	23.5	23.8	24.5	10.5
% Seniors	18.6	25.0	24.5	23.6	8.5
% 2-year	21.8	27.2	25.7	19.2	6.2

7. If I had to stay for an extended period of time in a country whose language I did not know at all, I would make an effort to learn that language even though I could get along in that country by using English.

	1	2	3	4	5
% Freshmen	46.6	42.1	6.3	4.3	0.7
% Seniors	56.0	37.7	3.0	2.1	1.1
% 2-year	51.0	43.3	4.5	0.9	0.4

8. Studying a foreign language can be important for me because other people will respect me more if I have knowledge of a foreign language.

	1	2	3	4	5
% Freshmen	8.1	25.9	38.0	22.7	5.4
% Seniors	11.4	26.4	38.5	17.4	6.2
% 2-year	11.2	26.3	37.7	19.0	5.8

9. I would study a foreign language in school even if it were not required.

	1	2	3	4	5
% Freshmen	20.5	31.8	23.4	20.5	3.9
% Seniors	23.5	31.5	20.0	18.6	6.4
% 2-year	20.4	34.1	21.2	19.3	4.9

10. Learning a foreign language is unnecessary because English is spoken almost everywhere.

	1	2	3	4	5
% Freshmen	1.7	5.7	14.8	43.4	34.4
% Seniors	0.7	5.7	9.1	46.9	37.6
% 2-year	2.0	6.8	12.9	44.1	34.2

11. Studying a foreign language can be important for me because it will allow me to meet and converse with more and varied people.

	1	2	3	4	5
% Freshmen	23.5	47.9	21.0	6.9	0.7
% Seniors	25.0	48.3	18.0	7.9	0.7
% 2-year	31.1	46.1	16.4	5.3	1.0

12. I would rather spend my time on subjects other than foreign languages.

	1	2	3	4	5
% Freshmen	11.8	38.7	26.6	19.1	3.9
% Seniors	13.4	35.4	27.0	20.1	4.1
% 2-year	10.4	39.1	29.3	14.6	6.6

13. Studying a foreign language can be important for me because I will be able to participate more freely in the activities of other cultural groups.

	1	2	3	4	5
% Freshmen	10.2	39.6	39.2	9.3	1.7
% Seniors	10.9	41.3	35.9	11.3	0.6
% 2-year	14.0	44.2	32.8	8.1	0.9

14. If I had the opportunity to study a foreign language in the future (or to continue my language study), I would take it.

	1	2	3	4	5
% Freshmen	20.1	35.5	24.9	17.0	2.4
% Seniors	25.8	39.0	21.5	11.4	2.3
% 2-year	25.7	41.6	20.6	8.8	3.3

15. Studying a foreign language can be important for me because it will make me a more knowledgeable person.

	1	2	3	4	5
% Freshmen	20.3	50.2	20.9	7.2	1.5
% Seniors	26.1	49.0	19.4	5.1	0.4
% 2-year	24.8	49.2	17.4	6.5	2.1

PART IV - ASSESSMENT OF WORLD ISSUES

We are interested in your perceptions of certain world problems. Please
indicate your view on each of them, using the scales on the following pages.

Examples:

If you think that the problem at the top of the page is very closely related
to one end of the scale, you should circle the number that is closest to
that end.

This problem is   1   2   3   4   5   This problem is
important.   unimportant.

                                    OR

This problem is   1   2   3   4   5   This problem is
important.   unimportant.

If you think that the problem is related to one or the other end of the scale
(but not closely), you should circle a number as follows.

This problem is   1   2   3   4   5   This problem is
important.   unimportant.

                                    OR

This problem is   1   2   3   4   5   This problem is
important.   unimportant.

If you consider the problem to be neutral on the scale, i.e., both sides of
the scale are equally associated with the problem, or if the scale is completely
unrelated to the problem, you should circle number 3.

This problem is   1   2   3   4   5   This problem is
important.   unimportant.

Environmental Pollution

	1	2	3	4	5

1. This problem is important.   This problem is unimportant.

	1	2	3	4	5
% Freshmen	64.2	30.8	3.2	1.4	0.4
% Seniors	69.6	26.5	2.4	1.3	0.2
% 2-year	66.3	24.8	7.9	0.4	0.6

2. I know very little about this problem.   I know a lot about this problem.

	1	2	3	4	5
% Freshmen	2.7	22.1	32.8	35.3	7.1
% Seniors	3.5	13.0	35.2	37.3	11.1
% 2-year	3.9	20.1	36.6	31.0	8.3

3. The American government can do a lot to solve this problem.   The American government can do very little to solve this problem.

	1	2	3	4	5
% Freshmen	30.6	47.6	15.9	4.5	1.5
% Seniors	37.3	46.2	11.2	4.8	0.5
% 2-year	36.4	41.7	14.1	7.2	0.6

4. This problem will decrease in the next twenty years.   This problem will increase in the next twenty years.

	1	2	3	4	5
% Freshmen	2.0	7.4	18.9	33.7	38.0
% Seniors	2.6	8.3	15.9	29.0	44.2
% 2-year	5.3	8.5	15.9	30.9	39.5

5. This problem is not interesting to learn about.   This problem is interesting to learn about.

	1	2	3	4	5
% Freshmen	2.4	6.6	15.9	40.8	34.2
% Seniors	2.2	5.7	13.2	41.6	37.3
% 2-year	3.6	9.3	16.2	32.7	38.2

177

		<u>1</u>	<u>2</u>	<u>3</u>	<u>4</u>	<u>5</u>	
6.	This problem is solvable.						This problem is unsolvable.
	% Freshmen	34.5	38.3	19.3	6.2	1.7	
	% Seniors	34.7	39.6	15.1	10.1	0.5	
	% 2-year	37.9	35.4	16.1	6.7	3.9	
7.	International organizations can do very little to solve this problem.						International organizations can do a lot to solve this problem.
	% Freshmen	2.8	8.6	21.6	39.0	28.0	
	% Seniors	3.9	9.3	12.2	42.4	32.2	
	% 2-year	5.1	7.1	24.5	29.5	33.7	
8.	This problem is unavoidable.						This problem is avoidable.
	% Freshmen	16.1	14.4	15.6	34.7	19.2	
	% Seniors	12.6	18.9	14.9	34.3	19.4	
	% 2-year	22.7	17.4	17.9	23.0	19.0	
9.	This problem is related to many other problems.						This problem is not related to many other problems.
	% Freshmen	47.0	38.7	11.3	2.2	0.9	
	% Seniors	59.4	29.5	8.1	1.6	1.4	
	% 2-year	51.8	29.6	11.6	5.0	2.0	
10.	This problem is temporary.						This problem is long-term.
	% Freshmen	1.2	3.0	11.5	30.3	54.0	
	% Seniors	1.5	2.5	7.9	28.8	59.3	
	% 2-year	3.8	2.4	11.8	27.1	54.9	
11.	This problem is of concern to people in many parts of the world.						This problem is of concern to people in only a few parts of the world.
	% Freshmen	61.8	21.3	7.7	6.4	2.9	
	% Seniors	58.8	25.7	6.2	7.3	2.0	
	% 2-year	56.2	22.4	11.5	6.4	3.5	

Denial of Basic Human Rights

		1	2	3	4	5	
1.	This problem is important.						This problem is unimportant.
	% Freshmen	66.9	25.2	5.5	1.7	0.7	
	% Seniors	68.2	22.5	6.5	2.1	0.6	
	% 2-year	68.4	21.0	9.3	0.8	0.6	
2.	I know very little about this problem.						I know a lot about this problem.
	% Freshmen	5.7	23.2	32.4	30.1	8.5	
	% Seniors	5.1	19.0	29.8	35.1	11.0	
	% 2-year	7.6	19.2	32.3	28.2	12.7	
3.	The American government can do a lot to solve this problem.						The American government can do very little to solve this problem.
	% Freshmen	29.0	39.8	21.2	7.9	2.1	
	% Seniors	23.1	44.0	20.6	11.1	1.3	
	% 2-year	31.0	32.3	25.6	10.3	0.8	
4.	This problem will decrease in the next twenty years.						This problem will increase in the next twenty years.
	% Freshmen	5.5	23.8	35.8	25.1	9.8	
	% Seniors	4.3	19.4	39.2	27.8	9.3	
	% 2-year	6.3	22.3	32.3	24.2	15.0	
5.	This problem is not interesting to learn about.						This problem is interesting to learn about.
	% Freshmen	2.4	7.9	18.6	36.3	34.8	
	% Seniors	3.2	8.1	14.8	40.1	33.9	
	% 2-year	4.2	7.9	20.1	35.9	31.9	

		1	2	3	4	5	
6.	This problem is solvable.						This problem is unsolvable.
	% Freshmen	35.3	36.1	19.4	6.9	2.4	
	% Seniors	22.8	43.9	21.5	10.5	1.3	
	% 2-year	36.4	29.7	25.2	7.0	1.7	
7.	International organizations can do very little to solve this problem.						International organizations can do a lot to solve this problem.
	% Freshmen	4.9	7.1	21.3	35.7	31.0	
	% Seniors	2.7	10.6	16.3	35.8	34.6	
	% 2-year	6.0	7.0	21.3	33.3	32.3	
8.	This problem is unavoidable.						This problem is avoidable.
	% Freshmen	12.2	20.9	17.2	28.3	21.3	
	% Seniors	9.3	21.0	20.5	28.7	20.4	
	% 2-year	18.4	21.0	18.8	22.4	19.3	
9.	This problem is related to many other problems.						This problem is not related to many other problems.
	% Freshmen	39.2	37.1	16.8	5.6	1.2	
	% Seniors	48.2	38.1	8.7	3.4	1.7	
	% 2-year	46.5	27.4	17.1	6.3	2.7	
10.	This problem is temporary.						This problem is long-term.
	% Freshmen	2.3	9.8	22.7	35.8	29.4	
	% Seniors	1.1	6.0	18.8	35.3	38.9	
	% 2-year	3.5	9.2	23.3	27.9	36.1	
11.	This problem is of concern to people in many parts of the world.						This problem is of concern to people in only a few parts of the world.
	% Freshmen	56.6	26.2	9.0	5.1	3.0	
	% Seniors	63.0	25.8	6.1	2.3	2.8	
	% 2-year	54.8	23.2	8.7	8.8	4.4	

		1	2	3	4	5	
1.	This problem is important.						This problem is unimportant.
	% Freshmen	74.9	20.6	2.6	1.1	0.8	
	% Seniors	71.4	24.2	2.4	1.4	0.6	
	% 2-year	77.4	19.6	1.6	0.7	0.8	
2.	I know very little about this problem.						I know a lot about this problem.
	% Freshmen	3.7	15.5	25.1	38.4	17.3	
	% Seniors	3.6	15.6	23.4	39.4	18.1	
	% 2-year	3.8	15.4	21.7	37.7	21.3	
3.	The American government can do a lot to solve this problem.						The American government can do very little to solve this problem.
	% Freshmen	43.6	39.2	11.4	4.4	1.3	
	% Seniors	35.9	38.3	18.2	6.2	1.5	
	% 2-year	43.9	32.4	14.5	7.2	1.9	
4.	This problem will decrease in the next twenty years.						This problem will increase in the next twenty years.
	% Freshmen	1.9	6.9	32.4	32.1	26.8	
	% Seniors	0.9	6.6	35.2	37.8	19.5	
	% 2-year	4.6	6.6	33.7	28.4	26.7	
5.	This problem is not interesting to learn about.						This problem is interesting to learn about.
	% Freshmen	4.2	9.4	27.6	35.5	23.4	
	% Seniors	2.8	11.0	25.2	36.8	24.2	
	% 2-year	5.3	9.8	26.0	30.7	28.2	

		1	2	3	4	5	
6.	This problem is solvable.						This problem is unsolvable.
	% Freshmen	26.3	43.1	19.1	9.4	2.0	
	% Seniors	21.3	44.1	22.6	9.2	2.8	
	% 2-year	32.3	36.2	18.9	9.7	3.0	
7.	International organizations can do very little to solve this problem.						International organizations can do a lot to solve this problem.
	% Freshmen	12.1	19.1	31.9	24.4	12.5	
	% Seniors	13.7	20.6	35.4	21.7	8.7	
	% 2-year	13.5	16.8	26.8	25.2	17.8	
8.	This problem is unavoidable.						This problem is avoidable.
	% Freshmen	19.2	28.9	18.6	24.5	8.8	
	% Seniors	13.5	33.0	20.5	24.4	8.6	
	% 2-year	24.6	23.0	18.3	22.9	11.2	
9.	This problem is related to many other problems.						This problem is not related to many other problems.
	% Freshmen	57.3	30.4	9.0	2.6	0.6	
	% Seniors	58.4	35.4	3.2	2.7	0.3	
	% 2-year	62.3	26.9	5.8	2.3	2.7	
10.	This problem is temporary.						This problem is long-term
	% Freshmen	1.4	9.5	22.4	37.8	29.0	
	% Seniors	2.1	5.5	19.4	37.4	35.6	
	% 2-year	3.5	8.3	25.1	30.8	32.3	
11.	This problem is of concern to people in many parts of the world.						This problem is of concern to people in only a few parts of the world.
	% Freshmen	52.8	25.9	12.4	5.7	3.1	
	% Seniors	52.2	30.0	8.4	6.7	2.7	
	% 2-year	52.6	24.5	14.3	4.3	4.2	

Intergroup Conflict

	1	2	3	4	5	
1. This problem is important.						This problem is unimportant.
% Freshmen	26.5	32.0	34.1	5.3	2.1	
% Seniors	33.4	33.5	25.5	6.0	1.6	
% 2-year	33.6	30.6	29.6	3.0	3.2	
2. I know very little about this problem.						I know a lot about this problem.
% Freshmen	34.2	24.9	26.0	12.0	2.9	
% Seniors	19.7	27.0	33.0	15.5	4.9	
2-year	24.9	23.8	30.6	14.8	5.8	
3. The American government can do a lot to solve this problem.						The American government can do very little to solve this problem.
% Freshmen	5.4	22.3	57.0	11.0	4.4	
% Seniors	7.0	27.2	43.2	17.6	5.0	
% 2-year	6.2	26.8	46.8	13.4	6.7	
4. This problem will decrease in the next twenty years.						This problem will increase in the next twenty years.
% Freshmen	0.9	9.0	57.8	25.0	7.3	
% Seniors	0.5	7.0	51.2	30.0	11.3	
% 2-year	2.7	7.5	55.1	22.9	11.9	
5. This problem is not interesting to learn about.						This problem is interesting to learn about.
% Freshmen	6.7	13.4	39.9	28.0	12.0	
% Seniors	4.6	13.6	33.4	31.8	16.6	
% 2-year	7.2	10.8	38.5	26.9	16.6	

	1	2	3	4	5

6. This problem is solvable.   This problem is unsolvable.

	1	2	3	4	5
% Freshmen	10.2	32.5	43.4	10.6	3.2
% Seniors	9.3	35.0	37.7	14.5	3.5
% 2-year	14.4	29.2	39.9	12.3	4.2

7. International organizations can do very little to solve this problem.   International organizations can do a lot to solve this problem.

	1	2	3	4	5
% Freshmen	4.7	11.8	44.9	25.0	13.6
% Seniors	7.0	11.8	35.6	29.7	15.9
% 2-year	9.1	13.2	41.3	22.8	13.6

8. This problem is unavoidable.   This problem is avoidable.

	1	2	3	4	5
% Freshmen	12.9	24.8	40.5	15.7	6.1
% Seniors	13.2	32.2	28.4	21.2	5.1
% 2-year	15.7	24.1	38.3	15.7	6.2

9. This problem is related to many other problems.   This problem is not related to many other problems.

	1	2	3	4	5
% Freshmen	28.6	33.4	33.2	3.5	1.2
% Seniors	38.9	35.3	21.5	3.3	1.0
% 2-year	34.7	27.8	30.9	5.1	1.5

10. This problem is temporary.   This problem is long-term.

	1	2	3	4	5
% Freshmen	1.5	5.2	46.5	29.4	17.3
% Seniors	0.4	6.4	34.3	34.2	24.7
% 2-year	1.9	5.1	46.1	25.1	22.0

11. This problem is of concern to people in many parts of the world.   This problem is of concern to people in only a few parts of the world.

	1	2	3	4	5
% Freshmen	37.3	24.7	31.5	5.0	1.5
% Seniors	44.8	25.1	24.6	5.0	0.6
% 2-year	38.3	22.2	30.9	5.9	2.6

Depletion of Natural Resources

	1	2	3	4	5	
1. This problem is important.						This problem is unimportant.
% Freshmen	85.6	11.3	2.3	0.1	0.7	
% Seniors	87.2	10.6	1.1	0.6	0.5	
% 2-year	83.0	11.6	4.5	0.5	0.3	
2. I know very little about this problem.						I know a lot about this problem.
% Freshmen	3.7	13.4	18.5	42.4	21.9	
% Seniors	3.0	15.3	15.5	41.8	24.4	
% 2-year	5.2	17.4	22.6	38.4	16.4	
3. The American government can do a lot to solve this problem.						The American government can do very little to solve this problem.
% Freshmen	48.0	32.9	10.2	7.0	1.9	
% Seniors	50.1	36.9	7.8	3.6	1.7	
% 2-year	44.5	31.5	17.7	4.9	1.4	
4. This problem will decrease in the next twenty years.						This problem will increase in the next twenty years.
% Freshmen	1.9	3.6	12.4	25.3	56.7	
% Seniors	1.0	3.2	9.6	20.4	65.8	
% 2-year	2.8	4.7	18.0	23.1	51.4	
5. This problem is not interesting to learn about.						This problem interesting to learn about.
% Freshmen	3.0	4.1	9.3	35.7	47.9	
% Seniors	3.5	5.3	10.2	32.7	48.3	
% 2-year	4.1	4.4	14.1	31.5	45.9	

		<u>1</u>	<u>2</u>	<u>3</u>	<u>4</u>	<u>5</u>	
6.	This problem is solvable.						This problem is unsolvable.
	% Freshmen	28.3	32.0	19.5	16.2	3.9	
	% Seniors	27.9	36.4	18.3	13.3	4.0	
	% 2-year	29.0	30.4	26.6	10.4	3.5	
7.	International organizations can do very little to solve this problem.						International organizations can do a lot to solve this problem.
	% Freshmen	5.8	10.8	20.8	30.5	32.1	
	% Seniors	5.5	8.6	15.1	34.8	36.0	
	% 2-year	5.9	9.5	23.0	27.4	34.2	
8.	This problem is unavoidable.						This problem is avoidable.
	% Freshmen	21.4	23.8	16.2	23.2	15.3	
	% Seniors	22.3	22.7	15.0	24.3	15.7	
	% 2-year	24.9	18.3	22.1	18.5	16.1	
9.	This problem is related to many other problems.						This problem is not related to many other problems.
	% Freshmen	48.0	33.7	11.9	5.1	1.4	
	% Seniors	56.2	31.4	8.1	3.0	1.2	
	% 2-year	50.0	30.2	13.1	3.1	3.6	
10.	This problem is temporary.						This problem is long-term.
	% Freshmen	1.7	5.0	15.7	24.4	53.2	
	% Seniors	0.9	1.8	7.4	23.1	66.7	
	% 2-year	1.9	4.6	19.3	23.4	50.8	
11.	This problem is of concern to people in many parts of the world.						This problem is of concern to people in only a few parts of the world.
	% Freshmen	68.0	16.1	7.6	5.2	3.1	
	% Seniors	74.5	14.1	4.8	4.4	2.2	
	% 2-year	59.9	17.9	11.4	5.4	5.4	

Inflation

		1	2	3	4	5	
1.	This problem is important.						This problem is unimportant.
	% Freshmen	79.9	16.1	1.5	1.6	0.9	
	% Seniors	77.1	19.2	2.5	0.7	0.5	
	% 2-year	84.4	12.8	2.1	0.2	0.5	
2.	I know very little about this problem.						I know a lot about this problem.
	% Freshmen	4.1	14.9	20.0	39.5	21.5	
	% Seniors	5.8	19.5	21.6	34.3	18.7	
	% 2-year	6.8	14.4	19.8	35.5	23.5	
3.	The American government can do a lot to solve this problem.						The American government can do very little to solve this problem.
	% Freshmen	47.8	34.5	11.2	4.0	2.4	
	% Seniors	40.6	39.1	14.3	4.1	1.9	
	% 2-year	52.9	30.0	11.3	3.0	2.8	
4.	This problem will decrease in the next twenty years.						This problem will increase in the next twenty years.
	% Freshmen	2.2	5.9	24.3	32.0	35.7	
	% Seniors	1.8	4.9	21.6	35.4	36.2	
	% 2-year	3.8	4.6	27.0	29.0	35.5	
5.	This problem is not interesting to learn about.						This problem interesting to learn about.
	% Freshmen	5.3	10.7	20.0	33.4	30.7	
	% Seniors	2.4	10.2	21.4	33.5	32.4	
	% 2-year	4.5	7.6	20.9	33.9	33.1	

	1	2	3	4	5	

6. This problem is solvable.

This problem is unsolvable.

	1	2	3	4	5
% Freshmen	26.6	39.4	20.9	9.8	3.3
% Seniors	20.1	38.7	24.3	15.1	1.9
% 2-year	30.7	37.6	22.0	7.6	2.0

7. International organizations can do very little to solve this problem.

International organizations can do a lot to solve this problem.

	1	2	3	4	5
% Freshmen	7.6	12.8	30.3	27.8	21.6
% Seniors	6.9	16.0	32.7	30.0	14.4
% 2-year	8.9	13.3	28.7	26.2	22.8

8. This problem is unavoidable.

This problem is avoidable.

	1	2	3	4	5
% Freshmen	17.3	23.0	22.4	22.8	14.5
% Seniors	12.6	21.0	22.7	35.0	8.7
% 2-year	20.7	16.0	23.3	24.6	15.4

9. This problem is related to many other problems.

This problem is not related to many other problems.

	1	2	3	4	5
% Freshmen	60.5	29.5	7.4	1.8	0.7
% Seniors	63.1	31.0	3.7	1.4	0.8
% 2-year	66.5	19.8	9.3	1.6	2.9

10. This problem is temporary.

This problem is long-term.

	1	2	3	4	5
% Freshmen	2.8	6.6	24.7	33.9	32.1
% Seniors	2.7	8.1	17.1	36.1	36.0
% 2-year	2.6	9.7	23.6	29.0	35.1

11. This problem is of concern to people in many parts of the world.

This problem is of concern to people in only a few parts of the world.

	1	2	3	4	5
% Freshmen	56.0	23.7	10.7	5.9	3.8
% Seniors	52.8	28.5	12.2	4.3	2.2
% 2-year	55.2	19.4	15.5	4.5	5.5

Malnutrition and Inadequate Health Care

		1	2	3	4	5	
1.	This problem is important.						This problem is unimportant.
	% Freshmen	74.7	20.0	3.7	1.0	0.5	
	% Seniors	74.9	20.4	3.0	1.2	0.5	
	% 2-year	73.7	19.0	5.0	0.5	1.7	
2.	I know very little about this problem.						I know a lot about this problem.
	% Freshmen	6.4	25.6	25.5	29.7	12.8	
	% Seniors	6.5	25.6	24.5	30.8	12.5	
	% 2-year	10.3	21.3	28.9	23.1	16.3	
3.	The American government can do a lot to solve this problem.						The American government can do very little to solve this problem.
	% Freshmen	34.6	37.2	21.2	5.5	1.3	
	% Seniors	34.6	44.0	14.6	5.6	1.1	
	% 2-year	40.2	32.7	19.8	4.6	2.7	
4.	This problem will decrease in the next twenty years.						This problem will increase in the next twenty years.
	% Freshmen	2.4	14.6	24.0	32.2	26.9	
	% Seniors	4.2	12.7	20.9	33.8	28.4	
	% 2-year	5.6	12.0	24.7	27.1	30.5	
5.	This problem is not interesting to learn about.						This problem is interesting to learn about.
	% Freshmen	5.1	9.1	23.0	32.7	30.0	
	% Seniors	3.4	9.9	23.2	36.7	26.9	
	% 2-year	7.5	7.9	20.9	32.5	31.2	

189

		1	2	3	4	5	
6.	This problem is solvable.						This problem is unsolvable.
	% Freshmen	33.5	41.4	16.6	5.4	3.1	
	% Seniors	34.5	43.5	13.4	7.4	1.3	
	% 2-year	35.9	37.4	17.9	5.8	2.9	
7.	International organizations can do very little to solve this problem.						International organizations can do a lot to solve this problem.
	% Freshmen	3.8	5.2	14.8	31.5	44.7	
	% Seniors	3.7	5.2	10.3	33.5	47.3	
	% 2-year	5.5	8.4	17.7	27.1	41.3	
8.	This problem is unavoidable.						This problem is avoidable.
	% Freshmen	15.7	17.0	17.6	28.2	21.5	
	% Seniors	10.1	15.8	15.8	29.5	28.8	
	% 2-year	16.6	18.2	18.2	23.7	23.3	
9.	This problem is related to many other problems.						This problem is not related to many other problems.
	% Freshmen	41.4	37.2	13.1	5.6	2.6	
	% Seniors	49.9	33.5	12.2	3.5	0.9	
	% 2-year	48.5	28.8	14.4	5.6	2.7	
10.	This problem is temporary.						This problem is long-term.
	% Freshmen	1.8	6.8	26.1	31.8	33.6	
	% Seniors	1.0	6.7	18.8	35.7	37.9	
	% 2-year	4.3	6.5	23.3	30.2	35.7	
11.	This problem is of concern to people in many parts of the world.						This problem is of concern to people in only a few parts of the world.
	% Freshmen	73.4	16.3	4.6	3.3	2.4	
	% Seniors	79.3	13.9	3.8	1.1	2.0	
	% 2-year	66.2	17.6	6.6	4.3	5.3	

International Conflict of War

		1	2	3	4	5	
1.	This problem is important.						This problem is unimportant.
	% Freshmen	92.3	5.7	0.7	0.1	1.1	
	% Seniors	90.3	7.6	0.9	0.2	1.0	
	% 2-year	90.0	7.0	2.0	0.4	0.6	
2.	I know very little about this problem.						I know a lot about this problem.
	% Freshmen	5.2	14.1	19.3	37.0	24.4	
	% Seniors	4.4	13.2	20.3	41.0	21.1	
	% 2-year	7.3	16.1	21.2	33.7	21.8	
3.	The American government can do a lot to solve this problem.						The American government can do very little to solve this problem.
	% Freshmen	47.6	30.3	15.0	4.6	2.4	
	% Seniors	47.0	29.7	16.4	5.7	1.3	
	% 2-year	47.7	25.4	17.0	6.9	3.1	
4.	This problem will decrease in the next twenty years.						This problem will increase in the next twenty years.
	% Freshmen	1.2	3.8	23.9	33.3	37.9	
	% Seniors	1.3	5.0	18.9	36.3	38.5	
	% 2-year	2.1	6.2	22.1	27.2	42.4	
5.	This problem is not interesting to learn about.						This problem is interesting to learn about.
	% Freshmen	3.4	5.8	7.0	30.6	53.2	
	% Seniors	4.5	5.8	10.3	26.5	52.9	
	% 2-year	4.3	4.9	12.7	22.3	55.8	

		1	2	3	4	5	
6.	This problem is solvable.						This problem is unsolvable.
	% Freshmen	34.2	27.9	22.6	9.8	5.5	
	% Seniors	23.6	32.5	24.6	14.9	4.3	
	% 2-year	29.0	30.5	22.9	8.9	8.7	
7.	International organizations can do very little to solve this problem.						International organizations can do a lot to solve this problem.
	% Freshmen	5.6	5.1	10.7	22.4	56.3	
	% Seniors	5.3	6.7	11.2	26.3	50.5	
	% 2-year	7.8	8.0	13.9	19.6	50.6	
8.	This problem is unavoidable.						This problem is avoidable.
	% Freshmen	19.5	16.8	18.6	18.4	26.6	
	% Seniors	13.3	19.8	19.9	25.3	21.7	
	% 2-year	22.2	17.6	18.1	19.2	22.9	
9.	This problem is related to many other problems.						This problem is not related to many other problems.
	% Freshmen	66.5	21.7	7.0	2.7	2.2	
	% Seniors	67.3	24.6	3.7	1.7	2.7	
	% 2-year	64.9	21.5	7.7	2.5	3.5	
10.	This problem is temporary.						This problem is long-term.
	% Freshmen	2.4	4.7	22.8	26.6	43.4	
	% Seniors	1.3	4.7	12.5	27.4	54.2	
	% 2-year	2.1	6.0	19.7	27.5	44.8	
11.	This problem is of concern to people in many parts of the world.						This problem is of concern to people in only a few parts of the world.
	% Freshmen	86.0	8.0	2.4	1.9	1.7	
	% Seniors	87.5	8.9	1.7	0.5	1.4	
	% 2-year	79.5	10.4	4.3	1.4	4.4	

PART V - OPINION SURVEY

On the following pages you will find a series of statements. Read each statement and decide whether or not you agree with it. At the top of each page numbered responses appear as follows:

STRONGLY AGREE	AGREE	INDIFFERENT	DISAGREE	STRONGLY DISAGREE
1	2	3	4	5

After you have read each statement, please circle the number (1, 2, 3, 4, or 5) that indicates your response to it.

	1	2	3	4	5

1. Pacifist demonstrations--picketing missile bases, peace walks, etc.-- are harmful to the best interests of the American people.

	1	2	3	4	5
% Freshmen	7.2	15.7	25.6	34.1	17.3
% Seniors	4.0	15.0	16.3	35.2	29.5
% 2-year	7.9	15.5	24.2	30.9	21.4

2. I believe that the United States should send food and materials to any country that needs them.

	1	2	3	4	5
% Freshmen	7.8	28.9	16.9	38.4	8.1
% Seniors	5.1	31.4	12.7	39.5	11.3
% 2-year	10.2	32.5	16.3	29.1	11.8

3. The best way to insure peace is to keep the United States stronger than any other nation in the world.

	1	2	3	4	5
% Freshmen	17.1	28.6	17.7	29.4	7.2
% Seniors	15.0	24.6	14.5	40.0	5.9
% 2-year	24.7	28.6	15.9	25.8	5.0

4. The immigration of foreigners to this country should be kept down so that we can provide for Americans first.

	1	2	3	4	5
% Freshmen	18.0	31.2	20.3	23.0	7.5
% Seniors	10.4	31.5	18.7	32.9	6.5
% 2-year	21.1	30.3	22.1	21.7	4.8

		1	2	3	4	5
5.	Political freedom is a basic human right and no government should be permitted to abridge it.					
	% Freshmen	39.6	40.6	12.8	5.9	1.1
	% Seniors	41.1	39.1	10.6	7.8	1.5
	% 2-year	46.3	37.1	11.0	5.1	0.5
6.	The main threat to basic American institutions during this century has come from the infiltration of foreign ideas and doctrines.					
	% Freshmen	3.4	15.1	36.7	31.6	13.2
	% Seniors	1.7	7.4	17.9	42.3	30.6
	% 2-year	7.0	16.7	31.6	29.3	15.5
7.	Since the world's supplies of essential minerals are limited, the mining and distribution of mineral resources should be controlled by an international authority.					
	% Freshmen	10.5	25.7	26.5	27.2	10.1
	% Seniors	6.7	25.0	19.4	36.4	12.5
	% 2-year	7.7	31.5	28.1	24.3	8.4
8.	Everyone should have the right to leave any country, including his own, and to return to his country.					
	% Freshmen	37.4	40.6	10.5	9.4	2.1
	% Seniors	41.4	39.4	9.1	8.5	1.7
	% 2-year	41.8	39.9	9.2	7.2	1.9
9.	We should be willing to settle all differences with other nations within the framework of a World Government.					
	% Freshmen	29.1	39.8	17.0	9.7	4.4
	% Seniors	23.4	45.2	14.0	12.6	4.8
	% 2-year	32.8	42.7	15.5	5.6	3.3
10.	War is a satisfactory way to solve international problems.					
	% Freshmen	0.7	3.2	4.3	22.9	69.0
	% Seniors	0.8	4.1	3.7	27.9	63.6
	% 2-year	1.6	1.7	5.7	23.7	67.3

		<u>1</u>	<u>2</u>	<u>3</u>	<u>4</u>	<u>5</u>
11.	No government should deny access to basic education to any of its citizens.					
	% Freshmen	69.3	25.0	2.7	2.6	0.5
	% Seniors	68.9	26.8	2.5	0.5	1.3
	% 2-year	68.8	22.2	5.5	2.8	0.8
12.	We should not allow foreign business enterprises to buy American farmland.					
	% Freshmen	28.7	37.7	21.7	9.7	2.2
	% Seniors	26.0	37.9	17.4	14.8	3.8
	% 2-year	30.1	32.6	21.7	11.7	3.9
13.	Under some conditions, war is necessary to maintain justice.					
	% Freshmen	7.3	40.4	13.0	21.7	17.6
	% Seniors	7.2	47.3	10.8	20.5	14.2
	% 2-year	9.0	37.5	14.0	21.2	18.4
14.	Patriotism and loyalty are the first and most important requirements of a good citizen.					
	% Freshmen	16.9	37.5	25.1	15.0	5.5
	% Seniors	11.3	32.2	25.5	23.1	7.8
	% 2-year	18.0	35.5	25.4	15.3	5.8
15.	Immigrants should not be permitted to come into our country if they compete with our own workers.					
	% Freshmen	7.8	21.3	26.5	37.0	7.3
	% Seniors	5.5	22.6	22.7	40.8	8.3
	% 2-year	8.9	17.4	28.7	38.3	6.7
16.	We should have a World Government with the power to make laws that would be binding to all its member nations.					
	% Freshmen	13.1	30.1	26.4	19.8	10.7
	% Seniors	11.8	33.0	20.0	25.6	9.5
	% 2-year	16.7	32.3	28.5	16.1	6.5

		1	2	3	4	5

17. Any healthy individual, regardless of race or religion, should be allowed to live in whatever country he chooses.

	1	2	3	4	5
% Freshmen	28.5	40.2	14.3	14.2	2.8
% Seniors	31.0	39.7	16.4	10.1	2.8
% 2-year	32.7	40.6	16.1	8.2	2.4

18. There is no conceivable justification for war.

	1	2	3	4	5
% Freshmen	24.4	20.6	17.3	32.0	5.7
% Seniors	20.2	17.3	10.5	41.4	10.6
% 2-year	22.1	23.3	19.7	26.5	8.4

19. Our country should have the right to prohibit certain racial and religious groups from immigrating.

	1	2	3	4	5
% Freshmen	5.0	13.0	17.2	37.1	27.1
% Seniors	4.6	11.2	14.0	40.1	30.1
% 2-year	5.0	13.1	21.4	34.9	25.7

20. An international authority should be established and given direct control over the production of nuclear energy in all countries, including the United States.

	1	2	3	4	5
% Freshmen	14.8	27.1	23.8	24.7	9.5
% Seniors	16.0	31.9	16.9	21.5	13.7
% 2-year	16.6	24.0	28.3	23.2	7.9

21. It is our responsibility to do everything possible to prevent people from starving anywhere in the world.

	1	2	3	4	5
% Freshmen	14.6	34.4	23.0	20.2	7.8
% Seniors	15.7	37.1	13.6	24.9	8.7
% 2-year	19.1	35.7	22.8	16.9	5.6

22. Changes in government should always be accomplished through peaceful means.

	1	2	3	4	5
% Freshmen	32.7	47.3	12.4	7.1	0.6
% Seniors	24.8	49.9	11.2	13.6	0.6
% 2-year	32.5	48.4	11.9	6.3	0.8

		1	2	3	4	5
23.	It is none of our business if other governments restrict the personal freedom of their citizens.					
	% Freshmen	4.6	15.1	23.7	40.3	16.3
	% Seniors	3.1	14.1	15.5	47.4	20.0
	% 2-year	4.9	16.9	25.3	36.7	16.1
24.	The only way peace can be maintained is to keep America so powerful and well-armed that no other nation will dare to attack us.					
	% Freshmen	8.9	22.7	18.8	38.9	10.7
	% Seniors	7.3	21.7	13.2	41.8	16.1
	% 2-year	10.6	26.8	18.7	34.1	9.8
25.	The United States should be open to all those who wish to settle here.					
	% Freshmen	7.4	31.4	22.4	32.1	6.7
	% Seniors	7.7	32.1	21.3	34.6	4.4
	% 2-year	9.7	28.0	25.9	29.1	7.2
26.	No duties are more important than duties toward one's country.					
	% Freshmen	10.7	29.1	25.5	29.1	5.6
	% Seniors	7.0	20.5	24.0	36.6	12.0
	% 2-year	12.3	26.9	26.9	26.3	7.6
27.	People should refuse to engage in any war, no matter how serious the consequences to their country may be.					
	% Freshmen	5.0	8.7	16.5	53.0	16.9
	% Seniors	3.8	9.1	12.3	53.7	21.0
	% 2-year	8.7	10.3	17.7	46.9	16.5
28.	I prefer to be a citizen of the world rather than of any country.					
	% Freshmen	8.0	12.3	21.2	37.8	20.6
	% Seniors	9.6	15.7	17.2	39.1	18.5
	% 2-year	13.8	18.4	21.4	31.0	15.4

	1	2	3	4	5

29. I'm for my country, right or wrong.

	1	2	3	4	5
% Freshmen	11.1	15.6	20.7	39.5	13.1
% Seniors	5.5	13.1	18.7	38.7	24.0
% 2-year	11.0	16.3	22.2	38.6	12.0

30. The United States ought to be willing to give up its independence and submit to the authority of a United States of the World.

	1	2	3	4	5
% Freshmen	2.4	8.0	23.8	33.7	32.2
% Seniors	4.0	10.1	20.8	35.6	29.5
% 2-year	3.8	10.3	28.2	30.0	27.7

31. Violent revolution is sometimes the only way to eliminate an oppressive government.

	1	2	3	4	5
% Freshmen	5.6	39.4	19.2	21.6	14.3
% Seniors	7.5	50.9	15.6	17.4	8.6
% 2-year	6.0	36.6	18.8	26.3	12.4

32. Well-fed people in developed nations should voluntarily cut back on their food consumption and contribute food to the inadequately fed in underdeveloped nations.

	1	2	3	4	5
% Freshmen	11.2	38.5	28.9	17.7	3.6
% Seniors	7.4	41.1	23.9	22.8	4.9
% 2-year	11.1	35.8	30.3	19.4	3.4

PART VI - STUDENT SELF-PERCEPTIONS

Listed below are several statements that one might use to describe oneself.
Read each statement and decide whether or not it describes you. Indicate
your response to each statement by circling one of the letters (T = True,
F = False) in front of the sentence.

	True	False
1. I am interested in international relations and acquire information about international developments whenever I can.		
% Freshmen	60.3	39.7
% Seniors	65.3	34.7
% 2-year	64.5	35.5
2. The fact that a flood can kill 25,000 people in India is very depressing to me.		
% Freshmen	70.5	29.5
% Seniors	69.0	31.0
% 2-year	71.5	28.5
3. I am most comfortable with people from my own culture.		
% Freshmen	78.6	21.4
% Seniors	77.9	22.1
% 2-year	70.7	29.3
4. I feel a strong kinship with the worldwide human family.		
% Freshmen	41.4	58.6
% Seniors	42.4	57.6
% 2-year	49.2	50.8
5. I rarely read news articles about international events.		
% Freshmen	26.0	74.0
% Seniors	20.3	79.7
% 2-year	21.6	78.4
6. I find the customs of foreigners difficult to understand.		
% Freshmen	27.8	72.2
% Seniors	22.8	77.2
% 2-year	28.7	71.3

	True	False

7. When I hear that thousands of people are
    starving in Cambodia, I feel very frustrated.

	True	False
% Freshmen	69.4	30.6
% Seniors	71.6	28.4
% 2-year	65.3	34.7

8. I am not interested in studying other cultures.

	True	False
% Freshmen	12.1	87.9
% Seniors	12.1	87.9
% 2-year	12.3	87.7

9. I have almost nothing in common with people in
    underdeveloped nations.

	True	False
% Freshmen	28.0	72.0
% Seniors	27.7	72.3
% 2-year	25.2	74.8

10. I make an effort to meet people from other
    countries.

	True	False
% Freshmen	60.0	40.0
% Seniors	58.6	41.4
% 2-year	63.8	36.2

Appendix B

Booklet B Item Responses

1. Most of the new nations that came into existence in the thirty-year period
   after the Second World War are located on which of the following pairs of
   continents?

   (1) Europe and Asia
   (2) Asia and Africa
   (3) Africa and South America
   (4) South America and Asia

		OMIT	1	2*	3	4	TOTAL		
Freshmen	PERCENT	2.41	38.01	33.74	18.41	7.43	100.00	R BIS = 0.3360	P+ = 0.3374
	MEAN SCORE	29.24	39.73	46.07	41.61	39.37	41.94	PT BIS = 0.2597	
Senior	PERCENT	0.78	26.48	51.58	18.07	3.09	100.00	R BIS = 0.4201	P+ = 0.5158
	MEAN SCORE	34.96	44.75	54.39	50.00	40.39	50.46	PT BIS = 0.3350	
2-Year	PERCENT	1.72	30.88	39.62	17.94	9.83	100.00	R BIS = 0.4473	P+ = 0.3962
	MEAN SCORE	27.05	36.33	45.91	40.44	33.82	40.45	PT BIS = 0.3524	

2. Which of the following aspects of Western education has had the most profound
    influence on revolutionary leaders of the Third World who were educated in the
    West?

    (1) Humanities
    (2) Physical and biological sciences
    (3) Industrial technology
    (4) Social and political theories

		OMIT	1	2	3	4*	TOTAL				
Freshmen	PERCENT	2.42	5.98	5.10	40.11	46.38	100.00	R BIS =	0.2344	P+ =	0.4638
	MEAN SCORE	27.89	40.44	35.15	41.24	44.21	41.94	PT BIS =	0.1866		
Senior	PERCENT	1.32	3.86	2.12	38.53	54.17	100.00	R BIS =	0.2152	P+ =	0.5417
	MEAN SCORE	37.74	49.40	4.92	48.85	52.37	50.46	PT BIS =	0.1713		
2-Year	PERCENT	3.00	7.36	3.86	38.54	47.24	100.00	R BIS =	0.2898	P+ =	0.4724
	MEAN SCORE	23.77	37.61	33.98	39.19	43.51	40.45	PT BIS =	0.2309		

3. Since the Second World War, the gap in per capita income between the world's
    richest and poorest countries has

    (1) widened
    (2) remained about the same
    (3) narrowed slightly
    (4) narrowed substantially

		OMIT	1*	2	3	4	TOTAL				
Freshmen	PERCENT	1.91	68.44	8.09	17.62	3.94	100.00	R BIS =	0.2023	P+ =	0.6844
	MEAN SCORE	29.73	43.13	38.59	40.80	39.08	41.94	PT BIS =	0.1548		
Senior	PERCENT	1.15	76.76	6.57	13.06	2.45	100.00	R BIS =	0.2215	P+ =	0.7676
	MEAN SCORE	37.40	51.53	49.55	47.70	40.33	50.46	PT BIS =	0.1601		
2-Year	PERCENT	1.15	66.82	8.25	18.00	5.78	100.00	R BIS =	0.2963	P+ =	0.6682
	MEAN SCORE	31.29	42.47	35.02	37.95	34.48	40.45	PT BIS =	0.2284		

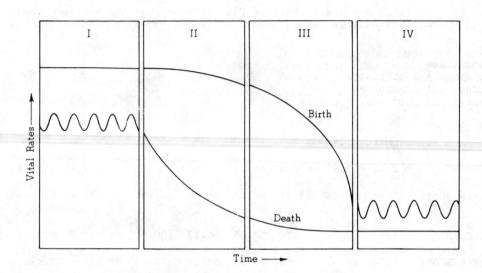

4. The birth and death rates in most of the world's countries today are best represented by which pattern(s) of curves in the diagram above?

   (1) III only
   (2) I and II only
   (3) II and III only
   (4) III and IV only

		OMIT	1	2	3*	4	TOTAL				
Freshmen	PERCENT	6.01	19.60	26.54	34.63	13.22	100.00	R BIS =	0.1852	P+ =	0.3463
	MEAN SCORE	36.37	38.89	42.33	44.18	42.31	41.94	PT BIS =	0.1436		
Senior	PERCENT	6.77	13.64	28.05	41.10	10.44	100.00	R BIS =	0.1430	P+ =	0.4110
	MEAN SCORE	49.66	48.57	50.79	52.10	46.10	50.46	PT BIS =	0.1130		
2-Year	PERCENT	6.30	12.14	25.19	39.52	16.85	100.00	R BIS =	0.1372	P+ =	0.3952
	MEAN SCORE	34.72	38.04	42.54	42.13	37.29	40.45	PT BIS =	0.1081		

5. Since the Second World War, most international migration has been from the

    (1) more developed to the less developed countries
    (2) more developed to the more developed countries
    (3) less developed to the less developed countries
    (4) less developed to the more developed countries

		OMIT	1	2	3	4*	TOTAL					
Freshmen	PERCENT	1.14	5.74	7.84	5.20	80.07	100.00	R BIS =	0.2071	P+ =	0.8007
	MEAN SCORE	20.83	36.15	41.82	40.50	42.76	41.94	PT BIS =	0.1449		
Senior	PERCENT	0.76	4.27	8.61	3.59	82.77	100.00	R BIS =	0.1064	P+ =	0.8277
	MEAN SCORE	36.88	43.98	48.48	56.63	50.86	50.46	PT BIS =	0.0720		
2-Year	PERCENT	1.30	4.17	11.44	4.63	78.45	100.00	R BIS =	0.2208	P+ =	0.7845
	MEAN SCORE	29.71	33.90	40.16	32.60	41.49	40.45	PT BIS =	0.1572		

6. The largest groups of people living outside their home countries in 1978-1979 were made up of

    (1) political refugees leaving or fleeing their countries
    (2) foreign workers and their families working and residing in West European countries
    (3) legal and illegal immigrants to the United States
    (4) military forces of the United States and the Soviet Union stationed in the territories of allied countries.

		OMIT	1	2*	3	4	TOTAL					
Freshmen	PERCENT	1.84	30.93	10.22	41.23	15.77	100.00	R BIS =	0.0010	P+ =	0.1022
	MEAN SCORE	26.54	43.97	41.96	40.15	44.38	41.94	PT BIS =	0.006		
Senior	PERCENT	1.99	36.04	10.93	31.19	19.85	100.00	R BIS =	0.1456	P+ =	0.1093
	MEAN SCORE	45.12	52.10	53.48	46.71	52.25	50.46	PT BIS =	0.0874		
2-Year	PERCENT	1.18	37.06	8.57	42.51	10.68	100.00	R BIS =	0.0389	P+ =	0.0857
	MEAN SCORE	28.63	42.29	41.35	38.35	43.08	40.45	PT BIS =	0.0217		

7. Since 1950, the percentage of total population in Africa, Asia, and Latin
   America living in cities has

   (1) increased
   (2) remained stable
   (3) decreased slightly
   (4) decreased greatly

		OMIT	1*	2	3	4	TOTAL					
Freshmen	PERCENT	2.01	82.52	7.43	7.00	1.03	100.00	R BIS =	0.3042	P+ =	0.8252
	MEAN SCORE	24.96	43.01	39.68	36.85	39.39	41.94	PT BIS =	0.2064		
Senior	PERCENT	1.04	92.95	3.38	2.58	0.06	100.00	R BIS =	0.4588	P+ =	0.9295
	MEAN SCORE	34.41	51.27	43.90	37.05	22.62	50.46	PT BIS =	0.2417		
2-Year	PERCENT	0.43	87.04	5.69	5.96	0.88	100.00	R BIS =	0.3299	P+ =	0.8704
	MEAN SCORE	27.63	41.46	34.49	33.82	30.85	40.45	PT BIS =	0.2075		

(Note: Error-choice items are omitted from this Appendix. See Table 3.4.1, p.)

9. The United States accounts for roughly 5 per cent of the world's population.
   The entries on which line (1, 2, 3 or 4) of the table below are approximately
   correct for the United States today?

	Percentage of World Consumption of Nonrenewable Resources	Percentage of World Producton of Economic Goods and Service
(1)	40	25
(2)	10	40
(3)	30	30
(4)	25	5

		OMIT	1*	2	3	4	TOTAL					
Freshmen	PERCENT	13.71	44.15	11.80	26.50	3.84	100.00	R BIS =	0.2913	P+ =	0.4415
	MEAN SCORE	34.40	44.89	38.33	42.55	41.70	41.94	PT BIS =	0.2314		
Senior	PERCENT	11.65	56.16	7.05	19.76	5.38	100.00	R BIS =	0.2272	P+ =	0.5616
	MEAN SCORE	45.34	52.39	42.85	50.60	50.87	50.46	PT BIS =	0.1804		
2-Year	PERCENT	19.02	40.62	12.43	22.47	5.46	100.00	R BIS =	0.2971	P+ =	0.4062
	MEAN SCORE	36.85	44.01	35.86	40.09	38.51	40.45	PT BIS =	0.2346		

10. The most important worldwide <u>commercial</u> source of energy today is

    (1) coal
    (2) nuclear power
    (3) petroleum
    (4) solar power

		OMIT	1	2	3*	4	TOTAL				
Freshmen	PERCENT	1.16	8.74	7.73	79.12	3.26	100.00	R BIS =	0.3800	P+ =	0.7912
	MEAN SCORE	25.77	38.59	35.24	43.50	34.48	41.94	PT BIS =	0.2685		
Senior	PERCENT	0.34	7.74	5.66	84.91	1.35	100.00	R BIS =	0.2188	P+ =	0.8491
	MEAN SCORE	25.63	50.38	42.36	51.19	45.09	50.46	PT BIS =	0.1432		
2-Year	PERCENT	0.76	10.22	11.32	73.20	4.49	100.00	R BIS =	0.4369	P+ =	0.7320
	MEAN SCORE	30.96	39.25	30.03	42.92	30.90	40.45	PT BIS =	0.3249		

11. The primary household fuel in Africa and Asia is

    (1) wood
    (2) coal
    (3) natural gas
    (4) petroleum

		OMIT	1*	2	3	4	TOTAL				
Freshmen	PERCENT	4.35	43.99	22.75	15.43	13.48	100.00	R BIS =	0.2903	P+ =	0.4399
	MEAN SCORE	33.24	44.89	41.53	38.89	39.27	41.94	PT BIS =	0.2306		
Senior	PERCENT	3.25	53.47	21.79	7.48	14.01	100.00	R BIS =	0.5087	P+ =	0.5347
	MEAN SCORE	44.09	55.04	47.23	42.21	43.90	50.46	PT BIS =	0.4051		
2-Year	PERCENT	3.36	48.93	21.42	9.57	16.73	100.00	R BIS =	0.3261	P+ =	0.4893
	MEAN SCORE	34.02	43.79	37.55	34.65	39.04	40.45	PT BIS =	0.2601		

13. The typical meal in the poor countries of the world consists of

    (1) meat, vegetables, and a dairy product
    (2) cereal grains and a side dish of vegetables
    (3) meat or fish and cereal grains
    (4) an egg or other dairy product, vegetables, and fruit

		OMIT	1	2*	3	4	TOTAL				
Freshmen	PERCENT	0.88	0.40	80.18	16.61	1.94	100.00	R BIS =	0.2553	P+ =	0.8018
	MEAN SCORE	21.53	26.14	42.94	39.25	35.76	41.94	PT BIS =	0.1784		
Senior	PERCENT	0.37	0.19	85.16	13.53	0.74	100.00	R BIS =	0.2343	P+ =	0.8516
	MEAN SCORE	27.77	31.34	51.23	46.72	46.26	50.46	PT BIS =	0.1527		
2-Year	PERCENT	0.56	0.93	79.25	17.50	1.76	100.00	R BIS =	0.3272	P+ =	0.7925
	MEAN SCORE	37.22	28.62	41.94	35.45	30.72	40.45	PT BIS =	0.2310		

14. Which of the following is the major reason why more and more countries in
Asia, Africa, and Latin America have become net food importers in the
last fifty years?

    (1) Generally they have not had the resources to grow enough
         food to feed their populations.
    (2) They have been encouraged to shift production from food crops to cash crops.
    (3) Importing food has seemed desirable as a hedge against frequent crop failures.
    (4) They have shifted a large part of the labor force to industrial production.

		OMIT	1	2*	3	4	TOTAL				
Freshmen	PERCENT	3.30	48.23	18.12	8.16	22.18	100.00	R BIS =	0.0467	P+ =	0.1812
	MEAN SCORE	27.00	43.29	42.71	38.28	41.93	41.94	PT BIS =	0.0320		
Senior	PERCENT	1.73	52.38	19.72	6.15	20.02	100.00	R BIS =	0.3368	P+ =	0.1972
	MEAN SCORE	38.25	50.14	56.21	43.93	48.71	50.46	PT BIS =	0.2350		
2-Year	PERCENT	2.31	48.47	13.25	10.88	25.09	100.00	R BIS =	0.0658	P+ =	0.1325
	MEAN SCORE	31.28	41.67	41.79	33.47	41.27	40.45	PT BIS =	0.0416		

15. During the last quarter century, the largest percentage of world trade has been

    (1) among the industrial or developed countries
    (2) among the less developed countries
    (3) between the industrial or developed countries and the less developed countries
    (4) between non-Communist countries and Communist countries

		OMIT	1*	2	3	4	TOTAL				
Freshmen	PERCENT	1.62	54.66	2.29	32.38	9.04	100.00	R BIS =	0.2766	P+ =	0.5466
	MEAN SCORE	23.71	44.21	31.31	41.31	36.39	41.94	PT BIS =	0.2200		
Senior	PERCENT	1.73	58.65	3.17	32.19	4.26	100.00	R BIS =	0.3313	P+ =	0.5865
	MEAN SCORE	33.75	53.13	37.90	49.16	39.70	50.46	PT BIS =	0.2620		
2-Year	PERCENT	1.44	53.15	3.03	34.00	8.38	100.00	R BIS =	0.2717	P+ =	0.5315
	MEAN SCORE	34.42	43.00	31.30	39.22	33.63	40.45	PT BIS =	0.2164		

16. Unlike trade negotiations in the 1940's, 1950's, and 1960's, the main purpose of the recently completed multilateral trade negotiations was to

    (1) lower tariffs and customs duties
    (2) establish stable prices for petroleum products
    (3) reduce nontariff barriers to trade
    (4) reduce the trade barriers of less developed countries

		OMIT	1	2	3*	4	TOTAL				
Freshmen	PERCENT	9.94	15.50	36.27	12.75	25.54	100.00	R BIS =	0.1746	P+ =	0.1275
	MEAN SCORE	36.72	39.87	41.34	45.18	44.44	41.94	PT BIS =	0.1093		
Senior	PERCENT	12.74	15.22	27.75	17.98	26.31	100.00	R BIS =	0.3034	P+ =	0.1798
	MEAN SCORE	51.15	50.86	47.27	55.82	49.59	50.46	PT BIS =	0.2072		
2-Year	PERCENT	8.97	19.41	32.39	13.03	26.20	100.00	R BIS =	0.1390	P+ =	0.1303
	MEAN SCORE	34.26	39.17	40.34	43.29	42.26	40.45	PT BIS =	0.0875		

17. Taiwan, Hong Kong, Singapore, and South Korea all experienced which of the following during the 1970's?

    (1) Rapid growth of light industry
    (2) Massive in-migration
    (3) Increasing poverty
    (4) Serious unemployment

		OMIT	1*	2	3	4	TOTAL				
Freshmen	PERCENT	3.46	47.25	9.57	25.11	14.61	100.00	R BIS =	0.2688	P+ =	0.4725
	MEAN SCORE	33.67	44.51	39.92	38.10	43.48	41.94	PT BIS =	0.2142		
Senior	PERCENT	4.25	61.21	9.44	13.56	11.54	100.00	R BIS =	0.3126	P+ =	0.6121
	MEAN SCORE	44.85	52.83	49.38	43.65	48.84	50.46	PT BIS =	0.2458		
2-Year	PERCENT	3.43	50.31	10.16	23.89	12.21	100.00	R BIS =	0.2450	P+ =	0.5031
	MEAN SCORE	31.57	42.89	41.00	36.94	39.32	40.45	PT BIS =	0.1955		

18. Which of the following did NOT contribute to United States balance-of-payments difficulties in the 1970's?

    (1) The costs of waging a war in Vietnam in the 1960's and early 1970's
    (2) The decline of United States agricultural output
    (3) The increase in oil prices resulting from the price policies of the Organization of Petroleum Exporting Countries (OPEC)
    (4) The growth of competitive manufacturing sectors in other countries

		OMIT	1	2*	3	4	TOTAL				
Freshmen	PERCENT	4.41	12.59	38.56	15.32	29.12	100.00	R BIS =	0.4493	P+ =	0.3856
	MEAN SCORE	29.48	38.97	47.00	37.67	40.65	41.94	PT BIS =	0.3530		
Senior	PERCENT	3.06	16.92	51.67	9.34	19.02	100.00	R BIS =	0.5103	P+ =	0.5167
	MEAN SCORE	36.99	48.88	55.23	43.58	44.46	50.46	PT BIS =	0.4069		
2-Year	PERCENT	4.84	17.95	31.78	20.89	24.53	100.00	R BIS =	0.5501	P+ =	0.3178
	MEAN SCORE	28.59	37.31	48.20	36.53	38.40	40.45	PT BIS =	0.4213		

19. A very high degree of interdependence is a basic fact of contemporary
    international life. Which of the following is NOT a significant consequence
    of interdependence?

    (1) Interdependence intermingles domestic with foreign policies.
    (2) Interdependence is associated with an increased willingness to
         renounce war as an instrument of national policy.
    (3) Interdependence makes it highly probable that significant events in,
         or actions by, nation A will have serious effects on nations B, C,
         D, etc., and vice versa.
    (4) Interdependence may make both self-sufficiency and dependency (e.g.,
         reliance on imports of essential raw materials) difficult and
         costly.

		OMIT	1	2*	3	4	TOTAL				
Freshmen	PERCENT	13.01	14.55	23.18	24.16	25.10	100.00	R BIS =	0.2780	P+ =	0.2318
	MEAN SCORE	33.29	43.66	46.09	39.09	44.32	41.94	PT BIS =	0.2009		
Senior	PERCENT	8.35	15.76	33.18	14.60	28.11	100.00	R BIS =	0.2603	P+ =	0.3318
	MEAN SCORE	43.91	49.48	53.91	45.58	51.42	50.46	PT BIS =	0.2007		
2-Year	PERCENT	8.30	13.76	28.27	25.21	24.46	100.00	R BIS =	0.2711	P+ =	0.2827
	MEAN SCORE	28.77	42.28	44.52	37.98	41.24	40.45	PT BIS =	0.2036		

20. On which of the following issues has there been the greatest success in
    achieving cross-cultural consensus on aims and policies?

    (1) Health, as exemplified by the activities of the World Health Organization (WHO)
    (2) Working conditions, as exemplified by the activities of the International
         Labour Organization (ILO)
    (3) Industrial development, as exemplified by the activities of the
         United Nations Industrial Development Organization (UNIDO)
    (4) Human rights, as exemplified by the activities of the United
         Nations Economic and Social Council (ECOSOC)

		OMIT	1*	2	3	4	TOTAL				
Freshmen	PERCENT	6.02	33.15	10.87	26.27	23.68	100.00	R BIS =	0.4129	P+ =	0.3315
	MEAN SCORE	30.43	47.07	36.22	41.10	41.22	41.94	PT BIS =	0.3183		
Senior	PERCENT	3.63	46.21	4.95	29.46	15.75	100.00	R BIS =	0.3983	P+ =	0.4621
	MEAN SCORE	37.78	54.61	40.18	49.47	46.31	50.46	PT BIS =	0.3171		
2-Year	PERCENT	5.88	29.26	14.45	25.47	24.93	100.00	R BIS =	0.4572	P+ =	0.2926
	MEAN SCORE	28.62	47.19	34.68	40.11	39.04	40.45	PT BIS =	0.3455		

21. The worldwide spread of human disease has been linked to all of the
    following EXCEPT

     (1)   advances in transportation technology and associated increases in
    the speed at which carriers of disease travel
     (2)   the development of super strains of bacteria and viruses or their
    vectors as unintended consequences of disease prevention measures
     (3)   increased contact among hitherto remote populations through voluntary
    and involuntary migrations
     (4)   the evolution of new insect species that sometimes carry human diseases

		OMIT	1	2	3	4*	TOTAL				
Freshmen	PERCENT	2.52	24.31	19.19	14.24	39.74	100.00	R BIS =	0.2720	P+ =	0.3974
	MEAN SCORE	21.64	41.49	40.82	39.42	44.93	41.94	PT BIS =	0.2144		
Senior	PERCENT	2.00	24.46	17.30	13.38	42.87	100.00	R BIS =	0.2910	P+ =	0.4287
	MEAN SCORE	33.82	48.86	47.98	48.73	53.69	50.46	PT BIS =	0.2308		
2-Year	PERCENT	4.01	24.10	23.58	16.09	32.22	100.00	R BIS =	0.3974	P+ =	0.3222
	MEAN SCORE	33.52	38.83	38.00	37.10	46.00	40.45	PT BIS =	0.3051		

24. The major factor in the elimination of smallpox in the 1970's as an
    epidemic threat to the world was

     (1)   the introduction of better sanitation
     (2)   the introduction of better methods of treatment
     (3)   a decline in the virulence of the virus
     (4)   the implementation of worldwide vaccination programs

		OMIT	1	2	3	4*	TOTAL				
Freshmen	PERCENT	2.41	2.66	8.21	3.78	82.93	100.00	R BIS =	0.4983	P+ =	0.8293
	MEAN SCORE	21.88	34.91	36.18	34.17	43.67	41.94	PT BIS =	0.3362		
Senior	PERCENT	1.16	4.53	4.51	3.87	85.93	100.00	R BIS =	0.2502	P+ =	0.8593
	MEAN SCORE	45.15	51.16	43.89	41.39	51.25	50.46	PT BIS =	0.1608		
2-Year	PERCENT	1.73	4.75	9.29	3.41	80.83	100.00	R BIS =	0.4651	P+ =	0.8083
	MEAN SCORE	28.74	33.05	31.40	34.69	42.42	40.45	PT BIS =	0.3225		

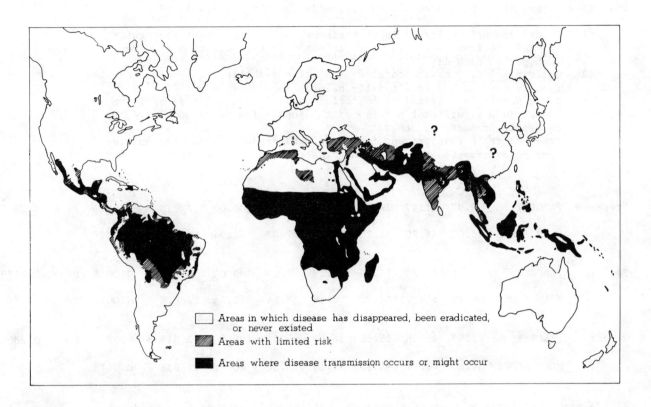

Areas in which disease has disappeared, been eradicated, or never existed

Areas with limited risk

Areas where disease transmission occurs or might occur

25. The map above shows the distribution in the world today of which of the following diseases?

(1) Bubonic plague
(2) Malaria
(3) Typhoid fever
(4) Cholera

		OMIT	1	2*	3	4	TOTAL					
Freshmen	PERCENT	7.51	5.90	61.19	15.80	9.60	100.00	R BIS =	0.2567	P+ =	0.6119
	MEAN SCORE	34.67	37.60	43.76	38.46	44.36	41.94	PT BIS =	0.2018		
Senior	PERCENT	7.08	1.67	63.74	13.18	14.33	100.00	R BIS =	0.1576	P+ =	0.6374
	MEAN SCORE	47.07	38.83	51.58	47.69	51.04	50.46	PT BIS =	0.1230		
2-Year	PERCENT	9.31	5.86	52.22	18.87	13.73	100.00	R BIS =	0.1998	P+ =	0.5222
	MEAN SCORE	40.05	34.66	42.36	36.19	41.79	40.45	PT BIS =	0.1592		

26. As a global problem, inadequate nutrition is largely the result of

   (1) large populations living in countries whose production of foodstuffs
       is insufficient to provide the minimum number of calories required by
       each person each day
   (2) world population having outgrown the world's ability to produce enough
       food to meet each person's daily caloric requirements
   (3) large populations living in countries in which inequalities of income
       result in a significant portion of the population being unable to buy
       the foods produced by others
   (4) trade controls that prevent food surpluses produced by some countries
       from being exported to other countries that want to buy them

		OMIT	1	2	3*	4	TOTAL				
Freshmen	PERCENT	2.93	51.47	14.42	26.94	4.25	100.00	R BIS = 0.0026	P+ =	0.2694
	MEAN SCORE	26.02	44.20	38.20	41.97	37.87	41.94	PT BIS = 0.0019		
Senior	PERCENT	1.11	61.26	10.44	24.29	2.90	100.00	R BIS = 0.0018	P+ =	0.2429
	MEAN SCORE	36.85	51.92	43.72	50.49	48.84	50.46	PT BIS = 0.0013		
2-Year	PERCENT	1.97	48.68	15.86	28.04	5.46	100.00	R BIS = -0.0897	P+ =	0.2804
	MEAN SCORE	31.89	43.51	5.98	39.10	36.28	40.45	PT BIS = -0.0673		

27. A major criticism of Western companies that persuade mothers in developing
    countries to substitute simulated milk for breast milk is that

   (1) many mothers are too poor to give their infants an adequate and/or
       sustained diet of simulated milk
   (2) the sale of simulated milk cuts into the market for domestically
       produced dairy products
   (3) the promotion of simulated milk presupposes that all infants have the
       same dietary needs as Western children
   (4) many mothers are indirectly encouraged to have more children because
       the use of simulated milk makes child-rearing easier

		OMIT	1*	2	3	4	TOTAL			
Freshmen	PERCENT	3.46	52.27	11.22	19.84	13.21	100.00	R BIS = 0.2470	P+ =	0.5227
	MEAN SCORE	25.16	44.07	38.68	41.63	41.09	41.94	PT BIS = 0.1969		
Senior	PERCENT	2.05	55.26	6.85	26.23	9.61	100.00	R BIS = 0.1735	P+ =	0.5526
	MEAN SCORE	46.38	51.96	43.58	50.91	46.38	50.46	PT BIS = 0.1380		
2-Year	PERCENT	2.02	53.01	9.42	22.90	12.65	100.00	R BIS = 0.0718	P+ =	0.5301
	MEAN SCORE	24.67	41.13	37.63	42.24	39.01	40.45	P+ BIS = 0.0572		

29. The most persuasive argument against livestock production in a densely
    populated world is that it

    (1)   entails feeding foodcrops that could be directly consumed by people
    to animals whose meat ultimately yields significantly less protein
    and calorie value than the food the animals consume
    (2)   attaches more importance to producing high quality cuts of meat than
    to maximizing the volume of output
    (3)   gives priority to beef cattle when goats, hogs, and chickens could
    better serve as exports to the rest of the world
    (4)   yields meat of high animal fat content when vegetable fats are better and cheaper

		OMIT	1*	2	3	4	TOTAL				
Freshmen	PERCENT	4.11	58.20	14.15	12.12	11.42	100.00	R BIS =	0.4991	P+ =	0.5820
	MEAN SCORE	23.12	45.74	37.30	36.80	40.52	41.94	PT BIS =	0.3951		
Senior	PERCENT	1.54	70.07	11.70	6.77	9.92	100.00	R BIS =	0.4157	P+ =	0.7007
	MEAN SCORE	38.06	52.96	45.76	42.13	45.97	50.46	PT BIS =	0.3153		
2-Year	PERCENT	4.61	54.46	16.72	12.02	12.20	100.00	R BIS =	0.5723	P+ =	0.5446
	MEAN SCORE	27.17	45.68	33.96	35.13	36.31	40.45	PT BIS =	0.4554		

30. At the end of the eighteenth century, Thomas Malthus first publicized the idea that

    (1)   rapid population growth is essential for economic stability
    (2)   world population growth tends to outstrip the earth's capacity to produce food
    (3)   population control programs should be initiated to keep population in
    balance with food supply
    (4)   technological innovations in food production allow the world to cope
    with increasing population growth

		OMIT	1	2*	3	4	TOTAL				
Freshmen	PERCENT	14.59	6.97	37.61	32.43	8.41	100.00	R BIS =	0.2891	P+ =	0.3761
	MEAN SCORE	36.85	39.27	45.25	42.07	37.63	41.94	PT BIS =	0.2265		
Senior	PERCENT	11.57	7.80	48.98	26.74	4.91	100.00	R BIS =	0.3982	P+ =	0.4898
	MEAN SCORE	46.73	47.34	54.39	46.33	47.52	50.46	PT BIS =	0.3176		
2-Year	PERCENT	11.53	9.46	38.75	31.21	9.06	100.00	R BIS =	0.3539	P+ =	0.3875
	MEAN SCORE	33.98	37.70	44.84	39.88	34.78	40.45	PT BIS =	0.2783		

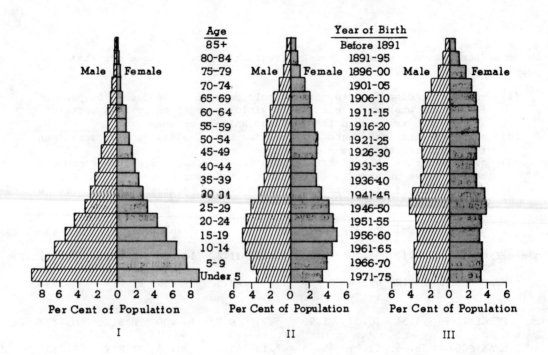

	Age		Year of Birth	
Male ⬛ Female	85+	Male ⬛ Female	Before 1891	Male ⬛ Female
	80-84		1891-95	
	75-79		1896-00	
	70-74		1901-05	
	65-69		1906-10	
	60-64		1911-15	
	55-59		1916-20	
	50-54		1921-25	
	45-49		1926-30	
	40-44		1931-35	
	35-39		1936-40	
	30-34		1941-45	
	25-29		1946-50	
	20-24		1951-55	
	15-19		1956-60	
	10-14		1961-65	
	5-9		1966-70	
	Under 5		1971-75	

```
  8 6 4 2 0 2 4 6 8        6 4 2 0 2 4 6        6 4 2 0 2 4 6
  Per Cent of Population   Per Cent of Population   Per Cent of Population
           I                        II                      III
```

31. The pyramids above represent the populations of Sweden, Mexico, and the
United States in 1975. Which of the following correctly matches each
pyramid with the country whose population it represents

	I	II	III
(1)	Mexico	United States	Sweden
(2)	United States	Mexico	Sweden
(3)	Mexico	Sweden	United States
(4)	Sweden	United States	Mexico

		OMIT	1*	2	3	4	TOTAL			
Freshmen	PERCENT	9.88	33.31	20.36	27.65	8.81	100.00	R BIS = 0.3473	P+ =	0.3331
	MEAN SCORE	33.24	46.24	38.53	43.17	39.39	41.94	PT BIS = 0.2679		
Senior	PERCENT	8.90	48.49	7.98	26.87	7.76	100.00	R BIS = 0.3357	P+ =	0.4849
	MEAN SCORE	44.02	53.80	42.02	49.93	47.49	50.46	PT BIS = 0.2677		
2-Year	PERCENT	13.39	29.14	21.12	25.62	10.72	100.00	R BIS = 0.4393	P+ =	0.2914
	MEAN SCORE	33.26	46.94	35.80	41.93	37.46	40.45	PT BIS = 0.3317		

32. Which of the following statements describes the trend in world population growth as of 1980?

(1) It is accelerating and total population is expected to triple by the year 2000.
(2) It is accelerating and total population is expected to double by the year 2000.
(3) It has begun to decelerate, but total population is still expected to increase substantially by the year 2000.
(4) It has started to decelerate, and therefore total population is expected to decline by the year 2000.

		OMIT	1	2	3*	4	TOTAL		
Freshmen	PERCENT	3.00	9.87	33.12	48.93	5.08	100.00	R BIS = 0.1645	P+ = 0.4893
	MEAN SCORE	21.47	39.86	43.15	43.46	35.43	41.94	PT BIS = 0.1312	
Senior	PERCENT	0.87	6.57	36.84	52.59	3.13	100.00	R BIS = 0.0944	P+ = 0.5259
	MEAN SCORE	21.06	50.10	51.00	51.33	38.61	50.46	PT BIS = 0.0752	
2-Year	PERCENT	1.88	10.73	33.86	46.09	7.43	100.00	R BIS = 0.1557	P+ = 0.4609
	MEAN SCORE	18.42	33.97	42.34	42.14	36.39	40.45	PT BIS = 0.1239	

34. During the course of history, which of the following human activities has contributed most directly to environmental alteration of the greatest area of the earth's surface?

(1) Urbanization
(2) Livestock raising
(3) Hunting and gathering
(4) Cultivation of crops

		OMIT	1	2	3	4*	TOTAL		
Freshmen	PERCENT	2.21	63.22	3.82	3.34	27.42	100.00	R BIS = 0.1562	P+ = 0.2742
	MEAN SCORE	15.13	42.57	36.70	36.00	44.09	41.94	PT BIS = 0.1166	
Senior	PERCENT	0.48	62.57	3.30	2.20	31.45	100.00	R BIS = 0.3677	P+ = 0.3145
	MEAN SCORE	19.10	48.88	46.97	35.63	55.49	50.46	PT BIS = 0.2812	
2-Year	PERCENT	0.93	61.03	5.92	6.52	25.60	100.00	R BIS = 0.0816	P+ = 0.2560
	MEAN SCORE	22.79	41.73	34.53	31.33	41.74	40.45	PT BIS = 0.0602	

35. Which of the following statements about the exhaustion of natural resources is most correct?

    (1) Worldwide population growth is the principal factor threatening to exhaust resources.
    (2) Because of their population growth, developing countries account for a disproportionate share of the increase in demands on resources.
    (3) Both increasing rates of per capita consumption and population growth are threatening to exhaust resources.
    (4) Technological change is the principal factor threatening to exhaust resources.

		OMIT	1	2	3*	4	TOTAL				
Freshmen	PERCENT	2.45	13.06	10.37	53.24	20.88	100.00	R BIS =	0.2088	P+ =	0.5324
	MEAN SCORE	21.29	42.90	37.31	43.71	41.53	41.94	PT BIS =	0.1663		
Senior	PERCENT	1.37	11.60	7.38	60.25	19.42	100.00	R BIS =	0.2787	P+ =	0.6025
	MEAN SCORE	32.92	48.71	41.94	52.62	49.27	50.46	PT BIS =	0.2196		
2-Year	PERCENT	3.80	13.34	12.62	51.49	18.74	100.00	R BIS =	0.2734	P+ =	0.5149
	MEAN SCORE	33.84	37.91	35.06	43.11	39.95	40.45	PT BIS =	0.2180		

36. Which of the following curves best represents the estimates of experts about the pattern of the world's past and possible future consumption of fossil fuels such as petroleum, natural gas, and coal?

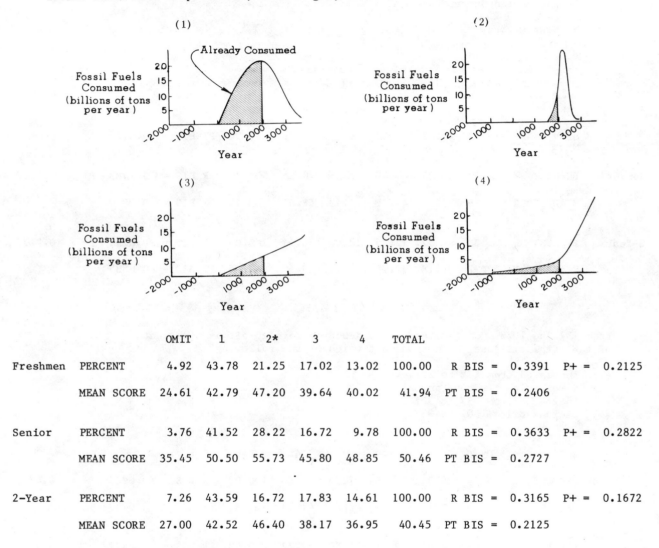

		OMIT	1	2*	3	4	TOTAL				
Freshmen	PERCENT	4.92	43.78	21.25	17.02	13.02	100.00	R BIS =	0.3391	P+ =	0.2125
	MEAN SCORE	24.61	42.79	47.20	39.64	40.02	41.94	PT BIS =	0.2406		
Senior	PERCENT	3.76	41.52	28.22	16.72	9.78	100.00	R BIS =	0.3633	P+ =	0.2822
	MEAN SCORE	35.45	50.50	55.73	45.80	48.85	50.46	PT BIS =	0.2727		
2-Year	PERCENT	7.26	43.59	16.72	17.83	14.61	100.00	R BIS =	0.3165	P+ =	0.1672
	MEAN SCORE	27.00	42.52	46.40	38.17	36.95	40.45	PT BIS =	0.2125		

37. The economy of which of the following is LEAST vulnerable to increases in the price of oil or to decreases in the supply of oil?

    (1) The United States
    (2) Japan
    (3) West Germany
    (4) Brazil

		OMIT	1*	2	3	4	TOTAL		
Freshmen	PERCENT	3.50	13.28	14.59	10.23	58.40	100.00	R BIS = −0.0280	P+ = 0.1328
	MEAN SCORE	19.47	41.42	38.63	38.72	44.79	41.94	PT BIS = −0.0177	
Senior	PERCENT	0.93	15.07	7.48	6.26	70.26	100.00	R BIS = 0.1483	P+ = 0.1507
	MEAN SCORE	28.39	53.25	43.71	44.42	51.41	50.46	PT BIS = 0.0970	
2-Year	PERCENT	1.33	21.72	12.25	12.60	52.11	100.00	R BIS = −0.0751	P+ = 0.2172
	MEAN SCORE	30.22	39.18	34.74	36.71	43.50	40.45	PT BIS = −0.0535	

39. From 1972 to 1978, United States dependence on foreign oil as a percentage of the total oil that it consumed did which of the following?

    (1) Increased from 10% to 25%.
    (2) Remained nearly constant at 25%.
    (3) Increased from 33% to 50%.
    (4) Decreased from 50% to 33%.

		OMIT	1	2	3*	4	TOTAL		
Freshmen	PERCENT	4.14	29.76	10.96	47.33	7.80	100.00	R BIS = 0.0925	P+ = 0.4733
	MEAN SCORE	23.48	42.11	43.69	42.82	43.23	41.94	PT BIS = 0.0737	
Senior	PERCENT	1.67	34.00	9.81	46.80	7.72	100.00	R BIS = 0.0472	PT = 0.4680
	MEAN SCORE	39.30	50.75	50.42	50.95	48.73	50.46	PT BIS = 0.0376	
2-Year	PERCENT	2.19	30.51	13.25	47.73	6.33	100.00	R BIS = 0.1529	P+ = 0.4773
	MEAN SCORE	25.82	39.64	39.45	42.05	39.50	40.45	PT BIS = 0.1219	

40. President Carter was primarily concerned about which of the following when he urged all nations to defer nuclear fuel reprocessing and the development of the breeder reactor?

    (1)   The possibility of nuclear weapons proliferation
    (2)   The occurrence of a catastrophic accident
    (3)   The emergency of a uranium cartel
    (4)   The distortion of economic development priorities

		OMIT	1*	2	3	4	TOTAL				
Freshmen	PERCENT	4.52	36.01	40.06	6.33	13.08	100.00	R BIS =	0.2222	P+ =	0.3601
	MEAN SCORE	23.19	44.56	43.15	39.62	38.58	41.94	PT BIS =	0.1732		
Senior	PERCENT	1.78	43.52	37.63	5.50	11.57	100.00	R BIS =	0.2735	P+ =	0.4352
	MEAN SCORE	36.01	53.46	48.44	50.47	47.99	50.46	PT BIS =	0.2171		
2-Year	PERCENT	3.27	44.27	35.17	5.31	11.97	100.00	R BIS =	0.1545	P+ =	0.4427
	MEAN SCORE	28.45	42.18	41.23	39.65	35.43	40.45	PT BIS =	0.1228		

41. The term "assured destruction" refers to which of the following?

    (1)   The notion, shared by many pacifists, that the destruction of all nuclear weapons will assure world peace
    (2)   A technical clause, contained in many peace treaties, referring to the destruction of the arsenals of defeated parties
    (3)   The likely fate of Western civilization in the event of a third world war
    (4)   A deterrence strategy that credibly threatens a significant level of population and industrial destruction should an adversary attack first

		OMIT	1	2	3	4*	TOTAL				
Freshmen	PERCENT	6.86	5.95	8.00	54.03	25.16	100.00	R BIS =	0.2939	P+ =	0.2516
	MEAN SCORE	29.02	37.35	39.05	42.54	46.17	41.94	PT BIS =	0.2159		
Senior	PERCENT	7.01	3.70	6.15	47.16	35.98	100.00	R BIS =	0.4312	P+ =	0.3598
	MEAN SCORE	44.11	37.85	44.48	49.03	55.89	50.46	PT BIS =	0.3362		
2-Year	PERCENT	6.85	8.85	7.65	44.96	31.68	100.00	R BIS =	0.3387	P+ =	0.3168
	MEAN SCORE	29.32	34.10	33.70	41.19	45.23	40.45	PT BIS =	0.2593		

43. Which of the following is true of the Salt II Treaty signed in 1979?

    (1) The members of NATO and the Warsaw Pact were the major signatory blocs.
    (2) It imposed significant controls on the development of new weapons technologies.
    (3) It sought to maintain an existing balance of forces between the signatories.
    (4) It imposed stringent limits on the weapon systems of powers other than
        the signatories.

		OMIT	1	2	3*	4	TOTAL				
Freshmen	PERCENT	7.80	9.53	26.67	42.46	13.55	100.00	R BIS =	0.3288	P+ =	0.4246
	MEAN SCORE	29.92	41.10	42.01	45.38	38.50	41.94	PT BIS =	0.2606		
Senior	PERCENT	5.34	7.55	28.48	50.92	7.71	100.00	R BIS =	0.3087	P+ =	0.5092
	MEAN SCORE	40.31	51.92	49.04	53.39	41.94	50.46	PT BIS =	0.2462		
2-Year	PERCENT	7.88	12.03	27.26	42.36	10.47	100.00	R BIS =	0.3648	P+ =	0.4236
	MEAN SCORE	28.92	38.42	40.42	44.68	34.45	40.45	PT BIS =	0.2891		

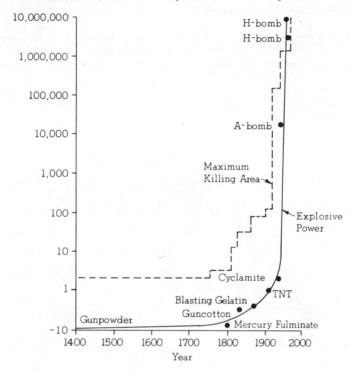

INCREASE IN EXPLOSIVE POWER AND KILLING AREA
(in tons of TNT equivalent and square miles of killing area)

44. Of the following, which is the most likely implication of the data recorded
     in the table above?

     (1) States today have greater independent military security than they did
          in former times because each can potentially command enormous firepower.
     (2) Warfare can no longer be limited in geographic scope, and most wars of
          the future are likely to be intercontinental.
     (3) Even strong states are losing their ability to defend their territories
          and populations effectively from military attack.
     (4) New weaponry is forcing states to concentrate on territorial defense
          rather than on deterrence of military attack.

		OMIT	1	2	3*	4	TOTAL				
Freshmen	PERCENT	6.53	12.30	48.66	18.88	13.64	100.00	R BIS =	0.0270	P+ =	0.1888
	MEAN SCORE	28.67	40.41	44.53	42.37	39.81	41.94	PT BIS =	0.0187		
Senior	PERCENT	3.87	8.21	60.83	17.04	10.05	100.00	R BIS =	0.1626	P+ =	0.1704
	MEAN SCORE	36.27	46.30	51.94	53.39	45.40	50.46	PT BIS =	0.1096		
2-Year	PERCENT	6.50	15.40	48.15	12.79	17.16	100.00	R BIS =	0.0513	P+ =	0.1279
	MEAN SCORE	26.19	40.21	43.05	41.51	38.00	40.45	PT BIS =	0.0322		

45. The establishment of the Western sovereign territorial state and the modern state system is usually dated from the

    (1) breakup of the Roman Empire in the fifth century
    (2) development of feudalism in the early Middle Ages
    (3) Peace of Westphalia in the mid-seventeenth century, which brought European conflicts fought in the name of religion to an end
    (4) Peace of Versailles in the early twentieth century, which dealt with the aftermath of the breakup of the Russian, German, Austro-Hungarian, and Ottoman empires

		OMIT	1	2	3*	4	TOTAL				
Freshmen	PERCENT	11.19	15.30	18.40	18.92	36.19	100.00	R BIS =	0.0891	P+ =	0.1892
	MEAN SCORE	33.27	40.41	43.53	43.38	43.69	41.94	PT BIS =	0.0616		
Senior	PERCENT	9.80	13.23	20.54	19.04	37.39	100.00	R BIS =	0.1910	P+ =	0.1904
	MEAN SCORE	44.54	50.30	50.78	53.76	50.21	50.46	PT BIS =	0.1322		
2-Year	PERCENT	9.82	16.76	21.42	17.60	34.41	100.00	R BIS =	0.0396	P+ =	0.1760
	MEAN SCORE	31.22	42.13	40.65	41.18	41.78	40.45	PT BIS =	0.0269		

46. In which of the following periods in European history did nationalist movements emerge as significant political forces?

    (1) The early Middle Ages
    (2) The late Middle Ages
    (3) The Renaissance
    (4) The nineteenth century

		OMIT	1	2	3	4*	TOTAL				
Freshmen	PERCENT	6.01	4.73	15.57	26.70	46.99	100.00	R BIS =	0.3131	P+ =	0.4699
	MEAN SCORE	30.04	35.70	41.34	40.77	44.95	41.94	PT BIS =	0.2494		
Senior	PERCENT	3.99	4.08	12.90	24.29	54.74	100.00	R BIS =	0.1811	P+ =	0.5474
	MEAN SCORE	45.54	48.41	45.82	50.50	52.05	50.46	PT BIS =	0.1440		
2-Year	PERCENT	6.85	5.97	16.40	23.76	47.02	100.00	R BIS =	0.1638	P+ =	0.4702
	MEAN SCORE	35.80	34.17	39.23	40.78	42.19	40.45	PT BIS =	0.1305		

47. Since 1945, political conflict and instability have often arisen as a
    result of racial, religious, ethnic, and linguistic differences within
    many states. Of the following, which three states contain within their
    boundaries the most ethno-linguistic diversity?

    (1) Italy, Jamaica, Japan
    (2) Czechoslovakia, Sri Lanka, the United States
    (3) India, Nigeria, Iran
    (4) Panama, Romania, Turkey

		OMIT	1	2	3*	4	TOTAL				
Freshmen	PERCENT	5.61	17.90	40.62	25.94	9.93	100.00	R BIS =	0.1744	P+ =	0.2594
	MEAN SCORE	27.62	39.25	44.38	44.41	38.42	41.94	PT BIS =	0.1289		
Senior	PERCENT	4.13	11.01	49.23	29.98	5.65	100.00	R BIS =	0.3533	P+ =	0.2998
	MEAN SCORE	39.36	44.33	50.11	55.42	47.23	50.46	PT BIS =	0.2681		
2-Year	PERCENT	6.11	17.21	42.24	25.71	8.73	100.00	R BIS =	0.1967	P+ =	0.2571
	MEAN SCORE	27.49	37.94	42.22	43.55	36.82	40.45	PT BIS =	0.1451		

48. The republics of the Soviet Union were formed primarily on the basis of

    (1) the ethnic groups or nationalities of the people
    (2) natural geographic boundaries
    (3) the political orientation of the people
    (4) agricultural and climatic zones

		OMIT	1*	2	3	4	TOTAL				
Freshmen	PERCENT	4.31	25.08	25.08	32.82	12.71	100.00	R BIS =	0.3300	P+ =	0.2508
	MEAN SCORE	25.75	46.69	42.01	40.24	42.26	41.94	PT BIS =	0.2423		
Senior	PERCENT	2.98	35.90	20.73	25.96	14.43	100.00	R BIS =	0.5719	P+ =	0.3590
	MEAN SCORE	36.83	57.67	49.38	44.35	47.87	50.46	PT BIS =	0.4457		
2-Year	PERCENT	4.74	24.10	22.56	34.85	13.76	100.00	R BIS =	0.4014	P+ =	0.2410
	MEAN SCORE	30.86	46.96	38.63	38.67	39.86	40.45	PT BIS =	0.2924		

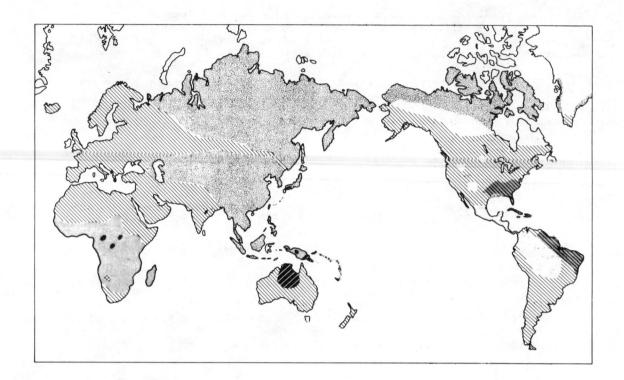

49. The general distribution of which of the following is shown on the map
    above dated 1960?

    (1) Human racial groups
    (2) Major world religions
    (3) Major world language groups
    (4) Cereal grains

		OMIT	1*	2	3	4	TOTAL				
Freshmen	PERCENT	6.82	26.14	18.38	15.59	33.06	100.00	R BIS =	0.1951	P+ =	0.2614
	MEAN	33.31	44.69	41.79	39.41	42.81	41.94	PT BIS =	0.1445		
Senior	PERCENT	7.39	30.05	11.91	11.34	39.31	100.00	R BIS =	0.1120	P+ =	0.3005
	MEAN	44.34	52.03	45.47	44.98	53.50	50.46	PT BIS =	0.0850		
2-Year	PERCENT	7.91	24.46	14.30	23.72	29.61	100.00	R BIS =	0.0522	P+ =	0.2446
	MEAN	33.39	41.29	38.98	39.94	42.77	40.45	PT BIS =	0.0381		

50. Since the Second World War, ethnic or religious groups that have engaged in violent conflict with one another include which of the following?

      I.   Jews and Arabs
     II. Hindus and Muslims
   III. Christians and Muslims
    IV. Catholics and Protestants

(1) I only
(2) I and IV only
(3) II and III only
(4) I, II, III, and IV

		OMIT	1	2	3	4*	TOTAL				
Freshmen	PERCENT	3.21	17.81	30.08	8.67	40.23	100.00	R BIS =	0.3666	P+ =	0.4023
	MEAN SCORE	22.61	38.92	42.52	34.66	45.94	41.94	PT BIS =	0.2893		
Senior	PERCENT	1.59	13.39	30.11	3.84	51.07	100.00	R BIS =	0.4709	P+ =	0.5107
	MEAN SCORE	26.51	43.23	48.94	38.31	54.91	50.46	PT BIS =	0.3756		
2-Year	PERCENT	3.13	20.54	30.66	7.58	38.09	100.00	R BIS =	0.4355	P+ =	0.3809
	MEAN SCORE	22.29	37.29	38.74	36.02	45.92	40.45	PT BIS =	0.3418		

51. Since 1947, successive Indian governments have regarded which of the following an an impediment to the realization of democratic ideals in India?

(1) Resistance to the modification of the traditional caste system
(2) Continuing political power of the former maharajahs
(3) Multiplicity of religious faiths within India
(4) Multiplicity of ethnic groups within India

		OMIT	1*	2	3	4	TOTAL				
Freshmen	PERCENT	10.56	42.49	15.39	22.37	9.18	100.00	R BIS =	0.5233	P+ =	0.4249
	MEAN SCORE	30.73	47.42	37.99	40.42	39.76	41.94	PT BIS =	0.4147		
Senior	PERCENT	5.55	54.26	11.40	19.91	8.88	100.00	R BIS =	0.3726	P+ =	0.5426
	MEAN SCORE	38.42	53.76	47.05	47.28	49.33	50.46	PT BIS =	0.2965		
2-Year	PERCENT	7.87	43.24	18.06	21.73	9.09	100.00	R BIS =	0.5277	P+ =	0.4324
	MEAN SCORE	29.19	46.47	37.72	37.03	35.24	40.45	PT BIS =	0.4187		

52. Apartheid in South Africa is a term designating which of the following?

    (1) The existence of widespread racial prejudice
    (2) A system of laws designed to separate the races
    (3) A system of laws designed to alleviate economic inequalities
    (4) Affirmative action against discrimination

		OMIT	1	2*	3	4	TOTAL			
Freshmen	PERCENT	15.34	13.88	44.09	17.45	9.24	100.00	R BIS = 0.5359	P+ =	0.4409
	MEAN SCORE	34.57	41.01	47.38	37.88	37.23	41.94	PT BIS = 0.4257		
Senior	PERCENT	11.42	10.16	64.11	9.26	5.05	100.00	R BIS = 0.5818	P+ =	0.6411
	MEAN SCORE	41.60	45.81	54.57	41.49	44.13	50.46	PT BIS = 0.4534		
2-Year	PERCENT	11.17	13.30	48.08	16.33	11.12	100.00	R BIS = 0.5226	P+ =	0.4808
	MEAN SCORE	30.98	38.08	45.88	35.52	36.59	40.45	PT BIS = 0.4166		

53. In the seventeenth and eighteenth centuries significant numbers of black slaves were brought from Africa to all of the following EXCEPT

    (1) British North America
    (2) The Caribbean Islands
    (3) Brazil
    (4) Argentina

		OMIT	1	2	3	4*	TOTAL			
Freshmen	PERCENT	4.59	14.59	18.44	15.32	47.07	100.00	R BIS = 0.4006	P+ =	0.4707
	MEAN SCORE	23.02	37.92	40.52	41.31	45.78	41.94	PT BIS = 0.3192		
Senior	PERCENT	2.46	11.20	17.67	12.61	56.05	100.00	R BIS = 0.4195	P+ =	0.5605
	MEAN SCORE	30.79	46.13	44.07	51.22	54.03	50.46	PT BIS = 0.3332		
2-Year	PERCENT	2.64	17.21	21.59	14.10	44.46	100.00	R BIS = 0.5144	P+ =	0.4446
	MEAN SCORE	21.01	36.84	35.83	37.51	46.19	40.45	PT BIS = 0.4088		

54. Which of the following is a correct statement about the historical sources of population in North and South America?

   (1) During the mid-eighteenth century struggle between England and France for dominance in Canada, the French were a minority of the Canadian white population.
   (2) By the beginning of the nineteenth century, all major areas of European settlement on the South American continent were under Spanish domination.
   (3) The first sizable number of people of Mexican descent in the United States were resident in areas conquered or annexed by the United States in the mid-nineteenth century.
   (4) In the massive influx of European immigrants into the United States during the late nineteenth and early twentieth centuries, Northern Europeans predominated over immigrants from Eastern and Southern Europe.

		OMIT	1	2	3*	4	TOTAL			
Freshmen	PERCENT	9.20	11.06	22.93	25.48	31.33	100.00	R BIS =	0.1880	P = 0.2548
	MEAN SCORE	29.00	39.72	42.54	44.63	43.89	41.94	PT BIS =	0.1385	
Senior	PERCENT	6.44	8.38	19.65	35.13	30.40	100.00	R BIS =	0.3017	P+ = 0.3513
	MEAN SCORE	40.79	47.51	48.00	54.32	50.46	50.46	PT BIS =	0.2345	
2-Year	PERCENT	7.73	13.39	21.23	30.26	27.39	100.00	R BIS =	0.3134	P+ = 0.3026
	MEAN SCORE	26.76	38.00	38.67	44.99	41.89	40.45	PT BIS =	0.2381	

55. Which of the following accounts for the death from infectious diseases of more than twenty million American Indians after their early contacts with white people?

   (1) An inadequate diet that made the Indians unhealthy
   (2) The fact that the Indians had low resistance to diseases previously unknown in the Americas
   (3) An increased virulence of disease organisms resulting from the crossing of European and American strains
   (4) Deliberate germ warfare waged by Europeans against the Indians

		OMIT	1	2*	3	4	TOTAL			
Freshmen	PERCENT	4.67	7.02	65.31	18.35	4.66	100.00	R BIS =	0.5663	P+ = 0.6531
	MEAN SCORE	21.63	35.01	45.57	38.37	35.74	41.94	PT BIS =	0.4394	
Senior	PERCENT	1.80	3.53	81.63	10.24	2.81	100.00	R BIS =	0.5974	P+ = 0.8163
	MEAN SCORE	29.50	38.27	52.82	43.20	37.12	50.46	PT BIS =	0.4102	
2-Year	PERCENT	3.88	7.93	64.61	18.71	4.86	100.00	R BIS =	0.5930	P+ = 0.6461
	MEAN SCORE	22.68	33.23	44.74	34.32	33.13	40.45	PT BIS =	0.4613	

56. Which of the following became the focus of a debate about human rights that led to a reform movement?

    (1) Slavery among the ancient Greeks
    (2) Serfdom in Europe in the Middle Ages
    (3) Punishment for heresy in early modern Europe
    (4) Slavery in nineteenth-century America

		OMIT	1	2	3	4*	TOTAL			
Freshmen	PERCENT	4.05	3.69	7.33	8.19	76.74	100.00	R BIS = 0.4248	P+ = 0.7674
	MEAN SCORE	21.91	35.77	41.03	37.42	43.86	41.94	PT BIS = 0.3072	
Senior	PERCENT	2.83	1.98	5.44	5.07	84.68	100.00	R BIS = 0.2348	P+ = 0.8468
	MEAN SCORE	38.38	39.84	48.83	49.82	51.26	50.46	PT BIS = 0.1543	
2-Year	PERCENT	4.91	4.04	9.12	9.35	72.59	100.00	R BIS = 0.2811	P+ = 0.7259
	MEAN SCORE	22.06	36.19	39.20	40.61	42.07	40.45	PT BIS = 0.2100	

57. Recent widespread deaths in Cambodia have been characterized by some persons as "genocide." This term was originally invented to describe the

    (1) Italian subjection of Ethiopia in the mid-1930's
    (2) Nazi extermination of Jews and others during the Second World War
    (3) imprisonment of Japanese-Americans in the United States during the Second World War
    (4) Chinese invasion of Tibet in the early 1950's

		OMIT	1	2*	3	4	TOTAL			
Freshmen	PERCENT	7.12	4.07	74.88	9.68	4.24	100.00	R BIS = 0.5941	P+ = 0.7488
	MEAN SCORE	28.22	35.75	44.81	35.48	34.94	41.94	PT BIS = 0.4364	
Senior	PERCENT	2.70	3.00	88.48	3.71	2.11	100.00	R BIS = 0.4877	P+ = 0.8848
	MEAN SCORE	31.40	51.16	51.76	36.70	43.63	50.46	PT BIS = 0.2970	
2-Year	PERCENT	9.04	4.41	73.01	8.87	4.67	100.00	R BIS = 0.5557	P+ = 0.7301
	MEAN SCORE	24.39	40.31	43.61	33.87	34.87	40.45	PT BIS = 0.4138	

58. Which of the following organizations promulgated the Universal Declaration
     of Human Rights?

     (1) The League of Nations in 1919 following the First World War
     (2) The World Council of Churches in 1936 following the outbreak of the Spanish
          Civil War
     (3) The United Nations in 1948 following the Second World War
     (4) Amnesty International in 1972 following a terrorist attack at the Olympic
          Games

		OMIT	1	2	3*	4	TOTAL						
Freshmen	PERCENT	10.46	21.03	7.92	49.92	10.67	100.00	R BIS	=	0.2825	P+ =		0.4992
	MEAN SCORE	31.68	42.86	37.29	44.50	41.61	41.94	PT BIS	=	0.2254			
Senior	PERCENT	10.57	21.57	5.94	51.58	10.34	100.00	R BIS	=	0.1328	P+ =		0.5158
	MEAN SCORE	45.59	49.95	45.92	51.70	52.92	50.46	PT BIS	=	0.1059			
2-Year	PERCENT	10.45	20.46	7.88	46.04	15.17	100.00	R BIS	=	0.1857	P+ =		0.4604
	MEAN SCORE	31.88	40.17	39.21	42.46	41.31	40.45	PT BIS	=	0.1478			

59. In the period between 1945 and 1975, the United Nations adopted nearly 20
     human rights treaties, such as the Genocide convention. These treaties
     must be ratified by a certain number of member countries before going
     into effect. About how many of these treaties did the United States
     ratify?

     (1) Nearly all of them
     (2) More than half of them
     (3) Fewer than half of them
     (4) Almost none of them

		OMIT	1	2	3*	4	TOTAL						
Freshmen	PERCENT	6.67	40.33	28.87	19.46	4.67	100.00	R BIS	=	-0.1193	P+ =		0.1946
	MEAN SCORE	27.44	46.58	40.36	40.02	40.24	41.94	PT BIS	=	-0.0830			
Senior	PERCENT	7.08	51.52	29.58	9.30	2.51	100.00	R BIS	=	-0.1906	P+ =		0.0930
	MEAN SCORE	42.65	53.97	47.35	46.33	52.44	50.46	PT BIS	=	-0.1092			
2-Year	PERCENT	7.35	38.63	29.91	19.12	4.99	100.00	R BIS	=	-0.0772	P+ =		0.1912
	MEAN SCORE	30.09	43.73	39.81	39.07	39.52	40.45	PT BIS	=	-0.0535			

0. In 1977 Amnesty International won the Nobel Peace Prize for

    (1) working against the death penalty
    (2) working for the freedom of political prisoners
    (3) supporting self-exiled draft resisters
    (4) working for disarmament

		OMIT	1	2*	3	4	TOTAL				
Freshmen	PERCENT	7.00	6.22	42.25	19.49	25.04	100.00	R BIS =	0.4430	P+ =	0.4225
	MEAN SCORE	27.41	33.80	46.60	40.39	40.86	41.94	PT BIS =	0.3510		
Senior	PERCENT	5.28	2.92	53.06	24.41	14.33	100.00	R BIS =	0.4018	P+ =	0.5306
	MEAN SCORE	41.21	40.80	54.11	47.90	46.69	50.46	PT BIS =	0.3201		
2-Year	PERCENT	6.25	6.96	42.21	27.96	16.62	100.00	R BIS =	0.2623	P+ =	0.4221
	MEAN SCORE	25.27	32.67	43.50	41.23	40.38	40.45	PT BIS =	0.2078		

61. Between 1900 and 1979, numerous conferences and agreements intended to establish the conditions of international peace through prevention and control of war as well as through arms limitation fell short of their aims. Which of the following is LEAST important in explaining the lack of substantial progress toward world peace?

    (1) Sequences of arms buildup, followed by perceived threat, followed by another arms build-up by two rival nations or blocs of nations
    (2) Failure to design and implement a system of collective security that nations can trust to preserve their safety and to protect their interests
    (3) Destabilizing effects of war-related science and technology on arms limitation agreements
    (4) The increase in the number of governments established by military coup and the number of governments currently dominated by military regimes

		OMIT	1	2	3	4*	TOTAL				
Freshmen	PERCENT	10.01	11.54	33.01	22.27	23.18	100.00	R BIS =	0.2686	P+ =	0.2318
	MEAN SCORE	31.39	41.54	41.25	43.72	45.95	41.94	PT BIS =	0.1941		
Senior	PERCENT	9.18	13.84	26.38	23.63	26.97	100.00	R BIS =	0.2341	P+ =	0.2697
	MEAN SCORE	41.78	48.36	49.19	52.51	53.93	50.46	PT BIS =	0.1743		
2-Year	PERCENT	10.72	12.76	32.64	22.46	21.42	100.00	R BIS =	0.3245	P+ =	0.2142
	MEAN SCORE	29.15	38.76	40.99	40.75	45.99	40.45	PT BIS =	0.2306		

62. Which country is currently the leading exporter of armaments in the world?

    (1) The Soviet Union
    (2) The Federal Republic of Germany (West Germany)
    (3) The United States
    (4) France

		OMIT	1	2	3*	4	TOTAL		
Freshmen	PERCENT	4.06	30.99	8.36	53.62	2.97	100.00	R BIS = 0.3570	P+ = 0.5362
	MEAN SCORE	22.81	41.11	36.88	44.94	36.66	41.94	PT BIS = 0.2843	
Senior	PERCENT	2.19	24.03	6.41	64.26	3.11	100.00	R BIS = 0.3314	P+ = 0.6426
	MEAN SCORE	29.83	47.89	43.97	52.79	50.02	50.46	PT BIS = 0.2581	
2-Year	PERCENT	5.16	28.26	8.18	52.58	5.82	100.00	R BIS = 0.4651	P+ = 0.5258
	MEAN SCORE	21.53	37.52	37.34	44.87	36.00	40.45	PT BIS = 0.3707	

63. Rapid developments in the weapons technologies of advanced industrial societies have had, in general, which of the following effects upon and among Third World countries?

    (1) An increase in arms competition but a reduction in military expenditures through the acquisition of weapons yielding "more bang for a buck"
    (2) Increases in arms competition, arms costs, and reliance upon arms suppliers
    (3) Stabilization of arms competition by the acquisition of weapons that, though costly, are less vulnerable, more reliable, and more easily maintained by Third World countries themselves
    (4) The development of high technology weapons industries in Third World countries

		OMIT	1	2*	3	4	TOTAL		
Freshmen	PERCENT	9.28	9.12	44.05	16.05	21.50	100.00	R BIS = 0.3887	P+ = 0.4405
	MEAN SCORE	29.17	42.77	45.89	38.92	41.24	41.94	PT BIS = 0.3088	
Senior	PERCENT	5.86	8.26	60.24	10.81	14.82	100.00	R BIS = 0.5231	P+ = 0.6024
	MEAN SCORE	38.87	44.95	54.52	46.19	44.75	50.46	PT BIS = 0.4123	
2-Year	PERCENT	8.84	10.57	39.02	17.05	24.52	100.00	R BIS = 0.4181	P+ = 0.3902
	MEAN SCORE	27.09	38.28	45.61	39.74	38.50	40.45	PT BIS = 0.3289	

64. By their use of the term "neo-colonialism" Third World political leaders
    mean that

    (1) historical relationships have been reversed and power is now in the
         hands of the Third World
    (2) political independence has not brought economic independence to Third
         World states
    (3) new Soviet imperialism has replaced traditional Western imperialism
    (4) China is expanding its control in Third World countries

		OMIT	1	2*	3	4	TOTAL		
Freshmen	PERCENT	11.35	13.01	47.00	21.80	6.84	100.00	R BIS = 0.3892	P+ = 0.4700
	MEAN SCORE	31.26	41.06	45.68	41.70	36.36	41.94	PT BIS = 0.3101	
Senior	PERCENT	6.30	11.42	65.12	14.43	2.73	100.00	R BIS = 0.5200	P+ = 0.6512
	MEAN SCORE	38.25	43.19	54.04	46.62	43.99	50.46	PT BIS = 0.4037	
2-Year	PERCENT	11.86	18.91	44.91	18.90	5.42	100.00	R BIS = 0.5708	P+ = 0.4491
	MEAN SCORE	27.73	38.05	46.76	37.40	35.10	40.45	PT BIS = 0.4539	

65. Nonalignment in international affairs can best be described as a movement

    (1) fostered by Nehru of India, Nasser of Egypt, and Tito of Yugoslavia,
         involving the refusal of some countries to be tied to a military
         alliance with either of the two Cold War blocs
    (2) among some Third World countries to create a third international
         economic system, neither capitalist nor socialist, aimed at extricating
         these countries from the economic domination of the United States or
         the Soviet Union
    (3) fostered by Chou En-lai of China, Castro of Cuba, and Allende of Chile
         to establish a third significant military bloc capable of restoring a
         global multipolar balance of power
    (4) among socialist democratic countries to establish their neutrality in
         the event of war between capitalist democratic powers and totalitarian
         socialist powers

		OMIT	1*	2	3	4	TOTAL		
Freshmen	PERCENT	16.86	17.32	28.61	13.19	24.03	100.00	R BIS = 0.5917	P+ = 0.1732
	MEAN SCORE	34.08	51.88	42.09	37.53	42.52	41.94	PT BIS = 0.4006	
Senior	PERCENT	11.43	29.45	25.83	8.60	24.69	100.00	R BIS = 0.5130	P+ = 0.2945
	MEAN SCORE	39.60	57.74	48.98	46.22	49.84	50.46	PT BIS = 0.3881	
2-Year	PERCENT	14.28	16.08	28.48	13.78	27.37	100.00	R BIS = 0.4104	P+ = 0.1608
	MEAN SCORE	30.89	48.27	39.63	36.44	43.72	40.45	PT BIS = 0.2729	

66. All of the following are examples of the emergence during the 1960's of a multipolar international system EXCEPT the

    (1) French withdrawal from the NATO command structure
    (2) Sino-Soviet rift
    (3) independent moves in international relations made by Romania
    (4) Cuban Missile Crisis

		OMIT	1	2	3	4*	TOTAL				
Freshmen	PERCENT	10.21	18.83	15.67	32.14	23.15	100.00	R BIS = 0.2170	P+ = 0.2315
	MEAN SCORE	31.12	43.27	40.78	42.81	45.18	41.94	PT BIS = 0.1568	
Senior	PERCENT	12.07	15.84	10.85	31.83	29.42	100.00	R BIS = 0.3749	P+ = 0.2942
	MEAN SCORE	46.07	48.25	46.01	49.83	55.78	50.46	PT BIS = 0.2835	
2-Year	PERCENT	10.84	17.95	14.01	34.40	22.80	100.00	R BIS = 0.1824	P+ = 0.2280
	MEAN SCORE	30.00	40.00	38.18	42.91	43.49	40.45	PT BIS = 0.1314	

67. In which of the following countries do the regional governments have the most authority?

    (1) The Soviet Union
    (2) Great Britain
    (3) The United States
    (4) France

		OMIT	1	2	3*	4	TOTAL				
Freshmen	PERCENT	4.96	33.49	11.28	39.73	10.53	100.00	R BIS = 0.3966	P+ = 0.3973
	MEAN SCORE	26.38	39.30	41.71	46.31	41.38	41.94	PT BIS = 0.3126	
Senior	PERCENT	5.11	18.83	13.91	52.76	9.39	100.00	R BIS = 0.4195	P+ = 0.5276
	MEAN SCORE	38.91	45.32	48.59	54.29	48.31	50.46	PT BIS = 0.3343	
2-Year	PERCENT	7.64	29.55	12.92	38.93	10.96	100.00	R BIS = 0.4620	P+ = 0.3893
	MEAN SCORE	30.01	36.36	39.07	46.16	40.13	40.45	PT BIS = 0.3634	

68. Which of the following poses the LEAST challenge to the predominance of
the contemporary nation-state?

    (1) The International Criminal Police Organization (Interpol) and its National
        Central Bureaus
    (2) Multinational corporations
    (3) International voluntary nongovernmental organizations
    (4) The United Nations and its specialized agencies

		OMIT	1*	2	3	4	TOTAL				
Freshmen	PERCENT	10.33	16.24	17.58	35.97	19.88	100.00	R BIS =	0.1776	P+ =	0.1624
	MEAN SCORE	31.70	44.99	40.17	44.16	42.30	41.94	PT BIS =	0.1184		
Senior	PERCENT	9.31	21.97	12.21	38.50	18.01	100.00	R BIS =	0.2781	P+ =	0.2197
	MEAN SCORE	41.76	55.00	46.76	51.55	49.61	50.46	PT BIS =	0.1987		
2-Year	PERCENT	11.35	14.80	17.53	36.38	19.93	100.00	R BIS =	0.1643	P+ =	0.1480
	MEAN SCORE	27.72	43.67	37.75	43.80	41.59	40.45	PT BIS =	0.1070		

69. Each of the following nations has an important film export industry EXCEPT

    (1) Poland
    (2) India
    (3) France
    (4) Saudi Arabia

		OMIT	1	2	3	4*	TOTAL				
Freshmen	PERCENT	5.42	20.32	35.19	2.54	36.53	100.00	R BIS =	0.2175	P+ =	0.3653
	MEAN SCORE	26.67	40.93	42.68	35.59	44.48	41.94	PT BIS =	0.1698		
Senior	PERCENT	4.41	13.15	39.22	2.08	41.13	100.00	R BIS =	0.4163	P+ =	0.4113
	MEAN SCORE	41.19	43.76	49.29	40.19	55.23	50.46	PT BIS =	0.3291		
2-Year	PERCENT	6.78	17.28	30.79	3.15	42.01	100.00	R BIS =	0.3203	P+ =	0.4201
	MEAN SCORE	23.97	37.65	41.29	33.26	44.19	40.45	PT BIS =	0.2537		

70. Which grouping of the religions below presents them in descending size of estimated world membership?

    (1) Chrisitanity, Buddhism, Islam, Hinduism, Judaism
    (2) Islam, Christianity, Hinduism, Buddhism, Judaism
    (3) Hinduism, Islam, Christianity, Judaism, Buddhism
    (4) Christianity, Islam, Hinduism, Buddhism, Judaism

		OMIT	1	2	3	4*	TOTAL			
Freshmen	PERCENT	4.18	20.88	21.81	17.16	35.97	100.00	R BIS = −0.0650	P+ =	0.3597
	MEAN SCORE	22.82	40.42	46.27	44.53	41.17	41.94	PT BIS = −0.0507		
Senior	PERCENT	3.33	16.24	23.94	24.69	31.81	100.00	R BIS = −0.0233	P+ =	0.3181
	MEAN SCORE	33.28	48.31	54.98	50.22	50.14	50.46	PT BIS = −0.0179		
2-Year	PERCENT	6.16	28.16	15.90	18.82	30.96	100.00	R BIS = 0.0588	P+ =	0.3096
	MEAN SCORE	24.33	39.44	45.97	41.22	41.29	40.45	PT BIS = 0.0448		

71. Which of the following is shared by Christianity, Judaism, Islam, Buddhism, and Hinduism?

    (1) The concept of a messiah
    (2) A general tendency to proselytize
    (3) A tradition of mysticism
    (4) Insistence on personal identification with a single religion

		OMIT	1	2	3*	4	TOTAL			
Freshmen	PERCENT	5.17	36.62	6.12	10.60	41.49	100.00	R BIS = 0.0061	P+ =	0.1060
	MEAN SCORE	27.67	42.75	41.67	42.06	43.00	41.94	PT BIS = 0.0036		
Senior	PERCENT	3.17	35.11	5.44	13.72	42.56	100.00	R BIS = 0.1813	P+ −	0.1372
	MEAN SCORE	39.23	48.14	51.17	53.98	51.98	50.46	PT BIS = 0.1157		
2-Year	PERCENT	6.59	34.88	6.22	9.34	42.97	100.00	R BIS = 0.0747	P+ =	0.0934
	MEAN SCORE	24.54	39.93	40.25	42.13	42.99	40.45	PT BIS = 0.0428		

72. Each religion below is correctly matched with countries in _each_ of which
    it either predominates or has a significant minority following EXCEPT

    (1) Christianity..Greece, Lebanon, the Philippines, Ethiopia
    (2) Islam..Saudi Arabia, the Soviet Union, Indonesia, Nigeria
    (3) Buddhism..Japan, Thailand, Vietnam, Sri Lanka (Ceylon)
    (4) Hinduism..India, Pakistan, Afghanistan, Kampuchea (Cambodia)

		OMIT	1	2	3	4*	TOTAL				
Freshmen	PERCENT	5.37	29.21	39.76	13.19	12.47	100.00	R BIS =	0.0923	P+ =	0.1247
	MEAN SCORE	24.73	42.65	44.29	38.63	43.66	41.94	PT BIS =	0.0574		
Senior	PERCENT	5.91	31.92	41.96	7.15	13.06	100.00	R BIS =	0.4518	P+ =	0.1306
	MEAN SCORE	40.25	48.55	51.63	44.33	59.36	50.46	PT BIS =	0.2848		
2-Year	PERCENT	9.49	33.41	31.05	14.32	11.73	100.00	R BIS =	0.1433	P+ =	0.1173
	MEAN SCORE	28.35	41.43	42.75	38.75	43.47	40.45	PT BIS =	0.0877		

73. The World Zionist Organization, which sought the creation of a Jewish
    state, was founded in response to

    (1) the anti-Semitism that surrounded the Dreyfus case at the end of the nine-
         teenth century
    (2) the British government's 1917 declaration in support of the concept of a
         Jewish national homeland
    (3) Stalin's anti-Semitic purges in the 1930's
    (4) Nazi persecution of the Jews

		OMIT	1*	2	3	4	TOTAL				
Freshmen	PERCENT	8.45	10.24	16.88	13.16	51.28	100.00	R BIS =	0.1092	P+ =	0.1024
	MEAN SCORE	29.15	44.10	41.61	41.58	43.81	41.94	PT BIS =	0.0643		
Senior	PERCENT	7.79	11.02	18.77	12.51	49.91	100.00	R BIS =	0.0345	P+ =	0.1102
	MEAN SCORE	42.29	51.18	55.54	48.97	50.04	50.46	PT BIS =	0.0208		
2-Year	PERCENT	11.03	9.73	12.27	11.08	55.89	100.00	R BIS =	-0.1940	P+ =	0.0973
	MEAN SCORE	27.35	36.15	42.13	42.41	43.03	40.45	PT BIS =	-0.1126		

74. All of the following are characteristics of Islam EXCEPT

    (1)   belief in an after-life
    (2)   monotheism
    (3)   recognition of Moses as an important prophet
    (4)   veneration of Jerusalem as the faith's most holy city

		OMIT	1	2	3	4*	TOTAL			
Freshmen	PERCENT	5.93	10.45	15.10	34.09	34.42	100.00	R BIS = 0.2863	P+ =	0.3442
	MEAN SCORE	24.83	40.08	39.55	43.02	45.42	41.94	PT BIS = 0.2219		
Senior	PERCENT	6.64	7.79	6.81	36.51	42.25	100.00	R BIS = 0.3578	P+ =	0.4225
	MEAN SCORE	42.03	46.68	45.12	49.15	54.48	50.46	PT BIS = 0.2835		
2-Year	PERCENT	9.44	6.79	15.94	37.36	30.46	100.00	R BIS = 0.3886	P+ =	0.3046
	MEAN SCORE	26.91	35.16	35.81	42.25	46.06	40.45	PT BIS = 0.2957		

75. One of Buddhism's most basic teachings is that

    (1)   one can be saved from sin if one learns to suppress anger and fear
    (2)   human life is a cycle of suffering caused by individual desires
    (3)   everyone who wishes to be saved from sin must become a monk or a nun
    (4)   the Buddha was the final divinely inspired prophet sent to the human race

		OMIT	1	2*	3	4	TOTAL			
Freshmen	PERCENT	6.44	9.59	29.81	11.31	42.85	100.00	R BIS = 0.3036	P+ =	0.2981
	MEAN SCORE	27.53	41.73	45.95	41.89	41.37	41.94	PT BIS = 0.2301		
Senior	PERCENT	5.00	11.61	39.49	9.46	34.44	100.00	R BIS = 0.3433	P+ =	0.3949
	MORE SCORE	40.64	51.11	54.52	47.31	47.88	50.46	PT BIS = 0.2704		
2-Year	PERCENT	8.95	12.09	29.19	9.68	40.10	100.00	R BIS = 0.4221	P+ =	0.2919
	MEAN SCORE	26.38	39.00	46.68	40.69	39.44	40.45	PT BIS = 0.3188		

Questions 76-77 refer to the following pictures of works by Western artists and artisans.

(1)

(2) Alinari/Editorial Photocolor Archives.

(3) Paul Gauguin: *Offerings of Gratitude*. Collection, The Museum of Modern Art, New York.

(4) Jacques Lipchitz: *Figure 1926-30*. Collection, The Museum of Modern Art, New York. Van Gogh Purchase Fund.

76. Each of the following correctly pairs one of the works with the homeland of
    the culture that inspired it EXCEPT

    (1)   I..China
    (2)   II..India
    (3)   III..Polynesia
    (4)   IV..Africa

		OMIT	1	2*	3	4	TOTAL				
Freshmen	PERCENT	3.80	8.67	61.77	18.20	7.55	100.00	R BIS =	0.4187	P+ =	0.6177
	MEAN SCORE	21.90	38.97	44.87	38.04	40.79	41.94	PT BIS =	0.3288		
Senior	PERCENT	2.54	10.73	67.72	11.00	8.02	100.00	R BIS =	0.3173	P+ =	0.6772
	MEAN SCORE	29.66	49.00	52.50	44.77	49.59	50.46	PT BIS =	0.2437		
2-Year	PERCENT	6.24	9.65	53.71	21.77	8.63	100.00	R BIS =	0.5293	P+ =	0.5371
	MEAN SCORE	22.73	38.86	45.36	34.96	38.37	40.45	PT BIS =	0.4215		

77. There is evidence in the works that the Western artists and artisans who
    created them did which of the following in appropriating the art styles of
    other cultures?

    (1)   Cheapened the art by pursuing commercial purposes.
    (2)   Improved the materials with which they worked by using scientific
          technology.
    (3)   Lacked the skill to reproduce the original accurately.
    (4)   Transformed what they chose to borrow by fitting it into the western
          tradition of art.

		OMIT	1	2	3	4*	TOTAL				
Freshmen	PERCENT	7.12	6.99	16.94	11.12	57.82	100.00	R BIS =	0.4689	P+ =	0.5782
	MEAN SCORE	28.02	39.38	40.27	36.25	45.54	41.94	PT BIS =	0.3714		
Senior	PERCENT	3.51	5.49	15.54	6.01	69.44	100.00	R BIS =	0.5059	P+ =	0.6944
	MEAN SCORE	32.72	43.27	45.76	43.79	53.56	50.46	PT BIS =	0.3851		
2-Year	PERCENT	8.83	7.43	19.09	12.13	52.53	100.00	R BIS =	0.5686	P+ =	0.5253
	MEAN SCORE	25.90	34.28	37.16	36.61	45.86	40.45	PT BIS =	0.4532		

78. Which of the following correctly ranks from numerically highest to
   numerically lowest the four languages that are most spoken in the world?

   (1) Chinese, English, Russian, Spanish
   (2) English, Chinese, Arabic, Hindi
   (3) Chinese, Russian, English, French
   (4) Spanish, English, Russian, Arabic

		OMIT	1*	2	3	4	TOTAL				
Freshmen	PERCENT	3.79	35.51	29.20	11.88	19.62	100.00	R BIS =	0.3896	P+ =	0.3331
	MEAN SCORE	19.30	46.58	40.26	43.10	39.69	41.94	PT BIS =	0.3032		
Senior	PERCENT	1.88	44.81	23.46	13.72	16.13	100.00	R BIS =	0.4167	P+ =	0.4481
	MEAN SCORE	26.99	54.92	47.73	48.14	46.76	50.46	PT BIS =	0.3313		
2-Year	PERCENT	5.10	31.98	29.27	11.11	22.54	100.00	R BIS =	0.3391	P+ =	0.3198
	MEAN SCORE	22.70	45.21	39.60	44.42	36.88	40.45	PT BIS =	0.2600		

79. Chinese culture has been characterized by all of the following EXCEPT:

   (1) a caste system
   (2) patriarchal control
   (3) a strong family cult
   (4) ancestral concern

		OMIT	1*	2	3	4	TOTAL				
Freshmen	PERCENT	4.31	56.13	27.37	7.36	4.82	100.00	R BIS =	0.3693	P+ =	0.5613
	MEAN SCORE	21.05	44.88	41.26	37.36	37.14	41.94	PT BIS =	0.2933		
Senior	PERCENT	4.05	67.50	18.42	7.81	2.21	100.00	R BIS =	0.3776	P+ =	0.6750
	MEAN SCORE	33.65	52.90	45.92	49.16	49.21	50.46	PT BIS =	0.2903		
2-Year	PERCENT	5.63	55.56	27.59	5.92	5.31	100.00	R BIS =	0.4974	P+ =	0.5556
	MEAN SCORE	21.39	44.89	37.07	36.03	36.76	40.45	PT BIS =	0.3953		

80. The "brain drain" refers to the

   (1) lack of opportunities for millions of high school students to receive
       a university education
   (2) large-scale migration of highly trained professionals to countries with
       higher standards of living
   (3) reluctance of many governments to employ in responsible positions
       nationals who have studied and received degrees abroad
   (4) lack of financial resources for the development of advanced research
       facilities in many of the newly independent countries

		OMIT	1	2*	3	4	TOTAL				
Freshmen	PERCENT	9.63	19.54	36.70	13.53	20.60	100.00	R BIS =	0.5298	P+ =	0.3670
	MEAN SCORE	30.73	39.75	48.11	39.90	39.58	41.94	PT BIS =	0.4140		
Senior	PERCENT	7.43	11.49	59.62	7.04	14.41	100.00	R BIS =	0.6512	P+ =	0.5962
	MEAN SCORE	39.00	43.29	55.59	41.53	45.26	50.46	PT BIS =	0.5140		
2-Year	PERCENT	10.16	17.47	36.90	15.20	20.27	100.00	R BIS =	0.6612	P+ =	0.3690
	MEAN SCORE	27.78	34.59	48.93	37.80	38.42	40.45	PT BIS =	0.5170		

82. The medium of communication that currently reaches the largest number of
persons throughout the world is

   (1) television
   (2) books
   (3) newspapers
   (4) radio

		OMIT	1	2	3	4*	TOTAL				
Freshmen	PERCENT	3.46	23.19	8.46	18.33	46.56	100.00	R BIS =	0.4119	P+ =	0.4656
	MEAN SCORE	19.37	38.56	40.76	40.86	45.93	41.94	PT BIS =	0.3281		
Senior	PERCENT	1.91	15.18	8.27	18.85	55.79	100.00	R BIS =	0.3542	P+ =	0.5579
	MEAN SCORE	26.89	46.81	46.02	48.75	53.50	50.46	PT BIS =	0.2814		
2-Year	PERCENT	6.29	26.14	9.33	19.48	38.76	100.00	R BIS =	0.4115	P+ =	0.3876
	MEAN SCORE	23.34	36.83	41.59	40.15	45.55	40.45	PT BIS =	0.3235		

83. Which of the following sports is the most popular worldwide?

    (1) Soccer
    (2) Baseball
    (3) Tennis
    (4) Basketball

		OMIT	1*	2	3	4	TOTAL				
Freshmen	PERCENT	3.43	72.95	11.67	7.02	4.92	100.00	R BIS =	0.6008	P+ =	0.7295
	MEAN SCORE	19.27	45.03	35.50	36.03	35.51	41.94	PT BIS =	0.4476		
Senior	PERCENT	1.70	86.89	6.75	2.85	1.82	100.00	R BIS =	0.5934	P+ =	0.8689
	MEAN SCORE	24.16	52.22	42.43	41.23	35.08	50.46	PT BIS =	0.3744		
2-Year	PERCENT	4.94	65.95	15.42	9.34	4.35	100.00	R BIS =	0.6109	P+ =	0.6595
	MEAN SCORE	23.02	44.71	32.43	36.75	32.06	40.45	PT BIS =	0.4727		

84. There have been several areas in which cooperation has led to major inter-
    national agreements offering some protection to the environment. All of the
    following are covered or embodied in international agreements EXCEPT

    (1) protection of the Antarctic ecosystem
    (2) long-term nuclear waste disposal
    (3) liability of ship owners for oil spills
    (4) limitations on the killing of certain species of whales

		OMIT	1	2*	3	4	TOTAL				
Freshmen	PERCENT	6.21	19.83	37.77	24.80	11.39	100.00	R BIS =	0.2468	P+ =	0.3777
	MEAN SCORE	23.02	41.75	44.76	42.72	41.51	41.94	PT BIS =	0.1935		
Senior	PERCENT	4.37	17.49	49.37	19.13	9.63	100.00	R BIS =	0.3936	P+ =	0.4937
	MEAN SCORE	32.98	47.18	54.31	48.74	48.02	50.46	PT BIS =	0.3141		
2-Year	PERCENT	9.22	15.51	43.71	17.52	14.05	100.00	R BIS =	0.3236	P+ =	0.4371
	MEAN SCORE	22.86	39.71	44.11	42.09	39.40	40.45	PR BIS =	0.2569		

Questions 85-87 refer to the following maps. For each stated geographical distribution, choose the appropriate map.

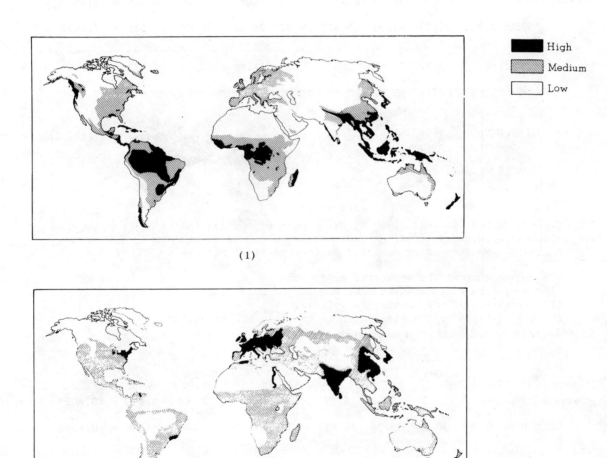

(1)

(2)

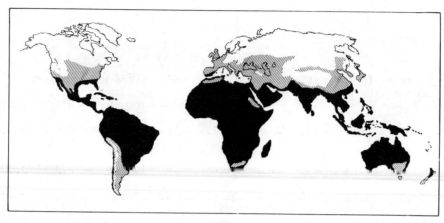

(3)

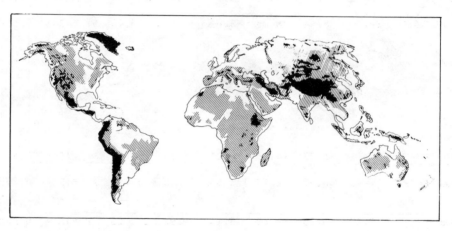

(4)

85. Average annual surface temperature

		OMIT	1	2	3*	4	TOTAL					
Freshmen	PERCENT	13.74	7.62	6.89	65.38	6.38	100.00	R BIS =	0.6029	P+ =	0.6538
	MEAN SCORE	30.24	39.16	36.81	45.80	36.36	41.94	PT BIS =	0.4676		
Senior	PERCENT	8.52	8.20	5.80	74.78	2.70	100.00	R BIS =	0.5683	P+ =	0.7478
	MEAN SCORE	35.28	45.52	47.69	53.40	37.92	50.46	PT BIS =	0.4177		
2-Year	PERCENT	21.48	10.43	8.52	54.32	5.25	100.00	R BIS =	0.6405	P+ =	0.5432
	MEAN SCORE	29.96	38.18	36.41	46.32	33.81	40.45	PT BIS =	0.5097		

86. Elevation above sea level

		OMIT	1	2	3	4*	TOTAL					
Freshmen	PERCENT	13.89	5.13	9.90	6.54	64.54	100.00	R BIS =	0.6285	P+ =	0.6454
	MEAN SCORE	30.40	38.58	38.41	33.75	46.05	41.94	PT BIS =	0.4890		
Senior	PERCENT	7.95	3.62	4.31	4.48	79.63	100.00	R BIS =	0.7008	P+ =	0.7963
	MEAN SCORE	33.84	46.45	41.02	38.67	53.48	50.46	PT BIS =	0.4926		
2-Year	PERCENT	21.26	7.63	7.43	12.58	51.11	100.00	R BIS =	0.7019	P+ =	0.5111
	MEAN SCORE	29.80	38.44	38.36	33.01	47.32	40.45	PT BIS =	0.5599		

87. Average annual precipitation

		OMIT	1*	2	3	4	TOTAL					
Freshmen	PERCENT	14.07	51.73	14.66	10.21	9.33	100.00	R BIS =	0.4734	P+ =	0.5173
	MEAN SCORE	30.43	46.08	42.79	39.65	37.48	41.94	PT BIS =	0.3775		
Senior	PERCENT	8.32	65.53	11.09	8.14	6.92	100.00	R BIS =	0.5481	P+ =	0.6553
	MEAN SCORE	34.37	54.19	48.35	44.91	44.35	50.46	PT BIS =	0.4249		
2-Year	PERCENT	22.08	39.32	17.44	10.63	10.53	100.00	R BIS =	0.5534	P+ =	0.3932
	MEAN SCORE	30.22	47.24	40.10	39.90	37.70	40.45	PT BIS =	0.4358		

88. Most countries that have a majority of their populations working in
agriculture and earn most of their foreign exchange from agriculture
exports are finding economic development difficult because

   (1) there is a declining world market for agricultural products
   (2) they can only develop through mechanization of agriculture, but this will
create large-scale unemployment
   (3) they are especially vulnerable to both crop failures and world price
fluctuations
   (4) the income of the majority of the population depends upon export earnings

		OMIT	1	2	3*	4	TOTAL		
Freshmen	PERCENT	7.20	6.24	19.50	57.86	9.19	100.00	R BIS = 0.3300	P+ = 0.5786
	MEAN SCORE	26.99	39.65	42.34	44.47	38.38	41.94	PT BIS = 0.2614	
Senior	PERCENT	3.28	2.52	21.50	65.84	6.86	100.00	R BIS = 0.1991	P+ = 0.6584
	MEAN SCORE	29.63	44.14	51.18	51.81	47.60	50.46	PT BIS = 0.1542	
2-Year	PERCENT	9.18	7.74	19.58	51.20	12.31	100.00	R BIS = 0.3881	P+ = 0.5120
	MEAN SCORE	25.84	34.50	41.85	44.24	37.11	40.45	PT BIS = 0.3096	

90. In China one-third of the farmland and sixty per cent of the rural labor force are devoted to growing rice. The major advantage to China of growing rice is that

   (1) China has surplus farm labor and few alternatives for employment
   (2) the weight, the nutrient, and the market value of rice per unit of land are much higher than those of other basic grain crops
   (3) rice, as the major grain involved in world trade, is principally grown for foreign markets to earn foreign exchange
   (4) the extra labor required for growing rice largely consists of women and children, a fact that makes the cost of growing rice less than that of growing other grains

		OMIT	1	2*	3	4	TOTAL				
Freshman	PERCENT	5.31	19.87	25.56	18.10	31.16	100.00	R BIS =	0.2749	P+ =	0.2556
	MEAN SCORE	23.04	45.97	45.86	37.55	41.92	41.94	PT BIS =	0.2026		
Senior	PERCENT	4.11	26.15	30.41	14.43	24.90	100.00	R BIS =	0.2585	P+ =	0.3041
	MEAN SCORE	34.25	53.95	54.06	42.50	49.69	50.46	PT BIS =	0.1966		
2-Year	PERCENT	6.17	17.36	22.33	25.77	28.37	100.00	R BIS =	0.4035	P+ =	0.2233
	MEAN SCORE	21.76	44.70	47.22	36.14	40.50	40.45	PT BIS =	0.2894		

91. An unanticipated consequence of the so-called green revolution in agriculture has been

   (1) increased economic and social inequality in rural areas
   (2) rising urban employment
   (3) a reduction of regional variations within same country
   (4) a lowering of the age of marriage among agricultural populations

		OMIT	1*	2	3	4	TOTAL				
Freshmen	PERCENT	10.90	31.11	23.90	29.05	5.04	100.00	R BIS =	0.2691	P+ =	0.3111
	MEAN SCORE	31.87	45.41	42.49	42.14	38.51	41.94	PT BIS =	0.2054		
Senior	PERCENT	11.42	38.47	24.18	22.24	3.69	100.00	R BIS =	0.2487	P+ =	0.3847
	MEAN SCORE	44.87	53.45	50.01	48.74	49.87	50.46	PT BIS =	0.1954		
2-Year	PERCENT	9.83	27.20	26.10	30.18	6.69	100.00	R BIS =	0.3046	P+ =	0.2720
	MEAN SCORE	29.84	45.12	40.06	40.92	36.51	40.45	PT BIS =	0.2272		

92. Although large areas of land are brought into cultivation each year,
    large amounts are also rendered useless or reduced in productive
    capacity for all of the following reasons EXCEPT

    (1) soil erosion
    (2) salinization, or salt buildup, in irrigated land
    (3) conversion of agricultural land to other purposes
    (4) lack of sufficient farm labor

		OMIT	1	2	3	4*	TOTAL			
Freshmen	PERCENT	6.11	11.46	15.94	20.11	46.37	100.00	R BIS = 0.4483	P+ = 0.4637
	MEAN SCORE	23.72	37.79	41.49	40.14	46.30	41.94	PT BIS = 0.3570	
Senior	PERCENT	3.12	6.00	13.72	18.87	58.29	100.00	R BIS = 0.4024	P+ = 0.5829
	MEAN SCORE	29.88	44.39	48.18	47.37	53.72	50.46	PT BIS = 0.3185	
2-Year	PERCENT	6.19	14.75	11.33	24.66	43.06	100.00	R BIS = 0.4549	P+ = 0.4306
	MEAN SCORE	22.69	35.35	38.99	39.56	45.66	40.45	PT BIS = 0.3608	

93. Which of the following statements best represents the position of
    the governments of Third World countries in regard to the pollution
    problems associated with economic development?

    (1) They are more concerned about pollution than the industrial countries are.
    (2) They are demanding installation of the most modern pollution control devices.
    (3) They express concern about pollution but believe economic development is
         more important.
    (4) They have so little pollution that they have not yet become concerned
         about the problem.

		OMIT	1	2	3*	4	TOTAL			
Freshmen	PERCENT	7.36	6.51	12.50	56.25	17.38	100.00	R BIS = 0.4400	P+ = 0.5625
	MEAN SCORE	24.14	39.49	36.19	45.44	43.19	41.94	PT BIS = 0.3493	
Senior	PERCENT	3.94	3.06	5.48	67.23	20.30	100.00	R BIS = 0.4253	P+ = 0.6723
	MEAN SCORE	29.96	36.40	41.36	53.23	49.84	50.46	PT BIS = 0.3273	
2-Year	PERCENT	9.48	7.59	12.39	52.37	18.16	100.00	R BIS = 0.5457	P+ = 0.5237
	MEAN SCORE	26.19	30.83	34.95	45.66	40.68	40.45	PT BIS = 0.4349	

94. In recent negotiations for a law of the sea treaty, concern for which of the
    following has been most obvious on the part of the participants?

    (1) Extension of national sovereignty over coastal waters
    (2) Environmental protection
    (3) Increased international cooperation
    (4) Protection of seabed mineral resources

		OMIT	1*	2	3	4	TOTAL					
Freshmen	PERCENT	7.71	34.20	21.60	21.99	14.50	100.00	R BIS =	0.4222	P+ =		0.3420
	MEAN SCORE	27.29	47.09	40.04	40.11	43.17	41.94	PT BIS =	0.3269			
Senior	PERCENT	5.92	46.85	15.65	16.83	14.75	100.00	R BIS =	0.3097	P+ =		0.4685
	MEAN SCORE	36.65	53.64	47.40	46.02	54.20	50.46	PT BIS =	0.2467			
2-Year	PERCENT	7.94	36.26	22.94	21.28	11.57	100.00	R BIS =	0.4716	P+ =		0.3626
	MEAN SCORE	25.14	46.57	39.01	38.42	38.39	40.45	PT BIS =	0.3680			

95. What action can the United Nations Security Council take under the United
    Nations charter if a member country is violating the human rights of its
    citizens on a massive scale?

    (1) Withdraw its guarantee to take effective collective measures if the
         country in question becomes the victim of international aggression.
    (2) Impose a fine on the country in question.
    (3) Require member countries to admit as immigrants citizens of the country
         in question who flee and become homeless refugees.
    (4) Call upon member countries to impose economic sanctions against the
         country in question.

		OMIT	1	2	3	4*	TOTAL					
Freshmen	PERCENT	7.92	19.43	10.20	8.88	53.58	100.00	R BIS =	0.5530	P+ =		0.5358
	MEAN SCORE	26.02	40.25	35.91	38.65	46.59	41.94	PT BIS =	0.4404			
Senior	PERCENT	4.93	11.51	5.50	5.57	72.49	100.00	R BIS =	0.5901	P+ =		0.7249
	MEAN SCORE	33.30	47.29	38.93	40.77	53.75	50.46	PT BIS =	0.4410			
2-Year	PERCENT	9.06	17.17	8.81	10.64	54.32	100.00	R BIS =	0.5845	P+ =		0.5432
	MEAN SCORE	26.01	38.48	34.19	33.81	45.80	40.45	PT BIS =	0.4651			

96. In the area of human rights, the major accomplishment of the Helsinki Accords
    was the

    (1) establishment of a court where human rights complaints can be heard
    (2) acknowledgment of the signatories' right to intercede in the event one
        of their members violates human rights
    (3) commitment made by the United States to admit as an immigrant any
        Eastern European who can show that his or her human rights have been
        violated
    (4) recognition accorded human rights as a legitimate subject of discussion
        in the East-West debate

		OMIT	1	2	3	4*	TOTAL		
Freshmen	PERCENT	19.18	26.11	15.58	19.32	19.81	100.00	R BIS = 0.3600	P+ = 0.1981
	MEAN SCORE	35.31	45.07	40.30	39.69	47.68	41.94	PT BIS = 0.2515	
Senior	PERCENT	17.90	27.41	13.94	12.18	28.57	100.00	R BIS = 0.5907	P+ = 0.2857
	MEAN SCORE	43.96	50.95	45.05	45.12	58.97	50.46	PT BIS = 0.4445	
2-Year	PERCENT	14.97	27.94	14.11	17.97	25.01	100.00	R BIS = 0.4902	P+ = 0.2501
	MEAN SCORE	30.23	42.05	39.51	36.36	48.27	40.45	PT BIS = 0.3597	

97. Which of the following statements about war crimes trials is true?

    (1) They have regularly been held after major wars to decide on the punish-
        ment of political leaders of the defeated side.
    (2) They have been based on the belief that war itself is a crime no matter
        how humanely it is conducted.
    (3) There were no cases of war crimes trials before the Second World War.
    (4) The Nuremberg trials were without precedent because of the types of crimes
        for which the political leaders of Nazi Germany were brought to trial.

		OMIT	1	2	3	4*	TOTAL		
Freshmen	PERCENT	6.35	24.63	12.98	11.52	44.52	100.00	R BIS = 0.4369	P+ = 0.4452
	MEAN SCORE	24.48	41.75	36.41	41.17	46.34	41.94	PT BIS = 0.3472	
Senior	PERCENT	5.79	18.93	5.96	11.99	57.33	100.00	R BIS = 0.3415	P+ = 0.5733
	MEAN SCORE	33.14	50.50	43.13	48.88	53.29	50.46	PT BIS = 0.2707	
2-Year	PERCENT	9.12	23.57	13.04	11.38	42.88	100.00	R BIS = 0.4900	P+ = 0.4288
	MEAN SCORE	26.18	40.73	34.52	36.92	46.08	40.45	PT BIS = 0.3886	

98. The announced aims of political groups that have espoused terrorist
     tactics include all of the following EXCEPT

     (1) gaining publicity for and recognition of their objectives by the
          general public and by other nations
     (2) drawing the regular armed forces of the government into major battles
          in order to destroy or capture the army's more sophisticated equipment
     (3) exposing the hypocrisy of constitutional governments by provoking
          violent repression
     (4) developing an identity, building partriotism, and enhancing the morale
          of the organization or people they claim to represent

		OMIT	1	2*	3	4	TOTAL				
Freshmen	PERCENT	9.70	9.34	49.13	16.74	15.10	100.00	R BIS =	0.5288	P+ =	0.4913
	MEAN SCORE	28.15	38.36	46.81	40.08	39.19	41.94	PT BIS =	0.4218		
Senior	PERCENT	9.45	7.40	61.05	11.60	10.50	100.00	R BIS =	0.4487	P+ =	0.6105
	MEAN SCORE	38.15	48.04	53.88	47.51	46.66	50.46	PT BIS =	0.3529		
2-Year	PERCENT	11.34	9.18	41.08	21.43	16.97	100.00	R BIS =	0.5191	P+ =	0.4108
	MEAN SCORE	27.42	37.48	46.62	37.00	40.22	40.45	PT BIS =	0.4103		

99. Which of the following best characterize the behavior of the United States
     and the Soviet Union during the era of detente in the 1970's?

          I.   Joint cooperation in solving Third World economic problems
          II. Greater restraint on both sides during international crises
          III. Movement toward improved economic relations
          IV. Suspension of the arms race

     (1) I and III only
     (2) I and IV only
     (3) II and III only
     (4) II, III, and IV only

		OMIT	1	2	3*	4	TOTAL				
Freshmen	PERCENT	7.15	14.22	10.55	33.61	34.47	100.00	R BIS =	0.3108	P+ =	0.3361
	MEAN SCORE	24.88	38.98	37.70	45.77	44.25	41.94	PT BIS =	0.2401		
Senior	PERCENT	6.29	8.48	6.61	47.71	30.91	100.00	R BIS =	0.4467	P+ =	0.4771
	MEAN SCORE	32.79	46.01	40.65	54.98	50.41	50.46	PT BIS =	0.3560		
2-Year	PERCENT	10.02	13.91	11.38	33.67	31.03	100.00	R BIS =	0.3891	P+ =	0.3367
	MEAN SCORE	26.28	36.01	34.18	45.75	43.58	40.45	PT BIS =	0.3006		

100. In its official interpretations of United States foreign policy,
Soviet doctrine tends to emphasize which of the following arguments?

(1) The United States is a democracy; consequently, its foreign policy
is driven by the aggressive aims of the masses.
(2) The United States is a state under the control of monopoly capitalists,
and as such, it is an imperialist power.
(3) The United States is a disguised dictatorship; therefore, its foreign
policy reflects the territorial ambitions of its military leaders.
(4) Internal divisions weaken the United States; hence, it is a paper
tiger and can safely be defied.

		OMIT	1	2*	3	4	TOTAL				
Freshmen	PERCENT	6.76	19.74	51.98	10.99	10.54	100.00	R BIS =	0.5094	P+ =	0.5198
	MEAN SCORE	26.26	38.41	46.37	36.68	42.20	41.94	PT BIS =	0.4061		
Senior	PERCENT	3.32	13.42	69.40	5.50	8.36	100.00	R BIS =	0.6668	P+ =	0.6940
	MEAN SCORE	29.15	41.50	54.54	42.95	44.33	50.46	PT BIS =	0.5076		
2-Year	PERCENT	8.17	19.93	49.96	9.20	12.75	100.00	R BIS =	0.5596	P+ =	0.4996
	MEAN SCORE	25.83	36.55	46.06	33.39	39.05	40.45	PT BIS =	0.4466		

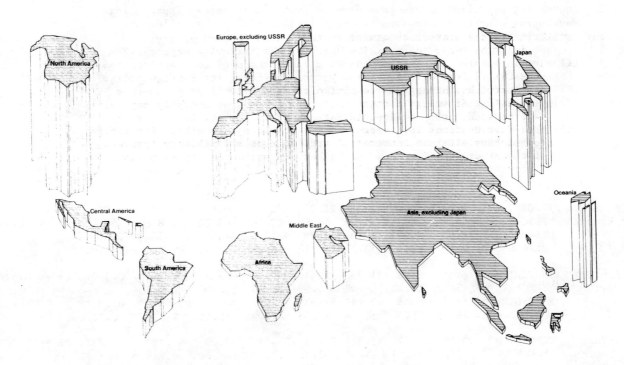

Note: Actual areas of regions were equalized befor they were
proportioned for the characteristic represented by the
surface area.

101. On the three-dimensional map above, one characteristic is represented
by the heights of the <u>regions</u> shown and another by their surface
areas. Respectively, these characteristics are

(1) population density and gross national product
(2) rate of population growth and total value of food produced
(3) per capita gross national product and population
(4) rate of inflation and total energy consumption

		OMIT	1	2	3*	4	TOTAL				
Freshmen	PERCENT	6.79	17.18	11.11	35.50	29.43	100.00	R BIS =	0.3250	P+ =	0.3550
	MEAN SCORE	27.44	42.21	36.60	45.81	42.46	41.94	PT BIS =	0.2529		
Senior	PERCENT	4.77	14.70	6.86	47.97	25.70	100.00	R BIS =	0.3956	P+ =	0.4797
	MEAN SCORE	33.90	47.59	48.51	54.44	48.27	50.46	PT BIS =	0.3154		
2-Year	PERCENT	9.55	18.26	12.26	34.68	25.25	100.00	R BIS =	0.4954	P+ =	0.3468
	MEAN SCORE	26.69	37.19	35.66	47.07	41.26	40.45	PT BIS =	0.3843		

255

102. Increasing petroleum prices have created problems for non-oil producing developing countries. Reasons for this include all of the following EXCEPT the fact that such countries

   (1) are integrated to world economies through the need for manufactured goods
   (2) are becoming increasingly committed to agricultural programs that require higher energy inputs
   (3) have received less foreign aid because of the impact of oil price increases on donor countries
   (4) do not have alternate domestic energy sources available to them in the short run

		OMIT	1	2	3*	4	TOTAL				
Freshmen	PERCENT	9.04	14.26	19.49	28.38	28.82	100.00	R BIS = 0.0992	P+ = 0.2838
	MEAN SCORE	28.95	44.05	44.26	43.28	42.07	41.94	PT BIS = 0.0745
Senior	PERCENT	6.31	13.72	21.36	31.44	27.17	100.00	R BIS = 0.1746	P+ = 0.3144
	MEAN SCORE	36.78	51.68	50.17	52.85	50.49	50.46	PT BIS = 0.1335
2-Year	PERCENT	10.61	15.62	19.32	30.01	24.44	100.00	R BIS = 0.2321	P+ = 0.3001
	MEAN SCORE	26.82	41.75	40.97	43.83	41.00	40.45	PT BIS = 0.1761

103. Which of the following helps to explain the ability of OPEC (Organization of Petroleum Exporting Countries) to raise oil prices since 1973?

   (1) OPEC countries have become controlled uniformly by groups hostile to capitalism and the West.
   (2) OPEC countries have experienced a significant growth in their military strength.
   (3) There has been a large increase in total world industrial production and transport since the early 1960's.
   (4) The value of the dollar has declined.

		OMIT	1	2	3*	4	TOTAL				
Freshmen	PERCENT	7.76	16.03	12.70	32.85	30.66	100.00	R BIS = 0.3052	P+ = 0.3285
	MEAN SCORE	28.28	42.90	39.23	45.75	41.92	41.94	PT BIS = 0.2350
Senior	PERCENT	5.59	21.99	8.41	40.18	23.83	100.00	R BIS = 0.2700	P+ = 0.4018
	MEAN SCORE	37.53	51.27	45.77	53.61	49.09	50.46	PT BIS = 0.2130
2-Year	PERCENT	8.67	14.37	13.41	31.12	32.44	100.00	R BIS = 0.3285	P+ = 0.3112
	MEAN SCORE	27.11	42.73	36.09	45.13	40.33	40.45	PT BIS = 0.2507

104. Which of the following lists is composed entirely of members of OPEC
(Organization of Petroleum Exporting Countries)?

(1) Iran, Iraq, Kuwait, Egypt
(2) Great Britain, Norway, Mexico, United Arab Emirates
(3) Syria, Lebanon, Libya, Ethiopia
(4) Venezuela, Indonesia, Nigeria, Saudi Arabia

		OMIT	1	2	3	4*	TOTAL			
Freshmen	PERCENT	7.01	56.19	7.33	8.47	20.99	100.00	R BIS = 0.2141	P+ =	0.2099
	MEAN SCORE	26.69	43.45	36.07	41.27	45.27	41.94	PT BIS = 0.1515		
Senior	PERCENT	4.61	57.50	2.14	6.69	29.06	100.00	R BIS = 0.3190	P+ =	0.2906
	MEAN SCORE	31.28	49.66	41.35	53.64	55.02	50.46	PT BIS = 0.2407		
2-Year	PERCENT	7.41	48.68	8.09	7.90	27.92	100.00	R BIS = 0.3598	P+ =	0.2792
	MEAN SCORE	26.03	40.69	34.16	39.79	45.89	40.45	PT BIS = 0.2696		

106. The world monetary system created after the Second World War
was fundamentally changed in 1971 when the United States found it
necessary to abandon the attempt to maintain a fixed United States
dollar price for gold. A major reason why the United States was
forced to take this action was the

(1) increase in gold production in the Soviet Union
(2) increase in gold production in South Africa
(3) increase in foreign holdings of United States dollars as a result of
deficits in the United States balance of payments
(4) increase in the price of oil charged by the OPEC countries

		OMIT	1	2	3*	4	TOTAL			
Freshmen	PERCENT	8.21	3.11	8.57	62.85	17.26	100.00	R BIS = 0.4911	P+ =	0.6285
	MEAN SCORE	27.68	32.07	38.80	45.29	39.83	41.94	PT BIS = 0.3843		
Senior	PERCENT	7.48	1.37	4.72	73.45	12.98	100.00	R BIS = 0.4778	P+ =	0.7345
	MEAN SCORE	37.98	32.54	44.64	53.04	47.04	50.46	PT BIS = 0.3547		
2-Year	PERCENT	9.74	4.80	7.90	57.89	19.67	100.00	R BIS = 0.5380	P+ =	0.5789
	MEAN SCORE	27.30	29.82	34.75	45.01	38.44	40.45	PT BIS = 0.4261		

107. Which of the following statements about the nineteenth-century gold
standard is NOT true?

(1) All transactions between one country's residents and another country's
residents were made in gold.
(2) The price of gold was set by the private market rather than by
governmental action.
(3) Net balances owed to and by a country were settled by gold movements.
(4) For purposes of international trade, the value of a country's currency
could be expressed in terms of gold.

		OMIT	1*	2	3	4	TOTAL				
Freshmen	PERCENT	7.73	33.16	24.80	16.59	17.71	100.00	R BIS =	0.2836	P+ =	0.3316
	MEAN SCORE	28.63	45.46	42.42	41.36	41.01	41.94	PT BIS =	0.2186		
Senior	PERCENT	8.13	47.45	18.68	11.97	13.76	100.00	R BIS =	0.4136	P+ =	0.4745
	MEAN SCORE	39.27	54.66	47.78	48.26	48.13	50.46	PT BIS =	0.3296		
2-Year	PERCENT	9.49	34.82	27.40	12.69	15.60	100.00	R BIS =	0.3697	P+ =	0.3482
	MEAN SCORE	26.49	45.38	40.73	39.52	38.24	40.45	PT BIS =	0.2870		

108. GATT (General Agreement on Tariffs and Trade), IMF (International
Monetary Fund), and the World Bank were established after the
Second World War to

(1) promote an open international economic system characterized by free
trade and convertible currencies
(2) safeguard the needs of developing countries
(3) act as supranational economic institutions that would have strong
authority over national economic policies
(4) operate the Marshall Plan and make loans to multinational corporations

		OMIT	1*	2	3	4	TOTAL				
Freshmen	PERCENT	10.78	44.33	19.56	17.61	7.72	100.00	R BIS =	0.3808	P+ =	0.4433
	MEAN SCORE	30.90	45.79	41.73	39.19	42.01	41.94	PT BIS =	0.3026		
Senior	PERCENT	12.81	55.89	11.02	13.61	6.67	100.00	R BIS =	0.3371	P+ =	0.5589
	MEAN SCORE	44.66	53.34	46.59	47.25	50.39	50.46	PT BIS =	0.2678		
2-Year	PERCENT	12.12	46.55	17.94	13.35	10.03	100.00	R BIS =	0.5061	P+ =	0.4655
	MEAN SCORE	26.89	45.87	39.13	39.49	35.37	40.45	PT BIS =	0.4030		

109. In the North-South talks, representatives of developing countries
    have demanded all of the following EXCEPT

    (1) the reduction of their level of economic interdependence with the
         industrialized countries
    (2) the stabilization of world prices for their basic commodity exports
    (3) increased control over monetary lending institutions such as the
         International Monetary Fund
    (4) lower tariffs in industrialized countries for their exports

		OMIT	1*	2	3	4	TOTAL				
Freshmen	PERCENT	14.41	22.40	18.15	29.36	15.67	100.00	R BIS =	0.3169	P+ =	0.2240
	MEAN SCORE	35.23	46.74	41.20	42.87	40.33	41.94	PT BIS =	0.2274		
Senior	PERCENT	18.67	24.91	16.85	27.49	12.08	100.00	R BIS =	0.3271	P+ =	0.2491
	MEAN SCORE	45.32	55.51	51.26	50.29	47.26	50.46	PT BIS =	0.2399		
2-Year	PERCENT	14.29	18.36	23.68	27.28	16.39	100.00	R BIS =	0.3590	P+ =	0.1836
	MEAN SCORE	30.20	46.97	40.93	40.70	40.99	40.45	PT BIS =	0.2465		

111. Which of the following is shared by all known culture groups?

    (1) A structured spoken language
    (2) A written language
    (3) A structured religion
    (4) A prison system

		OMIT	1*	2	3	4	TOTAL				
Freshmen	PERCENT	4.91	53.78	9.58	17.74	13.99	100.00	R BIS =	0.3805	P+ =	0.5378
	MEAN SCORE	24.69	45.13	39.72	40.60	38.94	41.94	PT BIS =	0.3029		
Senior	PERCENT	3.73	64.04	6.22	13.33	12.67	100.00	R BIS =	0.4490	P+ =	0.6404
	MEAN SCORE	32.02	53.64	43.93	46.48	47.23	50.46	PT BIS =	0.3500		
2-Year	PERCENT	5.96	49.75	10.85	16.03	17.40	100.00	R BIS =	0.3868	P+ =	0.4975
	MEAN SCORE	28.01	44.34	36.60	37.34	38.86	40.45	PT BIS =	0.3087		

112. Which country is in both Europe and Asia?

    (1) China
    (2) Russia/the Soviet Union
    (3) India
    (4) Poland

		OMIT	1	2*	3	4	TOTAL				
Freshmen	PERCENT	5.30	7.40	67.52	5.62	14.16	100.00	R BIS =	0.4909	P+ =	0.6752
	MEAN SCORE	23.72	36.75	44.91	34.37	40.29	41.94	PT BIS =	0.3773		
Senior	PERCENT	3.33	6.15	75.14	4.12	11.26	100.00	R BIS =	0.5447	P+ =	0.7514
	MEAN SCORE	31.35	40.90	53.24	41.51	46.05	50.46	PT BIS =	0.3992		
2-Year	PERCENT	6.33	9.83	67.14	7.24	9.46	100.00	R BIS =	0.4939	P+ =	0.6714
	MEAN SCORE	24.79	35.78	43.79	35.45	35.94	40.45	PT BIS =	0.3803		

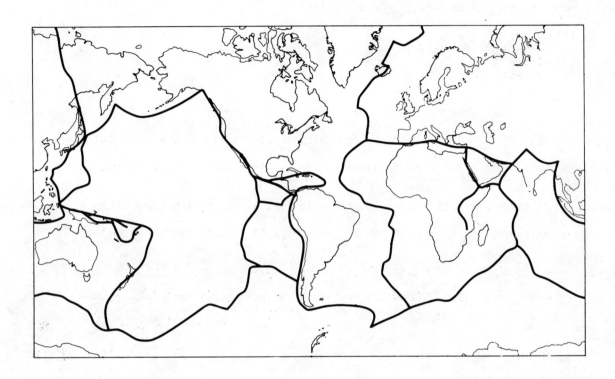

113. The heavy lines on the map above indicate major

    (1)   commercial fishing areas
    (2)   international trade routes
    (3)   earthquake belts
    (4)   flyways of bird migrations

		OMIT	1	2	3*	4	TOTAL			
Freshmen	PERCENT	4.99	11.90	41.99	38.31	2.81	100.00	R BIS =	0.3568	P+ = 0.3831
	MEAN SCORE	27.26	43.02	39.70	45.97	41.72	41.94	PT BIS =	0.2802	
Senior	PERCENT	4.16	10.82	33.10	50.01	1.91	100.00	R BIS =	0.5001	P+ = 0.5001
	MEAN SCORE	34.08	44.48	47.24	55.29	49.28	50.46	PT BIS =	0.3991	
2-Year	PERCENT	7.65	11.32	44.42	32.02	4.59	100.00	R BIS =	0.3754	P+ = 0.3202
	MEAN SCORE	27.15	44.67	38.49	45.72	34.51	40.45	PT BIS =	0.2879	

Appendix C

Foreign Language Questionnaire—Pretest

FOREIGN LANGUAGE QUESTIONNAIRE—PRETEST

This questionnaire, together with the language proficiency tests you have been asked to take, is part of a large-scale study of the relationships between foreign-language learning and other kinds of learning, especially in the areas of history, social studies, and international affairs.

The particular part of the study in which you have been asked to participate involves comparing actual language proficiency (as measured by the language tests) to answers to the language background questions and other items on this questionnaire.

The questionnaire should take about 15-20 minutes to complete, depending on your language background. Please take note of the amount of time you actually take, since this will be asked at the end of the questionnaire.

When you have finished the questionnaire, please put it in the envelope provided and seal the envelope. Put only *your name* and *today's date* on the envelope. (This information is needed to verify distribution and receipt of the questionnaire. The completed questionnaires will be forwarded unopened to the study staff, and your language teachers at your institution will *not* see your answers to the questions.)

Thank you for your cooperation.

PART I

Please use the following list of language codes to answer questions 1-7. On the line provided in front of each question, write in the code number which corresponds to the appropriate language.

1	Chinese	5	Greek	9	Polish	13	Tagalog
2	English	6	Hebrew	10	Portuguese	14	Yiddish
3	French	7	Italian	11	Russian	15	Other language not
4	German	8	Japanese	12	Spanish		listed
						16	I don't know

1.____ your own native language (mother tongue)

2.____ your father's native language

3.____ your mother's native language

4.____ your paternal grandfather's native language

5.____ your paternal grandmother's native language

6.____ your maternal grandfather's native language

7.____ your maternal grandmother's native language

For each of the questions below, please *circle* the code number to the left of the answer you select. In some cases, you may also be asked to write in additional explanatory information on the lines provided.

8.   Were you born in the United States?

1   Yes   2   No

9.   If you were not born in the United States, please *circle* the code number for the country of your birth:

1	Canada	7	England	13	Portugal
2	China (People's Republic)	8	Greece	14	Puerto Rico
3	Colombia	9	Italy	15	Taiwan
4	Cuba	10	Mexico	16	West Germany
5	Dominican Republic	11	The Philippines	17	Other (specify): _____
6	East Germany	12	Poland		

10.   If you were not born in the United States, please write in your age in years when you *first came to the United States*: (age in years)_____

11. At what school level(s) have you studied Latin? (Circle one or more code numbers for *all that apply*.)

  1 I have never studied Latin.
  2 I studied Latin in high school.
  3 I studied Latin in college.
  4 I studied Latin in some other situation.

12. At what school level(s) have you studied classical Greek? (Circle one or more code numbers for *all that apply*.)

  1 I have never studied classical Greek.
  2 I studied classical Greek in high school.
  3 I studied classical Greek in college.
  4 I studied classical Greek in some other situation.

13. Have you ever studied a modern language other than English in a formal classroom setting outside of the regular grade school/high school/college courses? (This would include such programs as Hebrew school, foreign language courses offered through cultural organizations such as the Alliance Française, Goethe House, and other similar learning activities.)

  1 YES (please give name of language and describe circumstances) _____
  _____
  _____

  2 NO

PART II

1. Have you ever been in a country other than the United States?

  1 YES (If you answered yes, please answer the remaining questions in this part.)
  2 NO (If you answered no, please go on to Part III.)

2. Please use the following codes to indicate the total length of time you have spent in each of the geographic areas below. Please write in a code number for each separate area on the line to the left of the area.

  1 no time or less than one month   5 1-2 years
  2 1-2 months   6 3-4 years
  3 3 months   7 5 years or more
  4 5-12 months

      _____ Canada (01)   _____ The Middle East (09)
      _____ Mexico (02)   _____ India (10)
      _____ Central America (03)   _____ China (11)
      _____ South America (04)   _____ Korea (12)
      _____ Scandinavia (05)   _____ Indochina (13)
      _____ The British Isles (06)   _____ Japan (14)
      _____ Europe (07)   _____ Australia; New Zealand (15)
      _____ Africa (08)   _____ Soviet Union (16)

3. Have you ever participated in an organized *summer-abroad* program in which you were required to live with a family whose native language was not English?

1 YES   Please write in the name of the country: _____   2 NO

4. Have you ever participated in an organized *year-abroad* program in which you were required to live with a family whose native language was not English?

1 YES   Please write in the name of the country: _____   2 NO

5. Have you ever participated in an organized *summer-abroad* program in which you lived alone or with native speakers of English?

1 YES   Please write in the name of the country: _____   2 NO

6. Have you ever participated in an organized *year-abroad* program in which you lived alone or with native speakers of English?

1 YES   Please write in the name of the country: _____   2 NO

7. Have you ever lived abroad for more than one month with members of your own family?

1 YES   Please write in the name of the country: _____   2 NO

8. Have you ever traveled abroad "on your own hook" (i.e., not with an organized tour program)?

1 YES   Please write in the name(s) of the country(ies): _____   2 NO

9. Have you ever been in the Peace Corps or other program involving similar kinds of service abroad?

1 YES   Please write in the name of the country: _____   2 NO

10. Which of the following best describes the extent to which you spoke a language other than English during your stay(s) outside the United States? Circle *one*.

1 I spoke only in English.
2 I used a few words of the foreign language.
3 I spoke the foreign language occasionally in social situations (greeting people, ordering a meal in a restaurant, asking directions, etc.), but except for this, used English.
4 I used the foreign language quite consistently in study or work situations.

PART III

1 .Have you ever studied a modern language other than English at any time from 3rd grade through college senior? (Do not count Latin or Classical Greek.)

1 YES   If you answered yes, please answer the remaining questions in this part.
2 NO   If you answered no, please go on to Part IV.

DIRECTIONS: This part of the questionnaire asks about any language(s) other than English you have studied in school. The example below has a number of rows showing the names of commonly taught languages, and additional rows with spaces where the names of other languages can be written in. The columns are grade levels going from 3rd grade through senior year college. The example shows the responses of a person who studies: French continuously from 3rd grade through 9th grade; Spanish in 9th, 10th, and 12th grades; and Japanese as a freshman and sophomore in college.

Example

Language	3rd	4th	5th	6th	7th	8th	9th	10th	11th	12th	Fr.	Soph.	Jr.	Sr.
French	X	X	X	X	X	X	X							
German														
Hebrew														
Italian														
Russian														
Spanish							X	X		X				
Other:														
Japanese											X	X		

On the similar diagram on the next page, please record your own language study history. First, if you have studied any language(s) other than English in school—at any time from 3rd grade through senior year college—which are not already listed on the rows of the diagram, please write the name(s) of the language(s) in the space(s) marked "Other."

Next, beginning with French and working horizontally across each row before going on to the next row, place an "X" in each language/grade level combination in which you studied that language at that grade level.

It is important for you to fill out this diagram carefully, so please give it all necessary attention. Please note that if you studied more than one language at a given grade level (for example, both French and Spanish in the 9th grade), there will be more than one "X" in the vertical column corresponding to that grade level.

Language	3rd	4th	5th	6th	7th	8th	9th	10th	11th	12th	Fr.	Soph.	Jr.	Sr.
French														
German														
Hebrew														
Italian														
Russian														
Spanish														
Other:														

If, in the figure above, you have marked only one language (i.e., if all of your "Xs" are in a single horizontal row), answer all of the remaining questions in this part in terms of that particular language.

If the figure above shows that you have studied more than one language, answer all of the remaining questions in this part in terms of the language in which you consider yourself currently most proficient. (For example, if you have studied both French and Spanish but feel that you are currently more proficient in Spanish, you should answer all of the remaining questions in this part in terms of Spanish only.) As another example, if you have studied both Italian and Portuguese (having written in "Portuguese" at the bottom of the figure) and feel that you are currently more proficient in Portuguese, you would answer the remaining questions in this part in terms of Portuguese.

Note that you do not have to be highly proficient in your "most proficient" language, but simply that, of the foreign language(s) you have studied, this is the one in which you feel best qualified at the present time.

After deciding on your "most proficient language" as described above, please circle the code number which corresponds to that language.

3	French	11	Russian
4	German	12	Spanish
6	Hebrew	15	Other (specify:_____)
7	Italian		

For convenience, we will use the letters "MPL" to signify your "most proficient language," whatever that language might be.

2. If you studied your MPL in *high school*, what grade, on the average, did you receive in your high school MPL course(s)? (If your high school did not use the letter system, please convert your system to letter terms.)

1	A to A-	4	Below C-
2	B+ to B-	5	I don't know
3	C+ to C-	6	I did not study the MPL in high school

3. If you studied your MPL in *college*, what grade, on the average, did you receive in your college MPL course(s)?

1	A to A-	4	Below C-
2	B+ to B-	5	I don't know
3	C+ to C-	6	I did not study the MPL in college

4. Considering the courses in your MPL that you have taken in both high school and college, which of the following best describes—on an overall basis—the kind of language study that you have had in that language. Circle *one*:

1 All in all, my courses in the MPL have concentrated more on *reading and writing* than on listening and speaking.
2 My courses in the MPL have concentrated on reading and writing about equally with listening and speaking.
3 My courses in the MPL have concentrated more on *listening and speaking* than on reading and writing.

PART IV

1. This question asks you to judge your own level of *speaking ability* in the language other than English in which you are most proficient (MPL). Please read each one of the six paragraphs below and decide which paragraph best describes

your ability to read the MPL (and to understand the spoken MPL). Please be as honest and as accurate as possible. Circle the number preceding only one of the paragraphs below:

1 My speech in the MPL is limited to a few words and I have great difficulty understanding the MPL, even when it is spoken very slowly. I cannot really communicate any information in the language.

2 I can ask and answer questions about very familiar subjects and can understand simple questions and statements if they are spoken slowly and sometimes repeated. My vocabulary is limited to basic needs (food, asking directions, greeting people, and so forth). I make many grammatical mistakes but my teachers can usually understand me. I can order food in a restaurant, get a room in a hotel, ask directions on the street, and introduce myself to people.

3 I can talk with native speakers of the MPL about myself and my family, my job or studies, hobbies, and current events. I can understand most conversations in the MPL except when the speech is very fast. My grammar is fairly good but I make mistakes with complicated constructions. If I do not know the word for a particular thought or object, I can usually describe it by using other, easier words.

4 I can understand almost everything spoken by native MPL users. My vocabulary is good enough that I usually know most or all of the words for what I want to say. My grammar is good and any mistakes I make are usually with the more complicated constructions. I can pronounce the MPL clearly but do not have a perfect accent.

5 I can understand native MPL speakers even when they are speaking quickly and using sophisticated or colloquial expressions. My vocabulary is very extensive, even for technical matters, and I can talk fluently and accurately about almost any subject with which I am familiar. I make only a very few grammatical errors and my pronunciation is very good but not completely native.

6 My speech is exactly like that of an educated native speaker of the MPL.

2. This question asks you to judge your own level of *reading ability* in your MPL. Please read each of the six paragraphs below and decide which paragraph best describes your ability to read the MPL. Circle the number preceding only one of the paragraphs below:

1 I cannot really read anything in the language, or can read only a few works that I have "memorized."

2 I can recognize the letters of the alphabet or the very common characters or printed syllables of the language. I can read some personal and place names, street signs, office and shop designations, numbers, and some isolated words and phrases.

3 I can get the general sense of routine business letters, news items, and articles in fields with which I am familiar, but I need to use a dictionary extensively in doing so.

4 I can grasp the essential meaning of newspaper items addressed to the general reader, and routine correspondence, reports, and technical material in fields with which I am familiar, without using a dictionary. However, I need to refer to the dictionary fairly often in order to work out the precise meaning of the entire text. I sometimes have difficulty with unusually complex structures or specialized expressions.

5 With occasional use of a dictionary, I can read without difficulty any prose directed at the general reader and all material in fields with which I am familiar.

6 I can read extremely difficult and abstract prose, as well as highly colloquial writing and the classic literary forms of the language.

3. Listed below are a number of "can do" statements about a person's speaking ability in the MPL. Please read each description carefully and indicate by circling the appropriate number in one of the three columns, whether you would be able—at the present time—to carry out this task "quite easily," "with some difficulty," or "with great difficulty or not at all."

		Quite Easily	With Some Difficulty	With Great Difficulty or Not at All
a)	Say the days of the week	1	2	3
b)	Count to 10 in the language	1	2	3
c)	Give the current date (month, day, year)	1	2	3
d)	Order a simple meal in a restaurant	1	2	3
e)	Ask directions on the street	1	2	3
f)	Buy clothes in a department store	1	2	3
g)	Introduce myself in social situations, and use appropriate greetings and leave-taking expressions	1	2	3
h)	Give simple biographical information about myself (place of birth, composition of family, early schooling, etc.)	1	2	3
i)	Talk about my favorite hobby at some length, using appropriate vocabulary	1	2	3
j)	Describe my present job, studies, or other major life activities accurately and in detail	1	2	3
k)	Tell what I plan to be doing 5 years from now, using appropriate future tenses	1	2	3
l)	Describe the U.S. educational system in some detail	1	2	3
m)	Describe the role played by Congress in the U.S. government system	1	2	3
n)	State and support with examples and reasons a position on a controversial topic (for example, birth control, nuclear safety, environmental pollution)	1	2	3

4. Regardless of how well you currently speak the MPL, please answer each of the following in terms of your present level of *listening comprehension* in the language:

	Quite Easily	With Some Difficulty	With Great Difficulty or Not at All
a) Understand very simple statements or questions in the language ("Hello," "How are you?", "What is your name?", "Where do you live?", etc.)	1	2	3
b) In face-to-face conversation, understand a native speaker who is speaking slowly and carefully (i.e., deliberately adapting his or her speech to suit me)	1	2	3
c) In face-to-face conversation with a native speaker who is speaking slowly and carefully to me, tell whether the speaker is referring to past, present, or future events	1	2	3
d) In face-to-face conversation, understand native speakers who are speaking to me as quickly and as colloquially as they would to another native speaker	1	2	3
e) On the telephone, understand a native speaker who is speaking to me slowly and carefully (i.e., deliberately adapting his or her speech to suit me)	1	2	3
f) On the telephone, understand a native speaker who is talking as quickly and as colloquially as he or she would to a native speaker of the language	1	2	3
g) Understand two native speakers when they are talking rapidly with one another	1	2	3
h) Understand movies without subtitles	1	2	3
i) Understand news broadcasts on the radio	1	2	3
j) Understand train departure announcements and similar kinds of "public address system" announcements	1	2	3
k) Understand the words of popular songs on the radio	1	2	3
l) Understand play-by-play descriptions of sports events (for example, a soccer match) on the radio	1	2	3

5. Please answer each of the following in terms of your present level of *reading proficiency* in the MPL:

	Quite Easily	With Some Difficulty	With Great Difficulty or Not at All
a) Read, on store fronts, the type of store or the services provided (for example, "dry cleaning," "bookstore," "butcher," etc.)	1	2	3
b) Read personal letters or notes written to me in which the writer has deliberately used simple words and constructions	1	2	3
c) Read personal letters and notes written as they would be to a native user of the language	1	2	3
d) Understand newspaper headlines	1	2	3
e) Read and understand magazine articles at a level similar to those found in *Time* or *Newsweek*, without using a dictionary	1	2	3
f) Read popular novels without using a dictionary	1	2	3
g) Read a highly technical material in a particular academic or professional field with no use or only very infrequent use of a dictionary	1	2	3
h) Read newspaper "want ads" with comprehension, even when many abbreviations are used	1	2	3

6. This question asks you to judge your own level of *writing ability* in the MPL. Please read each of the six paragraphs below and decide which paragraph best describes your ability to write the MPL. Circle the number preceding only one of the paragraphs below:

1 I cannot really communicate any information in the MPL through writing.
2 I can write a few sentences in the MPL using very basic vocabulary and structures.
3 I can write relatively simple items (such as a short note to a friend) that communicate basic messages but usually contain a considerable number of misspellings and/or grammatical errors.
4 I can write fairly long personal letters, as well as uncomplicated business letters, which convey meaning accurately and which contain relatively few errors, although they are not completely idiomatic in expression.
5 I can write complex personal and business letters, as well as many other kinds of documents (for example, a "letter to the editor" of the local newspaper), using in each case the particular vocabulary and style of expression appropriate to the particular writing situation. There is only an occasional hint that I am not a native writer of the language.
6 My writing, in all situations, cannot be distinguished from that of an educated native speaker.

PART V

1. Have you ever had a close friend whose native language was not English?

1 YES   (if yes, please write in the name of the language   )   2 NO

2. In your school studies, how enjoyable did you find your foreign language classes by comparison to your other academic subjects in general?

    1   I enjoyed the foreign language classes more than the classes in other subjects.
    2   I enjoyed the foreign language classes about as much as the classes in other subjects.
    3   I enjoyed the foreign language classes less than the classes in other subjects.

3. How important do you consider it to be for Americans to learn foreign languages?

    1 Very important   3 Of little importance
    2 Of some importance   4 Of no importance

4. If you had to stay for an extended period of time in another country whose language you did not know at all, would you make an effort to learn that language even though you could get along in that country by using English?

    1 Definitely   4 Probably not
    2 Probably   5 Definitely not
    3 Possibly

5. Some people feel uneasy, or are afraid to make mistakes, or think they will sound ridiculous when they try to speak a foreign language. Has this been a factor in your own language learning?

    1 No, not at all   3 Yes, somewhat
    2 Yes, but only slightly   4 Yes, to a considerable extent

6. If you had the opportunity to study a foreign language in the future (or to continue your language study), how would you react to this opportunity?

    1 I would definitely take the opportunity.
    2 I don't know whether I would take the opportunity or not.
    3 I would not take the opportunity

PART VI

Below and on the next page are a number of statements with which some people agree and others disagree. Please indicate *your own opinion* about each statement by circling the number in one of the 5 columns that best indicates the extent to which you disagree or agree with that statement. There are no right or wrong answers because many people have different opinions about identical matters, so please answer frankly in terms of your own personal opinion.

	Strongly Agree	Agree	Neutral	Disagree	Strongly Disagree
1. I enjoy meeting people who speak other languages.	1	2	3	4	5
2. I really enjoy learning languages.	1	2	3	4	5
3. Studying a foreign language can be important to me because I think it will someday be useful in getting a good job.	1	2	3	4	5
4. My parents feel that I should really try to learn a foreign language.	1	2	3	4	5
5. I wish that I could speak another language "like a native".	1	2	3	4	5
6. Foreign languages are an important part of the school program.	1	2	3	4	5
7. Studying a foreign language can be important for me because it will enable me to better understand and appreciate the art and literature of another country.	1	2	3	4	5
8. I plan to learn one or more foreign languages as thoroughly as possible.	1	2	3	4	5
9. Studying a foreign language can be important for me because other people will respect me more if I have knowledge of a foreign language.	1	2	3	4	5
10. Studying a foreign language is an enjoyable experience.	1	2	3	4	5
11. I would study a foreign language in school even if it were not required.	1	2	3	4	5
12. Studying a foreign language can be important for me because it will allow me to meet and converse with more and varied people.	1	2	3	4	5

	Strongly Agree	Agree	Neutral	Disagree	Strongly Disagree
13. I would rather spend my time on subjects other than foreign languages.	1	2	3	4	5
14. Studying a foreign language can be important for me because I will be able to participate more freely in the activities of other cultural groups.	1	2	3	4	5
15. I would rather read the literature of a foreign language in the original language than in an English translation.	1	2	3	4	5
16. Studying a foreign language can be important for me because it will make me a more knowledgeable person.	1	2	3	4	5

PART VII

Please answer the few remaining questions in terms of your experience with this questionnaire.

1. Do you feel that the questionnaire adequately covered your own language learning history, or were there other important ways in which you learned a language that were not covered?

1 The questionnaire adequately covered my language learning history.
2 I had other important language learning experiences that were not covered in the questionnaire. (Please describe briefly below:)_____

_____
_____
_____

2. In Part IV (where you were asked to judge your own level of speaking, reading, and writing ability in your most proficient language), how easy was it for you to select the proper answer to fit your own situation?

    1 Very easy   3 Somewhat difficult
    2 Fairly easy   4 Very difficult

3. Please use the spaces below to make any other comments concerning the questionnaire as a whole or particular questions. Although this question is "optional," we would appreciate any observations or suggestions you might have that would help us to improve the questionnaire or better analyze the results.

_____
_____
_____
_____
_____
_____

4. How long did it take you to complete the questionnaire?

    1 10 minutes or less   4 21-25 minutes
    2 11-15 minutes   5 more than 25 minutes
    3 16-20 minutes

Appendix D

Sources for Error-Choice Items

(Booklet B)

Item   8   Sivard, R. L. *World military and social expenditures 1979.* Leesburg, VA: World Priorities, 1979, pp. 28-30.

Item 12   Taylor, C. L., and Hudson, M. C. *World handbook of political and social indicators.* (2nd ed.). New Haven, CT: Yale University Press, 1972. p. 210.

Item 22   Sivard, R. L., p. 29.

Item 23   Sivard, R. L., p. 21.

Item 28   Sivard, R. L., p. 29.

Item 33   Sivard, R. L., p. 29.

Item 42   Sivard, R. L., p. 14.

Item 81   Taylor, C. L., and Hudson, M. C., p. 232. Sivard, R. L., pp. 28-31.

Item 89   Sivard, R. L., p. 20.

Item 110   Sivard, R. L., p. 28.

Appendix E

Institutional Correspondence
and
Administration Instructions

October , 1979

Dear

During this academic year, researchers at Educational Testing Service will conduct a national survey of 3,400 college freshmen and seniors to determine the degree to which undergraduates understand and appreciate international concepts and concerns. The "global awareness" to be assessed comprises many elements: knowledge of geography, anthropology, human ecology, civilizations-- and social, political, and economic systems, institutions, issues, and problems; the extent and influence of study of foreign languages will also be evaluated.

The survey stems from "Education and the World View," a program sponsored by the Council on Learning. The Council is a wholly independent nonprofit organization that acts as a catalytic force on issues of concern to academic professionals. It provides professional services and sponsors research and projects dealing with public policy issues in higher education. It is hoped that the present undertaking will stimulate debate in the postsecondary insti- tutions, and among the lay and professional communities, on whether under- graduate curricula should be revised to reflect the realities of increasing interdependence among nations. The Council plans to make an inventory of the range of pertinent programs and curricular approaches on the nation's campuses and will hold an invitational conference to challenge the academic, business, and government communities to a creative discussion of the findings. A special issue of Change magazine, an organ of the Council, will be devoted to the results of the ETS survey and will be distributed to every institution of higher education in the country. The National Endowment for the Humanities and the U.S. Office of Education are providing the main support for the several projects.

Educational Testing Service would very much like to include College in the survey, testing ten freshmen and ten seniors in February 1980.[1] We are hoping that you will be interested in this project and in obtaining the cooperation of your institution. The total survey, comprising cognitive, affective, and language components, will take about an hour and a half to complete; students will be paid $6.00 for their participation. Educational Testing Service will also provide an honorarium of $50.00 to each coordinator for recruiting the students and administering the survey.

_____

[1]Sets of institutions were asked to survey 10 or 20 and 15 or 30 students.

If you are interested in helping us in this study of global understanding, please complete and return the enclosed form. If you have any questions, please call either Lois Harris or Mary Bennett at (609) 921-9000, Ext 2711 or 2531. Once we have received notice of acceptance, we shall get back to you with further instructions. Since we are seeking a fully representative national sample, we sincerely hope that you will wish to join in this enterprise.

Very truly yours,

Thomas S. Barrows
Project Director

P.S. We are enclosing Update I so that you may have a full picture of the background, aim, and scope of "Education and the World View."

Mr. Thomas S. Barrows, Project Director
Global Awareness Project
Division of Educational Research
    and Evaluation
Educational Testing Service
Princeton, NJ 08541

_____ (will) (cannot) participate in the Global

Awareness Survey.

_____ will serve as Survey Coordinator
            (Name)

and may be reached at _____.
                        (Telephone)

January   , 1980

Dear Campus Coordinator:

Thank you for your willingness to help us with our national survey of Global Understanding. Our earlier letter suggested that we would ask you to recruit students and administer the survey, and this letter, with its attachments, is intended to provide instructions for carrying out these activities.

Attachment #1 is a form that should be completed and returned to us immediately. It asks for your Social Security number, which we will need in order to pay your honorarium. The form also has a space for you to fill in a mailing address. This may be left blank if our current address for you is a good one and is complete. Our experience suggests, on the one hand, that campus addresses often result in mail delays and, on the other, that home addresses can be a problem when no one is home to receive packages. We will be mailing survey materials to you and would like your suggestion as to the best address for receiving them. It is obviously important that the address be complete.

Attachment #2 consists of Student Sampling Instructions, a sheet of pressure-sensitive labels, and several worksheet pages. These documents provide a method for selecting random samples of students, and you should start on that process at your earliest convenience.

Attachment #3, Student Recruitment, provides general directions for securing student participation. The directions here are general so that you may tailor your efforts to your particular institution's characteristics.

Attachment #4 covers procedures for student payments and payment of your honorarium and expenses.

We will be shipping survey materials to you at the end of the third week in January and you should expect their arrival during the following week via United Parcel Service or UP Air. These materials will include two survey booklets for each student, general survey administration directions for you, and mailing materials for returning completed survey documents to ETS. You should plan to administer the survey between February 4 and 22. We expect all materials to be returned to us by the end of February.

Finally, you will probably note that the invitation letter for students describes a two-hour survey administration although we originally wrote you that it would be about one and one-half hours. We have found that Global Understanding encompasses a broader body of knowledge, attitudes, and concerns than we initially envisioned and that two hours is a better estimate of the time students will require to respond to the survey. We hope that this increase will not affect students' willingness to participate or seriously inconvenience you.

Should any of the enclosed materials or survey procedures raise questions or present problems, please phone us at 609-921-9000. Call collect and ask for Mrs. Harris at extension 2711 or Mrs. Bennett at extension 2431.

Thank you again for your help.

Sincerely,

Thomas S. Barrows
Project Director

Enclosures

STUDENT SAMPLING INSTRUMENTS

1) The first step in the sampling procedure is to locate a freshman class list. Next, determine the total number of students enrolled in the class and enter the figure in the appropriate space on page one of the attached blue worksheet. Divide the total freshman class enrollment by 20 an enter the result (N) in the space provided.

2) Now select a number between one and N (inclusive). This number will be your random starting point and should be entered in the appropriate space on the worksheet.

3) Turn to the sheet of pressure-sensitive labels enclosed in this package. Count down the freshman class list until you reach the random starting point you designated above. Copy down the name, address, and phone number of the student whose name appears at the random starting point on the first _numbered_ label in the left-hand column on the sheet of labels.

4) Count off every Nth student on the class list and copy down his or her name, address, and phone number on a pressure-sensitive label, working down the columns of labels _using only those which have numbers in the upper left-hand corners_. (The unnumbered labels are "extras." If you make a mistake on a numbered label, copy its number onto a blank label and discard the printed one.) Continue counting off every Nth student until you have 20 students.

5) Now locate a senior class list and determine the total number of students enrolled in the class. Divide the senior class enrollment by 20 to obtain N. Enter these figures on page one of the attached yellow worksheet.

6) Select a number between one and N (inclusive) and enter it in the space designated "random starting point."

7) Starting with the student whose name appears at the random starting point on the senior class list, count off every Nth student and copy down his or her name, address, and phone number on a pressure-sensitive label. Continue down the list until you have 20 students.

8) The numbers which appear on the pressure-sensitive labels will serve to randomize the samples you have drawn from the class lists. Blue worksheet pages two and three provide spaces for the freshman class labels. On the sheet of freshmen labels find the label with a "1." in the upper left-hand corner and affix it to the worksheet page in the space next to the number 1. Do the same for the labels numbered 2 through 20.

9) Yellow worksheet pages two and three provide spaces for the senior class labels. Repeat the above-described procedure for the senior class sample.

10) We have instructed you to draw a sample of 20 freshmen and 20 seniors even though you will be testing only 10 students from each class. We have directed you to oversample because we anticipate that some of the students you select will not wish to participate in the survey.

11) In order to protect students' anonymity and the confidentiality of their responses, please do not send your worksheets to ETS.

Number of enrolled freshmen: _____ divided by 22 = _____ (N)

Random starting point:_____

AFFIX PRESSURE-SENSITIVE LABELS BELOW:

1.   6.

2.   7.

3.   8.

4.   9.

5.   10.

STUDENT RECRUITMENT

The Survey of Global Understanding will be administered to 3,400 students at 185 colleges and universities around the country. Differences in student populations, institutional schedules, and physical facilities make it impractical for us to give you explicit instructions for recruiting students and administering the survey. As campus coordinator, you will determine the most efficient way to accomplish these tasks at your institution. Outlined below are general procedures which should serve as guidelines for your individual recruitment efforts.

1) As soon as you have drawn the sample you should begin recruiting students. We are enclosing letters of invitation to students for this purpose. Your initial mailing of these should go to 50 percent more students than you will test to allow for students who are unwilling to participate.

2) On the back of the form letter to students there is space for you to fill in your name and phone number and the day(s) and hour(s) you may be contacted. Space is also provided for you to fill in the date(s), time(s), and place(s) the survey will be administered. The letter asks the students to call you and let you know whether or not they will participate and if they will be available at the time(s) indicated for the administrations. We suggest that you set up two survey administrations in order to increase the chances of obtaining student cooperation. You may also administer the survey to individual students or to small groups of them if that is necessary and convenient for your schedule.

3) The majority of students who are going to respond to the first invitation letter will probably do so within two days of receiving it. Therefore, several days after mailing it you should consider the number of positive and negative responses you have received and the number of students who have not responded to the letter. Students who have not responded should be followed up with a note or phone call from you and students who have said that they will not participate should be replaced by sending an invitation letter to the next uninvited student on the randomized list.

4) You should follow the progress of your positive, negative, and no response results almost daily, judging when to follow up no response students with phone calls or personal notes. Negative responses should be followed quickly by issuing a new invitation to the next uninvited student and then following up if the newly invited student does not respond.

5) You may find that several students who said they would participate do not show up for their scheduled administrations. These students should be followed up with phone calls or notes in an attempt to reschedule. However, it is important to remember that participation is voluntary and we do not wish to intrude. Generally, every effort you are willing to make towards establishing a convenient administration time for students and making the survey's importance clear will pay off.

Dear*

    We would like to invite you to participate in an important national
survey of college students. This survey is supported by the National Endowment
for the Humanities and the U.S. Office of Education. It seeks to determine
college students' uderstanding of international and global problems and systems.
The survey will cover students' knowledge, foreign language abilities, and
their attitudes, perceptions, and concerns.

    The survey will be administered to a small number of randomly selected
students at each of 185 colleges throughout the U.S. You have been selected
as a potential participant, and we hope that you will be willing to make two
hours of your time available for this significant and timely survey. In
order to make participation more attractive, we are offering a $6.00 payment
for each student's participation and can assure you that your questionnaire
and test responses will be completely anonymous. To this latter end, the
survey's procedures assure that your name will not be sent to ETS at any
point.

    The date, time, and place of the survey administrations are given on the
back of this letter. Please call the survey administrator on your campus
to let him know whether you can take part in the survey. If you cannot
participate at the scheduled times, the campus survey administrator will try
to arrange an alternate time for you. The name, address, and telephone
number of the survey administrator also appear on the back of this letter.

    Since we are seeking a fully representative national sample, we sincerely
hope that you will make an earnest effort to help in this important survey.

    Thank you.

                                        Sincerely,

                                        Thomas S. Barrows
                                        Project Director

[*Survey administrator inserted student's name.]

The survey will be administered at the following times and places:

DATE:_____

TIME:_____

PLACE:_____

DATE:_____

TIME:_____

PLACE:_____

Survey Administrator:_____

Phone Number:_____

May be contacted:_____
                            (days)   (hours)

REIMBURSEMENT FOR SURVEY PARTICIPATION

1) Early in February, ETS will send you a check made out in an amount
   sufficient to cover $6.00 payments to the number of students we are
   asking you to test plus an additional sum to cover mailing and phone
   expenses.

2) This check will be made out to you, and you will be responsible for
   disbursing payments to students when they are tested. Because we are
   extremely anxious to maintain students' anonymity in this survey, we
   do not wish to receive the names of the students who participate. For
   each $6.00 that you disburse in the student payments, we will expect to
   receive a completed survey. An accounting of expenses such as postage
   should be mailed with the survey materials you return to us.

3) After we have received the completed survey booklets, we will send you
   a second check to cover your honorarium. Rather than asking you to
   return unused student payment or expense funds from the first check
   we will simply deduct any overpayment from the second or honorarium
   check.

SURVEY ADMINISTRATION INSTRUCTIONS

Enclosed in this package are the materials you will need to administer the Survey of Global Understanding to 10 freshmen and 10 seniors. Please look this material over carefully and follow the instructions provided below.

Survey Materials

    1) 20 copies of Student Instructions
    2) 20 copies of Survey Booklet A
    3) 20 copies of Survey Booklet B
    4) 20 ETS 9 x 12 envelopes
    5) 1 shipping label for returning survey materials

Survey Site

The survey should be administered in a quiet, well-lighted room. Students will need either desks or tables to sit at.

Distribution of Materials to Students

Each student should be given a copy of the "Student Instructions," one copy of Booklet A, one copy of Booklet B, and one envelope. Be sure that all students read the instructions before beginning the survey.

Institution Type and Student Class Identification

Students at two-year or community colleges should mark a "2" in the upper left-hand corner of Booklet A, Booklet B, and the envelope. Students at four-year institutions should mark the booklets and envelopes with a "1" if they are freshmen, or a "4" if they are seniors.

Survey Administration

Students should be instructed to start with Booklet A and work through it as rapidly as possible. You should monitor their progress as they work through Booklet A. At the end of one half hour, inform the students that they should be finishing the first booklet and moving on to Booklet B. Students who finish Booklet A in less than one half hour may go on to Booklet B immediately. If any student wishes to spend more than the allotted two hours on the survey, and if you are willing to stay at the administration site, the student should be allowed to do so.

Students should not be permitted to discuss survey questions with one another. If students have questions concerning Booklet A, you may assist them as much as possible. You should not, however, answer any questions regarding Booklet B.

When students have completed both booklets, they should place them in the envelope and seal it. Students should be paid when they hand in their sealed envelopes.

Returning Materials to ETS

As soon as you have collected all of the surveys, place the sealed envelopes with all unused materials back in the box. Include in this package a record of survey expenses. Seal the package and use the enclosed shipping label to return it to ETS as soon as possible.

INSTRUCTIONS TO STUDENTS

Thank you for your willingness to help us with your Survey of Global Understanding. In the next two hours, we ask that you complete two survey booklets. Please follow the specific instructions provided below:

Survey Materials

Your survey materials should consist of two survey booklets (A & B) and an envelope. Before proceeding, check to make sure you have each.

Institution Type and Student Class

If you are a student at a two-year or community college, mark a "2" in the upper left-hand corner of Booklet A, Booklet B, and the envelope. If you are a student at a four-year institution, mark Booklet A, Booklet B, and the envelope with a "1" in you are a freshman, or a "4" in you are a senior.

Survey Participation

Your participation in the survey is entirely voluntary and completely anonymous. If you find the survey personally objectionable, you may withdraw at any point. While we hope that you will answer every question in the survey, you may omit any question that you find objectionable. Please note that the survey procedures assure that no one will ever be able to identify your responses.

Instructions for Booklet A

Booklet A contains questions about your general and educational background, foreign language background and abilities, attitudes toward learning foreign languages, and your perceptions of and attitudes toward world issues and problems. You should be able to complete this booklet in about 30 minutes.

Instructions for Booklet B

Booklet B contains multiple-choice questions covering world issues and problems. A note at the beginning of the booklet explains that you must pace your work in order to consider each question in the time available. You should be able to complete Booklet B in about 90 minutes.

Survey Completion

When you have completed both of the survey booklets, please place them in the envelope and seal it. Return the sealed envelope to your Campus Coordinator and you will receive the six-dollar payment promised you for your participation in this survey.

Thank you for your cooperation.

Appendix F

Participating Colleges and Universities

(including pretest)

Adirondack Community College
Appalachian Bible College
Appalachian State University
Arkansas Tech University
Austin, Stephen F., State University
Ball State University
Bay Path Junior College
Beckley College
Belleville Area College
Bentley College
Bergen Community College
Bethany College
Bradley University
Brown University
California-Los Angeles, University of
California-Riverside, University of
California State University—Fresno
California State University—Hayward
California State University—Northridge
California State University—Sacramento
Carroll College
Central Piedmont Community College
Central Washington University
City University of New York Borough of Manhattan Community College
City University of New York Bronx Community College
City University of New York Hunter College
City University of New York Kingsborough Community College
City University of New York Queensborough Community College
Central Washington University
Charleston, College of
City Colleges of Chicago Kennedy-King College
City Colleges of Chicago Malcolm X College
City College of San Francisco
Clarion State College Venango Campus
Clarkson College of Technology
Cleveland Institute of Music
Colorado At Boulder, University of
Colorado State University
Columbia Basin Community College
Concordia College At Moorhead
Connecticut, University of
Coppin State College
County College of Morris
Cumberland College of Tennessee
Dayton, University of
Daytona Beach Community College
De Paul University
Delta State University
Denver North Campus, Community College of
Denver, University of
Detroit, University of
Duke University
Dutchess Community College
East Carolina University
East Tennessee State University

East Texas State University
El Camino College
El Centro College
Emporia State University
Faith Baptist Bible College
Felician College (NJ)
Florida Institute of Technology
Florida State University
Florida, University of
Fort Wayne Bible College
Georgetown University
Glassboro State College
Greenfield Community College
Gulf-Coast Bible College
Hawaii Kapiolani Community College, University of
Haywood Technical Institute
Hinds Junior College
Holy Cross, College of the
Holyoke Community College
Hood College
Hudson Valley Community College
Illinois Urbana Campus, University of
Illinois Valley Community College
Indiana University Bloomington
Iowa Wesleyan College
Jersey City State College
Kalamazoo Valley Community College
Kent State University Main Campus
Kirkwood Community College
Lakeland College
Lane Community College
Lehigh University
Lincoln University (MO)
Lipscomb, David, College
Livingston University
Loma Linda University
Los Angeles Pierce College
Los Angeles Valley College
Macomb County Community College
Marist College
Mars Hill College
Massachusetts Amherst Campus, University of
Massachusetts Institute of Technology
Memphis State University
Merced College
Miami-Dade Community College
Mid Plains Community College
Minnesota of Minneapolis St. Paul, University of
Mississippi State University
Mohawk Valley Community College
Monroe Community College
Montclair State College
Moorhead State University
Moravian College
Mount Hood Community College
Mount Mary College
Mount San Antonio College
Mount Senario College

Murray State University
Nassau Community College
Nebraska-Lincoln, University of
New Hampshire College
New Mexico State University Main Campus
North Alabama, University of
North Carolina At Chapel Hill, University of
North Dakota Main Campus, University of
Northwestern State University of Louisiana
Orange Coast College
Oregon State University
Ouachita Baptist College
Pacific Union College
Pan American University
Parkland College
Pasadena City College
Payne, Howard, University
Pennsylvania State University Main Campus
Philadelphia, Community College of
Pittsburgh Main Campus, University of
Reed College
Rhode Island Junior College
Rhode Island, University of
Ricks College
Rochester Institute of Technology—Eisenhower College
Rockingham Community College
Rockland Community College
Rogue Community College
Roosevelt University
San Francisco Art Institute
San Jose State University
Santa Monica College
Sauk Valley College
Sequoias, College of the
South Florida, University of
Southeastern Community College (NC)

Southeastern Oklahoma State University
Southern Illinois University at Carbondale
Southern Union State Junior College
Southern University in New Orleans
Southwestern Louisiana, University of
Southwestern at Memphis
State Fair Community College
State Technical Institute at Memphis
State University of New York Agricultural and Technical
    College at Farmingdale
State University of New York at Albany
State University of New York at Buffalo
State University of New York at Geneseo
State University of New York at New Paltz
Sullivan County Community College
Tennessee at Martin, University of
Texas A & M University Main Campus
Texas Southern University
Texas Tech University
Thornton Community College
Trenton State College
Tri-County Technical College
Trinity College (CT)
Trinity University
Utah, University of
Victoria College
Virginia Polytechnic Institute and State University
Washington State University
Waynesburg College
West Valley College
West Virginia State College
Western Nevada Community College
Wisconsin—Madison, University of
Wisconsin—Oshkosh, University of
Wisconsin—Stout, University of
Yale University

Bibliography

Barrows, T. S., S. F. Klein and J. L. D. Clark, with N. Hartshorne, *What College Students Know About Their World*. New Rochelle, NY: Change Magazine Press, 1981; E&WV Series V.

Bonham, G. W., "The Future Forsaken," *Change* Magazine (October 1978).

Carroll, J. B. *The Foreign Language Attainments of Language Majors in the Senior Year: A Survey Conducted in U.S. Colleges and Universities*. Cambridge, MA: Laboratory for Research and Instruction, Harvard Graduate School of Education, 1967.

Cochran, W. G. *Sampling Theory*. (2nd edition). New York : John Wiley and Sons, 1963.

"Council on Learning Proceedings," *Change* Magazine (April 1979).

————— , *Change* Magazine (February-March 1980).

Education and the World View. New Rochelle, NY: Change Magazine Press, 1980; E&WV Series IV.

Education for a Global Century: Handbook of Exemplary International Programs. New Rochelle, NY: Change Magazine Press, 1981; E&WV Series III.

"Educating for the World View," *Change* Magazine (May-June 1980).

Goldstein, L. S. and T. S. Barrows. *The Structure of Three Instruments Intended for Police Selection*. Progress Report 72-14. Princeton, NJ: Educational Testing Service, August 1972.

Harman, H. H. *Modern Factor Analysis*. (3rd edition revised). Chicago: The University of Chicago Press, 1976.

Kruskal, J. B. Multidimensional scaling by optimizing goodness of fit to a nonmetric hypothesis. *Psychometrika*, 1964a, 29, *1*, pp. 1-27.

————— ,Nonmetric multidimensional scaling: A numerical method. *Psychometrika*, 1964b, 29, *2*, pp. 115-129.

Lambert, R. D., ed. "New Directions in International Education," *The Annals* (AAPSS), v. 449 (May 1980).

MLA Cooperative Foreign Language Test. Princeton, NJ: Educational Testing Service, 1963.

MLA Foreign Language Proficiency Tests for Teachers and Advanced Students. Princeton, NJ: Educational Testing Service, 1964 ff.

Osgood, C. E., G. J. Suci, and P. H. Tannenbaum. *The Measurement of Meaning*. Urbana, IL: University of Illinois Press, 1957.

Pike, L. W. and T. S. Barrows, et al. *Other Nations, Other Peoples: A Survey of Student Interests, Knowledge, Attitudes, and Perceptions*. HEW Publication No. (OE) 78-19004. Washington, DC: U. S. Government Printing Office, 1979.

Pimsleur, P. *Pimsleur Modern Language Proficiency Tests*. New York: Harcourt-Brace, 1967.

Robinson, J. P., J. G. Rush, and K. B. Head. *Measures of Political Attitudes*. Ann Arbor, MI: Institute for Social Research, 1968.

The Role of the Scholarly Disciplines. New Rochelle, NY: Change Magazine Press, 1980; E&WV Series I.

Shaw, M. E. and J. M. Wright. *Scales for Measurement of Attitudes*. New York: McGraw-Hill, 1967.

Simon, P., *The Tongue-Tied American*. New York: Continuum, 1980.

Sward, R. L. *World Military and Social Expenditures 1979*. Leesburg, VA: World Priorities, 1979.

Taylor, C. L. and M. C. Hudson. *World Handbook of Political and Social Indicators*. (2nd edition). New Haven, CT: Yale University Press, 1972.

Tonkin, H. and J. Edwards, *The World in the Curriculum: Curricular Strategies for the 21st Century*. New Rochelle, NY: Change Magazine Press, 1981; E&WV Series II.

Wiley, D. E. Latent partition analysis. *Psychometrika*, 1967, 32 *2*, pp. 183-193.

Your Objectives, Guidelines, and Assessment: An Evaluation Form of Communicative Competence. Brattleboro, VT: Experiment in International Living, April 1974 (revised 1976).

Order Form

To order other volumes in the Council on Learning's Education and the World View series, fill in below and mail to Change Magazine Press, 271 North Avenue, New Rochelle, N.Y. 10801. (Add $1 for order without accompanying payment.)

indicate here number of each

The Role of the Scholarly Disciplines

This book focuses on the potential role of the disciplines in encouraging enlarged international dimensions in the undergraduate curriculum; it also provides useful insights into campus initiatives and effective curricular approaches. 44 pages. **$4.95**

The World in the Curriculum: Curricular Strategies for the 21st Century

Written by Humphrey Tonkin and Jane Edwards of the University of Pennsylvania, this volume considers concrete, feasible recommendations for strengthening the international perspective of the undergraduate curriculum at academic institutions; it provides a guide to meaningful curricular change for top administrators and faculty. Approximately 256 pages. **$6.95**

Education for a Global Century: Issues and Some Solutions

A reference handbook for faculty and administrators who wish to start or strengthen language and international programs, this contains descriptions of 62 exemplary programs, definitions of minimal competencies in students' international awareness and knowledge, and recommendations of the project's national task force. 168 pages. **$7.95**

Education and the World View

A book edition of Change's special issue on Education and the World View for use by trustees, faculty, and administrators; it also contains proceedings of a national conference that considered the implications of educational ethnocentrism and action to encourage change. 90 pages. **$6.95**

What College Students Know About Their World

Overview of an important new national assessment of American freshmen and seniors, conducted by the Educational Testing Service, that covers the strengths and weaknesses of American college students' global understanding; an aid to faculty and program directors, it pinpoints areas for improving international content. 48 pages. **$5.95**

Change Magazine Press
271 North Avenue
New Rochelle, N.Y. 10801

Please ship the following volumes to the address indicated below, with number of copies desired on each. Our payment is enclosed or please add $1 for this order and bill.

_____

name (and institution)

_____

address

_____

city, state, zip